LOVE YOUR WORK

BY

LOVING YOUR LIFE

(LwL²)

Martha R. A. Fields

Marmerv Press
Harvard Square, Cambridge, Massachusetts, USA

This book is intended to provide reliable, competent information on this subject. It is sold with the explicit understanding that the publisher and author are not engaged in rendering advice of a professional, legal, financial, or emotional nature.

If legal or other expert advice is needed and/or required, services of professionals should be procured. Laws and practices may vary from state to state. The publisher and author specifically disclaim any liability that is incurred from the application or use of this book.

Published by

Marmerv Press
124 Mount Auburn Street, Suite 200 North
Harvard Square, Cambridge, MA 02138 USA
(617) 576-5733

ISBN 0-9746802-0-6

Library of Congress Control Number: 2003114738

Visit us on our website at *www.MarthaRAFields.com*

Printed in the United States of America

Final book production by Accent Design, www.goaccent.com.

LOVE YOUR WORK BY LOVING YOUR LIFE

PRAISE FOR LWL²

Martha R. A. Fields is on the mark with the right message as we all need to discuss loving our work and life and relationships.

Edie Fraser—President, Business Women's Network (BWN) and Diversity Best Practices

Discovering your purpose in life is a critical factor to loving your worklife and Martha R. A. Fields provides valuable insights that will make it attainable in this remarkable but challenging time in which we are living.

Todd Campbell—Manager, Society for Human Resource Management

LwL² offers sage advice that any organization can use if it truly wants to help staff love their work and life.

Laura Avakian—Vice President Human Resources, Massachusetts Institute of Technology

This powerful book tells you about how to make a life, not just a living.

Jerome Smalls—Director of Diversity, TJX Companies (T.J. Maxx, Marshalls, HomeGoods, A.J. Wright)

This subject and book are right on target and should be of great use to organizations of all sectors.

Lt. General David Ohle—U.S. Army (Retired)

If you are doing something you don't enjoy, no money in the world will make you happy. LwL² is a fantastic book overflowing with wise words to help you and your company succeed.

Henry Ryan—Director of Human Resource Services, Harvard University

LOVE YOUR WORK BY
LOVING YOUR LIFE

The following companies are featured in LwL²:

Alexander, Wollman and Stark
American Airlines
American Program Bureau
Archdiocese of Boston
Arnold Worldwide
Barajas & Associates
Basic Diversity, Inc.
Bates Communications, Inc.
Beacon Network Technologies
Benjamin Franklin Institute of Technology
Bentley College
Beth Israel Deaconess Hospital
Blue Cross Blue Shield of Massachusetts
Booker's Rest Homes
Boston Bar Association
Boston Communications Group
Bright Horizons
Business Women's Network (BWN)
C. Thomas and Associates
Cambridge Trust
Cheetah Learning
Children's Hospital, Boston
Cisco Systems, Inc.
Clarks Companies, NA
The Commonwealth Institute
Commonwealth of Mass. Dept. of Mental Health
Couto Management Group, LLC
Concord Middle School—Peabody Building
Cromwell Consulting
Debora Bloom Associates
DiversityInc
Diversity Best Practices
Durham, North Carolina Police Department
Ecocentrix
Emerson Consulting

ENHEART Publishing
Feaster Enterprises
Ferguson Copeland Ltd.
Fields Associates, Inc.
Fisher College
FleetBoston Financial
Fidelity Investments
Gardenswartz & Rowe
Greater Boston Chamber of Commerce
Green Leaf Consulting Group, Inc.
Hairbraiding by Aisha & Fatou
Hanamura Consulting
Harvard Coop
Harvard John F. Kennedy School of Government
Harvard School of Public Health
Harvard University
High Impact Marketing Media
Highland Consulting
Hill & Associates
H.Q. Global Workplaces
Jobs For the Future
Kodak
Linkage, Inc.
Love Living Life (L³)
Massachusetts Institute of Technology (MIT)
Massachusetts Medical Society
Mathsoft Engineering & Education, Inc.
McWade Group, Inc.
Merck & Company, Inc.
Metro PowerNet, LLC
MITRE
Monica's Beauty Salon
MX2 Media
National Aeronautics Space Administration (NASA)
National Cooperative Bank

Network World
New Dimensions in Technology, Inc.
New England Journal of Medicine
New England Network Group, Inc.
New Tilt
North Carolina State University
Northeast Human Resources Association (NEHRA)
On-Purpose Partners
Package Machinery Company, Inc.
Partners Healthcare Systems, Inc.
The Partnership, Inc.
Party City of Raleigh
Raytheon Company
Results Marketing
Rosaline's SkinCare & Spa
Rosie's Bakery
Scotia Bank (Canada)
S.D.K. Financial
Sepracor
Shell Oil Company
Shipley Company, LLC
Small Business Dev. Center—Howard University
Society for Human Resource Management

Sprint
SRJ Enterprises
Staples
Stream Productions
Stybel Peabody & Associates, Inc.
Suffolk University Law School
Swift Murdock
The TJX Companies, Inc.—T.J. Maxx, Marshalls, HomeGoods
    and A.J. Wright
Tufts Health Plan
U.S. Air Force
U.S. Army
U.S. Marines
UnityFirst.com/ African American Newswire
Upper Room Church
Urban League of Eastern Massachusetts
Wachovia Bank
Watertown High School
Watertown Middle School
Willmott & Associates, Inc.
Women's Business
Women Presidents' Organization (WPO)
Yankee Partners, LLC

To Dad, Kiki, Mom, Richard, Shawna

and my brothers and sisters

and their families.

Thanks for helping me to

Love my work by Loving my Life.

TABLE OF CONTENTS

SECTION I   GET BACK TO AGE 7 AND CAN DO DOCTOR DANCING

SECTION II   FIND YOUR LIFE'S PURPOSE. FORM A ME, INC. AND HAVE STICK-TO-ITIVENESS

SECTION III   UNDERSTAND WORLD AND WORKPLACE CHANGES

SECTION IV   PUT THE WORLD INTO YOUR ADDRESS BOOK

SECTION V   EXCEL AT COMMUNICATIONS. NETWORK. BECOME A CORPORATE CUPID AND PRACTICE THE WALT DISNEY SCHOOL OF MARKETING

ACKNOWLEDGMENTS

AS I WAS WRITING THIS BOOK, I SAW A Bill Moyers PBS story on Bill Gates. I learned that at one time the King of Microsoft made a million dollars an hour. My bank account does not contain anywhere near that amount of money. I feel richer, however, than Mr. Gates, for my wealth is counted by the multitude of family, friends, and colleagues who have supported my writing and contributed to this book. I especially wish to thank the best daughter in the universe, Shawna I. Fields, and a man of extraordinary integrity, talent and desire to help the less fortunate, Dr. Richard K. Fields for hanging in there with me as I pursued my passion to help people make a memorable, positive difference in the world by loving their work and life.

I feel that my extended family is the best on the planet. Thanks to all of you for your unconditional love—Dad, Kiki, Mom, Betty, Binky, Bud, Chris M., Chris S., Dana, John, Opie and Pat, Adrienne, Chrissy, Della, K.D., Tasha, Sam and all my nieces and nephews. My lifetime friends are always there for me and I feel so blessed to have all of you in my universe. B.J., Janine, Jeffrey, Juliette, Nina, Regina, Robin and Torri—you're simply the best. Janine and Tom Fondon—thanks for allowing me to release this book at the Friar's Club. Robin and Mark Pedrelli—thanks for your support and referrals of Pauline and Mary-Lynne. Nina—I appreciate all of your hard work in putting together the FleetBoston book launch.

A cast of people—from CEOs, a college president, Harvard executives and MIT professors to individuals with little education but lots of street smarts—contributed their brain power to this book. Two people offered both their brains and their hands to this work—my deepest thanks to my two Executive Assistants: Jessie Shea worked endless hours on the book and also contributed a very informative and useful article. Her positive energy and drive kept my spirits high and helped me to stay on track. She is wise beyond her years. And Justin Lynch-Colameta is just a delight to work with and have on our team. He is a shining example of the hard work, integrity, and stick-to-itiveness of Generation X. Monica Calzolari, a woman with an undying thrust to help others, assisted me with the marketing and research of this book. I am forever grateful to her for her hard work and friendship. Steven and Ellie Kleinberg—thanks ever so much for keeping me positive and financially on track through thick and thin.

I'd also like to give thanks to the people behind the scenes who made this book look, feel and taste right. Pauline Kelly did an outstanding job in dotting the i's and crossing the t's with the overall editing of this book. She is so pleasant and professional and just a joy to be around. Martha Nichols, who claims she has never met a Martha she didn't like (and I'd have to concur), designed the wonderful front and back cover and initial layout. Several people pitched in at the last minute and offered their help. Thank you Miphi Hall, Lisa Jarvis, and Dana Mervin. The printers at Lightning Source did an outstanding job, and it was especially a delight to work with Shina Giles and Julia Houk. Mary-Lynne Bohn did an outstanding job of completing the typesetting for the book. I very much appreciated her willingness to take things on with such short notice.

I wish to thank all of the following people who contributed to this book:

- Francine Achbar—High Impact Marketing and Media/ Former CBS executive
- Dr. Barbara Addison Reid—Bentley College
- Laura Avakian—Massachusetts Institute of Technology
- Phyllis Barajas—Barajas and Associates
- Carol Bates, M.D.—Beth Israel Deaconess Hospital
- Suzanne Bates—Bates Communications, Inc.
- Pastor Franklin D. Battle, Sr.—Upper Room Church
- Art Berarducci—Alexander, Wollman and Stark
- Madelyn Battle—Upper Room Church
- Dima Berdiev—Cambridge Trust
- Danny Best—FleetBoston Financial
- Debora Bloom—Debora Bloom Associates
- Barry Bograd—Founder, Northeast Human Resource Association
- Dr. Bruce Bonnevier—Shipley Company, LLC
- Katie Booker—Booker's Rest Homes
- Corinne Broderick—Massachusetts Medical Society/ New England Journal of Medicine
- Darryl Brown—Durham, North Carolina Police Department
- Sharon Brown—Wachovia Bank
- Yolanda Brown—New England Culinary Institute
- Mark Browne—U.S. Marines
- Robert Browne—Cisco Systems, Inc.
- Andrina Buffong—MITRE
- Sarah Byrne-Ducharme—New England Network Group, Inc.
- Monica Calzolari—Results Marketing
- Todd Campbell—Society of Human Resource Management
- Michelle Chambers—New Tilt
- Paul Chin—Raytheon Company
- Justin Lynch-Colameta—Fields Associates, Inc.
- Diene Conde—Hairbraiding by Aisha & Fatou
- Carole Copeland Thomas—C. Thomas & Associates
- Pamela Covington—National Aeronautics Space Administration (NASA)
- Kim Cromwell—Cromwell Consulting
- Carmon Cunningham—Jobs For the Future
- Deborah Dagit—Merck & Company, Inc.
- Vanessa DeCampos—Watertown High School
- Regina DeTore—Sepracor
- John Dixon—Ferguson Copeland Ltd.
- Vicki Donlan—Women's Business
- Shaina DiGiacomo—Watertown Middle School
- Bob Eubank—Swift Murdock
- Carolyn Everette—Harvard School of Public Health
- Joseph Feaster, Esq.—Feaster Enterprises
- Haywood Fennell, Sr.—Author and Playwright
- Timothy Fenstermacher—Sepracor
- Benny Ferlazzo—Monica's Beauty Salon
- Dr. Ashley Fields—Shell Oil Company
- Dr. Richard K. Fields—Benjamin Franklin Institute of Technology
- Shawna Fields—Concord Middle School
- Marsha Firestone, P.h.D.—Women Presidents' Organization (WPO)
- Rod Flakes—Commonwealth of Massachusetts Dept. of Mental Health
- Janine Fondon—UnityFirst.com/African American Newswire
- Barbara Frankel—DiversityInc
- Edie Fraser—Business Women's Network (BWN) and Diversity Best Practices
- Thomas Glynn—Partners Healthcare Systems, Inc.
- Mindy Goodfriend—Yankee Partners, LLC
- Susan Gordon—FleetBoston Financial
- Betty Graves—Wachovia Bank
- Anthony Griffin—Metro Power Net, LLC
- Torri Griffin, Ph.D., LPC, NCC—Love Living Life (L³)
- Paul Guzzi—Greater Boston Chamber of Commerce
- Paula Hammond Cunningham—Massachusetts Institute of Technology (MIT)
- Steve Hanamura—Hanamura Consulting
- Susan Hancox—Children's Hospital, Boston
- Arthur Harris—Ecocentrix
- Michele Fantt Harris—National Cooperative Bank
- Richard Kaplan—Harvard Coop
- Sidrah Jackson—SRJ Enterprises
- Lisa Jarvis—Clarks Companies, NA
- Beverly Kahn—New Dimensions in Technology, Inc.
- John Kendzior—Harvard University
- Kristen Kennedy—Network World
- Janine Kilty—Kodak
- Ellie Kleinberg—S.D.K. Financial
- Steve Kleinberg—S.D.K. Financial
- Melissa Klinkhamer—Sepracor
- Michelle LaBrosse, PMP—Cheetah Learning
- Renee M. Landers, Esq.—Suffolk Law School and Boston Bar Association
- Kathleen Larsen—American Program Bureau
- Ina Lavin—Boston Communications Group, Inc.
- Jennifer Le—Watertown High School
- Nancy Leaming—Tufts Health Plan
- Jeremy Lew—Mathsoft Engineering & Education, Inc.
- Jacqueline Lewis—Linkage, Inc.
- Ken Lizotte—Emerson Consulting
- Rosaline Lowe—Rosaline's Skincare and Spa
- Thomas Lyons, M.D.—Beth Israel Deaconess Hospital
- Wayne Martin—Stream Productions
- Thomas C. Matera—Highland Consulting
- Darryl Mayers, Esq.
- Juliette Mayers—Blue Cross Blue Shield of Massachusetts
- Martha McNeil—Concord Middle School—Peabody Building
- Jessica McWade—McWade Group, Inc.
- Kevin W. McCarthy—On-Purpose Partners
- Laura Melville—H.Q. Global Workplaces
- Leland Melvin—NASA

- Chris Mervin—Party City of Raleigh
- Cira Mervin—North Carolina State University
- Dana V.C. Mervin—DAD/Author/Former Rocket Scientist
- Leonard Mervin, Jr.—U.S. Army, Retired
- Leonard Mervin, Sr.—U.S. Air Force, Retired
- Michael Mervin
- Marilyn Midyette—Sprint
- Nina Miller-Browne—FleetBoston Financial
- Sonia Miller—Ann Taylor
- Mike Millis—MX2 Media
- Virginia Nelson—TJX Companies (Marshalls, T.J. Maxx, HomeGoods, A.J. Wright)
- Lt. General Dave Ohle—U.S. Army, Retired
- Kevin O'Keefe, CNE, MCP—Beacon Network Technologies
- Clara Ooyama—Kodak
- Herb Pearce—Psychotherapist, Trainer, Ennegram Specialist
- Robin Pedrelli—Linkage, Inc.
- Mark Pedrelli—Arnold Worldwide
- Polly Price—Harvard University
- George Providakes—MITRE
- Katherine E. Putnam—Package Machinery Company, Inc.
- Lisa Roberts
- June Rokoff—The Commonwealth Institute
- Ted Roome—MITRE
- Judy Rosenberg—Rosie's Bakery
- Michael Rubner, Ph.D.—Massachusetts Institute of Technology (MIT)
- Jeffrey Rose, CPA
- Patricia Rose—Social Worker
- Monica Ross-Rustici—Monica's Beauty Salon
- Anita Rowe, Ph.D.—Gardenswartz & Rowe
- Henry Ryan—Harvard University
- Sal Sagarese—Cambridge Trust
- Fatou Samb—Hairbraiding by Aisha & Fatou
- Jessie Shea—Fields Associates, Inc.
- Kelly Shea—Couto Management Group, LLC
- Liming Shao—Sepracor
- Fredi Shonkoff—Blue Cross Blue Shield of Massachusetts
- Pat Shultz—ENHEART Publishing
- Dr. Mangalam Srinivasan—Harvard John F. Kennedy School of Government
- Jerome Smalls—TJX Companies (Marshalls, T.J. Maxx, HomeGoods, A.J. Wright)
- Martha Stephens—Green Leaf Consulting Group, Inc.
- Laura Stone—Stream Productions
- Dr. Lawrence J. Stybel—Stybel Peabody & Associates, Inc.
- Maureen Tacito—Civil Engineer
- Gloria Thompson—Former Nurse
- Henry J. Turner—Small Business Development Center— Howard University
- Pamela Turner—Blue Cross Blue Shield of Massachusetts
- TURTLE—Staples
- Albert Vivian—Basic Diversity, Inc.
- Reverend CT Vivian—Basic Diversity, Inc.
- Anne Volante—MITRE
- Marnee Walsh—Archdiocese of Boston
- Judy Weil—Northeast Human Resource Association
- Bennie Wiley—The Partnership, Inc.
- Darnell Williams—Urban League of Eastern Massachusetts
- Wendy Allen Williams
- Clark Willmott—Willmott & Associates, Inc.
- Alesia Wilson—Fidelity Investments
- Shanice Wilson—Watertown High School
- Patricia Whelchel—H.Q. Global Workplaces
- Adrienne Rumi White—Hill & Associates
- Carl Wooten—Sepracor
- Wen "Jasmine" Zhao—Scotia Bank (Canada)

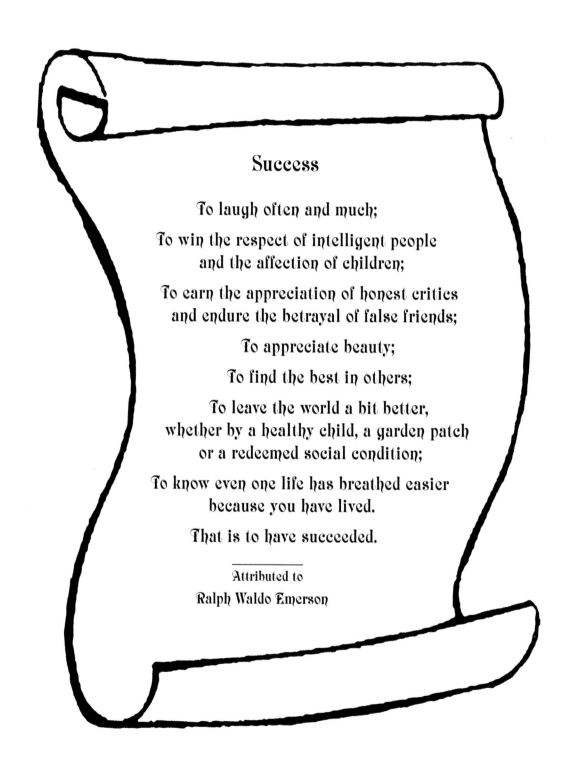

Success

To laugh often and much;

To win the respect of intelligent people
and the affection of children;

To earn the appreciation of honest critics
and endure the betrayal of false friends;

To appreciate beauty;

To find the best in others;

To leave the world a bit better,
whether by a healthy child, a garden patch
or a redeemed social condition;

To know even one life has breathed easier
because you have lived.

That is to have succeeded.

———————

Attributed to

Ralph Waldo Emerson

INTRODUCTION

AS I WAS PUTTING TOGETHER MY thoughts for this book, I was reminded of an interview I saw with Art Linkletter. If you even know who Art Linkletter is, you are seriously dating yourself. Art Linkletter is the originator of a show, "House Party," a TV series that began in the 1950s and was updated by Bill Cosby to "Kids Say the Darndest Things."

Art said something interesting when he was asked, "Which people make for the best interviews?" He replied that there were two groups. Can you guess who they are? ("Kids Say the Darndest Things"—HINT HINT.) If you answered kids, you are brilliant!

The second category is people who are 65 and older. Children who are ten years and younger make for great interviews because they tell the truth, but they don't necessarily know they're doing so. Individuals 65 years and older tell the truth, know they're telling the truth, and they don't care what you think! I am somewhere between the age of ten and 65, so I somewhat know the truth and I really do care what you think about this topic of Loving your work by Loving your Life.

There are several reasons why I wrote Love your work by *Loving your Life (LwL²)*. In my second book entitled *Indispensable Employees: How to Hire Them., How to Keep Them.*, I interviewed more than 26 major organizations from all over the United States, and revealed how they get and keep their top talents. When I was interviewed about the *Indispensable Employees*

> Note from the author: Throughout this book, I refer to the phrase *Love your work by Loving your Life* simply by using the LwL² designation. If I were correct in my capitalization, the word *work* in the title would be capitalized, but it is not. This was done on purpose. The lowercase *w* in work is to de-emphasize its importance. Here, the emphasis is on loving your life, and by loving your life you'll have a better chance at loving your work.

book, whether on radio or TV, or when I delivered keynote addresses and seminars, people would invariably ask, "What do I need to do to become that indispensable employee?" So I began to think that maybe I needed to write a book to tackle that subject from the perspective of what the individual needs to do to become a corporate most valuable player.

Another reason I wrote this book was that in the year 2003, I crossed over that proverbial hill: I turned 50 years old. I got a birthday card and small book from the love of my life, and for some reason it put into perspective exactly how *really* old one is when they have lived a half century. The card was about what things cost in 1953, the year I was born. Can you guess what the average yearly income was that year? $6,011! Just try to live on that today!

But even more significant, you won't believe what the minimum wage was at that time. It was 75 cents an hour. I said that to someone recently and they replied, "Oh my goodness, you are old!"

If you purchased a house it would cost $9,525, a car would be $1,651, and if you were hungry you could get a whole loaf of bread for 16 cents. A stamp set you back a costly three cents, and you could take in a hot movie for a mere 70 cents![1]

---

1 1953 *Pages of Time*, A Nostalgia New Report and Seek Publishing , Seek123.com Company, 1055 Ridgecrest Drive, Millersville, TN 37072-3621

FACING THE REALITY OF A CHANGING WORLD AND WORKPLACE

After reaching that milestone age of 50, I spent humongous amounts of brainpower focusing on the past, present and future of my life. I reflected hard on changes that occurred during that half-century in the globe, the marketplace, and society. In addition, I went into a deep analytical period that lasted for months. I tried to sort through the question, "Now that 50 years of my existence on this earth have transpired, what must I do to ensure that I position myself (barring any acts of God) so I can live to celebrate my 100th birthday?"

Many of my thoughts centered around the past and how substantially different life was in 1953. I also wondered about what life would be like in 2053. What did I need to do so I could continue to Love my work by Loving my Life? Here were some of my thoughts:

I read somewhere that there is more computer power in today's wristwatch or singing birthday card than existed in the entire world in 1953. As a kid, I watched black-and-white TV. We had three TV stations to select from—CBS, NBC, and ABC. There were no remote controls—you had to move from your couch potato position and change the channels using a knob on the TV. To make matters even more interesting, the stations in my town typically went off the air around midnight every night.

50 YEARS AND COUNTING

As I pondered on how substantially different the world and the workplace had become in my lifetime, I thought about the political ramifications of some of the things that happened in 1953, the year that I was born: John and Jacqueline Kennedy wed in a glamorous Newport, Rhode Island extravaganza in September of that year. Dwight David Eisenhower was President of the United States, and Richard Nixon was his second-in-command. In England, Elizabeth II had been queen only a few months, having ascended the throne the previous year after her father's death. What a difference 50 years makes!

Worklife was also interesting. In 1953, eight years had passed since the end of World War II in 1945. Most women who had worked in factories building items for the war had retired their blowtorches and hard hats as the "boys" came home from the war. These men reclaimed their places as the head of the household and sole family breadwinner.

June Cleaver, the popular mother-figure in the *Leave it to Beaver* television show, seemed to inhabit many of the households in America. These moms stayed home and took care of the children in their new suburban homes purchased using the GI Bill that rewarded WWII veterans for defending their country.

Primarily, white men inhabited the workforce. Women who did have a professional career were typically clerks, girl Fridays, secretaries, teachers or nurses. There were no laws banning discrimination based on race, gender, religion or pregnancy. Employers could ask you if you were planning to get pregnant, married, or using birth control.

Since 1953, we've watched as radio—which had until then been the predominant means of mass communication—surrendered that somewhat dubious honor to television, first black-and-white and then color, and now to communication systems that include cable and digital TV and many more than just three TV stations—and they don't go off the air every night at midnight anymore. Men have walked on the moon; animals have been cloned.

Besides turning 50, another seminal event prompted me to write this book: the tragic occurrences of September 11, 2001. Like many people, the events of that day made me take a 360° look at my work, my life and the world. I'm sure you remember where you were and what you were doing on that fateful day. I was at the Shell Oil Corporation in Houston, Texas, and I was right in the middle of giving a seminar on my book **Indispensable Employees** and doing a book-signing afterwards when I heard the news.

I was conducting a 3-hour seminar and had just completed about an hour of it when an official-looking individual knocked on the door. The person entered the room abruptly and said, "I'm really sorry to interrupt your seminar, but there is something that's happened that I need to tell you about." He went on to say, "Two planes from Logan Airport in Boston have been hijacked and crashed into the World Trade Center in New York, another one has crashed into the Pentagon, and a fourth one has gone down in Pennsylvania. I just wanted you to know about this and will keep you posted, so just continue with your seminar."

The room was filled with shocked Shell Oil executives, managers, and employees. Since I was the speaker, I tried with every muscle in my body to stay composed before saying, "Oh my goodness, did he just say Boston Logan Airport?!" I had just flown out of Logan two days before, and I was supposed to leave for home at 4 o'clock that afternoon. Little did I know that it would be days before I'd return to my beloved Boston.

In what seemed like endless hours following Tuesday, September 11—until I was eventually able to return by private jet to the Boston area on Friday, September 14th— my life passed in front of me. During that period, there were moments of doubt about whether or not I was ever going to see my loved ones again. I wasn't sure if Armageddon had not, in fact, finally arrived.

My thoughts during those uncertainty-plagued days centered around what and who was important in my life.

I pondered on what changes I'd make to my life if by the grace of God I survived that ordeal. I also thought about who was important to me in my life. I vowed that if I ever saw them again, I'd make sure they knew how special they were to me.

An insight I gained through those dark days from September 11 to September 14 was who the truly significant people in my life were. It was very revealing to me to analyze who the people were in the world that I had to call and talk to on September 11 so they would know I was fine and still existed. It was equally eye-opening to see which people in the universe made it a point to track me down in Houston because they wanted reassurance that I was safe and not in harm's way.

In the years after that September 11, it has been interesting to discover how many people went through a similar life-cleansing process. I've also uncovered a very intriguing fact as I've talked with people and interviewed them for this book: As nearly as I can tell, only about 2% of people are truly Loving their work by Loving their Life. This figure was reached by using a totally unscientific method—I based it on the thousands of people with whom I came into contact through corporations, organizations, and on people I work with, train, consult, and deliver motivational speeches to throughout the United States and the world.

Quite often when I mention that 2% statistic, some people exclaim, "That low?!" Then I challenge them to think about it by asking, "How many people do you know—your family, friends, colleagues, and peers—who get out of bed in the morning and about 80% of the time are humming, whistling or singing something like the song sung by the seven dwarfs in the Walt Disney classic *Snow White and the Seven Dwarfs*, 'Hi Ho, Hi Ho. It's off to work I go!'?"

Most people reply, "Very few." I point out that more than likely, those individuals are humming a tune that sounds like, "Hi Ho, Hi Ho. It's off to work I go," but the lyrics are more like "Oh no, oh no. It's off to work I go." Or "I owe, I owe. It's off to work I go."

What I want to accomplish in this book, is to get more people into that 2% number and widen the percentage so they are Loving their work by Loving their Life. Here is the formula I've devised to accomplish this feat:

$$Lw \ (Love\ work) \ L^2 \ (Love\ Life)$$
$$or$$
$$Lw \times L^2 = LwL^2$$
(Love your work by Loving your Life)

By the power vested in me by absolutely no one, I'm going to reveal 7 secrets of how you can Love your work by Loving your Life:

❦ Get Back to Age 7 and Can Do Doctor Dancing
❦ Find your Life's Purpose. Form a ME, Inc., and Have Stick-to-itiveness
❦ Understand World and Workplace Changes
❦ Put the World into Your Address Book
❦ Excel at Communications. Network. Become a Corporate Cupid and Practice the Walt Disney School of Marketing
❦ Make BOSS your Favorite 4-Letter Word and Don't Believe in Customer Satisfaction
❦ Plan to Fail. Learn as Much, if not More, from the Downs as from the Ups

The 7 "Love your work by Loving your Life" secrets were developed from insights gained by research and interviews with experts, average working people and companies willing to share their knowledge on the subject.

In addition, I've dug into my 25 years of working in the fields of Human Resource Management and management as practitioner, consultant, trainer and coach to produce this book. I hope it will help you to better Love your work by Loving your Life.

WHY READ LwL²?

LwL² will help you to align your work with your life. It provides insights that will position you for success in an ever-changing and turbulent world and workplace. If you don't love your job and/or life and are looking for answers on what to do, or if you are content with your life and/or work but could always use new, fresh and practical insights, then LwL² is the book for you. This thought-provoking, motivational book has helped people answer such questions as

• How can I better integrate my job into my life and vice-versa?
• How can my career choices become compatible with my personal life and life's work?
• What are the top jobs and occupations of the future?
• How can I stay gainfully employed over the long haul and better position myself for success in life?
• What skills, networks and relationships should I build at work and in my family life to secure my future?

The tips, profiles of success, stories and action exercises will help you if either of these statements applies to your life:

• I work so many hours that my work has become my life. I need to see that there is a light at the end of the tunnel.
• I hate my job and I am starting to dislike my life in general. What can I do to change that dynamic before it's too late?

In September of 2003, I attended the 40th birthday of a friend. I was seated on a plush over-stuffed couch in a corner with three accomplished individuals—an artist, a MIT professor who is also a department head, and a Boston University assistant professor. After we all introduced ourselves via elevator speeches, the question was posed to me, "Can you love your life, but not your work and vice-versa?"

I didn't have to answer the first part of the question because someone tackled it for me. "Of course you can love your life and not your work—a lot of people do that!" one woman exclaimed.

"I guess that's true," the woman who asked the original question replied, "but I'm not sure you can love your work and not your life."

"Sure you can," the third woman blurted out, then continued. "Some people hate their lives so much that they use their work as an escape. I've known professors who sleep in their labs because their personal lives stink so badly they don't want to go home."

I couldn't agree more with those comments. You can love your life but not your work, or you can adore your work but abhor your life. My idea, however, is to strike a balance, and about 80% of the time love both. My sincere hope is that when you finish reading this book, you will gain new insights to help you to Love your work by Loving your Life.

VALUE-ADDED BOOK FEATURES

LwL² contains the following "value-added" features:

Profiles of Success — Interviews with prominent, mega-successful people who are loving their life, their work, or both are featured.

Quotes of Note — Quotes from accomplished professionals, individuals with street smarts and experts in their fields offer their opinion on various LwL² topics. Individuals have weighed in on the LwL² subject from a number of "HOT" growth industries.

The "C Suites" Check In — A number of current and former Chief Executive Officers (CEOs) and Chief Operating Officers (COOs) representing different industries contributed quotes and their thoughts on LwL² to this book.

Get Up, Stand Up: Stories of Courageous People Who Took a Stand and Left a Legacy — You'll read the poignant stories of people who did what the old Bob Marley song challenged people to do — "Get up, Stand up. Stand up for your rights!" Included are the lives of courageous individuals who took a stand and established a legacy. Their work has helped generations of people fulfill their personal and professional dreams.

Opinions of Employees — You will hear a wide range of thoughts and opinions from executives and experts to employees from "HOT" industries that are expected to grow and thrive in the future such as, defense, health care, education, financial services, petroleum and pharmaceuticals. Individuals from a variety of for-profit and nonprofit companies, as well as government agencies, have contributed to the book.

Expert Articles — Numerous articles were written specifically for this book by experts in their respective fields. The articles are encapsulated within these boxes.

Wise Words — Thought-provoking, inspirational and motivational words of wisdom collected from people with book and/or street smarts. These mighty messages will stimulate your brain and spur your soul into action.

Fortune Cookie or Tea Bag Tag Messages

— The most memorable Fortune Cookie I've seen was opened back in the late 1970s. I was having lunch with some colleagues and one of the single ladies at our table opened a crunchy beige one that read: *"You're not ten pounds overweight, you're three months pregnant."*

Luckily for her, that fortune proved to be a false alarm.

In my journey through life, I've opened hundreds of fortune cookies that did or did not pan out and have also marveled at sage advice scribbled on the ends of the tea bags. I'm a collector of those fortunes and tea bag tag messages and decided to share some of my most favorite with you.

Quick Quizzes

— These fast-to-complete quizzes provide astonishing insights into trends and demographics which affect your ability to LwL^2. Knowledge of them will prepare you for the issues that will be flowing into the workforce and the world of the future.

Recommended Reading

— Books, articles, magazines and other resources highly recommended by people from all walks of life are presented throughout the book.

Web Browsers

— Websites to expand your knowledge of topics covered are indicated.

Corporate Cupid Contacts

— This includes contact information and/or websites of individuals in the book who will share information and wish to be contacted.

Best, Interesting and Radical Practices

— Policies, procedures, and benefits utilized by companies to help staff love their work and life are highlighted throughout the book.

Let's Rap: Young People Speak Out about LwL^2

— In the 1960s and 1970s, people used the word *rap* to describe conversations and dialogues that generally were of a controversial, out of the box, groovy or deep/heavy nature. Today, rap is a form of music which often expresses similar sentiments. In this section, people aged 12–25 rap about their perspective on LwL^2.

To begin this process, we will start by looking at the first of the 7 Secrets to LwL^2—Get Back to Age 7 and Can Do Doctor Dancing.

My fervent wish is that you will utilize the 7 Secrets revealed in this book to unlock your unique powers.

Best of luck as you strive to make a positive, memorable difference in the world that lasts to infinity—and beyond!

Chapter 1

Secret #1:
Get Back to Age 7 and Can Do Doctor Dancing

Get Back to Age 7 and Can Do Doctor Dancing

UNDERSTANDING WORKFORCE AND SOCIETAL CHANGES

WHEN MY DAUGHTER WAS SEVEN YEARS old, her teacher assigned her first grade class to think about what they wanted to do when they got older. They had one week to complete their work before revealing their answers to classmates. My daughter came home very upset. "Mom, I got this homework and I don't know what I'm going to do when I get older," she exclaimed.

Seeing the agony plastered across her face, I responded, "Why don't we talk about it every night, so by next week you'll know what you want to do?" She smiled a big toothy grin because that sounded like a fantastic approach to her.

So the first night I asked, "Shawna, what do you want to do when you get older?" and she replied, "Oh Mom… I don't know, but maybe I can be…Barbie's assistant." So she wants to be Barbie's assistant, I thought—I've got a lot of career coaching to do with her this week. Barbie's assistant—mmm-hmmm.

But then I put on my rose-colored contact lenses and became open-minded to my daughter possibly working for one of the most famous dolls in history. Well, Barbie *had* been around since 1959, and that could provide my little one with job security. Nevertheless, I wanted to work on expanding her career choices.

So every night that week we talked about job possibilities and she kept changing her answer as to what she wanted to be when she grew up. Her list was endless. I

was relieved that on subsequent nights she expanded her options to include a vet, a doctor, an astronaut, a ballerina, or any type of dancer.

On the night before the class where she would reveal what she wanted to do when she got older I asked, "Shawna, sweetheart, what are you going to tell everyone tomorrow about what you want to do when you get older?"

With tears almost seeping from the corners of her eyes, she pounded a fist gently on the table and mumbled, "I don't know. I want to be a doctor and a dancer."

I took a second to reflect on her decision, then said with conviction, "You can do that—and besides, it might be nice to have a dancing doctor in the family."

Every time I think of that construct—a doctor…dancing, doing the twist, waltz, tango or some hip hop dance around the operating room—it just puts a wide toothy smile on my face. It also reminds me that at age seven we open ourselves to all types of possibilities in our careers and lives. We can be a doctor. We can be a dancer. We can be a dancing doctor—and that's okay.

Whenever I remember that story, I ponder how nice it is to be seven years old and allow yourself to link the things you like in life with a career. At seven, you don't let your mind put up permanent roadblocks. Barriers aren't erected that bring those work possibilities to a screeching halt before they can even take to the road for a test drive.

The first tip to Love your work by Loving your Life is to get back to that "Can Do Doctor Dancing" attitude. As the world is evolving, shifting, churning and burning, in order to survive and thrive, we must stay open to the possibilities of what we can do in our lives and work. With these uncertain times in which we live, we are often called upon to shift our careers so they are consistent with world realities and economic times.

Who could have predicted that the booming dot-coms of the mid-to-late 90s would become the dot-bombs in the new millennium? Stories abound about dot-comers who were making millions in 1998. By 2003, many of those people were out of work and searching for jobs to replace their depleted incomes— only to come up empty-handed.

The positions of pilots, flight attendants, baggage x-ray technicians and postal workers changed significantly in a post-September 11, 2001 society. Almost monthly, the jobs of healthcare workers change as they prepare to combat the disease du jour, which since 2001 has ranged from anthrax to SARS and west nile virus to small pox, monkey pox, and mad cow disease, among others.

By staying open to "Can Do Doctor Dancing," we allow ourselves to remain connected to possibilities. We don't filter them through lenses that say "I'm too old/ young to do that." Instead, we remember people like John F. Kennedy, who died in his forties, and Martin Luther King, Jr., who was only 39 when he was killed, 5 years after he made his famous "I Have a Dream" speech. He prophesied to the world that he thought he may not get to the mountain top with them. These people weren't too young to leave their legacy for future generations.

On the other hand, John Glenn defied the notion that seniors aren't fit for certain assignments. The astronaut and politician, who in 1962 orbited the earth, soared to new heights by returning to space in a shuttle at age 70. He exemplifies the ideal that by keeping ourselves open to "Can Do Doctor Dancing" we grant ourselves permission to re-explore career options that may be more suitable in a changing world. As John Glenn

was in his era, Susan B. Anthony and Elizabeth Cady Stanton were also mature adults when they and others started the Women's Suffrage Movement in Seneca Falls, New York. Their efforts eventually led to women winning the right to vote in 1920. These remarkable people did not let the societal age bias of their respective times limit their possibilities.

Having made the case for why you should "Get Back to Age 7" and "Can Do Doctor Dancing," I will say that actually doing it is not easy. Why? you ask. I've got some theories that address that question. To understand more, read on.

YOUR FIRST CAREER DREAM—TO BE OR NOT TO BE?

1. What was your very first career dream? (Perhaps this was something from your childhood or teen years. Maybe it was a dream you had as a college student or young adult.)

2. At any point in your life, did you fulfill that career dream?

3. Are you living out that first career dream right now?

4. Do you have any interest in fulfilling it?

When I ask these questions to individuals and audiences, most people reply that they aren't living their career dream—some never did or ever will; others did, then moved on. When I asked this question at a seminar I delivered at Walt Disney World in Orlando, Florida, a woman quickly raised her hand and said that all her life she wanted to be an interior decorator and create lovely store windows. She exclaimed, "I guess I'm sort of living my first career dream now because I decorate funeral home showrooms."

If there is still a burning desire for you to accomplish your first career dream, why not think of a way to make it a reality. Take the attitude of the funeral home interior decorator and adapt the dream a little to your current circumstances. The most important thing is to listen to the message of the classic Nike commercial and "Just do it!"

Six Careers and Fifteen Jobs in a Lifetime

As we travel the path to LwL^2, we have to do more of that 7-year-old way of thinking. Here's why. The world as we know it is changing, and our careers must change with it. Most of us will not have just one job or work for the same company for a lifetime. In fact, experts will tell us that the average person is going to have multiple careers/professions and jobs throughout their lives.

The world has dramatically changed, but we treat our careers as if we were still living in the Industrial Revolution. Experts say that we may have as many as 6 careers and 15 jobs in a lifetime. When I mention that statistic, people often say something like, "That's unbelievable!" or "Are you sure?!" After hearing that reaction, I did something that you might want to try—I looked at my own life and counted up the number of jobs and careers I had undertaken.

As it turns out, since I started working—at 9 years old as a babysitter and then into the big league at 16, flipping burgers and preparing soft-serve ice cream cones at Cookies Dairy Bar and Burgers—I've had 11 careers and 17 jobs! If you're curious about my work history, here it is:

> Babysitter (first job)
> Burger flipper/order taker
> High school band—Martha and the Sensations

> Work study student for Financial Aid Office—Boston University
> After-school program teacher
> Research, teaching assistant
> Singer
> Seminar Coordinator for the National Fire Protection Association
> Engineering assistant
> Consultant and trainer—Contract Research Corporation
> Laid off
> Employee Relations and Training and Development Manager—Children's Hospital
> Director of Human Resources
> Director of Corporate Recruitment
> Vice President of Human Resources—Harvard Medical School-affiliated hospital
> Business Owner, CEO/President/Consultant
> Author and motivational speaker

Now that humans are living longer, there are greater opportunities for us to do more within our work lives. Many of us are working beyond age 65, partly because we are living longer (and healthier) lives, but also because financially we can't afford to be unemployed.

Why I Can't Do "Can Do"

Psychologists can provide us with 1,001 reasons why many of us aren't engaged in "Can Do Doctor Dancing." I'd like to suggest just a few more, then offer some solutions for getting out of the "I Can't Do 'Can Do Doctor Dancing'" syndrome.

I believe that many of us practiced "Can Do Doctor Dancing" as a child, then left it behind around age 25. I've met many people who sing a song about their life, and the tune sounds like this:

"I used to be wide open to different career and life opportunities, but then I _____."

The blank gets filled in by any number of excuses, such as

graduated from college/ vocational school	got married
got my first real job	purchased my first house
got my first car and/or apartment	had kids
	got into too much debt

Often, after filling in the blank, people proceed to the "coulda, woulda, shoulda" mode. The conversation often sounds like this:

"If I **coulda** just done *x*, I **woulda** reached *y*. I **shoulda** made that move years ago and now it's too late."

After the "coulda" and "woulda" parts of the dialogue, people just shut down regarding the "shoulda" options. We don't leave ourselves open to the fact that "shoulda" can still happen and it doesn't have to be a thing of the past. We have the power to make "shoulda" happen right NOW!

LIVING IN THE NOW AND NOT IN THE "COULDA, WOULDA, SHOULDA" MODE

How many times have you heard people say something like, "Don't worry about *xyz*—what will happen, will happen. Just enjoy this moment and live in the NOW." Living in the NOW is a difficult thing to do; I struggle with it daily. The conversation in my head when I'm trying to make myself stay in the NOW begins, "Today I'm going to make a promise to myself and God to live in the NOW." Then I make my decaf coffee and Yogi Green Tea with Energy. I'm okay and cooking with gas; then I make a wrong strategic move and turn on the TV. Some disease du jour is being discussed in lurid detail on the screen. One day it's SARS, then west nile virus—today it's monkey pox.

My mind starts playing games and I wonder, "Oh my goodness—what if I'm playing with a prairie dog and get bitten and contract monkey pox!" At this point the rational part of my brain kicks in and says, "Wait just one moment, Martha; you've never even seen a prairie dog,

so why do you think one would have the nerve to bite you? Snap out of it—you're not living in the NOW."

It is so very hard to keep our personal universe glued to the NOW and the very second in which we are living! A tip to help stay in the NOW is to think about a saying that I heard from humorist Loretta La Roche some 20 years ago at a Boston Human Resource Association seminar. It goes something like this:

Wise Words
Loretta La Roche

Yesterday is history, tomorrow is a mystery. Today is a gift, and that's why it's called the present.

To LwL² you have to begin to live in the NOW, but plan for the future. You'll find more on the planning part in the chapter where I discuss "Plan to Fail. Learning as Much, If Not More, From the Downs as From the Ups."

Don't worry so much about what you "coulda, woulda or shoulda" done in the past, or what you might not be able to do in the future. Instead, focus on what you are doing in the NOW. Sometimes, to have success you have to fire the downers and drainers who are keeping you in the "coulda, woulda, shoulda" mode.

The American Program Bureau has been setting the standard in the speakers industry for almost 40 years. Over the years, their diverse client list has included such luminaries as Martin Luther King, Jr., Yoko Ono, and Cesar Chavez. Kathleen Larsen, Program Consultant at the American Program Bureau, offers some insights into this subject in the following article, written exclusively for this book:

You Can Have Success, and The Importance of Firing Downers and Drainers To Help Get You There

Kathleen Larsen—Program Consultant,
American Program Bureau

THE OLDER I GET THE MORE I REALIZE JUST how much one should never stay at a job or in any relationship (whether it's with a loved one or a friend) if they are not truly happy. As unfathomable as it may seem, you really can fire someone or something from your life if you realize that it is a downer or drainer. Some people make a living sucking the life out of others. If you realize this is happening, I urge you to get rid of that person or thing. Trust me, you will feel so much better in the end, and have no idea just how much of a weight will be lifted from your everyday life.

As much of a cliche as it sounds, I really do try to live my life remembering that I literally could die tomorrow. And so could you. Wouldn't you then want to have lived every day as happily and effectively as possible? So why wait? Take charge of your life and career now. Take command of your destiny. Not only do you deserve it, but certainly no one else will do it for you.

There are some things in life you cannot control, such as certain illnesses, natural disasters, etc. But you CAN, however, control your attitude about what happens to you, the people you hang out with, and your job. Now I realize that not everyone is willing to make a leap from a job,

even if they aren't satisfied. Ok, then let's make it better. Take power to change your situation and how you are perceived at work. Be thoughtful, confident and good at what you do, and people will respect you regardless of your position. Get noticed! How many times have you read about someone who started out at the bottom, worked hard, and was eventually promoted to the top? It happens. And how do you think they did that? They certainly didn't climb the ladder of success by sitting quietly at their desk day after day, or by complaining to their colleagues and family of what they didn't like. They did it by taking action, initiative and sincere care.

In my role as a Program Consultant with the American Program Bureau, I place many impressively successful people in speaking engagements throughout the world. And I've noticed they have in common a positive attitude, persistence, and a genuine care, concern and interest in their work.

Whether you are trying to get a bill passed in your town, helping individuals with disabilities, or climbing the ladder of success, if it's not in your heart, chances are it's going to be much more difficult to be successful. Do what you love and the success will follow.

To Love your work by Loving your Life, take charge, and know that you CAN do it. You deserve to succeed!

MOVING FORWARD IN LIFE

After getting ourselves off and running with our "coulda, woulda, shoulda" dialogues, we then slide even deeper into the "I Can't Do the 'Can Do Doctor Dancing'" mode. We rationalize our ability to not move forward with new career and life possibilities because of our responsibilities and/or financial commitments. We articulate such reasons as

- I can't change my job because in this economy, where would I go to get the kind of money I'm making and not have to start all over again?
- I'm a father/mother now, and it's not just about me anymore. I have others to think about and support, so I can't make that kind of a bold move in my life or career and jeopardize everything.

LIFE LESSON—MARLON BRANDO ON HIS FAME

In an interview with Larry King, Marlon Brando revealed why he became an actor.[2] He stated in essence that it was the only job where he knew he could make a lot of money while deciding on what he really wanted to do with his life. He went on to say that regarding his fame, it made him feel isolated and alone.

How many of us can relate to Marlon Brando's statement? We fall into a certain career path and life rhythm. The job pays well, but in the final analysis the fame and/or success makes you feel isolated, alone and unfulfilled.

In that *Larry King Live* interview, Brando went on to say something profound. He said, "Unless we look inward, we can't clearly look outward." For those individuals who are feeling a sense of isolation around their lives or careers, this may be a wake-up call that you are *not* LwL[2].

Getting back to Can Do Doctor Dancing involves having the courage to explore career and life possibilities. It also involves having a clear vision about what you want to do and be as you get older. All of these require that we look both inward and outward. Before we examine how to begin this process, I'd like you to take this Quick Quiz that will begin to put these issues into perspective and give you a clearer understanding as to why you should be concerned about this issue.

 Quick Quiz

What is the fastest growing segment of the mature adult population according to the U.S. Census 2000?

a. 50–65 years old
b. 66–84 years old
c. 85+ years old

2 Larry King Live—King's Classics, CNN August 2, 2003

WHAT DO I WANT TO BE WHEN I GET OLDER?

Because we are living longer, the question "What do I want to be when I get older?" takes on even more significance. If the average retiring age is 70+, then you may have almost as many years in the workforce at the age of 50 as you did before 50.

To LwL[2], you must answer that question for yourself on two levels. First, you must look at what you do want to be and do in your career as you get older. As we age, our likes, desires, career aspirations and life goals change. What was important to our work and life at age 25 is not necessarily the same at age 52. This first aspect targets the "Loving your work" component as we answer for ourselves such questions as What type of career do I want to have? What skills must I possess to keep myself gainfully employed?

The second level of the question "What do I want to be when I get older?" addresses the "Loving your Life"

component. Here, you must ask yourself, "What do I want my life to be like when I get older?" The question you are striving to answer leads to an even deeper issue because it requires you to search and dig deep to reveal the style of living that you want (for example, a life of leisure and retirement, or one that allows you to sell your big house and move into a smaller condo in Florida, or the ability to live in an assisted living facility or independently in your own home). Here, the question becomes, "How—in the autumn and winter of my life—do I want to live, and what type of legacy do I want to leave so that the world and future generations to come will benefit from my life's journey?"

Later in this book, you will find a more detailed discussion on ways to create your legacy. Before you can begin to think about your legacy, you'll want to determine your life's purpose. In the next chapter, we'll explore that issue further.

Wise Words
A person who enters the workforce as a 22 year old will have worked 28 years by age 50. If they continue to work until age 70, they will have worked 20 more years. The math tells us that in their 48 years in the workforce, 28 years were spent below age 50, and 20 were spent above age 50.

Chapter 2

Find Your Life's Purpose. Form a ME, Inc., and Have Stick-to-itiveness

Secret #2
Find Your Life's Purpose. Form a ME, Inc., and Have Stick-to-itiveness

Quote of Note

Life's Purpose

Have you ever heard someone on their deathbed say, "I wish I had spent more time at the office. Why didn't I live long enough to send one more email or complete one more project?" Ask yourself, "When everything is said and done, what did my time in this world mean?"

—*Martha R. A. Fields*

FIND YOUR LIFE'S PURPOSE. FORM A ME, INC., and have stick-to-itiveness is the second secret to LwL[2]. Earlier I mentioned my unscientific notion that only 2% of people were truly loving their work and their lives. A study by the Conference Board, which surveyed 5,000 United States households, found that 50.7% of respondents said they're satisfied with their current jobs.[1]

Why are so many dissatisfied with their life and work? I believe it is because people do not understand the connection between the work they do on the job and their life's work or sense of purpose. "What is my life's work?" you might ask. I interviewed John Kendzior of Harvard University and he had a wonderful way of defining "life's work." Here's what he said:

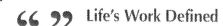

Life's Work Defined

I define sense of purpose and life's work as participating in a goal bigger and broader than one's self or one's agenda and immediate needs. Who I am and what I believe in is united with what I can do with a bigger group and purpose. This may include my family, partner, community, religion, country, or the world.

—*John Kendzior, Harvard University*

1 Anderson, Porter. '*Job Satisfaction': Oxymoron?* Oct. 24, 2000. http://www.cnn.com/2000/CAREER/trends/10/23/job.dissatisfaction/

LIFE'S WORK

Finding your life's work is about discovering what truly makes your heart smile and will make a memorable, positive difference in the world long after you're gone. It is greater than you.

Typically, one's life's work has a humanitarian, or spiritual tone. It is work that is satisfying to your soul and core values, yet ignites the lives of others.

When you have identified your life's work, you can answer these questions:

Life's Purpose/Work Is About

1. Who am I? What do I want to stand for in my life and work?
2. What is my higher calling? What am I suppose to do with my life and my work to make a positive memorable difference in the world and in the lives of others?
3. Where should I most focus my energies and efforts in life so I can accomplish what I was sent here to do?
4. When I leave this earth, what footprints will I leave on its landscape as a result of my life's work?
5. Why can or can't my "day job" and my "life's work" be one and the same?
6. What can I do to make the world a better place than what I found when I was born?
7. From my "little space on the planet," what can I do to change my life and that of others for the better?

HOW TO KNOW YOU'VE FOUND YOUR LIFE'S WORK

Finding your life's work requires that you have a vision and the ability to see the unknown. It's as if you possessed Supermanlike super vision and could see down the road of your life to your final destination. Through these lenses you begin to chart what routes you must take to end up at your dream location tomorrow.

When you find your life's purpose, you'll know it when you see it.

WORK EXAMPLES

Here is an example of how two people describe their *life's work*:

"To bring seemingly different people together and bring them towards a like understanding."

"To help organizations and individuals to make a memorable positive difference in the world."

Life's Work
Your life's work is the core of who you are—
your purpose and reason why
your presence graces this earth.

DO YOU HAVE PASSION AND FIRE IN YOUR BELLY FOR YOUR WORK AND LIFE?

Have you ever met people who seem to have it all? Their lives appear to be in perfect order. They feel fabulous. The air about them smells of success. They do get up about 80% of the time and sing and/or hum, "Hi Ho, Hi Ho. It's off to work I go!" Why? They truly love their work and their life. Watching them soar has you asking what drug they are on because you want some. Often, what they are high on is life. They have fire in their bellies and unlimited passion for their life and work. These people have found their life's work and understand how it connects with their day job.

LINKING YOUR LIFE'S WORK TO YOUR JOB

Linking your life's work to your career requires that you first determine your life's work/purpose, then find ways to realize it through your career and the world around you. You must recognize the role that your job and career play in accomplishing your life's work. In some instances, your job may be the mechanism used to carry out your life's work. In other cases, it is a means to financially support activities that are part of your life's work and becomes a method to support the activities that are part of your life's work.

We are blessed if our life's work and our jobs are one and the same. For most of us, they are not. If your life's work and your job are *not* the same, you may be wondering, "What should I do? I spend so many hours at my job, and it's really not connected to my life's work and what I enjoy doing most in my life."

I'd like to answer that question with this example. Let's say my life's work is about going to the Andes Mountains and the Amazon Jungle in Peru, and taking wonderful pictures of this glorious sight on the earth. When I return to my community, I love to conduct cultural understanding programs by showing people my Amazon Jungle pictures. That's where I have a lot of fire in my belly, but it costs a lot of money to go the Andes Mountains and to the Amazon Jungle and put on those programs.

Meanwhile, I'm the manager at this job that is just okay—however, it pays me a lot of money. My high income lets me buy the expensive equipment I need and pays for my airline ticket to Peru. Since I've been working there so long, I can take a month of vacation every year and spend my "free" time in Peru. My job isn't my life's work, but it allows me to do my life's work. Therefore, I can get up every day and sing, "Hi ho, Hi ho. It's off to work I go!" I know that by working every day, I'll have the means to visit Peru to do my life's work.

As this example illustrates, often our job becomes a means by which we can support our life's work. When we come to terms with that dynamic, our satisfaction at work starts to soar. We have finally made the connection between our job and our life's work.

People who have made this connection have a certain aura about them. They seem at peace and walk and talk with confidence and conviction. Their life's purpose is woven into the fabric of their work and life. It is seamless. It is incorporated into what they say and do and how they spend their waking moments in both their lives and their jobs. It is not an "on-call thing" where you call it up and it appears. It always is who you are and what your life is about.

Profile of Success
Judy Rosenberg—President and Founder, Rosie's Bakery

I started Rosie's Bakery in 1974 in Cambridge, Massachusetts, soon after I discovered—by chance—that I had a hidden talent for baking. Once I discovered this talent, I was so impassioned and all my creations came so naturally, as if I had known them all my life. I developed a whole new sense of empowerment and self and nothing could stop me from moving forward. I had no fears or insecurities about taking risks—I had such confidence in my ability to succeed that nothing I took on felt like a risk. I had tapped into something inside myself that I hadn't known existed. All the things I had done in my life came together—waitressing, eating, dieting, my art background, lusting after fattening desserts—everything seemed to come together to give birth to the "complete" me that I had been longing to discover. I found my personal expression, and it flowed right from the soul, from deep within me.

My art became my business: the colors, the cakes, the merchandising all became part of a large canvas which in turn was an expression of my soul and my natural rhythm which I so longed to express. You know when you find this passion that you can express yourself without fear of failing and that you must express yourself because the urge is so great and it feels so good!

Profile of Success
Pam Turner—Director, Learning and Professional Development
Blue Cross Blue Shield of Massachusetts

Thoughts on Loving Work

There are some people who have careers and jobs that truly fit into what they are passionate about. They are blessed to do things that are totally who they are. Others may not have a job that is the most passionate thing in their life, but they still enjoy their work. I'm always looking for the next thing that I haven't done or the next experience. That is really fresh and exciting for me.

What motivates me is not power, money, title or perks of the job. What motivates me is to be a guide and a helper. I like watching people grow and succeed. I surround myself with really successful people—it's fun and I get a lot of satisfaction watching them succeed. I don't need to be in the limelight but I get pleasure out of seeing others I help shine. What I like about working at Blue Cross Blue Shield is that we provide a lot of flexibility around the benefits we offer. We also accommodate peoples' personal circumstances so they can come to work and be focused.

How to Love your Life

This is defined a lot by what I give to others and what I give away. For example, giving them something that means more to them than me, or giving them knowledge or wisdom, or experience that I know will be helpful to them in their life's journey.

I have a strong sense of independence and know who I am without anyone else defining it for me. I'm perfectly capable of getting and doing things on my own. When all is said and done, the only person you can truly rely on is yourself. The only thing you can count on is that things are going to change. This reliance on myself gives me comfort because I am not afraid and fearful to do what I think is right.

The job I have allows me to do these things. Many people may say this, but I do like making a difference in what I do. My job and work do not necessarily define who or what I am. If I didn't have this job, I'd do something else that wouldn't detract from who I am.

Pam's Pearls of Wisdom

You need to be in charge of yourself and of what's happening and not be a bystander in your career and life choices. That's not something you abdicate and let someone else do for you. If you do, you're relinquishing your life and control over it. You cannot change and influence things that you can't control—it's wasted energy. What you can control is your attitude and how you respond to what happens to you, and how you make the most out of change and the opportunities it presents.

Recommended Reading

I like the magazine *Real Simple*. It provides helpful hints and tips for home, work, fun and relationships.

—Pam Turner

Wise Words

Jacqueline Lewis—Vice President, Program Director, Linkage, Inc.

Every time I reflect on what it means to "Love your work by Loving your Life," I think about thought leader Jim Collins, who offered a visual metaphor. According to Collins, we should pursue a place that represents the collective answer to three key questions; imagine each question as a circle of your life. First, what are you naturally gifted to do? Second, what are you passionate about? And, third, what can you do—professionally—that will enable you to meet your financial obligations? Live by working for what you love. Be true to yourself. Live and work in ways that make you better and stronger personally, professionally, and within your community. It's about balance, and—let's face it—you cannot separate "work" and "life."

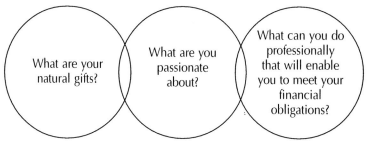

Quote of Note

If you have to put away your "moral compass" at work, there is going to be a disconnect, and it will spill over into your life. You can tolerate and endure it, but you won't flourish.

—*John Kendzior, Harvard University*

Wise Words

Pastor Franklin D. Battle, Sr.—Upper Room Church Atlanta, GA

To Love your work by Loving your Life, ask yourself these questions: What happens inside of you that makes you do what you do? What do you do that causes others to act the way they do around you? What causes people to perceive you the way they do? If everyone around you is stealing would you steal? If everyone around you was lying would you lie? What pleasures have you not fulfilled?

My advice: It's okay not to be what everyone else is. When you turn your back on something you believe in or that is good to or for you, it is hard to get back to it if you leave it behind too long. It is easy to be bad but oh so hard to be good. Know what you won't compromise on, then keep your vow to yourself.

To get your life straight and/or back on track, stop beating yourself up on your past. Angry words can perform inside of you for a long time.

How many people are you trying to clean and polish up, yet your life isn't in order? Work on getting yourself straight first with yourself then with God.

HOW DO I FIND MY LIFE'S WORK?

"How do I begin to define my life's work?" you may ask. There are many books to assist you. Here are a few examples of things that have helped people to find their life's work:

- Think about winning the billion-dollar lottery. There are many people who write about this as a method to find your life's work. So, if you won the billion-dollar lottery and money was no object, what would you begin doing with your time? How would you move your life forward? How would you spend the money?

- Imagine you're getting ready to die. Think about what you want written on your tombstone. Remember there can only be a few words on it.

Also, how would you want your obituary to read? When your life is over and everything is summed up, what will it say you stood for in life. When your loved ones are writing your obituary, what will be the major highlights? What do you want them to remember about your life? (Remember an obituary is brief and concise.)

- Think about your 100th birthday party. People are asking you to communicate the major accomplishments of your life. How do you want to be remembered?

- You have not had a bad hair *day*, but a bad hair *decade*. Despite that, when you think about a certain activity in your life, immediately your heart begins to smile. What is that activity? Could it be your life's purpose?

Wise Words
Laura Avakian—Vice President for Human Resources, Massachusetts Institute of Technology (MIT)

An MIT professor is credited with giving his students this career advice: "Imagine which relative died and gave you so much money you would never have to work for a living. Think about what you would do—then get a job doing that."

Wise Words
Mrs. Madelyn Battle

After all these years of challenges and failures, I've learned that I just have to be me.

You have to sweep away the cobwebs of the past in order to make way for your future.

To love your work and life, get up each morning with the attitude that you are going to make it a 'D' day—Delightful Day.

Quick Quiz

A person's life work/purpose may be accomplished through many avenues. Please check the items that apply and list the names of specific organizations.

Some ways that I might accomplish my life's work:

- ❑ my current job _____
- ❑ my career _____
- ❑ social/civic organizations _____
- ❑ hobbies _____
- ❑ religious organizations _____
- ❑ educational institutions _____
- ❑ charitable organizations _____
- ❑ community activities _____
- ❑ worldwide organizations _____
- ❑ social causes - local/national _____
- ❑ social causes - international _____
- ❑ the arts _____
- ❑ volunteer work _____
- ❑ fraternal organizations _____
- ❑ consulting work _____
- ❑ other _____
  _____

Quick Quiz
Finding Your Life's Purpose

Close your eyes tightly. Think of the happiest moment in your personal life. Don't open your eyes until you are clear about when that time occurred. After you open your eyes, write that thought down.

_____
_____
_____
_____

Repeat the above instructions, but ask yourself what the happiest moment in your work and career has been.

_____
_____
_____
_____

Interpreting This Exercise

Listen very hard for what your answers reveal about what makes you the happiest in life and at work. Perhaps this will literally shed some light about what your life's work entails.

LIFE'S WORK— SAMPLE LIFE AND WORK PHILOSOPHIES

To help you think about your personal philosophies regarding work and/or life, here are some that individuals I've interviewed have suggested:

- What you give out, you get back.
- Everything in its season.
- A little difference makes a big difference.
- Find the beauty in everything.

Sometimes people find it important to establish golden rules or boundaries of acceptable ways to operate in relation to their work. Except in rare occasions, they do not allow themselves or others to violate them. If you haven't established golden rules/boundaries, you may find it helpful to do so. Here are just a few examples that others have created:

- Work hard. Play harder.
- I'll finish my chores and work, then I will play and do whatever I want as long as it is not work.

- No phone calls after 11:00 P.M.
     or
- Phone calls are allowed from 6 A.M. to 10 P.M.
- My work and life are not separate. They have to be integrated.
- My work is my life and vice-versa.
- I'll make sure that my house is cleaned by Friday of every week so I don't have to worry about housework on the weekend and can enjoy my family time and do things for myself.
- No working at home on office-related issues. I will only grant an exception to this on rare occasions.
- I'll plan a summer and winter vacation every year regardless of my work schedule.

- I will take at least one day in my week to not talk or think about my job.
- I will meditate, pray, or attend a spiritual or religious event at least once a week.
- I will count my blessings at least once a day and will reserve a special time to do so.
- I will write an entry in my journal everyday before I go to sleep.
- At least twice a year, in January and June, I will review my progress on my work/life plan and the goals I've established for my life's work.

Developing a Professional Life that Mirrors Your *Core* Values

By John Kendzior—Harvard University

Love Your Work

Optimally, you should have a professional life that mirrors much of your core values and beliefs to love your work. Find an organization or group that supports and is not at odds with those principles. An organization shouldn't force you to divide and divorce you from your core values, especially your morals. If you have to put away your "moral compass" at work, there is going to be disconnect and it will spill over into your life. You can tolerate and endure it, but you won't flourish. To have this realization, you must take an attitude of "I know that I don't know."

About Jobs in Technology

There are jobs and competition is greater in technology fields. There are greater opportunities if you are able to move and be mobile. For example, Santa Fe, Texas, Florida, Nevada versus New England—to find a comparable job sometimes you have to reassess your expectations.

Here's a reality check: The year I graduated college was in 1984, one of the worst. We were at the peak of Reaganomics then. I left Business

School in 1988 and the market tanked in 1990 and 1991 with the recession. The market in 2003 was also one of the worst for college graduates and was among the toughest. So how do you stay gainfully employed with such fluctuations in the market? The answer is to concentrate on skills acquisition and the rest will follow. I also think it is important to find strong mentors and stay focused on your next career move.

Following Your Heart

People who come from great institutions, like Harvard and others, may consider nontraditional careers, like the Peace Corp, but the pressure they feel to go to work in places like Wall Street is great. This is a lot of the "herd" mentality and groupthink of what are the "in places to work." My advice to you is do not look to go miles with the herd, but follow what's in your heart. Success is what is named on your business card. Get a professional degree that's held in high esteem.

If you've been downsized, right-sized or supersized in your career, you must articulate why you want a degree. If it was to get away *from* something rather than move *toward* something, it may not work. A warning should go off around you when you hear statements such as "I fell into it," or "How did I get myself into this?!"

Love Your Life

Never run away *from* something. Run *toward* something with purpose. It reminds me of a Humanities course I took where I heard this statement: "The unexamined life is not worth living." (Aristotle on society)

There are elements of life that make us more human, such as the ability to have a sense of purpose. If you are always searching for something, but it doesn't include the search for knowledge or a larger ideal, then your search can have negative consequences.

I define *sense of purpose* and *life's work* as participating in a goal bigger or broader than oneself or one's agenda and immediate needs.

Who I am and what I believe in is united with what I can do with a bigger group and purpose.

This may include my family, partner or community, religion, country, or the world. All come together when you find your life's purpose.

LwL^2

LwL^2 is the ability to integrate these elements and express your system of beliefs; it is the ability to bring your moral compass to work, put it on your desk, and not have to put it away or hide it. For example, once I knew I had to leave a job where I wasn't being taken seriously—other things were not right and this crystallized things for me, and I knew I had to leave.

If you have to deny what's core to you based on years of what's taught to you by family, heroes, mentors—you won't be happy, fulfilled, and your success will be diminished.

Best, Interesting and Radical Practices

Some organizations help people by giving them volunteer time to do things, such as working for Habitat for Humanity, attending Urban League events, going into the community, or helping clean up the environment. This can help people connect with their purpose. This is also building goodwill for the corporation and for the community. For example, a cleaner community is better for the corporation and contributes to the social good.

A better-educated workforce with greater skills is a benefit to all.

Recommended Reading

I learn from history. A book I really like that was once given to me is *Siddhartha* by Hermann Hesse. This book speaks to our current condition and culture of "you are what you drive and where you live"—the "label mentality" part of our society. It also addresses what happiness is and how one finds it in the quest of life. This element of life is a continuous renewal and every day you should ask, "What have I done to express my inner beliefs?"

—John Kendzior

Wise Words

Dr. Lawrence J. Stybel—Cofounder of Stybel Peabody & Associates, Inc.
(a career consulting firm focusing on leaders and senior professionals)

I was a graduate student at Harvard and caught between three possible directions for my career. One way would take me to academia, another to consulting and a third to working for a corporation. The decision was really paralyzing me.

My wife was working for a company that had a work–life balance program we attended together. As part of an exercise, the instructor had us write down what an ideal day would be for ourselves 10 years from now. We had to write in excruciating detail—what the room would be like that we were sleeping in and where our home would be located, etc. The exercise would start with waking up and continue until the end of the ideal day.

The instructor told us that a guided missile doesn't know when it is on target. It's only programmed to know when it's off target and to take corrective action. At the time, he asked us to take our stories and put them in a file cabinet for 10 years. I am a psychologist by training so I said to myself, "This is foolish," but I did what he said.

Recently, I actually cleaned out a file cabinet and found that letter I had written not 10, but 15 years ago. Believe it or not, most of what I had written had come true. I realized that I had resolved the career choice dilemma because today I am a consultant. I always recommend that people do this exercise, and further, I do it every 10 years and share it with my wife. I wrote down my latest exercise three months ago.

Wise Words

Michele Fantt Harris—Human Resources Managing Director,
National Cooperative Bank

Since most people spend 50+ hours a week at work, it is important that you enjoy what you do. Your life purpose and you career goals should match. For when you love what you do for your career—you are a better person and happier person to yourself, your family, and your colleagues at work. You exude passion for your work and in your life and that passion is contagious for anyone who works with you.

Please notice that I use the word "career" and not job. When you only work at a job, you are limited. Your potential, your passion, and your results are also limited. When you love your career, it is not a day-by-day assignment but it becomes your life. Your career or life work is present in everything that you do.

In the next chapter, you'll discover how to put your life's work into action by forming a ME, Inc.

Chapter 3

FORM A ME, INC.

FORM A ME, INC.

TO IMPLEMENT YOUR LIFE'S WORK, YOU must become the CEO of your life and career and form yourself into a corporation called ME, Inc.

ME, Inc. is about

1. Acting like a business owner to find work, and marketing yourself in and outside your organization.
2. Knowing your life's work and how your job fits into it.
3. Seeking continuous personal improvement and life-long learning.
4. Seizing and maximizing opportunities while employed.
5. Letting go of a sense of entitlement and not waiting for someone else to make your career and life's dreams come true.
6. Taking responsibility for your career and life.

The ME, Inc. concept assumes that

1. You understand that the employee–employer contract has changed permanently from the pre-1990s concept of cradle-to-grave job security to a no guarantee of a job commitment.
2. Some organizations still offer career advancement opportunities and you should take advantage and tap into them.
3. You will not necessarily leave your current job to establish your ME, Inc.

4. If you develop a ME, Inc. you are not disloyal to your organization.
5. You must be loyal to your organization *and* yourself.

FOUR STEPS TO DEVELOP ME, INC.

There are four steps to take to develop a ME, Inc.:

1. Identify your ME, Inc. organizational structure and recruit your Senior Management Team and Board of Directors.
2. Take a Personal Skills Inventory.
3. Complete an Individual Development Plan.
4. Reinvent yourself regularly and acquire skills to survive and thrive in the new millennium.

Identify Members of Your ME, Inc. Organizational Structure

Any well-run corporation must have a competent staff and structure. A Senior Management Team and Board of Directors should be considered part of the ME, Inc. corporate structure. While most of the ME, Inc. structure and network will consist of non-paid family, colleagues and friends, they will assist you—the President, Chairperson and CEO—to implement your life's work. In

 **Quote of Note**
You must take control of your destiny and become the CEO of your life.

exchange for their services, you should also spend time helping those individuals to realize their life's work. The structure of your ME, Inc. organization should include these positions:

1. President, CEO, and Chairperson of the Board (that's ME)
2. A Senior Management Team with these members:
   VP Sales and Marketing
   VP Human Resources
   VP Training, Career Management, and Continuous Personal Quality Improvement
   VP Research and Development
   Chief Information Officer
   Chief Financial Officer
   Legal Counsel

3. A Board of Directors
   A diverse group of people of various ages, genders, religions and occupational, social, racial, economic, and cultural backgrounds

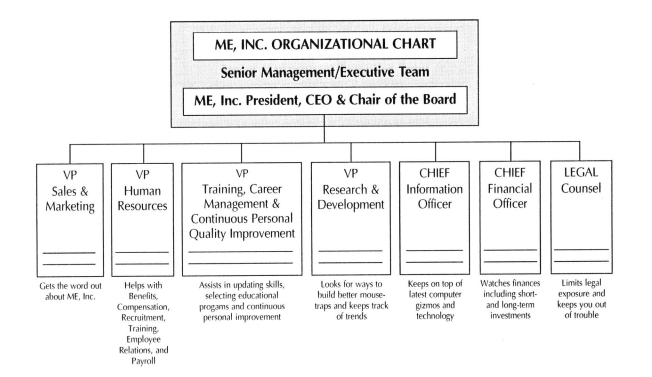

ME, INC. ORGANIZATIONAL CHART

Senior Management/Executive Team

ME, Inc. President, CEO & Chair of the Board

VP Sales & Marketing	VP Human Resources	VP Training, Career Management & Continuous Personal Quality Improvement	VP Research & Development	CHIEF Information Officer	CHIEF Financial Officer	LEGAL Counsel
Gets the word out about ME, Inc.	Helps with Benefits, Compensation, Recruitment, Training, Employee Relations, and Payroll	Assists in updating skills, selecting educational progams and continuous personal improvement	Looks for ways to build better mouse-traps and keeps track of trends	Keeps on top of latest computer gizmos and technology	Watches finances including short- and long-term investments	Limits legal exposure and keeps you out of trouble

Wise Words
Dr. Torri Griffin—President, Love Living Life (L³)

We all need people around us, especially during low points in our lives. Add people to your life who support you, particularly if you have a job or lifestyle where you are constantly giving. If you are the one always pouring out but never getting back, eventually you won't have anything left worth giving. You'll be at the bottom of your barrel where there's nothing there to distribute.

Love Living Life (L³)

By Torri Griffin, Ph.D., LPC, NCC

LOVING YOUR WORK BY LOVING YOUR LIFE is having such a fulfilling, purpose-driven life that the work you do is only another expression of your unique God-given talents that happens to pay you for what you would do all day for free.

LwL²

Be sure that your work is aligned with your personal mission statement and that it fulfills you.

Because work so often takes up so much of a person's daily life—up to and beyond eight hours each day in some cases—it is important to maintain balance. Work is usually seen as a necessary evil for many people, rather than an expression of the self. The person who understands who they are, what they want, and where they are going can use the workplace to enhance or express their personal mission, vision and goals.

Working in a place that violates an individual's principles and beliefs drains a person's life force and creates inner conflict that often radiates into other areas of their life. Likewise, working in a setting that supports and expresses one's values creates a satisfying balance in life that positively impacts the person beyond the professional setting.

Dr. Torri Griffin's Exercise to Love Living Life (L³)

Directions: Take a moment to answer the following questions as honestly as possible.

Part I. Who Am I and What Must Change or Remain the Same?

1. What do I love to do? List activities that you find enjoyable and fulfilling. List as many as you can, regardless of whether or not you are currently doing them.

    _____
    _____
    _____
    _____

2. What would I do every day if I were free to do exactly what I wanted to do? List your answers below. (This question is in relation to activities that have a positive effect on others.)

    _____
    _____
    _____
    _____

3. What is my personal mission statement? (This process can be somewhat time-consuming, but careful thought will help you answer the question "What am I created to do specifically with my life—large or small?")

    _____
    _____
    _____
    _____

4. What am I doing that I am NOT SUPPOSED to be doing? Look throughout your life and relationships to determine what things you have become complacent in doing that are not enhancing your life. List them below.

    _____
    _____
    _____
    _____

5. Now, review your answers and determine if you are going to continue doing the above or replace them with other things that are more fulfilling.

    I will continue to…

    _____
    _____
    _____
    _____

6. I will replace these things with something more fulfilling (list items and how you will change them):

    _____
    _____
    _____
    _____

Part II. My Dream Work Day

What do I really, really want to do? The answer to this question is a paragraph that describes your dream workday. Feel free to fill in the blanks, or create your own dream workday paragraph.

I want to spend my day in a _____ environment, doing _____ work and alongside _____ people. I want to be perceived as _____, and able to _____.

Part III. Reintroducing Myself to Myself

The next step is to reintroduce yourself to yourself. Complete the sentences with at least five responses:

"Hi, I'm _____ (state your name)…

My talents and gifts are
1. _____
2. _____
3. _____
4. _____
5. _____

I am told that I am skilled at
1. _____
2. _____
3. _____
4. _____
5. _____

I am a _____ person (state your qualities)
1. _____
2. _____
3. _____
4. _____
5. _____

My favorite things to do are
1. _____
2. _____
3. _____
4. _____
5. _____

My favorite topics to talk about are
1. _____
2. _____
3. _____
4. _____
5. _____

People say that I make them feel
1. _____
2. _____
3. _____
4. _____
5. _____

My friends say that I'm good at
1. _____
2. _____
3. _____
4. _____
5. _____

With this new information, you can choose to do something you love each day. The more of these activities that you participate in, the better you will love your life. The more you do them while on the job, the more you will love your work.

Loving your work by Loving your Life
starts with loving yourself enough to do
something you love to do daily.
—Dr. Torri L. Griffin

Best, Interesting and Radical Practices

To help staff LwL[2], organizations should properly access their unique talents. Allow workers the opportunity to investigate different aspects of the company. Inquire about their true interests and abilities. Base transfers on talent and desire rather than on standard means of promotion. Ensure that staff understands the value they bring to the workplace and how their individual contribution supports the mission, vision and strategy of the organization.

—Dr. Torri L. Griffin

Wise Words

Paul L. Chin—Manager, Diversity & EEO Compliance,
Raytheon Company, Integrated Defense Systems

My favorite quote in concert with this book is "Find something that you love to do, and you'll never have to work a day in your life." (Confucius)

Profile of Success

Darnell Williams—President and CEO,
Urban League of Eastern Massachusetts

Loving my life and loving my work has to come from assessing how far from where I came to where I am today. I came from the projects in Gary, Indiana. If you were to look at me 40 years ago, there was nothing you would have seen or associated with me that would have said I'd be included in a "most likely to succeed" category. I was not even on that short or long list. Yet, I'm at a point in my life now, that success has come along. Today, I need to look out for individuals like myself. Regardless of whether they are male or female, black, white or any race, I have to ask myself how I can give them opportunities to grow and develop as someone did for me. I can't guarantee their success, but I can point them in the direction of opportunity.

I do this by trying to get people to understand:

What do you like?
What do you do well?
When you feel good about yourself, what are you doing?

For example, some people feel good when they work with their hands, children, the elderly, mathematics or music—whatever turns them on.

There is also the opposite side of the ledger. I also inquire about the things they do not like. People must dig deep when answering these questions. They must ask about such things as, do I like working by myself, or with my boss hanging over my shoulder?

Once you've pinpointed your likes and dislikes, we've made some progress. The next step is to look at the jobs, occupations and careers that are connected to those likes and dislikes. This is about finding a job that is more in line with what you like to do. As a kid, people would laugh at me because I used to *love* to talk. I told them that one day someone would pay me to talk. They didn't believe me, but today someone does pay me to talk and that's a true story.

At the Urban League we have an intake and assessment process. Unfortunately, there are a lot of people who come to us and they have been psychologically battered. They have to be deprogrammed and deconstructed. Societal barriers exist for them and there is a lack of educational skills. They may not have strong writing or networking and interface skills. Some people hide behind street toughness and not trusting people. A person who is street savvy, tough and hip hop may need those qualities to navigate in the world outside of work. These same people, however, may need additional skill sets in order to maneuver successfully in corporate channels. It's not about losing your identity, but it's about acquiring another set of skills for you to be successful in different areas.

It's also about acquiring the knowledge that there is more that goes on at the office water bubbler than people drinking water. It's the subtleties of office politics. You won't find this stuff written in the policies and procedures manual. These are the unwritten rules of survival in the workplace. In short, how to play the game.

At the Urban League we tell people to get in contact with mentors inside and outside their organizations and ask them what it takes to be successful in their organization. You must ask people who have been around in an organization about the values and norms that speak to how a person can be successful in that company. You really have to play detective and have the Columbo approach. This means you may have to act dumber than you are. Sometimes, in some organizations, if you come across as being assertive, ambitious, articulate, politically savvy and a fast tracker, you are bound to create some enemies. Until you figure out the norms, you may have to take the Columbo approach. The character Columbo on TV was more calculating and smart than he let on. Sometimes you have to cloak your ambitions and by the time the adversaries figure out what you're doing, it is too late to stop the train. You've created so many allies there is too much energy and inertia to stop you from moving forward.

My final advice is that in spite of the shortcomings of both men and women, you have to have a steadfast walk with a higher power, regardless of the name you call it.

Some of what we've just discussed is easier said than accomplished. Next, you'll discover how to reinvent yourself and mutate regularly, a necessary component of success.

Chapter 4

Tips on How to Reinvent Yourself and Mutate Regularly

TIPS ON HOW TO REINVENT YOURSELF AND MUTATE REGULARLY

HERE ARE SOME TIPS TO HELP YOU REINvent yourself and mutate regularly. By practicing them, you improve the chances that your ME, Inc. will survive and thrive into infinity—and beyond!

1. Hold meetings with your Senior Management Team, ME, Inc. Board of Directors (individually and collectively) to see if they think you are on the right track and also to know where they are with their careers.
2. Keep abreast of changes in the world, the United States, and the workplace.
3. Mutate regularly so you can adapt to these changes in your career and the environment that surrounds you.
4. Keep yourself on track by completing an Individual Development Plan (IDP).
5. Evaluate your IDP every three to six months. Then:

   - Determine what needs to change.
   - Review what progress you are making to accomplish your IDP.
   - Make any needed corrections to the plan, then proceed with its implementation.

What Is an IDP?

An IDP is a written career management plan that identifies short- and long-term career goals and the training and education needed to accomplish them.

What Will an IDP Do for You?

An IDP can assist you to

- Develop short- and long-term career goals that are realistic, attainable, and compatible with your life's work/purpose.
- Identify what Knowledge, Skills, and Abilities (KSA) are needed to meet personal career goals, life's work/purpose, and organizational needs.
- Design a plan of action and timetable to acquire training and skills needed to achieve desired career goals and life's work/purpose.
- Better communicate your life's work/purpose and career desires to mentors, superiors, and others who may be instrumental in helping you achieve your goals.

Before Completing Your IDP Think About...

- Your skills and abilities
- Jobs and skills needed by organizations both now and in the future
- How do you make your career plans match with the jobs and skills needed in the future
- Ask yourself questions about your current and future job and how your life's work/purpose fits into the scheme

---

Wise Words

Controlling Your Actions

If you're reading this message on your computer, here's a simple exercise. With your left index finger, lightly touch, but do not press, the "C" key on your keyboard.

Though it may seem quick, easy and intuitive, you've just accomplished some very powerful and sophisticated things. You've exercised precise control, aiming at and reaching a target less than one-half inch in size. You've also exercised restraint, by touching the key without pressing it.

The point of this exercise is to demonstrate and remind you of a powerful and important truth—that you are in control of your actions. Every moment of the day, you control and direct yourself to the finest degree. You control what food and drink you put in your mouth and also what words come out of your mouth. You control when you get out of bed in the morning, and every action that follows.

The control you exercised in the past has brought you to precisely where you are right now. By controlling your actions, you can take yourself to wherever it is you wish to go. Anytime you get to thinking that something is out of reach or that you "just can't" bring yourself to act, reach over and touch that "C" key. Remember, you're in control. You can do it if you really wish.

Source: Ralph Marston, "Control", *THE DAILY MOTIVATOR*, Monday, Oct. 25, 1999

Part of reinventing yourself regularly involves having stick-to-itiveness, the topic of our next chapter.

Chapter 5

STICK-TO-ITIVENESS

STICK-TO-ITIVENESS

ONCE YOU ARE FOCUSED ABOUT YOUR life's work and how your job fits into it, you have to possess Stick-to-itiveness when it comes to accomplishing those career goals and your life's work.

A common quality of people who are successful and of those who LwL² is that they have Stick-to-itiveness. Their ability to persevere hinges on the philosophy that says, "When the going gets tough, the tough get going." I'd like to share the story of two men who fell down many times in their life but got up, dusted themselves off and picked up the pieces over and over again before they were rewarded with "mega-success." In so doing, they were able to LwL² and motivate, improve and entertain the lives of millions of people around the world.

STICK-TO-ITIVENESS: FROM OSWALD THE LUCKY RABBIT TO MORTIMER THE MOUSE

There was a gentleman who was born in 1901, and he was a cartoonist. He created a cartoon bunny rabbit named Oswald the Lucky Rabbit. Oswald the Lucky Rabbit actually did bring him good luck. He sold his Oswald the Lucky Rabbit cartoons to Universal Pictures and a gentleman by the name of Charlie Mintz.

His character was a phenomenal success. When his contract was ready to be renewed, he went to Mr. Mintz and Universal—feeling he was in a position of power—to ask them for substantially more money. He and his wife Lily boarded a train and went to New York, confident and prepared to negotiate. Once in New York, the man talked with the movie moguls about how Oswald the Lucky Rabbit had made so much money that he should also share more in the profits since the little rabbit had been his brainchild.

Universal and Mr. Mintz had also been thinking about this matter. They replied that they wanted total control over Oswald's future. The man was surprised and stated, "You can't do that. I own Oswald." Unfortunately, the man hadn't read the fine print in the contract: Universal, in fact, owned the rights to Oswald the Lucky Rabbit.

The artist was then asked if he wanted to come to New York, give up his business back home in California and work as their employee.

"Well, I can't do that. I have all these employees," the man stated.

"Well, we've taken care of that, too," Universal replied. "We have talked to most of your employees and almost all of them are coming to work for us. Since we own Oswald, you have two options: working for us—and therefore continuing to work with your employees—or leaving with nothing."

This gentleman just couldn't work for someone else. After all, he was an entrepreneur and that's what he wanted to be. He had no desire to work for someone else, so he took them up on their second option and left.

He and his wife boarded the train in New York to return to their home in California. On that train ride he pondered what he was going to do next. He decided that this incident was not going bring him down because he had Stick-to-itiveness. "I've got to invent another character," he decided.

Knowing that at that time a character named Felix the Cat was very popular, he set about finding something to compete with Felix the Cat. He finally had a wonderful brainstorm—how about a mouse? So, with his wife by his side on the train, he told her, "I think I want to create a mouse and I want to call it Mortimer."

She said, "Mortimer the mouse?! I don't think so! How about…Mickey?" By putting on his thinking cap and having Stick-to-itiveness, Walt Disney created Mickey Mouse and the rest, as they say, is history. Throughout his life, he never lost sight of how his empire got started. Legend has it that he was fond of saying, "If you can dream it, you can do it. Never forget that this whole thing was started by a mouse."

Wise Words
Walt Disney

"I think it's important to have a good hard failure when you're young. I learned a lot out of that. Because of it I have never had any fear. In my whole life when we've been near collapse and all of that, I've never been afraid. I've never had the feeling I couldn't walk out and get a job doing something.

You may not realize it when it happens, but a kick in the teeth may be the best thing in the world for you."

Source: Smith, Dave. *The Quotable Walt Disney*, page 106. Disney Editions New York, NY 2001

 ## Web Browser
Check out this website for more information: www.disneyeditions.com

---

 ## Recommended Reading
For more on the life of Walt Disney, check out these books by Dave Smith, director of the Walt Disney Archives:

- *The Quotable Walt Disney*
- *Disney A to Z*
- *The Ultimate Disney Trivia Book (1 through 4)*
- *Disney: The First 100 Years*

STICK-TO-ITIVENESS: FROM FORD FACTORY TO FAME

The second story on Stick-to-itiveness is about a man born in Detroit, Michigan. By all accounts, this individual said that many of the entrepreneurial and career efforts in the early part of his life seemed to end in failure. He had been in the Army, worked at a Ford Motors plant, and had been a boxer. He loved music. He wrote songs. He had actually opened a music store and wanted to sell the new upbeat form of music called jazz. But the people in Detroit didn't want to hear Charlie Parker and other great jazz musicians; they wanted to continue to wallow in the blues. So that business didn't work either.

In his community, he noticed poor but extremely talented children and young people on the street corners of Detroit. They were singing and dancing doo-wop and a capella songs that stirred the soul. He began to think about promoting this top talent. Doing that was something he could definitely sink his teeth into and be his life's work.

He borrowed some money, and he built a recording studio in his house that he lovingly called Hitsville USA. He took some of those talented teens off the streets and signed them for his record label. He decided to give his talent glorious names so that people would know his company and protégés stood for quality. He called them things like Smokey Robinson and the Miracles. He found a ten-year-old blind boy and dubbed him Little Stevie Wonder. The Temptations and three ladies he called The Supremes were also part of his stable of stars. This legendary man, Berry Gordy, created Motown Records by having Stick-to-itiveness.

The moral of the Berry Gordy and Walt Disney stories is if you're going to Love your work by Loving your Life you have to have Stick-to-itiveness.

CONFRONTING OUR FEARS

Having Stick-to-itiveness is also about not being afraid to take chances and risks and not being paralyzed by fear. I have a friend who, for almost 23 months after September 11, 2001, refused to get on a plane. He knew the statistic that he would be more likely to die in a car accident than in a plane crash, but he just wouldn't fly. So many of us have become victims of our own fears, and this can limit our ability to LwL[2].

To LwL[2], you have to realize that tomorrow is not promised to anyone. So why not use whatever time you've been granted today to live your life to the fullest as if it were your last day.

To accomplish this goal, you must live in the NOW and if you are worried about dying or some tragedy happening to you, ask yourself this: What am I doing today to make sure that when I breathe my final breath, I've left the world better than I found it when I was born? If you're spiritually inclined, you also want to make sure that you have made peace with your God.

Instead of worrying about when the next terrorist will strike or tragedy will occur, why not see every day as a gift and opportunity to do more to accomplish your life's work? That way, when that inevitable day arrives and you are at the end of this life's journey, both you and those left behind with only your memory will be able to say with warmth and happiness that "you did good" with the time you graced the earth.

Fortune Cookie or Tea Bag Tag Message

There are three values: Feel good, Be good, and Do good.

—Yogi Tea Bag, 9/3/03 (Wed.)

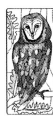

Wise Words

Attitude

The longer I live, the more I realize the impact of attitude on life. Attitude, to me, is more important than facts. It is more important than the past, than education, than money, than circumstances, than failures, than successes, than what other people think or say or do. It is more important than appearance, giftedness, or skill. It will make or break a company … a church … a home.

The remarkable thing is we have a choice everyday regarding the attitude we will embrace for that day. We can not change our past…. We cannot change the fact that people will act in a certain way. We can not change the inevitable. The only thing we can do is plan on the one thing we have, and that is our attitude…. I am convinced that life is 10% what happens to me and 90% how I react to it. And so it is with you…. We are in charge of our Attitudes.

Author Unknown
Contributed by Monica Calzolari

Wise Words

Contributed by Monica Calzolari

Ten Ways To Give Yourself Permission To Achieve Your Wildest Dreams

Give yourself permission to

> Seize the moment.
> Not be judgmental.
> Cultivate friendships.
> Laugh it off.
> Plan to have fun—regularly.
> Not spend your life getting ready.
> Be assertive and like it.
> Eliminate guilt—now.
> Like yourself.
> Live your life for YOU.

66 99 Quote of Note

Finding Your Life's Purpose

If you could rewrite your life's book from start to finish—how would it begin and end? What would the chapters say you did?

4/5/03 (Saturday)

If you could see down the road of your life and know what and where your final destination will be—where do you think you will end up? What routes should you take now to arrive at your ideal destination spot?

4/6/03 (Sunday) 7:55 a.m.

66 99 Quote of Note

Sometimes we're looking for things that other people seem to have. We ask ourselves, "Why don't I have what they have? What's wrong with ME?" We think it will radically change our life and make everything BETTER. In reality, they don't have what you think they have nor is it what we REALLY want.

—Dr. Torri Griffin

Forming a ME, Inc., finding your life's purpose and having Stick-to-itiveness requires that you constantly reevaluate your life then alter it accordingly. In the next chapter, you will learn insights on how to keep abreast of world and workplace changes.

SECRET #3:
UNDERSTAND WORLD
AND WORKPLACE CHANGES

Secret #3

Understand World and Workplace Changes

SOMEONE ONCE SAID THAT THE ONLY thing we know for sure in life is that we will

- Die
- Pay taxes and
- Be exposed to more change.

In recent years, adapting to the whims of change in both the world and workplace has become a way of life. In fact, some believe we've experienced more change over this past decade than we did during the Industrial Revolution.

Not only have we wallowed in change, but the rate and pace of change have also accelerated. Change happens more frequently and we must "get with it or perish" at lightning-like speed. Regarding the rate of change, I frequently reflect on the number of monumental changes that have occurred during my 50 years. I separate such occurrences by those that happened in the first 40 years of my life (1953–1993) and those that transpired after age 40.

World and life-altering events certainly occurred during those initial decades. Men walked on the moon for the first time, Camelot and the era of John F. Kennedy flourished and fell, civil rights statutes protecting the rights of blacks, women, and individuals with disabilities came into existence. The personal computer changed the way information was processed and exchanged, and the list goes on and on.

When I contrast the events and the rate and pace (frequency) of change that happened in the world and workplace from the 40-year period 1953–1993 with that which occurred after 1993, I immediately understand why so many people are feeling "change-weary."

To illustrate my point, reflect for a moment on the changes that occurred in a particular 1-year period: from September 11, 2001 to September 11, 2002. The chart which follows outlines some of those events, which affected our lives and the workplace. Take a moment to review this diagram, then reflect on how events since September 11, 2001 have affected your life and ability to LwL[2].

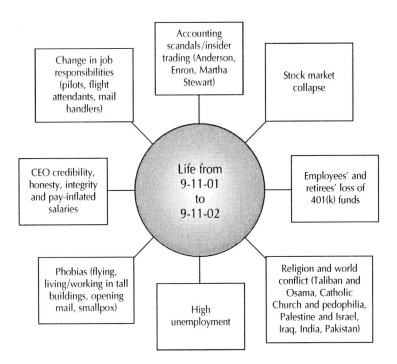

Without a doubt, the rate (how much) and pace (frequency) of change are occurring at a substantially higher rate than they occurred in the past. What, then, does this tell us about the implications of these phenomena on how we LwL2? What it says to me is that we must begin to understand why the changes occurred, then move to position ourselves to better accept them and move on with our lives.

In the pages that follow, we will begin by exploring

- What are the changes that have occurred in the world that affect the workplace, our lives and our ability to LwL2?
- How you can control and/or mitigate the effects of change on your ability to LwL2 if you understand the predictable stages of change.
- Are you ready or not for change?

Secret #3: Understand World and Workplace Changes
So the $1 billion question is if we want to be successful at LwL2, what must we do to adapt to a world character-ized by what Peter Vaill calls "Permanent White Water" change? Clara Ooyama, a Chief Operating Officer (COO) at Kodak, told me something interesting about her approach to change. She stated:

If I'm not willing to invest energy in doing something about it, why would I invest energy in complaining about it? My philosophy is that: if I'm not going to do something to change the situation, then I don't complain about it. If I can't or won't take time to work on correcting it, I'm not going to dwell on it and spend a whole lot of time not moving on.
—Clara Ooyama, Kodak Chief Operating Officer Global Diversity Office

---

In the pages ahead, we will examine the changes in the world that have affected the workplace, our lives and our ability to LwL2 both now and in the future.

Analyzing the WHAT and WHY of World and Workplace Change

When I begin to analyze WHAT changes have occurred in the workplace that affect our current ability to LwL², an image pops into my mind of my desk when I started my first professional job after college and graduate school.

The year was 1977, and I can visualize the oak desk and the items perched on top of it. The late-1970s objects I needed to perform my job are in front of me. There is a piece of equipment used to transmit information to others. What do you think it was? The latest PC perhaps? If that's what you're thinking…sorry…wrong answer. It's an IBM Selectric typewriter. Since the PC wouldn't even come into existence until a few years later in the early 1980s, a machine on which I could hunt and peck had to suffice.

While that typewriter did have a backspace key, it did not allow me to correct a mistake easily because it did not possess delete and insert functions. Instead, I had to rely on the help of a few office products to do so—namely liquid white-out or correcto tape.

Needless to say, because of this time-intensive correction process, sometimes if I was in a time crunch, I became overly tired because I just couldn't let the tiny errors go. If, however, I was busy making a change to an important document that my boss needed right away and the phone rang, I had a few choices of what I could do with the call. My options were

- Have my secretary take the call and write down a message for me on a pink message pad that contained carbon paper so she could give me the original and keep a copy for permanent records, or
- Let the phone ring and know that they'd call back because they couldn't leave a message on an answering machine which was yet to be invented.

When I did have a moment to answer my phone calls, I'd use my top-of-the-line rotary dial telephone. Push-button and cellular phones had not been mass-marketed yet. When I had time to return those calls, if someone else tried to reach me, they were simply out of luck and heard a busy signal rather than a beep, followed by a voice urging them to leave a brief message because their call was important to me.

The thought of owning a VCR, remote control, or having e-mail and a palm pilot would have been on an equal reality level as thinking that there really was a Santa Claus or an Easter Bunny. "Yeah, right," I'm sure I would have said, "There's no way machines could do those things for us."

After thinking about how radically different the desk and tools are that I use to perform my tasks today, I begin to shift my thoughts to an even deeper retrospective of how the workplace has changed since I entered the professional ranks in 1977.

At that time, companies such as IBM and the now-defunct Digital Equipment Corporation (DEC) operated in strict "no-layoffs" corporate cultures. These were places where staff were almost guaranteed tenure if they performed their job well and were not a disciplinary problem.

In the event a job disappeared because it was no longer needed, the expectation was that the company would reassign the employee to another job within the confines of their corporate structure. Throughout America in the late 1970s, it was not uncommon for the average worker to feel that if they worked hard and did a good job, their company would offer them job security in exchange. Rarely did people know what the term lay-off meant or even know anyone who had experienced the proverbial employment axe. Every now and then, however, someone would recall knowing someone who experienced a job reduction during the Great Depression, which occurred after the stock market collapsed in 1929!

Cradle-to-grave employment, in the late 1970s, was alive, well, and considered by many the expectation and societal norm. Employees didn't "job hop" from one company to another—in fact, that was frowned upon strongly. At that time, a recruiter or hiring manager looked on a candidate with a history of changing jobs every two to three years as a liability, not an asset. Further, that individual probably wouldn't be offered a position. The thinking back then was that if Mr. Joe GO is constantly changing jobs, he must not be stable. Many companies wanted someone who would come into their organization and retire with them after 25 or 30 years of service.

The "my-way-or-the-highway" school of management was alive and well as was the concept of resting on your laurels. For example, people needed credentials such as a high school, college or advanced degree to gain entry into certain jobs, but not necessarily to keep them. The skill sets one obtained through a college degree in 1975 could be the only ticket you needed to show that you had obtained a certain level of educational proficiency for life.

In the early 1980s, after Jimmy Carter lost the Presidency to Ronald Reagan, changes started to occur in the marketplace, which ultimately affected the job security dynamic. At that time, a mild recession (by today's standards) occurred and some people began to lose their jobs. I vividly remember that time because I began to see the use of that new word *layoff* in the vocabulary as some companies started to downsize. I was a layoff victim then, and for the first time in my life, I found myself as a young educated professional out of work. You'll learn more about that experience later. It wasn't until 1987 that the vast majority of businesses began to reframe their cradle-to-grave and no-layoff policies as a result of an event that happened on Black Monday in October of 1987. On that dark day, the stock market took a deep nose dive from its 1980's high-flying heights and crashed.

The deafening noise of the 1987 stock market collapse was heard not only in this country, but shock waves were felt around the world. The aftershocks of the stock market crash continued to build, reaching a peak in 1990 and 1991, when one of the worst recessions in the United States occurred.

Mega-changes were experienced in the workforce as companies literally fought for their corporate lives during that period. Terms like re-engineering and re-tooling, were the business terms du jour. Leaders like Lee Iacocca and W. Edwards Demming surfaced with new concepts of doing business. Iaccoca helped the automotive industry realize that quality would have to be Number One if they were to outperform their Japanese and other foreign competitors in the sale of well-built automobiles. Meanwhile, Demming, an American import to Japan, helped the Japanese learn how to structure their business philosophies and infrastructures. Ironically, Demming became the proverbial prophet who wasn't well recognized in his own land until outside forces rediscovered him.

During this period, other business leaders emerged, like Jack Welch who was given the nickname "Neutron Jack." He earned that distinction when he rebuilt General Electric by acting like a neutron bomb. The properties of a neutron bomb are such that they destroy/eliminate people—but leave buildings intact. Jack Welch, like a lot of CEOs throughout the country at that time, did a humongous amount of eliminating people and separating them from their jobs in the early years of the 1990s.

Recommended Reading

Welch, Jack with Bryne, John A. *Jack: Straight from the Gut.* New York: Warner Business Books, An AOL Time Warner Company, 2001.

Companies went from cradle-to-grave employment and no-layoff policies and not even knowing how to form their lips to say the word *layoff* to developing a plethora of terms to describe the process. Terms surfaced:

Downsizing	Right-sizing
Ostracizing	Reduction-in-force
"Giving people the axe"	Permanent sabbaticals

People, over time, were also told that they were "surplussed" or "deselected." Imagine telling someone that they are "deselected!"

As the year 1995 approached, the philosophies of Demming, Iaccoca, Welch and others proved to be just what the economy needed to boost itself out of the economic dumps.

I am a devotee of business magazines such as *FORTUNE*. Articles in three of their publications—June 13, 1994; March 16, 1998; and February 1, 1999— clearly tell the story of what transpired in workplaces throughout America from the mid-to late 1990s. Here's what they said:

There will never be job security. You will be employed by us as long as you add value to the organization, and you are continuously responsible for finding ways to add value. In return, you have the right to demand interesting and important work, the freedom and resources to perform it well, pay that reflects your contribution, and the experience and training needed to be employable here or elsewhere.
Source: FORTUNE, *June 13, 1994*

YO! Corporate America! I want a fat salary, a signing bonus, and a cappuccino machine—oh, and I'm bringing my bird to work. I'm the New Organization Man. You need me.
Roberto Ziche
Source: FORTUNE, *March 16, 1998*

Finished at 40
Companies used to pay for experience. Now they want potential— on the cheap. Just ask veteran marketing executive Mike Bellick, 46. He lost his job to a 28-year-old.
Source: FORTUNE, *February 1, 1999*

As these pieces illustrate, the workplace took a whirlwind tour through peaks and valleys of tossing and teasing employees. Following the stock market crash and then the recession of 1990–1991, employers announced that cradle-to-grave employment had expired. They announced new employment agreements, such as the one that appeared in the *FORTUNE* June 13, 1994 edition. Such contracts clearly included an implicit or explicit clause stating that the new rules of the workplace did NOT include a guarantee of job security.

By the late 1990s, this pact was well into effect and yet another landscape change took place in the world of work. As the March 16, 1998 cover of FORTUNE pointed out, "employees ruled!" Demands from signing bonuses to cappuccino machines and policies that allowed staff to bring pets to work were now in effect—anything to keep the scarce but highly prized and valued employee happy!

A year before the "New Millennium," it was clear that a new day had dawned. The rules of the workplace had undergone major surgery. In 1999, as the nation prepared to be counted in Census 2000, the changing demographics of the workplace had already weighed in. The February 1, 1999 issue of *FORTUNE* shows how workers were starting to look very different. MTV (Music Television) collided with AARP (American Association of Retired Persons) as young people began to more and more take jobs from individuals who were their mother's and father's—and even Grandma's and Grandpa's—age. As the February 1, 1999 *FORTUNE* magazine exclaimed, many middle-aged workers were finding themselves "finished at 40."

The New Millennium: From Dot-Com to Dot-Bomb

On January 1, 2000, when the new millennium "arrived," American workers (and organizations) had plenty to celebrate:

- A robust economy; stock market returns on investments were at some of the highest rates in history.
- Millions of jobs had been created during the Clinton administration.
- Workers in "HOT" demand and dot-com companies were making bountiful cash as the technology revolution ruled!
- High-wheeling stockbrokers and 23-year-old dot-com millionaires were able to hold employers hostage as they demanded ransoms consisting of sign-on bonuses as high as $100,000. As was reported in the *Wall Street Journal,* one company was giving new recruits and employees BMWs...in the color of their choice!

This high-yielding point in history came to a screeching halt in March 2001 as stock prices began to slip and the "R" words—recession and reduction-in-force—slipped into the lexicon and onto the tongues of business leaders, politicians, economists, financial analysts, TV commentators, and media moguls.

By September 11, 2001, the wheels of change had most definitely accelerated in the world and workplace. In fact, we are feeling the effects of that momentum today. What does all this have to do with LwL[2]? I'd like to answer that question by sharing with you my personal account of Lessons Learned from September 11, 2001 about LwL[2].

Chapter 7

Lessons Learned from September 11, 2001 About LwL²

ALMOST EVERYONE REMEMBERS WHERE they were on Tuesday, September 11, 2001. As previously mentioned, I was delivering a seminar, which was to be followed by a book-signing of my book, *Indispensable Employees: How to Hire Them. How to Keep Them.* These events were taking place at a Shell Oil Company conference in Houston, Texas. I had flown in to Hobby International Airport on Sunday September 9 from Boston's Logan Airport. My flight was on Delta, but out of habit, I had mistakenly gone to the American Airlines terminal, passing the infamous parking lot where a 9-11 terrorist's car eventually was located. This was to have been a short, routine business trip—out on Sunday (September 9) and back late Tuesday (September 11) night.

My 11-year-old daughter was left under the watchful eye of my 22-year-old niece, Yolanda Brown. Her father was on a business trip to Switzerland. Funny, the two of us were never out of Massachusetts on business trips at the same time. No problem. My daughter would hardly miss her mom and dad's presence. She had just started back to school and was busy on the phone and internet with her chums catching up on who did what, where and when in school. As you can probably guess, that business trip turned out to be neither routine nor short.

About an hour into my September 11 three-hour Shell Oil seminar, a rather official-looking person bolted through the door and politely announced: "I'm sorry to interrupt your seminar, but we wanted to keep you posted on something important. Two planes have been hijacked from Boston and have crashed into the World Trade Center in New York. Another plane has hit the Pentagon and a fourth went down somewhere in Pennsylvania. We'll continue to give you updates, but just continue on." The gentleman quickly exited the "you could hear a pin drop" seminar room.

Looking out into a misty sea of Shell Oil executives, managers and employees, I blurted out off the top of my head, "Did he say the plane was hijacked from Boston?" As if I were questioning myself, I muttered, "That's where I'm from." My next statement was even dumber: "Do you think anyone was killed?" A snide remark echoed from the audience, "I think if a plane hit a building like the World Trade Center, there would be some casualties." I replied, "Of course, duh!"

After pausing and shaking my head for a long minute, the cliché the show must go on became real for me. I had two hours left in my seminar and autographs of my *Indispensable Employees: How to Hire Them. How to Keep Them.* book yet to do. Taking three very deep breaths, I went back to my PowerPoint slides and somehow the show did proceed.

On several occasions during the year after September 11, 2001, I listened to two of my favorite media moguls, Larry King and Oprah, ask their guests, "Where were you on September 11?" Each time I heard that question, I reflected on where I was and how utterly frightened I was not only when I heard the news, but also when I realized the horrendous implications of that event.

Of course, I didn't make my flight out of Houston that Tuesday, September 11. I also didn't spend time that evening hugging my 11-year-old and giving her my surprise gift she has come to expect from each city that I visit. Instead, I huddled around the TV watching CNN with a colleague from Boston, Ms. Kim Cromwell. Thank God, as fate would have it, Kim also happened to be giving a seminar for Shell Oil at the same conference. I took comfort in having someone with me that evening who was familiar and from home. That night, I truly felt that the Bible's chapter of Revelations might actually be taking place. Could this be the Armageddon that movies had so graphically depicted? Like Dorothy from the Wizard of Oz, I wondered if I'd ever see my home and Kansas again. Would I ever be with my family, loved ones, business associates and my beloved cats, Neena and Nikki, again in this life?

The days immediately following September 11 did nothing to dispel those thoughts. As my 24/7 TV and newspaper vigil continued, hopes of ever reaching my "Kansas" again were dashed over and over.

Slowly details were revealed. Pictures appeared of President Bush riding the "not so friendly skies of United."

"Imagine that," I thought. "I can't go home to my house and our Commander in Chief is not able to go home to his White House either." That thought, however, didn't bring me solace. If the Chief Executive of the United States can't go to his domicile at the White House, why would an average citizen like me think I'd ever see my gray house again? Doubt really began to fog my thinking when the pictures of White House staff—some dressed in the uniforms of their professions—were huffing and puffing their way down the White House driveway. I remember vividly thinking, "If the cooks, butlers, maids, correspondents and others are fleeing the White House, who's left to take care of the First Family even if they could go back to their home?"

I was among the lucky ones. On Friday, September 14, just three long days after I was supposed to have returned home, my colleague Kim and I, along with two other people—John Truex, a famous New York shoe designer and Allen Abelow, an executive from Accenture—were on one of the first private planes out of Houston. Dr. Ashley Fields (no relation) of Shell Oil; Felicia, the concierge at the Houstonian Hotel; and Allen Abelow were all instrumental in helping to maneuver us out of Texas. Oh, how grateful I felt when I was finally heading to my home in the Bay State—and also worried about a newfound friend, Erika Zack, a manager at the famous Golden Door spa, who was left behind. We couldn't fly into Logan Airport because it was a crime scene and closed for an indefinite period, but that was just fine with me. I wasn't sure that I was ready to come face to face with that much tragedy.

I remember getting out of the private plane on Friday, September 14 and how utterly fabulous it felt as my feet hit the runway of TF Green Airport in Rhode Island. My impulse was to drop to my knees and kiss the ground like Pope John Paul II used to do in his younger days, but I held that urge in check. Somehow it didn't seem the proper thing to do after disembarking from a private plane. I vividly remember also wanting to hug the Boston Coach limo driver who cheerfully greeted my colleague and me and was ready to do whatever it took to get us back home safely to our "Kansas."

I recall my thoughts as we left TF Green Airport. I wasn't familiar with that particular section of Rhode Island, and all I wanted was to see something familiar—anything: a sign that said Massachusetts or better still, the familiar Boston skyline.

When that moment finally arrived, my heart was joyous and smiled. After reaching my gray house, I don't even remember ringing the doorbell or putting the key in the lock. I just recall saying goodbye to the Boston Coach limo driver and thanking him profusely for getting me home safely. My daughter, Shawna, and niece, Yolanda, suddenly appeared at the front door along with Neena and Nikki, our beloved cats, in tow. I hugged and kissed them as if I had been granted one last wish by a genie who would let me see them for my last time on earth.

Walking inside, I continued to caress them and the cats. "It's SO good to be home," I repeated for what seemed like the thousandth time. At that moment, I truly understood what Dorothy meant in one of my favorite movie classics, "The Wizard of Oz," when she finally made it back to Kansas. There truly is no place like home.

LIFE A YEAR LATER

It was a few days before we were to celebrate the one-year anniversary of September 11, 2001—that day that not only changed the course of history, but the direction of all our lives and our ability to LwL². I felt compelled at that time to get my thoughts out. It was amazing how different life had become just one short year later. I thought about the fact that the close to 3,000 people who lost their lives in the tragic events of that day had still been alive then. Little did they know that they had only a few days left to give their final hugs and kisses to their families and cats.

I wondered how many people the previous year thought that their patriotism would be rekindled and slogans like "Let's roll" would become part of the lexicon. Several friends and family members had still not been able to get onto a plane since 9-11. They weren't yet ready to face—as the old TV commercial used to say—those "friendly skies." I wondered at the time if anyone had quantified how much the income of therapists had soared as a result of the phobias people acquired after 9-11. I bet those who specialize in fears of flying, entering tall buildings, and visiting places like New York, Boston and Washington, D.C. had improved their bottom lines significantly that year.

I have a favorite saying—"You learn as much, if not more, from the downs as you do from the ups." This message has been particularly real for me in the years following 9-11-01. What knowledge have I acquired from those downs? Volumes. Here goes my list of the top five things I've learned from the post 9/11 downs:

1. ***Working is only one aspect of my life.*** I've vowed to take time to show loved ones I care as much about them as I do my job and career. Did the people going to work at the World Trade Center in New York City for the last time know that the stacks of emails they were rushing to send out on September 11 or the stock prices they were checking weren't going to be the most important things they would do during their final day on this earth? Did they have time before they left for their World Trade Center office to kiss or tell their children, spouses, or significant others how much they loved them? So many of us are wrapped up into making a living that we forget how to live. To LwL² means taking time to perk, smell, and share the coffee with family and friends. I don't always get it right, but I'm trying harder to make sure that everyday the special people in my life know I love them. I don't want a cell phone call or answering machine to be how they find out in the end how much I really cared for and adored them.

2. ***Approach each day as if it were my last.*** I've often wondered if any of the almost 3,000 people who perished as a result of the 9-11 events had a clue that their end was near. Some believe that if you're really in tune with the universe there can be tell tale signs that your life is ending. I've wondered if I'd recognize those signals when my number is up. Just in case I don't get the clues, I've started to try and live up to this statement and make it a way of life. I'll admit, I'm not successful everyday in "approaching each day as if it were my last," but I am trying.

Here's how it works for me: The days leading up to the one-year anniversary of September 11 felt like Yogi Berra's saying: "Déjà vu all over again." Believe it or not, as fate would have it, I had to take the same business trip I took in the days preceding September 11, 2001. My plans were to fly on Delta from Boston's Logan Airport on Sunday September 8. Once again I drove near the central parking area where the September 11 terrorists' car was found. I flew into Houston's Hobby Airport, as I had last year. I spoke again at the Shell Oil conference and flew out as planned on this routine business trip on Tuesday September 10th.

I've had to fly many times since September 11, including the path that several victims of 9-11 flew, such as several American Airlines flights to New York City and United flights to Washington, D.C. and Pennsylvania. During the week of February 24, 2002—five months after September 11—I had the pleasure of visiting the Big Apple and watched as workers cleaned up the World Trade Center Ground Zero site.

I took a shuttle from Boston to New York. I don't have a problem with getting onto a plane; however, I was actually relieved when it was a smaller plane—a less attractive option for any hijacker-wannabe because it carried less fuel than those that transport passengers to, say, Los Angeles.

Once on board the plane, I carefully scrutinized every man, woman, and child (including babies) along with their carry-ons. I checked for the exit signs. Although I've heard it a zillion times and usually don't pay it much mind, I listened attentively to the flight attendants' spiel about the features of the plane and what to do "in the unlikely event" of an emergency.

I admit that all the visualization techniques I know went into high gear. I took the time to play out in my mind's eye what I would do if the cabin lost pressure and I had to put on one of those thingamajigs before helping someone else. In addition, I rehearsed how I would use my seat cushion as a flotation device just in case everyone on the plane had to observe the "do not panic" instructions and walk (do not run) to the nearest exit and proceed down the evacuation slide.

Once in New York, the social anthropologist in me came out, and I wanted to take a big chomp out of the Apple and digest how 9-11 had altered it. I conducted some business at *FORTUNE* and Warner Brothers then spent the rest of the week attending a Women Presidents' Organization

(WPO) Conference at the Marriott Financial Center—down the street from Ground Zero.

The newly renovated hotel had just opened so our group was one of its first conferences after 9-11. The week of February 24, 2002 was an awesome time to taste the Big Apple. Like Rip Van Winkle waking up from his long nap, the city was reawakening. Schools that had been closed reopened that week. Not only had the Marriott Hotel Financial Center dug itself out from the ashes, but so had businesses and department stores like Century 21, a shopaholic's heaven, located across the street from Ground Zero.

I had many emotions when I visited Ground Zero for the first time. To me, the site itself looked a little smaller than it had on CNN, FOX, ABC, NBC and CBS. On the other hand, the true enormity of what happened in that space hadn't been captured thoroughly in any television camera lens.

I stood directly across the street from the Ground Zero site, zombie-like, with hoards of other onlookers, including my niece, Yolanda, who had accompanied me on my business trip. I took in all the sights, sounds and emotions of the workers who were cleaning up the site. The air was somber and a "can't quite put your finger on it" smell; perhaps it was a concoction of smoke, ashes, debris and sacred human remains that lingered in my nostrils. The clacking and hacking of large equipment and smaller shovels mixed with reverent whispers and hushed conversations of bystanders who shook their heads in disbelief or closed their eyes tightly in prayer. Many people were muttering things like "I can't believe it," "Why," or "How could they have been so cruel?" For about 30 minutes, my niece and I stood frozen in time, internalizing everything around us. A light gray powderlike substance clung to many of the buildings in the area. There were American flags in assorted sizes and in various frazzled conditions, many of which were coated in that light gray film.

Three images of Ground Zero are still prominent in my brain. One is of a very tall skyscraper draped in black. Another is of an abandoned building that had a steam-like substance spewing from its interior. My niece pointed it out to me. "Can you believe that building is still smoldering?" She asked into the cool February air. The third image was that of the workers—firefighters, police, and an array of construction workers. Many were busy at work, others looked like they were on break and "shooting the breeze."

"What a difference a year and a big tragedy can make," I thought. Twelve months before, for some people those guys were zeros, but that day they were heroes. Who would have thought that FDNY and NYPD T-shirts, baseball caps and other paraphernalia would become top sellers in the New York City street vendor stalls?

On Friday, March 1, 2002, my WPO group went to see the hot Broadway musical, "Urinetown." I remember that night, walking in Times Square past the popular Broadway theaters. The air was electric, so alive and vibrant. The streets were jammed wall-to-wall with people. My mind floated back to Friday, September 14, 2001, the night I finally got home from my Houston trip. I recall how utterly fabulous it felt to finally curl up into my own bed and twinkle my toes under my soft sheets with my cats, Neena and Nikki, curled up around me. I got my nightly CNN fix on the latest happening in the war on terrorism. As I watched the footage of the workers cleaning up Ground Zero and the reruns of the planes crashing then exploding into the Twin Towers, I recall wondering what it was like for the people in New York to be under a curfew. How did Broadway and Times Square look when the lights were turned out and theater goers couldn't get tickets to any hot Broadway show even if they had the means? After leaving the "Urinetown" musical on Friday, March 1, 2002, I still contemplated what a people-less Times Square and Broadway must have smelled, tasted and felt like. The actions of 18 men and their behind-the-scenes cohort Osama bin Laden had in many ways brought New York City and the United States to its knees, but it

hadn't destroyed the spirit and will of its people to rebuild. But, without a doubt, this 9-11 event had changed many individuals' ability to LwL^2.

I've traveled to New York numerous times over the years. My overall impression of New York on this post-9-11 trip was that it had become a kinder, gentler place. While the pace of the city continued to keep up with that of a rocket, I was pleasantly surprised at the number of people on the street, from Central Park to Rockefeller Center— shopkeepers, cab drivers and hotel staff who deliberately took time to chit chat and joke around with me. I left New York City with a much greater appreciation for the enormity of the toll that 9-11 took on the city as well as how big the resolve was of its people to rise again from the Ground Zero ashes to LwL^2. I must admit that even though I'm attempting to live each day as if it were my last, I don't want to hasten the process. I chose not to spend the night in lovely Houston, but to catch a plane out of Hobby on Tuesday night after speaking at the Shell Oil Conference, instead of waiting to leave on Wednesday, September 11, 2002.

Many people asked me, "Weren't you afraid that lightning would strike twice? What if terrorists had tried something before the September 11 first anniversary?" My standard reply went something like this: "When my times comes, I'm gone whether I want to be dead or not. I could be sitting in my home when some terrorist decides to blow up all the houses on my street. I have no control over that. I can't worry about such things. Instead, I need to make sure that I'm working on making my life right so when my time comes to meet my maker, I'll be in good shape. I want my God to tell me that I've 'done good' and that my job on earth has been well done. To LwL^2, that's what I have to be concerned about, not about whether or not my plane will be hijacked."

Usually after I finish this speech, the person(s) I'm talking to stares at me with a "deer-in-the-headlights" look and, depending on their age, usually replies, "That makes sense," or "Whatever." While I do truly believe in my heart what I've just articulated, if the truth be known, I struggle everyday to make sure I abide by those words.

3. ***Remember the people in the days following September 11 who tried to reach you and make sure you were alive and safe and vice versa.*** When I was stranded in Houston and unable to return to the Boston and Cambridge, Massachusetts area, it left deep psychological scars in my soul. They were not the bad kind of "psycho" wounds that leave you paralyzed and unable to cope, but the good ones. In the immediate days after that horrendous event, my eyes were opened as it became clear who was truly important in my life. What was so revealing was my choice of who to call in those tense Armageddon-feeling post 9-11 hours and days. It was equally astonishing to find out who felt the need to locate me in the universe and make sure I was still breathing and out of harms way. Of course I communicated with my brothers and sisters, dad, stepmother, my child and niece I had left in Boston and my significant other who was trapped in Switzerland. Beyond that, it was equally revealing to me who I didn't speak to directly or hear from at all.

I call myself a "corporate cupid" and as such, I am always looking to shoot my darts and bring organizations and people together to make a memorable, positive difference in the world. The corporate cupiding career can be a tiring one and leave you sometimes focusing on relationships that consume too much of your time, but nevertheless—duty calls and you respond. What September 11 taught me was a new outlook on my corporate cupiding position and on how I needed to view relationships in general. Before September 11, I had so many corporate couples to bring together that I hardly had time to spend with the people *I* cared about the most, and who shared that view about *me*. In giving so much to others, there was precious little time left to devote to myself.

Those calls I made from Houston during the days following September 11 and those I received from people worried about my post 9-11 where-abouts spoke volumes. One story really stands out. Before leaving for Houston on September 9, 2001, I had told a friend and colleague who works at Gillette—Deborah Perry—that I would be away on business. A neighbor of hers who attended my daughter's school told her that my daughter had left the school in tears on September 11 because her dad called from Europe and said she needed to go home immediately.

My friend from Gillette tried to put two and two together. She thought: Martha told me she was flying out on business. Her daughter was called home from school and left crying. That equals to Martha must have been on one of those planes that crashed. I was stunned on the evening of September 11 when yet another friend reached me in Houston. "I heard that you were on one of those planes, and even though your niece told me you weren't, I had to call and make sure you were fine," Janine said. She then told me how she arrived at that conclusion after speaking with Deborah. I was stunned. Then I laughed. "They can't get rid of me yet," I said. I hung up the phone and knew I was blessed to have colleagues and friends in the world who were so concerned about me.

4. ***Tomorrow's paycheck is promised to no one, so learn how to reinvent yourself regularly.*** Before 2002, who could have predicted that the vast majority of Enron or Arthur Anderson employees would no longer work for what had been two of the world's most prestigious and profitable companies? What retired persons from Polaroid, or individuals age 65+ who were living off their 401(k) plans would have dreamed that they'd need to come out of retirement and get a job as a department store greeter or grocery bagger in order to make ends meet or pay for health insurance?

What pre-2002 college student would have contemplated *not* going into a career such as an auditor/accountant, priest or bishop because it no longer stood for ethics, integrity and morals? What parents would have dreamed about a next door neighbor slipping into their home to rape, murder or, as in the case of Elizabeth Smart, kidnap their child while they slept? Somehow the commercial "like a good neighbor, State Farm is there" takes on a different meaning after September 11, 2001.

But what about job security? Many people feared the worst, especially with company after company laying off people after September 11 and stock prices collapsing and consumers not purchasing goods because, in their belt-tightening process, they discovered it was possible to do without them. Even in good economic times, job security is certainly not promised to any of us, but now more than ever I ask myself, What must I do to reinvent myself if I want to stay gainfully employed and LwL[2]?

5. ***Understand that to be gainfully employed, you may need to mutate regularly.*** The winners in the job security game are those who understand that there really is no job security, but that to thrive and survive you must mutate regularly.

Another interesting fallout of September 11 was that so many jobs changed. Take, for example, the jobs of people like pilots and flight attendants. What about postal workers and mail clerks who sort mail and found out that, if exposed to anthrax, their jobs could lead to their deaths? The value of a job, the price tag we are willing to pay someone to perform certain tasks, also came under fire and closer scrutiny. We've started to question why many CEOs are paid millions of dollars through prenuptial-like golden parachutes and severance arrangements, even after they've run companies into the ground, leaving workers unemployed, shareholders stockless, and retirees pensionless.

For employers, mutating regularly calls for the need to look more closely at the salaries of people who perform seemingly simple tasks like screening baggage at airline terminals. Before September 11, their salaries were close to minimum wage. Now

that people understand that a person's job can determine if the security of the world is violated, their wages have increased. In addition, the skills that are required to do the job have also become more robust. Currently, individuals must also possess some background in law enforcement, but such a breed of workers is scarce.

After September 11, many of us truly realized that no one is promised job security. Questions, however, still abound about whether we can produce enough skilled workers in the future to perform all of the jobs in our country. We must answer some very tough questions in the months and years ahead, like how much is a job really worth, and what are we truly willing to pay to get an important job done.

David Angell, the producer of the popular TV show *Frazier*, was killed with his wife on one of the Boston planes that crashed into the World Trade Center. In the weeks leading up to September 11, I had seen a report on one of those evening Hollywood entertainment shows about how much money Kelsey Grammer, the star of Frazier, had negotiated in his contract. The commentator mentioned that Grammer received at least $1 million per episode. When I heard about David Angell, I was saddened and thought, imagine that—all the money he was making and paying others, and in the end it didn't matter—his life couldn't be bought. I was also struck by the disparity of what someone like a movie star makes in relation to an individual like a baggage x-ray technician whose job can potentially determine whether a plane is hijacked and innocent people, places and things are destroyed.

I was shocked by a report I heard in 2002 which talked about the Major League Baseball strike that took place that year and that the average player made about $2.5 million a year. Imagine that, I thought, $2.5 million to hit a ball with a bat? In another report, I learned that some of the top playing boys of summer are paid a tad more— between $10 million and $25 million per year. Why is it that we don't pay our childcare workers or teachers so handsomely? Aren't they also playing with the lives of our kids and our future?

At the time, I didn't know whether I was ready to face the first anniversary of September 11, 2001 or not, but it arrived and left just as the sun and moon do daily. I'm resolved to try and live each day as if it were my last. In July and again in August of 2002, I visited Washington, D.C. for a week. As I walked past the White House, the Washington Monument and the Mall and on to the Capitol, I felt very patriotic as I thought about the national symbols that the terrorists had tried unsuccessfully to destroy but didn't on that September morning in 2001. I took the DC DUC tour while I was there and remember one thing the tour guide said about the Capitol Building. On the dome of the Capitol is a statue. That statue faces the east and represents Freedom. "Where does the sun rise?" The tour guide asked us. "In the east," we replied in unison. "Freedom faces the east so the sun will never set on it," the guide responded. In this post-September 11 world, I sure hope he is right.

Once again on November 14 (Friday), 2003, I visited the site of the World Trade Center in New York. One day before, I had announced the release of this book at the famous Friars Club. The event, hosted by Tom and Janine Fondon along with Alicia Evans and Gina Russell Stevens, also included insightful remarks by Cynthia D. Brown of the New York Friars Club and Lori Ioannou of FORTUNE.

I saw the abandoned building, that when I visited New York in February 2002, had a steam-like substance still smoldering from September 11, 2001. Progress had been made and nothing was spewing from the building. Next door to the building a sign was displayed prominently. It read:

Wise Words

"The human spirit is not measured by the size of the act, but by the size of the heart."

I crossed the street to go shopping at Century 21 and was looking at some beautiful crystal paperweights when the street vendor, named Willie, stated, "You don't have to be a Rockefeller to help a fellow." I believe Willie's words are a valuable message for anyone in a post-9-11 environment who wants to LwL[2].

In the next chapter, we will explore ways to bounce back after tragedy and mega-change in the workplace.

Chapter 8

Bouncing Back After Tragedy and Mega-Change in the Workplace

A FTER READING THE PRECEDING CHAPTERS you may be thinking that the workplace seems incredibly schizophrenic. Mixed messages dominate the organizational landscape. Organizations are downsizing while at the same time conducting mergers and acquisitions. Some companies and industries are at death's door or a heartbeat away from placement on the "Do Not Resuscitate" list while others are flourishing.

Many organizations are "hanging in there," knowing that it's just a matter of time before revenues rebound. Even within companies, disparate messages abound. It is not uncommon for a company to layoff staff in one department while hiring heavily in another.

All of these conflicting events may cause you to wonder about how to better bulletproof your career during uncertain times. With all these issues floating around the corridors of companies, it is no wonder that at the end of the day a lot of us look and feel like the woman in the picture on the next page.

TODAY'S EMPLOYEE

Since events such as downsizings, mergers, and acquisitions are guaranteed to cause stress and anxiety that ultimately impact your ability to LwL^2, it is important to learn about ways to cope with such situations before, during, and after the occurrences. In the pages ahead, I'll provide insights and suggestions to approaches you can take to minimize your stress when the death of your job, or that of others, occurs. We will begin by exploring ways to deal with the death of a job, company, or career.

DEALING WITH THE DEATH OF A JOB, A COMPANY OR A CAREER

As mentioned previously, before 1980 few people or organizations had expertise in conducting layoffs. Cradle-to-grave organizational philosophies allowed legions of workers to retire from their jobs after 25, 30, 40+ years with a gold watch or a rocking chair. Today, the notion of a company taking care of a person from work-infancy to death is an idea that has been buried like dinosaur relics. Whether you exist in an organization that truly cares about their staff before, after, and during major changes in the workplace—mergers, acquisitions, downsizing and leadership shifts—or one that couldn't care a hill of beans about the aftermath of its business decisions, here are some tips to consider when dealing with these situations so you can continue down the path of LwL^2.

Tip #1—Whether you are the initiator, recipient or survivor of a pink slip, understand that everyone is afraid of losing their job.

When I was the head of a Human Resources department and our organization went through the first layoff in its recent history, you could breathe the tension that swirled in the air the day before the announcement was to be made. As the senior Human Resources executive, I was the only person in the entire organization who had the master list containing the names of all the individuals who would no longer have a job.

Survivor Syndrome issues   Terrorist concerns

Weak leadership

Computer literacy   Future uncertainty

Job plateauing   **Employee**   Multidisciplinary and
                                                        self-directed teams

Retirement   Elder- and
concerns   childcare issues

Diversity and   Merger, acquisition
globalization   and downsizing

Continuous learning   **Concerns**   Loss of job security
and change

Working 1.5 jobs   Do more with less

Balancing work, family,
personal life

I've always thought of that particular Human Resource job responsibility as a blessing and a curse. On the one hand, I knew if my name or one of my staff was on that list. I also knew that invariably I'd run into someone whose job fate I knew but he didn't. When that would happen, I'd cringe thinking about how devastated that individual was probably about to become and how un-fun it was to know someone's future when he didn't have a clue that his life was about to change radically.

On the day before layoff notices were to be distributed to the unsuspecting recipients, I telephoned my boss, the Chief Operating Officer and second-in-command of this prestigious organization. I wanted to speak with him in person about a sensitive issue and asked for about ten minutes of his time. When I arrived at my boss' office, he looked extremely anxious and nervous. Sweat was dripping from his brow and huge rings had formed under the armpits of his starched blue button-down collar shirt. I told my boss what I needed to tell him, then got up to leave. Sitting on the edge of his executive leather chair, my boss blurted out, "Is that ALL you have to tell me?"

"Why yes," I replied. Wiping his sweaty forehead with the back of his hand, he exclaimed, "Whew, I thought you were going to tell me that I was going to be laid off."

I couldn't believe my ears. My own boss was afraid that he might not escape the blade of the layoff axe. The moral of the story is that regardless of your position, when there are layoffs in an organization, everyone is concerned about job security. This concern, if not kept in check, can radically affect your ability to LwL².

Tip #2—To properly recover from a layoff, you must mourn, then move on. To put yourself in position to LwL² again, allow yourself time to process through the stages of change.

To Love your work by Loving your Life, you need to understand that there are predictable stages of change. You must also learn how to deal with change effectively over time. In the changing world and workplace, we must constantly know how to adapt to, accept, or reject changes around us. With the rapid pace of change, we are often called upon to very quickly understand and absorb changes that often are beyond our wildest and raciest imaginations. Here is some advice to help you better cope with the changes of the workplace or world.

Understanding Stages of Grief and the Death of a Job

Countless authors and experts have dispensed information on the stages that an individual and/or organization go through when change occurs. It is crucial to understand and accept that when a change happens you must go through these stages in order to move on. Awareness of this notion also provides useful insights for those who must respond to the psychological and personal needs of individuals who lose their livelihood.

There is one model of change that I particularly like, although many others exist. This construct is commonly used by people who are dealing with stages of death and dying or grief as stages or steps. It is also applied to situations where an individual suffers a loss or social identity change. Elizabeth Kübler-Ross, M.D., wrote a very important book, *On Death and Dying,* based on her research in which she observed the stages that evolved as patients became aware of a terminal illness.

I first discovered this model when I worked in a Harvard Medical School-affiliated teaching hospital. While it is most commonly used to help people through the death and mourning process for a person, many have found it useful to describe the process one must undertake to accept almost any type of monumental, unexpected death-like experience. Since so many of us define ourselves (and some of us even derive our self-esteem) through our job, the loss of it can be devastating. For some, it is like a death.

Before you can accept and move on when a change occurs—particularly one that is horrendous and life-shattering—you may go through stages. It should be noted that some experts believe that not everyone goes through this process or that they experience it in a different order than that described by the Kübler-Ross model.

The Kübler-Ross stages are[1]

1. **Denial and Isolation**—You will experience strong shock and doubt that what occurred did in fact happen. Here you hope against all odds that what took place really and truly did not transpire. Perhaps you heard the news wrong, or this is a bad dream and you'll wake up and find it was just a nightmare; or maybe someone made a mistake and the information given to you was false—you rationalize that they *will* come back and retract that awful news about you no longer having a job. In addition, you experience isolation as others around you may avoid contact with you about what has occurred. In some cases, this is because individuals do not know what to say and/or what help they can offer you.

2. **Anger**—Once reality finally seeps in and you realize that what you heard is true, the next phase you will encounter is that of anger. The rage you experience can be directed outwardly towards the change itself or to the people and/or circumstances that caused the change, including anger with God. The anger can also be directed inward and cause almost every aspect of your life to be colored by it. Your ability to LwL[2] can seem nonexistent.

3. **Bargaining**—At some point in your journey, you start to tire of the anger or reach the conclusion that perhaps if you try harder and/or bargain with your God or the powers that be, you can postpone or delay what is about to happen. Some Human Resource professionals and managers report that employees who have been laid off often try to find

---

1 Source: Critiques of the Kübler-Ross Model—
  http://imc.gsm.com/demos/dddemo/consult/kublcrit.htm

a way to communicate with executives in their organization so that they can plead their own case as to why the organization needs them and why they shouldn't be laid off or should be brought back into the company.

Finally, you realize the life-altering change *did* occur and start to come to terms with how and why it took place. More importantly, you begin to delve deeper into the reasons for the change and assess what you'll need to cope with the reality and its aftermath.

4. **Depression**—At this stage, people finally come to grips with the fact that the death of the job is permanent and irreversible. The complete blow of the loss is felt, and depression—or what some term "the blues"—may rise to the surface.

5. **Acceptance**—In this phase, you finally reach the point where the change has been sufficiently processed for you to let go of the feeling that things will return to the way they were before the change. You reach the conclusion that new attitudes, behaviors, and lifestyle changes must

take place so you can cope, and—you hope—peacefully coexist with this change in your universe.

In this last step of the change process, you have accepted or adapted to the change and begin to live in a new reality. Your ability to LwL^2 may be restored. Some people, however, never reach this stage but continue to languish in the pain of what has happened to them and the unfairness of it all.

KÜBLER-ROSS MODEL APPLICABILITY TO THE DEATH OF A JOB

It is important to note that while many would agree with my view that the Kübler-Ross model on death and dying is a useful tool to understand the effect that layoffs have on individuals, others take exception to that approach. The following passage, found on a website (*http://imc.gsm.com/demos/dddemo/consult/kublcrit.htm*), demonstrates one opinion.

Critiques of the Kübler-Ross Model

THE KÜBLER-ROSS MODEL FOR DESCRIBING the grief process is widely accepted, but it is not without its critics. Schneidman emphasizes that "stages" oversimplifies the process, and describes dying as "a complicated clustering of intellectual and affective states." The stages of dying often do not unfold in a linear fashion, but are overlapping, emerging, retreating and re-emerging in different guises over time. Some have charged that conceptualizing five successive stages of dying makes even the process of dying something to be "rated," and puts pressure on patients to resolve their more "primitive" responses and move toward a so-called "healthy" death, comfortable in the final stage of acceptance.

Additionally, this model may not be applicable to the majority who die in old age, where a

terminal diagnosis may be more acceptable to the individual.

Many of the aged have experienced a gradual diminution of health and abilities which predates any knowledge of impending death. Such a diagnosis may be better accepted by the elderly both because of gradual infirmity and because approaching death is not viewed as a "surprise," but rather as part of a long and total life experience.

There are, of course, other models for understanding this important process which are well-worth your reading. One which deserves your special consideration is in the more recent work of Backer, Hannon and Russell.

References:
Backer, B., Hannon, R., & Russell, N. (1994). *Death and Dying: Understanding and Care*, 2nd ed. Albany, NY: Delmar Pub.
Schneidman, E. (1983) *Deaths of Man*. New York: Jason Aronson, Inc.

Recommended Reading

For more information on this subject, you many want to read Elizabeth Kübler-Ross' book, *On Death and Dying—What the Dying Have to Teach Doctors, Nurses, Clergy and Their Own Families.*

I still maintain that the Kübler-Ross model is a useful tool for any of us experiencing the valleys—and peaks—associated with job loss. However, it is important to know the limitations of this model for all situations.

10 Positive Ways to Look at Loss

By Herb Pearce—Psychotherapist, Trainer, Enneagram Specialist

1. Remember the summer ends on September 21 (not the end of August), so keep playing and having fun. Remember to have fun and enjoy life no matter what time of the day or year or even when you are feeling down!
2. Have faith that something positive will happen from change, even while you may be grieving or are afraid.
3. See loss and change as natural growth cycles that all living things go through. Surrender to what is natural and learn how to be with it.
4. Loss makes room for richness even beyond the loss. Have faith that life supports evolution.
5. Empathize with others who are experiencing loss, change and reactions to change.
6. Create security more and more from deeper things in your life and less from things that come and go.
7. Money, how a relationship is or will be, your possessions, even your health will change in time—can you enjoy these things and yet be less attached to them and how they have to be?
8. Reflect on your history of losses and see if any treasures came from them in time.
9. Watch how your mind tries to control things— let go of your mind being in total charge—have your clarity and choices become something bigger, more inclusive, more free.
10. Whether you are down, in pain, grief or anger, remember to look around and love and enjoy life at the same time—bring all your feelings with you—don't deny them, experience them and yet stay open too.

Tip #3—Understand how layoff decisions are made and whose court the ball lands in after a downsizing.

I've had the distinct privilege of learning about layoff decisions from many vantage points. Throughout my career as an employee, Human Resources executive and Management consultant, I've had to experience the ins and outs of how people get downsized. If you aren't a manager or in Human Resources, you may not know the painstaking steps that many organizations go through before handing out those proverbial pink slips. I'd like to give you an insight into how those decisions are sometimes made. I believe this will help you to better understand whose court the ball is in after certain team members are let go in the layoff game.

Regardless of how quickly a layoff decision is made, someone in an organization has to take the time to assess current talent in order to decide who stays on the team and who gets the pink slip to involuntarily become a free agent. Organizations vary regarding which individuals in the company are involved in that decision making process. Sometimes it is the manager, a Human Resources professional or executive, a lawyer, the President/CEO, a senior manager and/or a combination of people.

Typically, layoff decisions involve conversations around criteria that should be used to lay off an individual. These dialogues may include discussions about individual employees or departments and divisions. Topics discussed may or may not include the following:

- Seniority
- Last hired/first fired
- Performance
- Legal concerns
- Skill sets needed after the layoff
- Revenue-makers or people who have job skills or skill sets necessary for the survival of the company or who have invaluable information, an institutional memory and/or know where the organizational skeletons are buried

In most organizations, the decisions to eliminate a job are not taken lightly or made easily. Many organizations go to great lengths to try other solutions before resorting to layoffs. This can include such things as

- Cutting salaries
- Mandating a hiring freeze
- Eliminating or cutting back on overtime
- Eliminating frills such as free coffee, food at meetings, company parties, and free holiday events
- Changing or increasing the employees' contributions to benefits such as health care
- Decreasing vacations and other time-off benefits
- Eliminating bonuses
- Cutting hours
- Early retirement programs
- Voluntary layoffs

In the sad event that layoffs must occur, before they are announced, work must be done to prepare the organization and those who will be laid off for the news. A series of activities must occur, including preparing layoff lists, notices and various security issues. Most companies also train and/or notify the individuals who will deliver the bad news on how to communicate the messages. A large array of benefit and pay issues must be resolved such as

- Payouts for unused vacation or other time off
- Benefits that will be continued or discontinued (health and life insurance, 401(k)/pension plans)
- Outplacement resources outside of the organization
- Internal assistance to find a new job
- The criteria for making the layoff decisions/explanation of layoff process
- Resolution of the work the individual is leaving behind
- Severance pay agreements and policies
- How to apply for unemployment benefits
- Procedures for returning company property
- Security procedures and changes in computer security passwords, etc.

Depending on the organization, other issues and considerations must be addressed. As you can see, it is a laborious process to eliminate labor in an organization!

So, once the deed is done, where does that leave those who are left behind? They must now pick up and carry the ball so that revenue can continue to be made and no further layoffs occur.

Most of the people left behind are also greatly affected in a negative way by layoff activities. Experts have conducted mountains of research on the aftermath of layoffs and how staff react. Generally, the scene after the death of jobs is not a pretty picture. In fact, it's usually downright gruesome.

While staff who survive are typically relieved that their work life has been spared from the layoff axe, others would have preferred to have "gotten the layoff package." Research tells us that many people who are left behind suffer from what is called, "The Survivor's Syndrome." The Center for Creative Leadership has conducted some interesting work in this area and if you are interested in learning more about this subject, they might be a source for you.

SURVIVOR'S SYNDROME

I'd like to give you a brief overview about what people who have the Survivor's Syndrome experience. Believe it or not, they go through the same type of trauma that individuals experience after a major horrific event, such as a

- Plane crash
- Holocaust
- Natural disaster like a flood or tornado
- Terrorist bombing

They are marked by the event and have a range of conflicting emotions. For example, they may feel very lucky to have survived but still experience pain that it was someone they cared about who is gone and not them. They may be happy to have a job, but not so thrilled about the fact that their coworkers are out of work.

Most people heal from Survivor's Syndrome at their own pace but, in fact, some never do. Organizations are filled with people who never get better; they become the "working wounded" who have checked out emotionally but stayed physically because the job pays the bills.

Layoffs, whether they are a result of poor economic times, mergers, acquisitions, or businesses folding, seem to be with us for the long haul. If you are an employee, it is essential that you learn how to cope before, during and after a layoff. If, however, you are in a management position, learning how to conduct layoffs with grace is an important skill to acquire. Laura Avakian, Vice President of Human Resources at the Massachusetts Institute of Technology (MIT), sheds some light on how to say good-bye with grace.

Goodbye with Grace

By Laura Avakian—Vice President Human Resources, Massachusetts Institute of Technology (MIT)

"FUNERALS ARE FOR THE LIVING" IS A TRUISM. Throughout history, people have recognized that a farewell ritual for the deceased is important to loved ones and friends. We are consoled by the act of celebrating a life that touched us and by grieving side by side with others who share our loss.

When employees leave their jobs, particularly those who have been with an organization for some time, their co-workers may experience many of the same emotions as those that accompany death and dying. This is true even when an employee leaves for a happy reason, such as accepting a promotion elsewhere or having a baby. But it is even more profound when an employee is laid-off, "downsized," or otherwise terminated without cause.

David M. Noer, author of *Healing the Wounds* (Jossey-Bass 1993) addresses the phenomenon he terms "layoff survivor sickness." He notes that this "disease" is "widespread and toxic to both the human spirit and organizational survival." He says that while "organizations institute layoffs to cut costs and promote competitiveness…all they have gained is a depressed, anxious and angry workforce."

Most survivors of a layoff express a variety of feelings about the action—none of them positive. They may look for someone or something to blame: bad administrators, poor financial planning and performance, as examples. They may begin to fear for their own jobs, thereby becoming depressed, less willing to take risks, less productive. They may feel enormous guilt: "Why was poor Susie laid off and not me?"

There is no way to sugarcoat the reality of what happens during a layoff any more than there is a way to obliterate the sadness accompanying the loss of a loved one. However, there are actions an organization can take when downsizing that helps both the victims and survivors, and that ultimately helps the entire organization become a better workplace.

Here are some suggested actions:

- First, conduct the layoffs in a personal way. Notices should not be sent by email or memo. The manager closest to the employee should deliver the message. It should be compassionate and offer specific kinds of transitional support.
- Departing employees should be given the opportunity to say goodbye, and where possible to have suitable thank-you "parties."
- Administrators should be visible and sympathetic. If they cannot meet with the laid-off employees, they should send a personal note or make a phone call.
- Severance benefits should be as generous as possible.
- Conduct training for managers in how to deliver the news of a layoff to both victims and to surviving staff; let managers help train and support each other.
- Overcommunicate. We tend to hear selectively in traumatic situations, so be redundant with as much information as possible about the reason for the layoff, how it will be conducted and what support will be provided to those who go and those who stay.
- Provide professional outplacement services, but work with the company to make certain the programs are tailored to your culture and that they are individualized.
- Conduct appropriate interventions that facilitate the grieving process for the survivors. Talk openly about the sadness of loss, but also about the kind of organization you want to be.

- Provide career development programs or services that encourage employees to begin more aggressive self-management of their careers. This is empowering. It helps reduce the fear of downsizing and other organizational change.

Remember that all your actions toward the downsized employees send strong messages to the survivors—as well as to your customers and community—about the kind of place your organization is and how vital and viable it will be in the long run.

Personalized, generously supported and compassionate partings allow employees to exit with dignity and grace. They enable co-workers to grieve in ways that ultimately build a stronger team with greater energy and resilience. And, finally, they are a statement of recognition that our organizations will and should be judged by the way we treat our people, by the way we treat each other.

Best, Interesting and Radical Practices
Companies Helping Staff Cope with Change, Loss and Tragedy

When I think what best practices companies used to help individuals cope with loss after September 11, 2001, two companies come to mind:

- The TJX Companies (Marshalls, HomeGoods, T.J. Maxx and A.J. Wright)
- Shell Oil Company

Here's what they did.

The TJX Companies

Buyers from The TJX Companies, most of them young mothers with small children, boarded a United Airlines flight headed for Los Angeles. Little did they know that that fateful flight would be their last business trip. They were among those killed when their plane slammed into New York's World Trade Center.

The employees from TJX were devastated when they heard the news about their co-workers. President Ted English and his staff decided that not only should something be done to memorialize the staff who were killed, but a living memorial should be erected to remind staff about the need for peace in the world.

On the day that the company planned a memorial service for the slain staff, TJX stores across the country shut down so all staff could properly pay their respects and remember their coworkers. The company was obviously more concerned about souls than sales.

Aside from making sure that families of the victims were well taken care of, the company also erected a living memorial in the form of a peace garden at their corporate headquarters in Natick, Massachusetts.

The Shell Oil Company

As mentioned previously, I was stuck in Houston, Texas, doing work for the Shell Oil Company on September 11, 2001. There were a number of other out-of-state experts and professional speakers who were also stranded and couldn't return home after that event. I found it very interesting to watch how the employees of Shell Oil Company treated each other as well as me, a vendor/subcontractor, during that period.

The organization, in my opinion, exhibited concern, passion, and a genuine interest in making sure that I was well taken care of by a company representative, Dr. Ashley Fields. Although we share the same last name, we are not related. After my ordeal, I did, however, feel like he was my cousin or close friend. He constantly checked up on me, providing me with the necessary resources so I could return home to Boston as soon as the skies were cleared for travel.

On September 12, I had the opportunity to visit their corporate headquarters and meet with their Vice President of Human Resources. It provided me the perfect vantage point to view how a company and the people inside were treated during that ordeal. I was amazed at the warmth and concern that staff there, in their Human Resources and Diversity Departments, shared with each other as well as with me.

How companies treat people during the good as well as the bad times speaks volumes and is very telling as to whether or not they truly value their most precious asset, their staff. If you're working for an organization and/or individual who makes it difficult to love your work or life during trying times, you might want to consider whether or not it is worth wasting your precious time on this earth in that situation.

Chapter 9

WHOSE COURT IS
THE BALL IN
AFTER A LAYOFF?

THE QUESTION THAT PEOPLE WHO SURvive a layoff and want to continue to LwL[2] must answer after the downsizing madness has occurred is this:

WHOSE COURT IS THE BALL IN NOW THAT THE LAYOFF IS OVER?

I would venture to guess that after a layoff, employees who remain would probably answer that question with a resounding, "It certainly isn't in my court!" I'd like to throw out something for people who would respond in that manner to think about.

While there is no doubt that generally after a layoff, those left behind are told things like

"You'll have to do more with less."

"We had to lay off your coworkers, so you'll have to do their job and yours but, unfortunately, money is tight and revenue down so we don't have the cash to pay you more."

"We won't be able to give any raises or bonuses this year."

After hearing this news, of course, most people are inspired to be energized, their productivity rises to the occasion, and they want to do more work for less money, right? In addition, the Ain't-it-awful crowd coalesces and even if you're feeling positive and want to give it that ol' Ronald Reagan "Win one for the Gipper" try, this group does everything in its power to prevent you from delivering. After all, "It probably isn't over and when the next shoe drops, we will all probably be gone!" they remind you. Although the things mentioned above are swirling around the workplace after a layoff,

the reality is that the post-layoff ball really can be in the court of the employees who survive. WHAT?!

Think about it. Remember when I said earlier that even before a layoff decision is made, many companies agonize and go to great lengths to determine who will go or stay? If you are on the "List to Remain" then there is a BIG reason why you were selected to stay put. You have some important value to that company whether it is because of the skills or skeletons in the organizational closet of knowledge you possess. It may not seem like the ball is in your court, but in reality it is firmly in your hands. You have the power to decide if you want to run with the ball or retire your jersey and move on to another company league.

Tip #4—If you are the boss, never let these words cross your lips after a layoff, merger or acquisition: "Just be glad you have a job."

I often wonder if managers who consistently tell their staff or threaten them with the words "Just be glad you have a job" realize what a morale buster those words are? Have you ever known anyone to be pumped up and ready to perform to their maximum potential after hearing such a statement from a manager?

Don't forget how the layoff decisions were made. In the post-layoff environment, you need people who are willing to do more with fewer resources, and with no extra money for additional work. Executives and many managers have a tendency to want to move on after a layoff. Generally, they've had time before the announcement to process things and are ready to charge forward once the word "comes down." If you are managing people, allow staff time to absorb the enormity of what's happened so they too can properly mourn and move on.

Tip #5—At all cost, avoid paying your membership dues to the Ain't-it-awful crowd.

During mega-changes in the workforce—mergers, acquisitions, layoffs or shifts in leadership—one thing is guaranteed: The rumor mill *will* work overtime. In addition, the ol' mill is fueled by comments coming from a very powerful force within the organization which will undoubtedly form during this time—the Ain't-it-awful crowd. This non-upbeat in-crowd makes it its business to show the hows and whys the changes are bad for everyone and everything. The pressure to join it is also extremely strong, and even if you are positive and okay with the change, by the time they finish with you, you're trying to decide whether you should become a card-carrying member.

Don't be dragged down into the dirt and weeds with the Ain't-it-awful crowd.

Should you decide to join this group, membership benefits will definitely include the guaranteed eroding of your morale. Participation in the group's activities will zap your positive energy while turning it into negative, unproductive behaviors and actions.

Why not avoid membership at all costs? The dues just ain't worth it in terms of what it will do to your ability to LwL^2.

ATTITUDE CHANGES TO SURVIVE MEGA-CHANGES

An employee I knew who worked for the Bank of Boston when it merged with Fleet Bank once told me about how she adjusted to all the mega-changes inside her organization. I'll never forget the positive attitude she displayed when she told me her strategy for dealing with such change. Watchen stated, "I see this as an opportunity to start with a new company without leaving my old one. I'm going to make sure I identify, then acquire, new skill sets that I can use if I decide to stay

with the new company or progress elsewhere at a later time in my career."

Tip #6—Take a "What-can-I-learn-from-the-change-to-enhance-my-ability-to-LwL^2-and-expand-my-skill-set-toolkit?" attitude.

Get away from these attitudes:

- I won't do it if it's not in my job description.
- They don't pay me to do that.
- Why should I bother to kill myself or take on that assignment, or join that committee? They're not paying me to do that.

Instead:

- Figure out how you can use the knowledge and/or new skills you will obtain from an assignment to your advantage. Think about how this will help you to expand your ME, Inc. portfolio of skills and services.
- Volunteer and join a professional association—it can help you acquire needed skills that you're not getting on the job or through other aspects of your life.

Tips for Surviving a Job Transition

By Ina Lavin—Manager of Human Resources
Boston Communications Group

INA LAVIN WAS UNEMPLOYED FOR NINE-AND-a-half months in 2002 and 2003. She has since landed a wonderful job as the Manager of Human Resources at Boston Communications Group, Inc. Here, she provides some insights she gained on how to survive a job transition:

1. **Have a really good support group.** I created my own board of directors and if they weren't participating, I'd call and let them know they were shirking their responsibilities.

2. **Make sure that you have a balance and are not solely focused on finding a job 24/7.** For example, I did volunteer work at the Wellness Community, a social service agency that helps people with cancer. They also provide support groups. This gave me a perspective about life beyond being unemployed. The miracle work they did made me see that even though my situation was bad, there were others in the world who were worse off.

3. **Seek out people who are in similar situations so you don't feel alone.** This has another benefit—you come out of your unemployment experience with some really good friends.

4. **Take care of yourself.** I went to the gym regularly. This can be difficult to do, but you have to play the tapes in your mind, reminding you to get up and go.

5. **Have faith that things will work out.** Someone will recognize you for who you are and all that you can contribute. Just have faith and patience that this will occur.

6. **When interviewing, remember to have fun with it.** A friend said this to me and I remembered her words when I was interviewing. It really is good to have a support group to remind you of these things.

Knowing When to Put Yourself in a Job Transition

If you are doing work that you don't enjoy, you must know when to say to yourself, "I must quit and not stay in a rut. I must have the courage to move on." Sometimes if you are in an unsatisfactory situation too long, later in your life you will regret that period.

Finding a Job

It's really important to focus on the things that really matter to you in life. When you are looking for a position, don't just look for a job. Find a place that feels like home, one where you can be nurtured. You really need to do your homework when you are searching for a job so you can land in the right place.

Let's begin to look at when a job and/or profession changes on you, what steps you can take to LwL[2].

Chapter 10

What to do When a Job or Profession Changes on You

WHEN A JOB OR PROFESSION CHANGES ON YOU

WHAT CAN YOU DO IF YOUR JOB OR profession changes on you? The first thing you should do is explore your options. Don't wait for your boss or the Human Resources department to come to you with a job opportunity. Be proactive and check out job postings on a regular basis and identify career options both in and outside your organization.

If you are in business, do the same by checking out different industries that are in the growth mode both now and in the future. Start to cultivate relationships and attend events related to that field and read journals and information about them. Consider joining a professional organization where you can network with others in your field. In a later chapter, you will learn more information about the benefits of participating in professional associations. You also need to understand what skills to possess and how the world of work may be structured in the future. The following profile of executive search guru and business owner, Clark Willmott, will shed more light on this important subject.

Profile of Success

Clark Willmott—President and CEO, Willmott & Associates, Inc.

My passion involves helping people in transition. We've gone through an enormous change in the workplace and we've moved from employment for life to temporary employment. My father worked at a company for 35 years and got his gold watch and retired. Look at Human Resources: The average length of service has gone from life to two or three years in the 30+ years I've been in the business. We've moved to temporary employment because of technology, globalization, and company mergers. We don't understand that the implication of being a temporary employee is emotional. We understand it intellectually, but not emotionally.

The work environment has changed radically. It used to be you worked for a corporation, but with outsourcing you move in and out of different worlds. For example, in your work lifetime you might work for corporations, for a third party or in your own business or consulting firm. In your career you may have to work in these areas:

If we're all becoming temporary employees and moving in and out of different job structures, what competencies should we have and what skills do we need that we don't possess? Regardless, you have to be on top of your game just like a football player. For example, if you are in Human Resources, this means you must be more quantitative and able to act like a business person; you need to be not only tactical but more strategic.

The competency that is most missing is selling. The new world is about selling. Employees and employers must be re-educated and know that it is no longer a "I don't want to do it" skill. Employers must understand that by training their employees how to sell, they benefit. For example, people need to learn how to sell themselves—everyone should have a database of at least 1,000 people and use it to send out e-mails and newsletters to brand themselves. I recommend everyone take 5% of their time to sell. Update people about what's going on with you. You have to brand yourself. If you don't see a person for three years, you must keep up the relationship because "out of sight, out of mind."

The challenge is to get people to understand that this is the reality of the working world now, and although we are all temporary employees, we can generate revenue and have fun.

Companies of the future are the ones that build the "trusting environment." They allow people to work at home and trust they will get the job done.

What is the corporation's responsibility? How do we integrate an employee into the corporate world? Are we telling them they are an employee for life? If the company is truly responsible they should put every employee into sales training. This will help generate revenue in terms of customers and increase staff productivity.

I feel that in the future we will all have contracts and the executive coach will become your agent. More and more people are negotiating their severance agreement upfront. I see people who negotiate with their employers to have an executive coach who makes sure that their skill sets are kept up and that an individual brand is developed.

The whole thing about finding your passion is that you have to feel you are marketable. One of the things about life is that "life is the pursuit of rejections." Think about your pursuits for a job, a mate, a house—and possibly you may want to meet someone. To do this, go to Starbucks and approach anyone that is attractive to you and ask if they will have coffee with you. Eventually someone will say yes, but a lot will reject you. Statistically for every rejection we get, we are closer to achieving a yes answer.

The problem is we don't know how many no's we'll have to get to arrive at the yes. We need to reorient our whole thinking. In my business everyone who comes to see us is a customer.

Lessons for Corporations

A lesson for corporations: The reality is that people will leave you in three to four years, so how you treat people who leave is equally important as how you treat those who stay. Everyone is eventually a customer. We are so driven by quarterly results and we don't take the time to process people through changes. Revenue doesn't have to be defined as money ($), it can be defined as time off, recognition, or status. Employers need to look at how to become an employer of choice, not just today, but for the future. Retention is about increasing the employee life cycle and productivity from four years to five years.

How Do I Want to be Remembered?

How do you take your core passions and do something that will generate revenue for you? How I get the greatest satisfaction is helping people in career transition. The greatest joy I have in my job is when people look at me and say, "He's a great guy." I want my obituary to read, "He cared."

In the following article, Dr. Lawrence J. Stybel, Ed.D., and Maryanne Peabody offer yet another look at some models for employment that are emerging. They discuss a "free agent" model for executives in which they have careers that resemble those of professional sports stars.

Consulting with Clients When Good Jobs Are Perishable

By Lawrence J. Stybel, Ed.D. and
Maryanne Peabody—Stybel Peabody &
Associates, Inc.

TWENTY-FIVE YEARS AGO, CHANGING ECO-nomic times and the need for companies to develop nimble, leaner workforces shattered the model of the lifelong career at a single company. Executive job tenure began to shrink along with product life cycles, and time frames for achieving corporate exit strategies.

Good jobs had become perishable.

A second trend is the rise of enforcement of strict non-compete contracts. This situation makes it important that one's reputation extend beyond the narrow industry niche that consumes professional time.

In advising your clients and thinking about your own careers as consultants, what career model will fit the first twenty-five years of the 21st Century?

Free Agency Is Both True and Misleading

Economists like Robert Reich and popular business magazines like *BUSINESS 2.0* began to write about Free Agent Nation: Under a free agent model, executives have careers that resemble professional sports stars, smoothly shifting from one major league team to another through the work of third parties. In the sports and entertainment sectors, these third parties are called Agents. In other sectors, these third parties are called recruiters.

This model implied executives smoothly move from one senior executive position to another. The Free Agent model may work for "name brand" executives who come from "name brand" companies. But, it would be misleading to assume it works for all executives.

To make an analogy, professional sports players represent an elite segment of the general population. But only the top 10–15% of this elite can count on the Free Agent model to work in their favor. For the 85th percentile and below of this elite group, when their contract with one major league team is not renewed, it is the beginning of the end of their professional sports career (i.e., Minor League or overseas teams) or the end.

And even if we disregard performance, there is always the issue of age. At some point, the free agent model will stop working for even the highest performing athlete.

In business sectors beyond sports and entertainment, the model is similar: Free Agent works for the top 10–15% of an elite group of executives. And even the top performers within this elite group will find that free agent will stop working for them when they reach the "awkward age:" Too old to find opportunities in employment assignments but too young to find retirement attractive.

The notion of moving from a "good" corporate job to "temporary help" as a consultant or an interim executive can be both humiliating and painful. The Free Agent model says "winners" leap from job to job. On the other hand, failure to grasp the realities of the marketplace can make life even more painful. Consider the case of Jack:

> Jack was CFO of a FORTUNE 1000 company in a declining industry. A larger player acquired Jack's company, and he received a one-year severance agreement as part of his exit package. Jack spent the first nine months aggressively networking for a full-time CFO job in his geographic area, while making it clear that a full-time CFO position requiring relocation would be a second choice. By month ten, Jack became concerned about his family cash flow situation and began looking for interim CFO assignments or project consulting assignments.
>
> Jack found his network unresponsive, and the reason was obvious. Jack had clearly signaled early in his job search that project assignments were not on his original career agenda. Jack's network reasonably concluded that he

had failed to achieve his goals and was now desperate. Jack is now approaching month 24 without either employment assignments or project assignments. He refers to himself as feeling like a bottle of milk at a supermarket whose freshness date has expired.

We work with executives like Jack every day. His story is both unhappy and common. It need not have ended this way. Jack needed to understand and accept that his career may have begun as an employee but it would most certainly end as a consultant. Nor did he understand that a lifetime of work does not involve managing a single career comprising a series of corporate jobs. It is more like managing two careers—one focusing on employment assignments and the other focusing on project assignments.

In our experience, less than fifty of the eight hundred executives we have worked with have mastered the discipline and flexibility required to be successful in managing two careers that crisscross over time.

What can these fifty executives teach you about the skills to be mastered?

The four crisscross career management agendas:

- Mastery of professional identity
- Mastery of affiliation needs
- Mastery of job content
- Mastery of relationship management

Mastery of Professional Identity: From "You Are What You Do" to "You Do What You Are"

James is an example of one of our 50 executives:

After receiving his MBA from Columbia University, James went into banking. Various assignments at Mellon Bank and Bank of America eventually led to James' being hired as President/CEO of an Oregon bank. In 1990, James' bank was acquired and he was without employment, so James created a one-person consulting firm, whose initial focus was on what James called "credit dependent companies." Using his personal relationships with West Coast bank presidents, James was able to negotiate settlements so that both sides could have something of value.

By 1994, the recession had lifted, and one of James' clients came to him for consulting assistance. One consulting opportunity led to an offer to become Chief Operating Officer. His assignment was to double the size of this medical products distribution company and then sell the company to a national player in the industry during a time when rollups were attractive IPOs.

This assignment was completed within 18 months. Once again James opened his consulting practice. One of his clients was a non-profit organization. This consulting assignment brought him exposure to new areas like fundraising and working with agencies in Washington, D.C. This assignment was completed after two years. The contacts James developed brought him to the notice of a board member of a non-profit company in his town. James was offered the position of Chief Executive Officer for an Oregon human services organization. It has a budget of $265 million and its impact is felt statewide.

James has been a bank president, a distribution company COO, and a nonprofit CEO. Between these employment assignments, there has been a constant theme of project assignment work that leads him to the next employment assignment. Could it be that James has no career strategy?

If one assumes "You Are What You Do," the answer is "yes."

However, James would turn the statement on its head by saying, "You Do What You Are":

"I have centered my professional life on one strong theme: I solve financial/organizational problems. Had I identified myself as a 'banker,' my goose would have been cooked as the banking industry continued its consolidation. Instead, I have worked with medical products, retail companies, construction companies, a giftware company, and healthcare products.

"It has been fun, a real learning experience. But, my core identity remains the same. That never changes."

Ted is another executive with a You-Do-What-You-Are framework:

Ted began his IT career working with a variety of large corporations, beginning with EDS, the global IT outsourcing firm and Honeywell. Five years later, he moved to Monchik Weber, a consulting firm. His success as a consultant in an assignment involving ocean cargo issues led to an opportunity to become CIO for a company in the ocean freight transportation industry. Five years later, he was once again consulting. But the consulting assignment helped him gain credibility in the financial services sector. Ted is now CIO for a global financial services company."

In commenting on his professional life, Ted finds himself a solid constant in a series of ever-changing employment assignments and project assignments:

"My skills are coaching and developing people in technical environments. Internal or external, I use the same tools. I just apply those tools in different way."

Moving into a You-Do-What-You-Are framework is easy to write about and hard to implement. It requires both an intellectual and an emotional leap from prevailing norms that say, "You Are What You Do."

Mastery of Affiliation Needs: From Company-centric to Company-centric *and* Guild-centric

The management of affiliation needs is the most difficult skill for our clients to master. In employment assignments, moderate affiliation needs are a good thing at the senior executive levels. On the other hand, when moving into the project assignment phase, even moderate affiliation needs can

be dysfunctional: Your gift to your client is your objectivity. Constant angling to figure out ways of remaining as a permanent guest detracts from that gift.

When you are in the employment assignment trajectory, the members of your team are your allies for the duration of the assignment. On the other hand, the peer relationships you develop at your guild are with you for the duration of your professional life.

By guild we are referring to a work-related reference groups outside the corporation. These reference groups focus on functions, industry, or specific problems/opportunities. For example:

Functional: Financial Executives International, Young President's Organization, The Executive Committee, Society for Human Resource Management, Turnaround Management Association, California Association of Radiologists, Society for Information Management, American Marketing Association.

Industry: Massachusetts Hospital Association, California Biotech Council, National Association of Manufacturers, Florida Orange Grower's Association, Georgia Medical Association, Institute for Management Consulting, Society for Professional Consulting.

Problem/Opportunity: Association for Corporate Growth, MIT Enterprise Forum, Senior Executive Networking Group, Harvard Business School Alumni Association, American Chamber of Commerce in Berlin.

We earlier spoke about Ted's career trajectory from employment assignment to project assignment to employment assignment. Ted is a member of the Society for Information Management (SIM) and is past president of his city's chapter. He claims that he has been "fed" by SIM in two ways. Ted's SIM contacts have given him the last four out of five assignments. Thus, guild relationships provide a critical transition mechanism to move from one assignment to the next. A second way in which Ted is "fed" is that SIM provides

Ted a database of disinterested but competent peers for new ideas when he is working on assignments.

You Give to Your Guild and Your Guild Feeds You

Joining a guild and showing up for meetings is not the way to get fed. Having your guild feed you requires that you have an explicit guild management strategy. That strategy has guild and committee components.

Which Guilds to Join. We recommend to our clients that they confine participation to two associations. One group should represent the employment assignment phase. Many of the industry-related guilds noted above would fall into this category. The second guild would represent the assignment cycle phase. Many of the function-oriented guilds or the problem/opportunity guilds meet these objectives.

The demands of family may require involvement in a third association. For example, your child may be attending Sunday School and you have been asked to join the Religious Education Committee of your church. If you elect to join the Religious Education Committee, this membership would substitute for one of the two guilds. Spreading yourself too thin by being a marginal player in many guilds is not a strategy. It is a waste of precious time.

Committee Assignments. Once you join a guild, volunteer to be a member of an externally focused Committee of the Board. Externally focused committees are the "outreach" arms. Such involvement gives you a legitimate platform to be visible to the external world. Examples of good committee assignments would be marketing/membership, program, and legislative affairs. Avoid inwardly focused committees that get you too deep within guild politics. Examples might include a committee to draft a new constitution, planning the holiday party, etc.

An alternative structure to guilds would be a new breed of organizations that provide a consistent source of affiliation while traveling between assignments. Tatum CFO and Tatum CIO are examples of this new breed. (See "A New Structure for Crisscross Career Management.")

Mastery of Job Content: From Managerial/Provincial to Technical/Cosmopolitan *and* Managerial/Provincial

In the employment assignment trajectory, managers don't do line work themselves, but manage the line work of others; typically, the higher one moves up the corporate ladder towards corporate leadership, mastery of management becomes more important than mastery of technical content. Mastery of the unique political and cultural issues in accomplishing goals within the company is critical. We call this combination of knowledge managerial/provincial.

Mastery of managerial/provincial perspectives seldom is an asset in project assignment. Consultants and interim executives are hired because of specific content expertise. They are appreciated because they provide an understanding of how other companies in other industries handle similar problems. We call this type of knowledge technical/cosmopolitan.

It is a cliché to state that education is an ongoing process throughout life. What we are saying, however, is that the pull of managerial/provincial versus technical/cosmopolitan should guide your selection for how to spend your scarce time in a crisscross career. Let's return to the case of Ted, the CIO of a global financial services company:

Ted's company would be supportive of him taking executive education programs in strategy or the management of R&D at highly ranked business schools. Instead, Ted is taking a course on technology related to large database applications at a local community college. This is the type of course Ted would normally encourage for subordinates three or four suites below him within the company. What is the logic behind Ted spending time at a community college?

Ted knows that his company is actively considering it being acquired by one of three larger competitors. Achievement of that exit strategy would probably mean the end of Ted's employment assignment as CIO. If that happens, Ted believes that his next assignment would be a project assignment and he will get the opportunity through a guild. To prepare himself for that next assignment, Ted wants to be on top of the latest technology issues.

Once you get used to a crisscross framework, the value of hockey great Wayne Gretzky's comment becomes even more obvious: 'skate to where the puck is going to be.'

There also is an ageism issue in moving from Managerial/provincial to Managerial/provincial AND Technical/cosmopolitan.

Mastery of Relationship Management: From Narrow Banding to Broad Banding of Relationships

Senior executives are used to having the outside world knock at their doors, and having executive assistants take messages. The demands of scarce time frequently move such executives into what we call a narrow band framework of relationship management: external relationships are mostly confined to large, branded vendors. Bringing in well-known names for consideration is an easy decision and reduces political risks. All executives know the saying, "Nobody was ever fired for bringing in IBM." Time saved through narrow banding of external relationships can be applied for critical internal relationship management issues.

Based on our work with clients over the years, we believe narrow banding of external relationships is not in the company's interests and certainly not in the interests of executives whose careers will crisscross through employment and project assignments.

It is true that senior executives seldom get fired for bringing in well-known name brand names into their companies. It is also true that senior executives seldom are promoted because they know how to instruct their secretaries to program their speed dial for the "usual suspects."

Taking the necessary time for broad banding of relationships is a win/win situation for the company and for our clients.

When in the employment assignment trajectory, we recommend that our clients take the time to learn the best, most cost effective interim and consulting resources for their company's needs. For example:

> A company in the food distribution industry wants to look at its sales compensation plan. There is no glory or savings in calling one of the four national compensation firms and asking for a proposal. On the other hand, the Chief HR Officer knows that there is a boutique firm in Miami that focuses on sales compensation for the food distribution industry. Its fees are 30% less than the large compensation firms. The Chief HR Officer knows he will be dealing with the owner and not a junior consultant.

In an era where more non-core business functions are getting outsourced, senior executives with broadband relationships know that they can provide unique value to their employers. One executive we know allocates one day a month from 4:30–6:00 p.m. to meet new vendors and get a sense of what is going on.

The sparkling executives avoid narrowing external relationships into a few large vendor buckets. They want many relationships with many outstanding vendors, both large and small. One of those relationships can help them move to their next assignment.

Mastery of Relationship Management: Keeping the Network Warm versus Letting the Network Get Cold

Executives' failure to grasp the criss-cross nature of careers management is most powerfully felt when leaders in the employment assignment phase let great networks grow cold. People are not enthusiastic about helping executives who only contact them when they need favors. On the other hand, the time demands of full time employment provide little ability to keep good networks warm.

Scarce time needs to be allocated strategically. One CEO has hired a firm to outsource keeping the network warm. The firm has created a one-year "keep in touch" campaign that involves the firm designing and initiating a contact program for the executive. For example, the firm will send out six mailings per year. The firm designed each campaign on the CEO's personal stationary. The CEO only had to sign the letters with a personal note at the bottom of each letter. One campaign went out to CEO colleagues and included an enclosure about the CEO's company. But another mailing campaign went out to executive recruiters on the topic of how the CEO is building his management team. A third mailing campaign to the venture community focuses on an article dealing with industry IPO trends.

Earlier in this article we spoke about James, the former bank president who is now CEO of a non-profit. James designed his employment agreement to allow him to keep his network warm. That agreement allows for a defined number of days per year to be available to consult with non-competing firms.

The design of the employment contract reflects that James is accepting a reduction in base salary for working at a non-profit in return for the opportunity to generate additional income through project assignments and the security of knowing that he is keeping his network warm for the future. Is it possible to craft such arrangements in your next employment agreement? At the very least, it may be possible to craft an employment agreement to allow you to serve on the Board of one non-competing for-profit company. Such an agreement helps to broaden your industry perspective and keep your network warm.

Keeping the network warm is hard to implement. To move from good intentions to good actions, we recommend that clients schedule one hour a month in their calendars to make calls to 20% of their network list. If an executive has a contact list of 200, this means staying in touch by phone with 40 people over a 1-year period. This can easily be accomplished by reserving one hour a month. The agenda of such conversations is simply to remain in contact and to inquire how you might help the other person. But the time needs to be scheduled in advance.

Exhilaration and Terror

You may have begun your career as an employee. You most certainly will end it as a consultant. In between, you will criss-cross the employment and project assignment trajectories several times.

The cases of James and Ted illustrate people who combine flexibility with discipline. That mixture of flexibility and discipline is not unlike skiing down a mountain in a criss-cross mode, as you navigate through different types of snow and different terrain.

The payoff of skiing with flexibility and discipline are the simultaneous emotions of exhilaration and terror. Career management also provides those same emotions. As James says:

> "If you only focus on what is expected of you in your job, your ability is restricted to the next run in the ladder. The trick is to learn how to rapidly change ladders!"

In a world where good jobs are perishable, learning how to rapidly change ladders is the closest thing to job security most readers will have in the twenty-first century—the security of knowing you can maneuver between the two careers of your professional life. And having that security gives a sense of confidence in making the next selection when the crisscross opportunities emerge. Consider the case of Larry Gibson:

> Larry Gibson was Chief HR Officer with Harvard Pilgrim Health Plan in Boston. Prior to that, he was head of HR for a division of Motorola. For the past three years, he has been earning an income in project assignments: "My life as a consultant has broadened my professional perspective and given me a broader industry expertise. This makes me

more marketable. I enjoy consulting. I know how to make a living at it. If a full-time job opportunity came, I'd certainly look at the opportunity. But, it would have to go over a higher hurdle before I would sign on."

A New Structure for Crisscross Career Management

The crisscross nature of career management implies external relationship management is a never-ending task. Not everybody relishes this thought. The loss of income during the transition between assignments can be scary. The legitimate affiliation needs of senior executives are seldom fully met.

One corporate solution to the problem of career management is Tatum CFO Partners, LLP (www.tatumcfo.com). Founded in 1993, Tatum CFO Partners currently has 350 partners and offices in 28 cities in the United States. It offers project assignment solutions for corporate clients. After the projects are over, Tatum provides a structure for partners to move into employment assignments. According to CEO Doug Tatum, approximately 50% of Tatum CFO's Partners are engaged in employment assignments.

Partners admitted to Tatum CFO Partners LLP are referred by other partners. The historic acceptance rate is 10%.

Acceptance into the partnership has both liabilities and benefits.

Like any legal partnership, there is joint liability.

Part of each partner's compensation is allocated to the partnership pool. This is true regardless of whether the partner is in an employment assignment or a project assignment. The pooling takes place regardless of whether Tatum had a direct hand in securing the assignment or not. While working on project or employment assignments, partners have the benefits of a structured Broad Band Network and an infrastructure that keeps their network warm. Partners have constant access to other partners and exposure to the full intellectual capital of the firm, thus meeting some of their affiliation needs.

During periods of employment, Tatum CFO partners receive two streams of income: salaries, fees, and bonuses directly from clients or employers, and Tatum CFO partnership bonus/profit sharing. When partners find themselves "between assignments," they still participate in firm-wide bonus/profit-sharing. The financial structure of Tatum CFO LLP provides a structure to help smooth the financial risks of career management.

Being a member of formalized partnership can also function as a wealth enhancer. Tatum CFO partners can take equity as part of the compensation mix. A portion of the equity received by partners is also put into the partnership pool. Doug Tatum says, "You can build wealth with lots of pooled singles and doubles with good companies. You don't have to spend your life looking for that once-in-a-lifetime start up."

The success of Tatum CFO has spawned a sister firm, Tatum CIO Partners, LLP (www.tatumcio.com). In 2002, there were approximately 100 Tatum CIO partners.

The Tatum structure is designed to create career management opportunities within a single partnership structure. Doug Tatum says another benefit for both corporate clients and Tatum CFO is a structure that permits the partner to make the right ethical decision:

"When partners have confidence that they have the security of a career that covers them in project assignments as well as employment, they are more likely to make the right call when business issues get into the area of ethics and integrity. Our partners don't invest their entire careers with any one company. And that gives them the financial and emotional freedom to raise issues of ethics and integrity. That's good for our partners and that's good for our clients."

The authors thank the following colleagues for improving earlier versions of this text:
Laura Avakian, Lewis Rambo, and Larry Stone.

What do you need to learn and know if you want to become a consultant and/or business owner? In the following pages, you'll find one approach that involves not leaving your day job.

LEARNING HOW TO ACT LIKE A CONSULTANT OR BUSINESS OWNER

So You Want to Be a Business Owner or Consultant

ARE YOU TIRED OF YOUR DAY JOB AND want to start your own business or become a big-name consultant? What an easy life I'd have as a consultant, you think. Maybe it's a business you want to start so you can get away from a 4-letter word: BOSS. You can be your own boss and the CEO of ME, Inc. You know you can do it. You're sure you are ready for a change. Maybe you'll just give your notice tomorrow—tell them where they can take the job and shove it. Think again.

Before you leave your steady position and become a business owner or consultant, I offer the following advice: Don't leave your "day" job until you are positive that you can make a living out of your business and can pay your bills as you start it up. Instead of packing your bags, think about staying in your position but reframing your relationship to it. For example, you may want to think of your job as a major client that provides you with benefits like health care, life insurance, and the ability to get free training in-house or to use tuition reimbursement to acquire skills needed to run a business. This can include those involving finance, budgeting, marketing, sales, management, business writing, and communication skills.

Think about your current job as your major client; however, it is not your only client. In this approach, you use your spare time (mornings, nights, weekends, holidays) to concentrate on your business plan. Quite often, people who adopt this attitude change their mindset and begin to realize how their job can help them travel down that entrepreneurial path.

You should do the appropriate marketing research and business plan development before you step out on your own without a job or source of adequate income. Many people are finding success by easing into entrepreneurship and not leaving their jobs until this preparation work is completed.

In the following articles by marketing guru and business owner, Monica Calzolari, and Henry Turner, Executive Director of the Small Business Development Center at Howard University, you will find some pragmatic tips on how to start and stay in business for yourself.

Marketing Yourself When the Corporate Mold No Longer Fits

By Monica Calzolari—President, Results Marketing

TO BE FINANCIALLY SUCCESSFUL IN YOUR OWN BUSINESS, YOU MUST ADOPT A "1099" ATTITUDE and unlearn the "W2" mentality that comes from being an employee with a steady paycheck and benefits. The Internal Revenue Service tracks income from independent contractors using the "1099" form. As a self-employed business owner, your income will be directly proportional to your sales skills.

The learning curve is steep for the self-employed, and a salaried job in corporate America is not the best preparation you can have. I should know. I've worked for three FORTUNE 500 companies. Because I have learned many of these lessons the hard way over 22 years, I am eager to share what I have acquired with others, especially women, to accelerate their success. Be clear about the skills you will need to become profitable in a business of your own. Do work you enjoy and get paid for providing value to others.

I hope the following two lists provide enough contrast to help you see the skills and commitment required to own a business.

Adopt a 1099 Attitude	Skills in the W2 World
#1 Priority—generate revenue	Make your boss look good
#1 Skill—sales	Project management
Goal setting is essential	Meet goals set by company
Manage your time according to ROI	Execute your boss' priorities
Prioritize so that work is not 24/7	Work minimum of 40 hours
Be aggressive	Don't rock the boat
"If it's to be, it's up to me!"	Work the system and form allies
Accept full responsibility, 24/7	Become like Teflon: nothing sticks
Listen to your customers	Listen to your bosses
Flex to the market	Flex to reorganizations, downsizing
Learn to negotiate	Learn to bite your tongue
Get paid for producing value	Work around meetings and e-mail
Know what you are worth daily	Prepare for annual reviews

A final word of advice is that if you want a steady paycheck, then stick with a salaried position and receive a W2 form from your employer each January. To succeed as an entrepreneur, surround yourself with other 1099 people, books, tapes and seminars on success and self-employment.

Corporate Cupid
Monica Calzolari is President of Results Marketing, a consulting firm that specializes in marketing strategy and execution. She brings more than 20 years of direct marketing expertise in multiple industries and geographies to solve client challenges. Monica is a gifted writer and strategic marketing communicator who produces measurable results.

The Keys to Starting a Successful Business

By Henry J. Turner—Executive Director, Small Business Development Center at Howard University

I LOVE TO HELP PEOPLE CREATE entrepreneurial businesses as opposed to Mom-and-Pop operations. I like assisting people to step outside of the box with their businesses. My success comes from seeing clients and my students at Howard University become successful. When I see a business that I've helped to establish, grow and blossom, it makes me feel so good. I also like to help people make a decision not to go into business. The life of an entrepreneur is not for everyone. 85-90% of businesses will not exist longer than five years. If you are in the right business and profitable, you can make a reasonable living and be happy at doing it. Therefore, if you've been in business three or four years and it is not going well, by year five you're ready to quit. Many people invest the family funds into the business and that can cause friction in a marriage, especially if one individual is a risk taker and entrepreneurial and the other is conservative in approach. Here are four simple tips if you want to start a business:

1. Make sure to have some positive net worth because you have to invest so much money into the business up front. You will also need money to live off while the business is ramping up. No one will fund you 100%. Also, procuring a loan when you begin can be difficult. If you have a house, cash or some form of equity, banks are more apt to loan you money.

2. Only leave your day job to start a business if you have the following
   - family support
   - a good marketing plan
   - sufficient money for at least six months' cash flow.

3. Be ready to have lots of psychological and physical strength. They are needed to deal with the stresses and strains of entrepreneurship.

4. Know how to manage resources—people, time and money!

Believe it or not, the fastest-growing segment of the business market is women. Take this Quick Quiz to test your knowledge about Women's Buying Power.

Quick Quiz

Take this Quick Quiz on Women's Buying Power.

1. ___% of the private wealth in the U.S. is controlled by women.

    a. 5%   b. 27%   c. 47%   d. 51.3%

    Source: Federal Reserve in PBS online

2. ___% of individuals with assets worth more than $500,000 are women.

    a. 5%   b. 27%   c. 47%   d. 51.3%

    Source: U.S. Labor Department as reported in The Wall Street Journal 11/24/97

3. ___% of households in the U.S. are headed by single females.

    a. 5%   b. 27%   c. 47%   d. 51.3%

    Source: www.trendsight.com/gender/trends/spendingpower.html

Answer to Quick Quiz

1. d - 51.3%; 2. b - 27%; 3. c - 47%

" " Quotes of Note

"I started my own business because I didn't want to wait for someone to open a door for me. I decided to do it myself."

Source: Mike Millis, President, MX2 Media

Perspectives from Female Business Owners in the Women Presidents' Organization

Because I am a woman entrepreneur and women are the fastest-growing segment of the business market, I thought it would be interesting to hear the perspectives of women entrepreneurs about LwL². In the next section, you will read about Marsha Firestone, Founder and President of the Women Presidents' Organization. Her professional association's members are highly successful women whose businesses average $11 million in yearly revenue. She provides some practical insights for individuals who want to lead a business and maintain a healthy and happy lifestyle. Several successful business women, many of whom are WPO members, also weigh in on their thoughts and suggestions on how to LwL².

Profile of Success

Marsha Firestone, Ph.D.

Dr. Firestone is founder and president of the Women Presidents' Organization (WPO) for women whose businesses annually gross over 2 million dollars. WPO member businesses have an average of $11 million in revenues. The WPO is currently operating in 29 locations nationwide and in Canada. Before her involvement in women's economic development, she oversaw all operations and established educational direction as president of a for-profit educational institution. In 1998, Dr. Firestone was Executive Director of The Women's Economic Summit whose work resulted in a master plan for accelerating the growth of women's business and it was presented to Congress and the public in March 1999.

A study of the National Foundation for Women Business Owners found that between 1997 and 2000, women-owned businesses with $1 million or more in revenue grew 31.6%. Those with $10 million or more in revenue grew 36.8%. The WPO was developed with these women in mind. It brings together these highly successful women in a forum where they can discuss strategies to grow, sell or maintain their businesses.

Dr. Firestone has published research on adult learning theory, nonverbal communication, and managerial competency, which appeared in both business and educational journals. She also wrote The Busy Woman's Guide to Successful Self-Employment, an interactive, easy-to-read resource. She is the recipient of a special achievement award from Woman, Inc. of Jamaica and the Applause Award from WBENC for breaking down barriers for women in business.

She earned a Master's degree in communication from Teacher's College of New York, as well as a Ph.D. in communication from Columbia University.

Source: WPO Directory, 2002

Here are some of Dr. Firestone's thoughts about Loving your work by Loving your Life:

☆ My work provides great satisfaction and momentum in my life.

What people need to do to love their work:

☆ Believe in their mission and infuse it with integrity.

What people need to do to love their life:

☆ Have a well balanced life with satisfying work, family, friends and interests!

What people need to do to Love their work by Loving their Life:

☆ Have a passion for your business and keep the flame in your heart alive.

How organizations can help staff to love their work and life:

☆ Involve staff in planning and decision-making.

A number of WPO members shared their thoughts about Loving your work by Loving your Life.

 ## "C Suites" Check In

Mindy Goodfriend—President, Yankee Partners, L.L.C.; WPO member

☆ In my opinion, the key to the meaning is the word your—your work…your life. The most powerful positive changes for me have all been connected to my personal growth—introspection, awareness, action.
When my values, goals and priorities are aligned, and when I am learning and enjoying, I'm in the zone.

☆ My advice would be to make sure your work is congruent with your values, goals, priorities. Do you feel good about what you do? Does your work provide whatever is important to you?

☆ Keep asking the question: What's really important to me?

Tips on loving your work or life that have worked for me:

☆ Willingness to change; continuous learning; staying true to my values.

How organizations can help staff to love their work and life:

☆ Support people to grow. It might require change. Everyone will benefit.

Wise Words

Beverly A. Kahn—President and CEO, New Dimensions in Technology, Inc.;
WPO member

"From my personal experience, business people, when growing a company, spend an inordinate amount of time in their business life, and the remaining time is spent with their family. Thus, there is not a lot of time for play—to build friendships and explore personal interests. My advice: Take time to nurture your outside interests. Build that third part of your life."

"Life doesn't happen in a straight line. If it did, life would be boring and sterile. No, there are disruptions and interruptions in life, and that is where creativity and progress are born."

"Life is like an open canvas and you're adding to the picture."

"Have patience. Life is like a puzzle, as you get older all the pieces begin to fit together."

"If you can't get rid of the skeletons in your closet, you'd best teach them to dance."

—Anonymous; Provided by Beverly Kahn

Katherine E. Putnam—President, Package Machinery Company, Inc.; WPO member

If you are the boss, to build an effective team, you must ask yourself: Where do I find people who can be what I am not, and how do we function as a team? Do you like your team? Or is being with them a downer? If the answer to the former question is no, then you need to change the chemistry or someone must move on.

Profile of Success

Debora Bloom—President, Debora Bloom Associates

The world is going through cataclysmic change so it is more critical than ever that each person know what's important. We have to be clear on who we are and what our own priorities are.

We should pick a line of work that draws on our strengths. In the 70's, there were people who took a job just to make ends meet. They referred to their employment as work (with a small "w"). Their day job subsidized what was REALLY important to them. That meaningful work, usually voluntary (work with a big "W"), had to do with political or social agendas. What is really great is to be able to earn a living at whatever happens to be our own big "W."

Today, regardless of our job, we're going to experience uncertainty. That's why I chose to run my own business. If I have to feel uncertainty, I might as well have it with myself and not worry about whether or not I'm going to keep my job. As a diversity and organization development consultant, I usually have multiple projects happening at once. I regularly spend time creating new business. I have contracts ending, beginning and delayed. I like the variety, the excitement and the independence. I much prefer that to worrying about lay-offs.

Whether we work for ourselves or someone else, whether our focus is job, home, social issues, or spiritual development, we need to take time daily to appreciate what we are doing right and pat ourselves on the back for it. Life is smoother that way.

Wise Words

Vicki Donlan—Publisher, Women's Business

I learned from both my parents that by focusing my attention on helping others succeed I would achieve greatness and happiness in my work. Having created a newspaper promoting women in business, I live each day knowing that I am assisting women reach greater success by having the visibility they need and deserve.

Loving my work means having the opportunity to create a lasting impact for others.

Wise Words

Fatou Samb—Owner, Hairbraiding by Aisha & Fatou

I've loved braiding hair since I was a little girl. I love meeting new people, and my business allows me to do that. I can work hard and make people happy and my customers thrilled so they will come back and bring a lot of friends.

Wise Words

Diene Conde—African hairbraider & student at Bunker Hill Community College

When you really want something you have to be willing to work hard to get it. You need to love what you are doing in life and in your job or you will be very unhappy throughout your life.

Profile of Success

June Rokoff—Formerly SVP Lotus Development Corporation. Today: President, The Commonwealth Institute—a nonprofit organization that works with women CEOs and entrepreneurs to help them grow their businesses

For close to 30 years, I loved my work in the computer industry. I had the luxury of picking the companies I wanted to work for, and making a difference on the projects on which I worked. I worked with wonderful people who had similar ideals and goals. It was my pleasure to get up each day and work with a talented team of people on new technologies and help develop a corporate culture that was supportive of diversity.

Wise Words

Henry J. Turner—Executive Director, Small Business Development Center at Howard University

In the entrepreneurial company, the owner has to see the entire forest, not just a few trees. Some business owners neglect to look for and manage resources because they are so inundated with day-to-day operational matters. These owners are unable to see beyond the details of an issue.

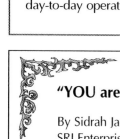

"YOU are the CORE of YOUR Success!!"

By Sidrah Jackson, President and CEO,
SRJ Enterprises

WHEN MY FRIEND AND AUTHOR OF *LOVE your work by Loving your Life* asked me to include a comment about my response to this affirmation, I went back and pulled out a speech that she had helped me design, called: YOU are the CORE of Your Success!! As I share with you a few salient points, I want you to know that starting my own business and formulating my speaking plan was a demonstration of how well Martha lives out her belief: "Love your work by Loving your Life," and a testimony to my belief in CORE.

Up until 3 months ago, I was a career banker, helping customers open checking accounts and get full access to the services and information that was available to them as business owners and clients. I have viewed many a business plan, and always sought to "get to the CORE" of who that business owner was. I could see what motivated them, what stopped them, and what challenged them. This was always an exercise of great appreciation—I felt that I was Alice looking through the looking glass—looking for something for myself that I couldn't quite see!

Well, three months ago I left my 23 year career in banking to do Development and Fundraising. I had to stand on my belief and teaching: Your are the CORE of Your Success! So let me share with you what CORE means and why it is Loving your work by Loving your Life!

Learning to Love your work by Loving your Life is a process. It is a CORE process: CORE stands for Center, Opportunity, Right, Energy. Getting to the CORE is about preparing for transformation. God had been preparing me for a time like this when everything came together to create the right opportunity. I launched SRJ Consulting, a consulting business specializing in development & fundraising. Who knew that my working with women-owned businesses, community health organizations, and ethnic and urban businesses would lead me here!

First, I had to get to my Center. And this isn't an easy job! As my brother Javier Jackson said many years ago: "It's a tough job being me but someone has got to do it!" Getting to the Center is being focused on getting to the truth about YOU! This means not always going with the crowd, taking the hits, and sometimes just going on when others would have thrown in the towel. It means confronting what we don't know and confronting what we must change about what we do know!! Getting to the Center and going through the storm generates understanding. It allows us to honor and accept our strengths and weaknesses. It means discovering our values, passion, and vision.

This is not a process for the faint-hearted!! It demands a commitment to personal growth and is available to everyone! For the business owner, however, the most poignant setting is his or her own business. Success is the result of this process, and the business owner not only experiences this, but those whom he or she mentors are encouraged to start their own transformation! Center brings us to the natural beauty of who we are—it is tedious and requires steadfast commitment. We must peel back layers of behaviors and thought patterns that have become comfortable for us. Therefore, it is PAINFUL and sometimes it STINKS!! It produces tears—sometimes of regret, but mostly of just letting go. I'm describing an onion! However, the process goes further than the onion peel, for when we have been matured by it—it produces a wonderful fragrance—and we can smell like a rose! The rose matures, there are notches and thorns, unexpected places that pierce and hurt. But without those demonstrations of growth, we won't benefit from the pain. In the end, we'll come out with a sweet smelling aroma and in all splendor!

Once we have dealt with our Center then we have new lenses through which to view our Opportunities! We have clarity of vision where challenges become opportunities. Clear vision yields abundance and consistent results. So, we can put on the new lenses!

All opportunities are not Right for us. So, having visited our Center, and viewed Opportunities through a new lens, we can now choose the Right opportunity! With clear vision and self-knowledge we become open to the right opportunity! It may have been there all along but we didn't see it!

Finally, the "E" in CORE represents that everything has come into alignment. This stage demands focus, full and complete attention and complete alignment for dynamic, consistent results!!

I have shared with you my definition of how going through the transformation from an onion to a rose is CORE to your Loving your work by Loving your Life! This personal transformation is available to all who commit to it. Successful business owners do this on a personal level, and the speed with which their business grows is a direct correlation to their personal transformation.

I encourage you to start Loving your work by Loving your Life!! It's all Connected!!

Sidrah's Keys to CORE Success
C enter
O pportunity
R ight
E nergy
"YOU are the CORE of YOUR Success"

CORE Questions EVERY Business Owner Should Ask Their Banker

- Exit Strategy - *How will we manage when difficulty occurs?*
- Team Approach vs. Hierarchy - *Who in the bank makes the final decision?*
- Risk Level - *What is the bank's risk tolerance for early, growth, & mature stage companies & types of industries?*
- Follow-through - *How responsive & dedicated is your banker?*
- Reputation - *What does the market say about how this banker delivers?*
- Referrals - *Will this banker refer you business from their network?*
- Flexibility - *How far can & will the banker stretch?*
- Focus - *How is the banker motivated? What are their goals? How are they compensated?*

DECIDING WHETHER OR NOT TO EMBRACE CHANGE

Many of us struggle with our decision about whether to embrace or reject a change when it occurs. When you are in a "limbo state" about your decision on what to do about the change—this is often a very anxious, chaotic and confusion-ridden time in your life—remember that in the final analysis, you only have a few options about what you can do about the change. Spend some time doing the necessary work needed to analyze your position and then move on. Remember the steps of the Kübler-Ross model on death and dying. In the end, know that your approach to change will fall into one of the following boxes in our next Quick Quiz. The decision is yours as to which one you check off.

Quick Quiz

What Is Your General Attitude Towards Change?

When faced with figuring out how you will or won't adapt to a change, determine which one of the four categories BEST describes your attitude towards the change.

- ❑ I accept change and embrace it. It's time to find the opportunities and take the challenges brought about by the change.
- ❑ I accept change and will cope with it—it's not how or what I would have wanted, but I must adjust to the change because it is what it is. It's not worth fighting it because it would be a losing battle.
- ❑ I may accept the change but I need to think about it for awhile before I make my decision on what to do about it.
- ❑ I do not accept the change and will never do so.

Analyzing This Quiz

Once you've completed your answers, decide whether or not to embrace the change. Your options are

- ❑ Accept and embrace the change as it is.
- ❑ Find ways to adapt to it and re-shape your life and/or work accordingly.
- ❑ Decide not to endorse the change.

Decide what the pros and cons are of your decision then prepare yourself to tackle any fallout from the path you've taken.

WHAT ARE THE JOBS OF THE FUTURE?

Whether you want to become a consultant or business owner or you already are one, you'll want to identify the "hot" jobs of the future. If you have no intention of becoming a budding entrepreneur, or can't feel self-employment in your bones and toes, the next chapter will also be of interest. You'll learn about future job growth and long range industry trends that can help to keep you gainfully employed both now as well as in the future so you can continue to LwL².

Chapter 12

JOBS FOR THE FUTURE

Future Job Outlook

TAKE THIS QUICK QUIZ TO LEARN MORE INTERESTING FACTS ABOUT THE FUTURE JOB outlook.

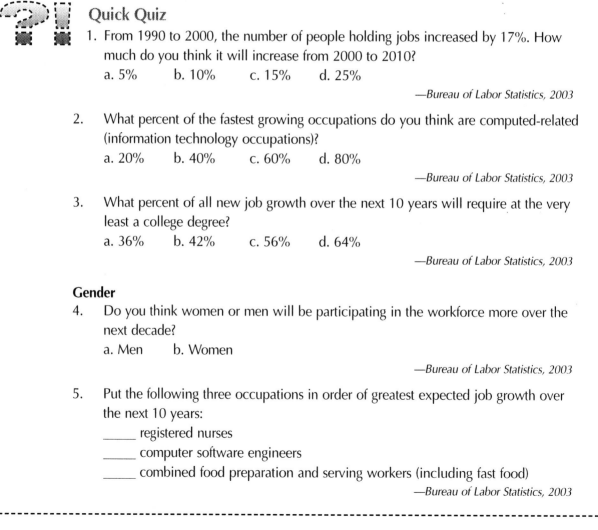

Quick Quiz

1. From 1990 to 2000, the number of people holding jobs increased by 17%. How much do you think it will increase from 2000 to 2010?
   a. 5%   b. 10%   c. 15%   d. 25%

   —Bureau of Labor Statistics, 2003

2. What percent of the fastest growing occupations do you think are computed-related (information technology occupations)?
   a. 20%   b. 40%   c. 60%   d. 80%

   —Bureau of Labor Statistics, 2003

3. What percent of all new job growth over the next 10 years will require at the very least a college degree?
   a. 36%   b. 42%   c. 56%   d. 64%

   —Bureau of Labor Statistics, 2003

Gender

4. Do you think women or men will be participating in the workforce more over the next decade?
   a. Men   b. Women

   —Bureau of Labor Statistics, 2003

5. Put the following three occupations in order of greatest expected job growth over the next 10 years:

   _____ registered nurses

   _____ computer software engineers

   _____ combined food preparation and serving workers (including fast food)

   —Bureau of Labor Statistics, 2003

6. By 2010, the total labor force is expected to reach 158 million. Within this labor force, which age group will be the fastest growing demographic?

a. 16 to 24   b. 25 to 54   c. 55 and older

—Bureau of Labor Statistics, 2003

7. What percent of the total labor force will consist of women by 2010?

a. 35%   b. 48%   c. 75%

—Bureau of Labor Statistics, 2003

Answers to Quick Quiz

1. c. 15%   **2.** d. 80%   **3.** b. 42%

4. b. Women   **5.** combined food preparation and serving workers (including fast food); registered nurses; computer software engineers

6. c. 55 and older   **7.** b. 48%

Job Outlook in Economic Highs and Lows

In terms of job growth, we must always remember that even in bad or volatile economic times, good jobs are available.

A fascinating article appeared in the *Boston Globe* on July 4, 2003. That date was the day after the largest increase in unemployment, 6.2%, in nine years was announced. The article discussed good jobs that were available during a harsh economy. Jobs were plentiful in construction because new housing construction and remodeling of homes was booming. This was due in part to low mortgage rates and increased refinancing activity.

The temporary help sector also increased during that low economic slump period. Some employers were beginning to see business pick up but didn't want to begin hiring full-time staff just yet. We also know that despite economic blips, according to *Business Week,* 53% of federal workers are eligible to retire during the next few years. With that high number of people leaving the Federal Government, job opportunities will undoubtedly abound in that sector during future years. As the population increases in age, so will the incidence of people with declining health problems. Health care and home health care will become growing fields. This is especially true since some 400,000 nursing vacancies by 2010 are projected.

So, part of what we have to look at if we want to continue to be gainfully employed is where are those jobs and what can we do to prepare ourselves for employment in high growth areas. This next article, by my assistant, Jessie Shea, explores what is in store for the workplace in the years to come.

Jobs for the Future

By Jessie Shea—Executive Assistant,
Fields Associates, Inc.

IN LIGHT OF ALL THE CHANGES IN THE WORLD and workplace, to LwL[2] over the long haul, it is very important to determine future job growth and long-range industry trends. This process is equally important if you are examining your current career and your ability to LwL[2] and/or the potential for a career change. To aid in that examination, the Bureau of Labor Statistics has provided 10-year employment projections by industry and occupation. This includes information on educational attainment and labor force statistics. Although these projections were issued in December, 2001, the results remain unchanged because of the unknown long-term consequences of demographic population shifts such as an aging population with low birth rates. However, as such consequences become clearer, projections will more than likely be adjusted accordingly.

The Bureau of Labor Statistics projects that the total number of people holding jobs between 2000 and 2010 is expected to increase by 15 percent, a slightly lesser growth than last decade. Projections for the service-producing industry—which includes[1] transportation, communications, and utilities; wholesale trade; retail trade; finance, insurance, and real estate; services, and government—shows a 19% increase in employment by 2010 with an addition of 20.5 million jobs—the largest increase in any industry.

A large portion of the fastest-growing sectors include[2] health services; business services; social services; engineering; management and related services. On the other hand, the goods-producing industry—including mining, construction, and durable and nondurable manufacturing—will only add about 1.3 million jobs, a 5 percent increase. In this industry, the construction and durable manufacturing sectors have the greatest gains over the 10-year period.

All occupations will increase by a total of about 15 percent. More than half the total job growth over the next 10 years is expected to come in the form of professional and related occupations as well as service occupations. Seven million jobs are expected to be added in the professional and related sectors, whereas the service sector is expected to increase by five million jobs. With advancements in computer technology, it is no surprise that administrative support and office occupations as well as production occupations will be growing more slowly than the average. Computers and machines will replace the need for people. In fact, despite the dot-com bomb of the years following March 2001, eighty percent of the fastest-growing occupations are computer-related (information technology occupations). Medical assistants and personal home care aides make up the other 20 percent of the fastest-growing occupations.

The ten occupations with the largest job growth over the next ten years include, in descending order of greatest increase in jobs[3]:

---

1 Source: Bureau of Labor Statistics, U.S. Department of Labor—Employment Projections for 2000–2010 (*http://www.bls.gov/emp*)

2 Source: Bureau of Labor Statistics, U.S. Department of Labor—Employment Projections for 2000–2010 (*http://www.bls.gov/emp*)

3 Source: Bureau of Labor Statistics, U.S. Department of Labor—Employment Projections for 2000-2010 (*http://www.bls.gov/emp*)

- Combined food preparation and serving workers, including fast food
- Customer service representatives
- Registered nurses
- Retail salespersons
- Computer support specialists
- Cashiers, except gaming
- Office clerks, general
- Security guards
- Computer software engineers, applications
- Waiters and waitresses

A basic college education, or even higher achievement, is extremely important in the future, almost a necessity. In fact, employment in such categories—with a Bachelor's degree, a Bachelor's degree and work experience, a Master's degree, Doctoral degree, first professional degree, Associate degree, or Postsecondary vocational award—is expected to grow faster than the average of all occupations. Ultimately, the job growth surrounding such education will increase by 13 percent more compared to that in 2000, occupying 42 percent of all new job growth.

By 2010, the total labor force is expected to grow by about 17 million people, reaching a total of 158 million. As the population ages, the demographics of this labor force will also change as rates of workforce participation among different age groups fluctuate. For example, according to the Bureau of Labor Statistics, "the youth labor force (aged 16 to 24) is expected to grow more rapidly than the overall labor force for the first time in 25 years." In addition, the baby-boomers aged 46 to 64 will dominate the workplace as the 55-and-older age group increases the most.

When considering the makeup of the labor force, women's participation will grow faster than men's. By 2010, women will comprise 48 percent of the total workforce. In addition, the Asian and other labor force group (including Asians and Pacific Islanders and American Indians and Native Alaskans) will increase the fastest by 44 percent, followed by the Hispanic labor force which will expand by 36 percent. Finally, "the black labor force is expected to grow by 21 percent, more

than twice as fast as the nine percent growth rate for the white labor force[4]."

Now that I have done all this research, what purpose does it serve besides offering an interesting peek into the future? Well, realizing what jobs will be hot in the future allows you to plan accordingly in the present. If anyone else is simply trying to get their foot in the door, they'll understand the frustration of trying to get their first job (or first professional job) in today's economy. This also holds true for those trying to break into a new industry. For those first timers, I am talking about the vicious cycle of "Experience Needed." Let me just throw this out: If I don't have the experience in the industry yet, and you won't give me a chance to gain any, then how am I ever going to be qualified for the position?! Are ability and skills irrelevant without experience?

After researching this future job assignment for the book (a perfect fit for a recent college grad), I had an epiphany. I realized that by being aware of the future job market, I can position myself now to gain the experience I will need for those jobs in the future. Hallelujah! Well, you may be thinking, that's just great if my interests and skills happen to coincide with those future jobs—but what if they don't? I figure that knowing the trends will allow me to find alternative work that is at least in the same industry, regardless of the field I end up in. I don't have to fit that exact job, but I can find a job that is related. For example, retail salespersons is number four on the list. Hence, with an increase in retail salespersons, there will undoubtedly be a need for retail managers to manage those salespersons. By understanding and being aware of where the occupation trends are going, you can position yourself early, plan ahead and begin to Love your work by Loving your Life, whether at 22 or 52!

However, don't base your entire life's work on these predictions. As we all know, unexpected

4 Source: Bureau of Labor Statistics, U.S. Department of Labor—Employment Projections for 2000-2010 (http://www.bls.gov/emp)

events and major changes in the world and workplace are inevitable. Such forecasts should be used as a general guide through an unknown and otherwise unpredictable future. On a career path that may have taken/or will take many wrong turns and detours, it doesn't hurt to stop and ask for a little direction along the way (unless, of course, you are a man!).

In addition to knowing where the greatest job growth will occur, others are simply interested in learning where the largest salary growth will occur. (Just a reminder—in order to Love your work by Loving your Life, remember that money isn't everything, and although it can buy you a lot of things, money cannot guarantee you happiness.) In my opinion, it is extremely important that you love the work you are doing regardless of the salary. In other words, you don't dread the arrival of Monday every Sunday night. So, for those of you with interests that match the following "Top 10 Highest Paying Jobs in the U.S.," you're the lucky ones. According to the 2001 Occupational Employment Statistics Survey conducted by the Department of Labor's Bureau of Labor Statistics (BLS), the biggest breadwinners are as follows.

The Actual Top 10 Highest Paying Professions in the U.S.[5]

1. Surgeons	$65.89/hr	$137,050/yr
2. Obstetricians and gynecologists		
	$64.15/hr	$133,430/yr
3. Anesthesiologists	$63.31/hr	$131,680/yr
4. Internists, general	$61.03/hr	$126,940/yr
5. Pediatricians, general	$56.03/hr	$116,550/yr
6. Psychiatrists	$54.60/hr	$113,570/yr
7. Family and general practitioners		
	$52.89/hr	$110,020/yr
8. Dentists	$53.28/hr	$110,820/yr

9. Chief Executives	$51.77/hr	$107,670/yr
10. Airline pilots, copilots and flight engineers		
	(N/A)	$99,400/yr

(Figures reflect mean hourly pay projected out to a year-round, full-time annual average)

You may have noticed that seven out of the top ten occupations listed above are in the medical field—hey, no one said it would be easy to make the big bucks! However, if medicine isn't your forte, the list continues with a variety of jobs from numerous fields[6]:

11. Podiatrists	$45.43/hr	$94,500/yr
12. Lawyers	$44.19/hr	$91,920/yr
13. Optometrists	$42.35/hr	$88,100/yr
14. Computer and information systems managers		
	$40.33/hr	$83,890/yr
15. Physicists	$40.26/hr	$83,750/yr
16. Air traffic controllers	$40.07/hr	$83,350/yr
17. Petroleum Engineers	$39.33/hr	$81,800/yr
18. Nuclear Engineers	$38.56/hr	$80,200/yr
19. Judges, magistrate judges, and magistrates		
	$38.24/hr	$79,540/yr
20. Marketing Managers	$37.70/hr	$78,410/yr

(Figures reflect mean hourly pay projected out to a year-round, full-time annual average)

If you are like me and still don't know what you want to be when you grow up, it doesn't hurt to do a little research on your own and learn where the current "hot" jobs are and where they are forecasted to be in the future.

As you will learn more about later, if you fail to plan, you plan to fail!

5 Source: *http://editorial.careers.msn.com/articles/highestpay/*

6 Source: *http://editorial.careers.msn.com/articles/highestpay/*

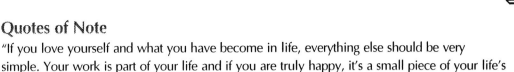

66 99 Quotes of Note

"If you love yourself and what you have become in life, everything else should be very simple. Your work is part of your life and if you are truly happy, it's a small piece of your life's puzzle. Friends, family and loved ones should be the major part of your life—the rest fills in the blanks. Therefore, loving your work is very simple if you have your life in order."

—*Anthony Pizzimenti, Sales Professional*

Profile of Success

Thomas Lyons, M.D.—Beth Israel Deaconess Hospital

Podiatrists are among the top 20 highest paying professions. Podiatrist Thomas Lyons, M.D. tells a most interesting story about why he became a doctor.

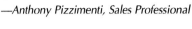

It is not always good to get comfortable with the excesses of life. As Thoreau alluded to, people live lives of quiet desperation. People, however, who live modest lifestyles and have good basic survival instincts know that they will survive. I believe they have less of a sense of quiet desperation. They know they can take care of themselves in even the worst of situations.

When I grew up, I had these lousy jobs—at Paragon Amusement Park, a gas station attendant, and a paperboy. The gas station job was the worst and the paperboy position was a close second. The least attractive part of being a paperboy was when my fingers and toes would freeze in the New England winters. They would begin to hurt and then go numb. When I arrived home, they would hurt more as they were warming up.

There was a man in my neighborhood who I delivered papers to and his name was Henry Tremaine. He was a cop and his claim to fame in our community was that he was the one who gave out traffic tickets to just about everyone in Hull, Massachusetts. Needless to say, he was not the most popular or loved person in the town. He used to sit in a recliner with his legs elevated trying to heal the ulcers on them. I would stop at his home and find myself in long conversations with this man.

Despite his reputation, I had come to know him as kind and compassionate. One day, he asked, "Do you like being a paperboy?" I responded with a resounding, "**No!**" Then, he told me something that I will never forget. He said, "*Whatever it takes, get a good job so you won't have to work at a bad one for 40 or 50 years.*" I took his words to heart and became a doctor and surgeon.

"C Suites" Check In

Health care is one of the fastest growing industries. Here is what "C Suite" health care executives have to say about LwL[2]:

"I always have believed that to 'love your work,' you must understand how your contribution ultimately makes a difference. It's easy to get caught up in the pressure and day-to-day hassles, but if you focus on the end result, you can feel inspired, even in the most difficult times. This has been my guide, and it certainly has helped to work with people who share these values!"

—Corinne Broderick, Executive Vice President, Massachusetts Medical Society/*New England Journal of Medicine*

"Loving your work is key for success in healthcare. If you don't love the mission, it is very hard to do a great job day after day after day."

—Thomas P. Glynn, Chief Operating Officer, Partners Healthcare System, Inc.

"Each one of us was born with innate talents and abilities, so the key to satisfaction at work—and in life—is taking the time to learn about yourself, and feeling confident in who you are as a person. Getting a college degree is relatively easy. What is infinitely more difficult is finding a career you're passionate about—one that maximizes your talents, keeps you challenged, allows you to constantly learn from others—but doesn't consume your entire life. Finding that life balance is key, not just for your own well being, but for others too. It sets an example for everyone around you—both at work and in your personal life."

— Nancy L. Leaming, President & Chief Executive Officer, Tufts Health Plan

Wise Words
Deborah Dagit—Executive Director Diversity & Work Environment, Merck & Co., Inc.

What people need to do to love their work:
Do something you care about more than organizational politics, and more than sleeping in. What you do at work should put a light in your eyes, a bounce in your step, and a fire in your heart.

What people need to do to love their life:
Realize there is no such thing as perfection. *The Brady Bunch* and *Father Knows Best* were TV shows and bear no resemblance to reality. Appreciate the small victories and tell the people you love how important they are every day.

Tips on loving your work or life that have worked for me:
Set achievable goals and celebrate their accomplishment. Cut yourself slack and realize you won't be perfect at everything every day. Have the courage of your convictions. Stand up for what is right whether or not it is popular. Have fun and laugh. Build authentic relationships with people, whether or not they share your passion and point of view.

How organizations can help staff to love their work and life:
Give praise whenever deserved in a timely fashion. Provide individual and unique rewards and recognition that fit the person not just a company process or tool. Trust your people and allow them the room to innovate. Make sure everyone in your organization feels challenged, valued, and capable of making a difference.

Wise Words
Arthur Harris—Hair Stylist and Cosmetologist Extraordinaire, Ecocentrix Salon

Arthur Harris, of Newbury St. Boston's trendy hair salon Ecocentrix, maintains that he has a fool-proof way to spot economic highs and lows and whether the economy is on the rebound or fully recovered. Arthur says to just check in with him and he can tell you whether the market is a Bull or a Bear. Customers get their hair cut, permed and dyed less frequently during bad economic times. "When the market is in a slump, so is our business," he proclaims.

Next time the Federal Reserve needs some advice, perhaps they should check in with Arthur.

A Practical Meaning Moment

Understand economic highs and lows and the impact on jobs now and in the future

To LwL[2] you must understand where the world of work is going and begin to analyze how your job/career and life must adapt to any changes or new directions in the world and workplace, and population/demographic trends.

It is important to keep up with trends regarding fastest growing careers/occupations and industries as well as those which are becoming obsolete. Take that information and make informed decisions around what, if any, new skills, attitudes or behaviors you must adapt to cope with such changes both in your work and life.

Another issue that many of us will face if we want to be gainfully employed is a real understanding about the world changes and diversity. We'll begin to understand more about how to put the world into our address books in the next chapter.

Chapter 13

Secret #4:
Put the World into
Your Address Book

UNDERSTANDING WORKFORCE AND SOCIETAL CHANGES

*"Despite the corporate and personal life perils generated by this tumultuous
year in our nation's history, many top organizations have demonstrated that
they've learned as much from the downs as they did from the economic boom
of the late '90s. Progressive organizations saw the horrific events as a wake-up call....
All agree: An investment in diversity is an investment that will pay corporations handsome
dividends in employee recruitment and retention, in the community
and in the marketplace today, tomorrow and in the future."*

—*Martha R. A. Fields, FORTUNE magazine,*
September 30, 2002

ON JULY 4, 2003, I WENT TO A VERY American event—an American Indian Pow Wow in Mashpee, Massachusetts. It was sponsored by the Wampanoag Indians. Sound familiar? They were the group who helped the Pilgrims when they first landed at nearby Plymouth and Pilgrim Rock.

My family and I ran into some people from Boston who we hadn't seen in a while. I was asked the common question, "How are you doing"?

I started to answer that with a ho-hum response of "Very well, thank you," then I stopped myself. Taking a moment to collect my thoughts, I replied with gusto, "Considering I don't have SARS, west nile virus, smallpox, monkey pox, and haven't opened an anthrax-ridden envelope or been hit by a SCUD missile or terrorist attack, I'm doing excellent!"

After saying that, I became very reflective and thought about how different life and work had become for us on that Fourth of July where Americans were celebrating their independence from England. I pondered the effect that diseases, spread from far away places, had on my life.

Just one year before that 2003 Fourth of July, the term SARS (Severe Acute Respiratory Syndrome) wasn't even part of the world's vocabulary. On that day, it was prominently embedded on the tongues of the Pow Wow attendees. There were people who would not visit Chinatown in any U.S. city, or fly to China or any other Asian country for fear of contracting that disease. The effect of that disease was not exclusively felt in the Chinese economy. American companies doing business in China, and industries such as the airline and travel business, also felt the pinch.

Events around the world have always had some affect on our lives and the workforce, but increasingly the occurrences are having a greater effect upon our way of life. Understanding the role that societal and workforce changes play in our lives helps us to better Love our work by Loving our Life. In this chapter, we will explore the impact that societal world and workforce changes have on our ability to Love our work by Loving our Life.

Secret #4

Put the World into Your Address Book

Put the World into Your Address Book is Secret #4. This concept refers to the need for you to expand your address book and circle of acquaintances to include people with backgrounds dissimilar from your own. It is also about including individuals from around the world into your life's little black book. Understanding these groups may include learning about how different life in the United States is from that in other parts of the world.

Previously, we learned that, since September 11, 2001, it is a small world after all. Events, activities, and actions that transpire around the world in "far away places with strange sounding names" do greatly affect us and our ability to LwL[2].

Attitudes about Americans differ around the world and I believe it behooves anyone who wants to LwL[2] to better understand how and why different segments of the universe view us in the way they do.

I first learned about how differently Americans are viewed when I was a child living in Okinawa, an island off the coast of Japan, in the early 1960s, about 15 years after WW II ended. I grew up as a military Air Force brat, and during that time my life was very global. People in the military and their families were always coming in or going out of various places in the world.

Although racial segregation was alive and very well in the United States, it was less so in my world at Kadena Air Force Base in Okinawa. There, you were not considered black or white, but American. In addition, everything was focused on patriotism. In Okinawa, I loved to go to the movies on Saturdays to see Roy Rogers and Dale Evans cowboy films. (You can see I'm really dating myself.) At the base theatre, an American flag would always be on stage. Before the movie started, our national anthem, "The Star-Spangled Banner," would play and the audience had to stand up and put their hands over their hearts. Only after this ritual could we enjoy Roy Rogers and Dale Evans singing songs like "Happy Trails To You…Until We Meet Again."

My family first landed in the United States at Anchorage, Alaska, and then in San Francisco just after the big earthquake of 1964. From there, we took the Greyhound bus across the country to North Carolina.

I'll never forget that trip; it was the year after our nation's beloved President John F. Kennedy had been shot in Dallas. One of the stops on our cross-country bus trip was in Dallas, Texas. The city's wounds had not yet healed from the tragedy that would forever mark that city in the annals of history as the site where young President Kennedy was assassinated over 40 years ago on November 22, 1963.

After living overseas for several years, the domestic landscape looked very foreign to me. The year before in August of 1963, Martin Luther King, Jr. had led the march on Washington. Then the Civil Rights Act of 1964 was passed. As we traveled by bus across the country I could see why it was necessary to have such legislation. In some bus stations in the south, there were signs at water fountains and bathrooms that said "For Whites Only" or "For Coloreds Only."

"For Whites or For Coloreds Only"

When I saw people being separated in "For Coloreds" or "For Whites Only" sections, I had a strong impulse to do something to those people who created those rules. The imagination of my child's mind would flourish as I thought of creative and appropriate means of punishment for the guilty parties who invented those concepts. One form of punishment back in those 1960's was to put a child in a corner and place a cylindrical hat on his head which read "Dunce."

When I saw those signs, indicating that just because your skin was white or beige-colored, you had to use one facility, and if it was black or brown, another, I wanted to correct that awful injustice that had been put in place to separate people simply by the color of their white and black skin. This wasn't cool, and I couldn't dig it Daddy-O, as the beatniks of the time would say. I wanted to round up all those people who had made those rules and put them en masse in a huge corner with the biggest dunce hat I could find placed squarely between their ears and those pea-sized brains that caused them to think up such a ridiculous concept.

Aren't We All Americans?

After my family returned to the United States in that summer of 1964, we went to visit my grandparents' house at the foothills of the Blue Ridge Mountains in Lenoir, North Carolina.

I'll always remember the first time I went to see a Roy Rogers and Dale Evans cowboy movie with my cousin; I was so excited. We entered the tiny theater where the lobby smelled of freshly popped popcorn and walked up a long set of stairs until we reached the bad seats in the back of the balcony. Huffing and puffing, I looked out over the balcony and asked my cousin, "What are we doing up here? Those are the good seats down there, and these are bad seats."

She looked at me like I was crazy and said, "Don't you know? That's for the li'l white kids; these are for the colored chillun."

Whoa! For the colored children? I couldn't believe my ears. The movie started. There was no American flag. No "Star-Spangled Banner" played. I was so baffled by everything that I couldn't even enjoy Roy and Dale singing one of my favorite songs, "Happy Trails to You…Until We Meet Again." I remember going home to my mom and saying with tears in my eyes and a lump in my throat, "Mom, I can't believe this. Aren't we all Americans?"

Quick Quiz

To better understand the people in the world who may be potential candidates to put into your address book, I'd like you to take these Quick Quizzes to give you some perspective on U.S. vs. world demographics.

World Population—A Village-of-100 Exercise

Directions: If the world's population were to shrink proportionally to a village of 100 people, what would the demographics look like? Circle the correct answer for each statement.

1. This is the number of non-whites:
   a. 20   b. 50   c. 70

2. This number would be not be able to read:
   a. 20   b. 70   c. 90

3. This number would be university (college) educated:
   a. 1   b. 25   c. 80

4. This number would live in substandard housing:
   a. 20   b. 80   c. 90

5. Seventeen would speak this widely spoken language:
   a. Mandarin b. English   c. Hindi or Urdu

6. These individuals would not have access to clean, safe drinking water:
   a. 33   b. 53   c. 73

Source: Exercise based on information from Unheard Voices:
Celebrating Cultures from the Developing World, ERIC Search—United Nations

Village-of-100 Answers

Something to think about:

If the world's population were to shrink proportionally to a village of 100 people, it would look something like this:

1. c. 70 of the 100 would be non-white
2. b. 70 of the 100 would be unable to read
3. a. only 1 would be university-educated
4. b. 80 would live in sub-standard housing
5. a. 17 people would speak Mandarin
6. a. 33 would not have clean, safe drinking water

Source: Excerpted from Unheard Voices: Celebrating Cultures from the Developing World, and ERIC Search—United Nations Demographic Data

US Village

Something to think about:

If the U.S. population were to shrink proportionally to a village of 100 people, it would look something like this:

75 would be white
12 would be African American
1 would be American Indian
4 would be Asian
1 would be a Pacific Islander
5 would be another race
2 would be two or more races

83 would speak English only
17 would speak other than English
10 would speak Spanish
4 would speak other Indo-European languages
3 would speak Asian languages

7 would be under 5 years old
7 would be 20 to 24 years old
14 would be 25 to 34 years old
16 would be 35 to 44 years old
13 would be 45 to 54 years old
21 would be 55 and over

81 would have a high school diploma
25 would have a bachelors degree or higher

Source: 1990 and 2000 Census Data

As you can see from these two examples, we are extremely fortunate in the United States compared with many people in the rest of the world. The freedom and lifestyles engaged in this country, however, are at times resented or not understood by others in the world. Several studies point to a growing lack of tolerance for the American way of life. A fascinating study conducted by the Pew Research Center shed some light on how Americans are viewed around the world.

Views of a Changing World

A study entitled "Views of a Changing World 2003," released by the Pew Research Center, explores world attitudes about the United States. Below are some excerpts from the study that I found particularly relevant to Americans who want to better understand the world and how they can use that information to LwL2.[1]

1. "The speed of the war in Iraq [that occurred in 2003] and the prevailing belief that the Iraqi people are better off as a result have modestly improved the image of America. But in most countries, opinions of the U.S. are markedly lower than they were a year ago. The war has widened the rift between Americans and Western Europeans, further inflamed the Muslim world, softened support for the war on terrorism, and significantly weakened global public support for the pillars of the post-World War II era—the U.N. and the North Atlantic alliance."

2. "While the postwar poll paints a mostly negative picture of the image of America, its people and policies, the broader Pew Global Attitudes Survey shows wide support for the fundamental economic and political values that the U.S. has long promoted."

3. "Globalization, the free market model and democratic ideals are accepted in all corners of the world. Most notably, the 44-nation survey found strong democratic aspirations in most of the Muslim publics surveyed. The postwar update confirms that these aspirations remain intact despite the war and its attendant controversies."

4. "Beyond their common desire for democracy and free markets, people in emerging nations also generally acknowledge and accept globalization. People worldwide have become aware of the effect of increasing interconnectedness on their countries

---

1 Source: "Views of a Changing World 2003, War with Iraq Further Divides Global Policies," June 3, 2003. Pew Research Center for the People and Press Survey Reports. *http://peoplepress.org/reports/print-php3?pageID=712*

and their own lives. Majorities in 41 of 44 countries surveyed say that international trade and business contacts have increased in the past 5 years."

5. "The survey finds broad acceptance of the increasing interconnectedness of the world. Three-quarters or more of those interviewed in almost every country think children need to learn English to succeed in the world today. People generally view the growth in foreign trade, global communication and international popular culture as good for them and their families as well as their countries. For most of the world's people, however, this approval is guarded. Increased trade and business ties and other changes are viewed as somewhat positive, not very positive."

6. "People around the world generally have a positive view of the symbols of globalization. Large corporations from other countries get a favorable review in much of the world, as do international organizations.

   In Africa, people express highly favorable opinions of foreign corporations, while the Middle East is more divided. Dislike of foreign firms is mostly limited to people in the major advanced economies of Western Europe, the U.S. and Canada. Even in these countries, however, positive evaluations of multinationals outweigh negative assessments."

GLOBALIZATION ISSUES

Diversity issues differ in other parts of the world. Getting managers accustomed to doing business around the world and dealing with global employees sometimes produces a problem. Culture classes in which managers are taught to value the differences and similarities between American culture and other cultures can help with these problems.

Another problem is acclimating global workers into the U.S. workforce. As more cultures invade the workforce, employers will need to handle additional issues related to English as a Second Language, including policies regarding speaking English only.

I also believe that Americans may need to become more multi-lingual. I once took a trip to the Amazon Jungle in Iquitos, Peru with my husband. We were tourists with a very international group of travelers. Our guide, whose name was Segundo, kept speaking to people in their native languages—Spanish, French, Italian, German and English.

I was amazed by his talents because he had told us that he had been born and grew up in the jungle. I was so intrigued by his linguistic mastery that I had finally asked him, "Segundo, how many lenguas (languages) do you habla (speak)?"

He replied, apologetically, "Only five. I'm just starting to learn a sixth—Japanese—because we're starting to see so many more tourists here from Japan."

I was struck by the fact that he was apologizing for only speaking almost six languages. I knew plenty of native-born people in the United States who could barely speak English correctly.

I've traveled extensively throughout the world and have observed Segundo-like people in many parts of the globe. People outside of the U.S. often speak multiple languages, including English, which they use to link themselves with others whether that be on a personal, professional or work level. Later, we will see how the demographics in our country are changing and why we may need to begin learning other languages if we intend to keep up with the world and LwL[2].

Richard Kaplan, a career U.S. Diplomat and host of Author Events at the Harvard Coop, offers two intriguing insights into the relationship of the globe to our work and lives.

Globalization: The Whole is Greater Than the Sum of Its Parts

By Richard Kaplan—Career U.S. Diplomat and
host of Author Events,
Harvard Coop

"THE WORLD," THE POET WILLIAM Wordsworth wrote, "is too much with us." Globalization is that way today. Almost everybody talks about it. People write and read about it. They worry, fret and argue over it too. Many support it and condemn it. It is demonized on one hand, idealized on the other. Columnists, editors, and pundits ponder and opine about it. But few can agree on what it is.

Is it good or bad? Devoutly to be sought or anxiously to be avoided? A promise or a threat? An affliction or a cure? Utopia or dystopia? Can we take it or lump it, embrace or reject it? Or, is globalization—the global economy, the global culture, the global globe—beyond our control? Even out of control?

It is not a simple or single phenomenon. Is globalization Starbucks and McDonalds? Hollywood? The Internet? Air Jordan? Transnationals? The IMF? Free trade? Technology transfer? "McWorld?"

All of the above—but the whole is greater than the sum of its parts.

A fifteenth-century Florentine could not have grasped the significance of the Renaissance. He was busy living it and didn't know that the Renaissance was the Renaissance. He didn't comprehend where the Renaissance brick fit into history's wall.

The future will tell us what globalization is, but it may not be called by that name. One thing the future historian does not have to tell us, though: globalization is changing the way we live and work. How we play and may stay alive in the future. It has altered the way we think and link with others in the universe. Put differently: the way we live, work, play, think and link is changing. "Globalization" is the name we give that phenomenon.

The contemporary manager has no choice. He or she must be global. The times demand it. She knows that cultural competence—or ignorance—can make or break a deal, a project, a company itself (not to mention her career). She is fluid, adaptable, sensitive to signals, culturally quick on her feet—negotiating one week in Rio or Caracas, troubleshooting in Riyadh, Bombay or Manila the next. She knows that companies, like cars, need oil to run. Cultures, like components, have to work in tandem smoothly. The alternative is that the engine breaks and the corporation melts down.

Savvy businesses, from the corporate behemoths to mom and pop corner stores, grasp the central paradox of the global age: the closer together that business and technology bring us, the more critical understanding cultural differences becomes.

Widely separated cultures never clash. Bring them closer together, though, and like techtonic plates they grate and grind in sync. Cultures come together or collide everywhere today—in the office and the school, the gym and the street, the subway and the mall.

Managing across cultures, therefore, is not always the same as managing in other cultures. Suppose that you don't have to manage in Rio; or entertain clients in Riyadh. You never have to leave home. You're still not off the hook. The world is not "out there" anymore. The world is here. America isn't safe—or insulated—from it's borders. Chances are, you have to communicate across cultures. Translation: understand (which does not mean identify with) other cultures—as much in Dallas, or Nashville, or Los Angeles, as you would in Tokyo, Moscow or Berlin.

America, for better or worse, is an empire. It is not an empire of conquest and legions, but of opportunities. Those who join it, do so freely. America, for them, is a species of forgetting. It allows them to forget the old constraints and biases and prohibitions, the strangulating of old formalities. It doesn't have to conquer: by its very nature, by its breadth, verve, speed and freedoms, America seduces.

It is the New Way; an enlightened approach; a breath of fresh air. Many who don't have it want to immigrate into it. They long to breathe it, and if only superficially—in style, dress, attitude—enjoy the American way of life. Even terrorists wear Nikes, after all. And Harvard sweatshirts sell from Tokyo to Brazzaville.

Superficial similarities: there's the rub. We're talking Nikes, sweatshirts, cell phones, U.S. MBAs and SUVs. U.S. movies are on the screens from Tokyo to Brazzaville and English is the "link language" of the business and entertainment worlds.

Born and raised a Congolese or Japanese, whatever sweatshirt you might wear or hip-hop pop you listen to, you will remain your ethnicity or race, but also be influenced by that of another. An American in Paris, after all, is an American, Pernod, beret and all, and not a Frenchman.

Surface similarities deceive because true differences run deep. People often mistake similarities for commonality of purpose. Many in different parts of the globe experience time and space, present, past and future, in similar, but different ways. A "long time" in the United States may be 350 years. Other parts of the globe may view 3,500 years as a figure which constitutes a "long time."

Cultural competence, at the very least, is an issue of profit-and-loss. It can be an issue of life-and-death.

9/11 exposed more than the structural shortcomings of the World Trade Center. More than the shockingly soft underbelly of airport security. It exposed our cluelessness as well. Not all Americans inhabit Norman Rockwell-like, smiley-face, church-social, corner barber-shop small towns. Rockwell's portraits of American life are lovely and beguiling but don't represent all of America or the views shared by certain groups around the world.

What shocked us that September morning in 2001, wasn't just our enemies' capacity for murderous fanaticism—we've dealt with and defeated enemies like that before—but some people's HATRED for anything looking, breathing or smelling American. We discovered that this HATRED ran so deep that individuals were willing to take their own lives and that they were willing to commit suicide bombings so that the American way of life could eventually be blown away off the face of this earth.

We were blindered—just like some junkman's horse, not looking right or left but only straight ahead. We were culturally short-sighted and didn't know what might be coming at us from our right or left. We didn't even think much about our right or left. We misjudged our enemies and gave them about half a minute's thought on the evening news. Many of them, however, spent decades thinking almost every waking minute about how to mentally and physically defeat us. When they moved from thinking to action mode, they made towers and minds burn and crash.

Some believe that culture doesn't really matter any more than—despite what our teachers kept telling us in grammar school—penmanship and posture really mattered. But it really does—and must—to the country and to companies. It matters to our national survival and our continued ability to love our life and our work.

Globalization has been linked to a sea of change in the nature of business—indeed, of society as a whole. If so, then the modern manager has to sink or swim. Just floating along won't do! You can either love the new global economy or hate it—but you can't afford to ignore it. Wherever you work these days and in whatever field—from high-tech to services, from academia to agriculture, from medicine to banking—chances are you are working in a global and a multicultural environment. Global negotiation and communication skills, once merely useful, are increasingly critical to corporate success. Even critical to success in our daily lives. A challenge? Yes—but an exciting opportunity as well.

Baseball and the Global Manager

By Richard Kaplan—Career U.S. Diplomat and
host of Author Events,
Harvard Coop

As a manager in today's workplace, you're Joe Torre. You're Dusty Baker. The color of your infielders' skin, the shape of your outfielders' eyes—these are the least of your concerns. Winning, teamwork, chemistry, momentum, pitching, hitting, running and defense are your concerns. They have to be. You wouldn't be manager otherwise. Not for long!

Baseball is American. It is e pluribus unum in action. It celebrates the individual as well as the collective effort. A player, a good player, is never a cog in a machine. Babe Ruth, Ted Williams and Ty Cobb were not cogs. All pitchers throw differently. All hitters hit differently. Their differences give baseball flavor: differences in style and differences, increasingly, in culture.

Baseball is not only American. It is global, too: global, multicultural, international, color-blind, culture-tolerant and race-indifferent. It wasn't always the case. There was a time when the Major Leagues were (1) American and (2) lily white. Light-skinned blacks were smuggled onto teams as "Cubans."

Then came Jackie Robinson, and baseball, while still entirely American, was at least white and black American. Today, they are American and non-American and white and black and brown and yellow. Where you come from doesn't matter. What music you listen to in the clubhouse doesn't matter. Just what you can do and how well you fit in does. You don't have to eat, look, talk and worship the same to be part of that "in" crowd. Broody, me-first, screw-you loners of whatever nationality or background, domestic or imported, won't, in the end, succeed. They'll have

the flashy stats. They'll get their RBI's. But their teams won't win, nor be sad to see them go.

Baseball managers are global manages today. Offer them a Martian from outer space with a 97-mile-an-hour fastball and a decent curve and change-up and they'd play him (it?) too. But it may take a while to teach the Martian earthly ways. Managers know that team cohesion and cultural uniformity are not the same. The team uniform is uniformity enough. The Martian must become a Red Sox, Yankee or Brave first. Once he does, who cares how green he is?

Ichiro is a thorough going Japanese. He's made American concessions just as U.S. players in Japan have made them. Concessions and adaptations make not only for survival but for daily sanity as well. But Ichiro is otherwise 100% Japanese—and 100% Seattle Mariner.

It isn't an either/or. It's both. The modern manager is American and global. Globalization is not a zero-sum game. A manager is not less American for becoming more global any more than Ichiro is any less Japanese for being the star of an American baseball team.

Culture differences cannot, should not, be ironed out like wrinkles. Life would be too boring if they were! All cultures are human; therefore, somehow bridgeable. However perplexing, however impenetrable, however alien to the uninitiated, they share, or can be taught to share, a common ground. Dominicans, Japanese, Koreans, Nicaraguans, Midwest farmboys and southern good old boys and city ethnics and African-Americans have all found common ground in the game—and culture—of baseball. They are true to themselves in one sense; they transcend themselves in another.

An engineer in the United States makes on the average $90,000 per year. The average salary of an engineer with comparable education and experience in India is $23,000 per year.

Source: NBC Evening News, 10/27/03

Half of the doctoral and masters degrees in the United States are granted to foreign nationals. In additional, one half of the computer science and engineering degrees are also given to foreign students. The highest percentage of degrees are given to people from India (22%) followed by China, Korea and Japan. These individuals contribute $12 billion to the U.S. economy through tuition and living expenses.

Source: CNN—Lou Dobbs Moneyline, 10/17/03

In the pages ahead, you will hear some valuable perspectives on LwL[2] from individuals who have immigrated to the United States from a variety of areas around the globe.

Wise Words

Robert Browne—Barbados; Systems Engineer, Cisco Systems

I came here when I was young. On the island of Barbados, we were brought up with a lot of discipline and respect. The U.S. isn't as disciplined with kids as are a lot of foreign countries. My immediate effect was seen on many levels. Teachers love people who respect them, and I already had that in the islands. That was a no-brainer. The teachers immediately fell in love with me. I said, "Yes, sir" and "No, sir" and even stood up and addressed them. One teacher told me he wanted a dozen students like me.

From a work perspective, in the islands you had to do your homework or you would be disciplined and flogged. So coming here, to do the homework was nothing out of the ordinary for me.

The hardest part was relationships with other people. You are coming from a different background and environment. That's the biggest stop gap. You don't want to be better than everybody else or make yourself look bad. You just want to fit in. My approach was different. I laid the blame completely on my parents. So, if kids wanted to lead me down any path I didn't want to go, I could use them as the best out and say my mom would kill me if I did that or I'd say I was grounded for doing something and couldn't go.

My parents became the ultimate source of authority—even if they weren't. I used them as my cop out. As a kid, you're put into challenging spots. For example, your friends may want to skip school and go to the movies. If I was in that situation, I couldn't say no to them, but I could say that I had to be home and therefore I'm out of that predicament. I'd blame it on my parents. I hope my kids will do the same thing and use me as their "way out" when it comes to dealing with their peers.

Profiles of Success

Nina Miller-Browne—Jamaica; Senior Business Analyst, FleetBoston Financial

For me, coming to America was arriving in the Land of Opportunity. Being from Jamaica, a very different country, I wanted to capitalize on those opportunities. I started to research how I could go to work for a company that would pay for me to go to college because I couldn't afford to do so on my own. When I arrived in this country 13 years ago, I only had a high school education. I knew that to succeed, education was the key. I've been very lucky to work for good organizations that paid for my undergrad and graduate degrees and a graduate certificate and a CFA. I now have a Masters in Economics and Finance and a Graduate Certificate in Financial Markets and Services from Boston University. I also have an undergraduate degree in Management and Finance from Bentley College. All I had to do was work and they paid for me to learn and grow. That is the basis of my success.

I don't necessarily believe it's all about hard work, but it is about smart work. You have to be willing to invest the time and the effort to be a success in this country. That's all it is. It really isn't rocket science.

Profiles of Success

Benny Ferlazzo—Sicily; Cosmetologist, Monica's Beauty Salon

I am happy with everything I have done ever since I came to America (I was 18 months old when I arrived from Sicily). All I've done is hairdressing. I don't know anything else. I like everything about it, cutting and coloring hair, the prestige and atmosphere of it all and people. I've had people say, aren't you sick and tired of your work? I reply, No! I have wonderful customers and I get along with them. The best part is that I get paid for what I love to do.

Liming Shao—China; Associate Director of Drug Discovery, Sepracor

Loving your work by Loving your Life is all about pursuing your dream. I want to discover a drug that helps people to live a better quality of life. I really enjoy the research and coming up with new ideas and developing something that will lead to a new drug. I enjoy the process of discovery and research and I like working with people. In my field, to be successful you need to work with people from different areas. They teach you and you teach them.

I came to this country ten years ago from Shanghai, China by way of Japan, where I finished my Ph.D. My advice to people who immigrate to this country is to be confident. This is the basis and foundation to build your career and a happy life.

Chapter 14

WHY BECOME MORE DIVERSE?

Why Become More Diverse?

IN BOTH THE WORKPLACE AND THE MARketplace, we are becoming acutely aware of America's diversity. This is occurring as we share space at school, work, and in our personal lives with people of different genders, races, ages, sexual orientations and backgrounds. Technological advances, such as the computer, have brought the global village closer together. Online, customers are color-blind. Everyone vying for their dollar can look, feel, smell, taste and cost the same. To be successful at LwL[2], it is essential to acquire cultural competencies—skills that will help you relate to a variety of people both in the United States as well as around the world.

In the pages that follow, you will learn some practical tips on how to become more diverse. Serving customers from around the world can get tricky. A customer in Australia or Africa may require different customer service and marketing or sales focus than one in Japan, China, France, Great Britain, Brazil or Chile. Customers in New York may have different needs and service expectations than those in New Orleans or New Mexico.

The road to putting the world into your address book is paved with multiple challenges and opportunities. It requires you to learn about cultures, beliefs, traditions, and values that may be different from your own. As we have found, you may need to do this in a world where some do not embrace your values and way of life.

To begin, let's test your knowledge about diversity and the needs of multicultural consumers.

Quick Quiz
Diversity

1. Which of the following racial groups do you think will grow the fastest in the workforce by 2010?
   a. Asian and other*   b. Black   c. White   d. Hispanic
   —*Bureau of Labor Statistics*

2. According to the Census 2000, Whites make up this percentage of the population of the United States:
   a. 25.1%   b. 45.1%   c. 50.1%   d. 75.1%

3. True or False: In the past, the man of the house was responsible for the family budget and spending, and this still holds true today.
   —*"The Power of the Purse", www.trendsight.com/gendertrends/spendingpower.html*

4. According to *FORTUNE* magazine, this is the combined buying power of African-Americans, Asian Americans and Hispanic Americans:
   a. $1.5 million   b. $1.5 billion   c. $1.5 trillion   d. $1.5 kazillion

5. This is the largest ethnic group in the United States and has 60 million members:
   a. Italians   b. Germans   c. Irish   d. Mexicans
   —*WGBH TV*

6. By 2050, what percent of the total U.S. population will be of Hispanic origin?
   a.10%   b. 15%   c. 25%   d. 35%
   —*Sonia M. Perez, Council of La Raza to the House of Representatives*

7. What percentage of the Chinese elderly are fully supported by their children?
   a. 15%   b. 25%   c. 35%   d. 45%
   —*Hong Kong Trade Development Council*

8. This group has a population of 17 million and the buying power of $450 billion:
   a. White males   b. Gays, lesbians, bisexuals, transexuals   c. Women   d. Individuals with a disability
   —*FORTUNE magazine, October 13, 2003*

9. What group has rice as a staple dinner item?
   a. Hispanics   b. African-Americans   c. Asians
   --*The Market Segment Group Multicultural Snapshot 10/28/03, snapshots@marketsegment.com*

10. This rapidly growing group has a population of 50 million and a buying power of $175 billion:
    a. White males   b. Gays, lesbians, bisexuals, transexuals   c. Women   d. Individuals with a disability
    —*FORTUNE magazine, October 13, 2003*

(*includes Asians, Pacific Islanders, American Indians and Alaska Natives)

Web Browsers

These sites are great for information related to diversity and multicultural marketing:

www.bwni.com — Corporate membership optional

www.diversitybestpractices.com — Membership required

www.diversityinc.com — Registration or membership required

www.marketsegment.com/snapshot — Registration required

www.UnityFirst.com — Registration required

Wise Words

Barbara Frankel—Vice President, Executive Editor, DiversityInc

Work should be a vital component of one's ability to feel fulfilled and productive in society. It never should be the only way by which we define ourselves, but it always should be a significant way to add meaning and value to life. My work (20 years as a newspaper executive, three years as editor of DiversityInc) has given my life a richness and a purpose that has enabled me to be a better daughter, wife, mother and friend.

WHAT IS DIVERSITY?

Putting the world into your address book also requires that you understand and respect the diversity of others.

Today, the word diversity is everywhere. You can't turn on the television or radio, or read a newspaper or magazine without someone referring to the issue of diversity. What exactly is diversity? What does "diversity" really mean?

DIVERSITY DEFINED

Diversity is defined as "variety, medley, heterogeneity, multiplicity, and individuality." It is about valuing the differences and similarities that we all possess. Diversity may refer to individual characteristics including, but not limited to

- Gender
- Job function
- Sexual orientation
- Length of service and experience
- Race
- Personality
- Ethnicity
- Health
- National origin
- Physical and cognitive disabilities
- Age
- Balancing work, family and personal life
- Socioeconomic status
- Education
- Religion
- Background

Each one of us is unique and while that is important, we must also focus on how we are similar. People often spend a lot of time reflecting on their differences, but we have many similarities, regardless of age, race, or gender. For example, most of us want the best in life. We all have red blood and a heart that beats. Our similarities, as well as our differences, are what help make us so special.

Almost everyone can think of something they value that other people may not like or accept. In order to survive and thrive not only in your personal, but professional relationships, you must learn to respect individuals and their beliefs even when you do not necessarily agree with them.

Many of us think that diversity involves only people of color (African-Americans/Blacks, Asians, Hispanics/Latinos and Native Americans) when in fact, diversity includes everyone: Italians, Irish, Germans, the elderly, men, women, the physically challenged... everyone!

HOW TO BECOME MORE DIVERSE

"The journey of a thousand miles begins with the first step."
—Lao Tse, Chinese philosopher

To begin our diversity journey, we must open ourselves up to having conversations with a variety of people. This, however, may be easier said than done. Diversity conversations may be difficult because they challenge

- Individual beliefs, values, behavior and our way of life.
- Organizations, traditions, policies, procedures and culture.

Bear in mind that the road to becoming more diverse is a long one that takes a lifetime to travel.

OUT OF MANY, ONE PEOPLE

Recognize that

- We are not all the same.
- We have different cultures, beliefs, values, but as the motto for Jamaica—"Out of many, one people"—suggests, the uniqueness of many people composes the whole.
- *E Pluribus Unum,* the statement written on the great seal of the United States of America, also echoes this sentiment—"Out of Many, One."

THE PLATINUM RULE

To become more diverse, consider practicing the Platinum Rule. The Platinum Rule requires individuals to go beyond the Golden Rule:

"Do unto others as you would have things done unto you."

The Platinum Rule encourages people to "Do unto others as *they* would have things done. Respect the ways of others, even when they are not around."

This may sound confusing, but the concept is really quite simple. You may think you are being a good person or a good Samaritan by practicing the Golden Rule and treating another individual the way that you would like to be treated. However, the Platinum Rule is a higher order that requires you to treat someone else as they, rather than as you, would like to be treated.

Not only does the Platinum Rule apply when you are talking to the individual face-to-face, but it also implies respecting the way that person would like to be treated or referred to when they are not around. To practice the Platinum Rule, you have to become knowledgeable about other races, cultures, religions, ages, genders, socioeconomic groups, etc.

CULTURAL AND RACIAL CHARACTERISTICS

Quite often when people first embark on their journey to become more diverse, they take time to learn more about the characteristics of various cultural or racial groups.

This may be a good starting point and can provide a framework within which to understand information, or gain another perspective on a given culture, race, gender, etc. There is, however, a downside to that approach. Such generalizations may lead people to believe that ALL people in a given group possess certain characteristics.

TO STEREOTYPE OR NOT TO STEREOTYPE?

Try Not to Over-Generalize About Any Group of People

- Who said all white people have no rhythm and cannot dance?
- Do all Asian people love math and are very smart?
- Do not confuse people from Asian cultures because you think, "they all look alike." There are many Asian nationalities. China has a population of 1.2 billion; India has a population of close to a billion people. The Chinese people differ from Indian and Japanese people, who differ from Filipinos, Koreans and so on.
- Recognize individuals for both their racial and cultural heritage.
- Leave room for individual differences.

Think Smart

- Take stock of your thinking and do not always assume that African-Americans, Native Americans, and Latinos come from impoverished backgrounds.
- Just because you may not understand what someone is saying to you or they cannot understand what you are communicating to them, do not fast forward to the conclusion that they are less intelligent.
- Don't assume that when a person from an ethnic or racial group talks that they are speaking for the whole race.

- A single leader may have different views from others in the group that they appear to represent.
- Consider this: People would never think that when Bill Clinton, George W. Bush or Howard Stern speaks, they represent the views of all White people. Why, then, should Jesse Jackson, or Al Sharpton represent the views of all African-Americans?

Make Room for Individual Differences
- Realize that individuals make up a group.
- Not all people in a group are the same: people of the same race, gender, and age are also diverse. For example, consider how different individuals from these various Caucasian groups are: Italians, Germans, Australians; people of African descent: Jamaicans, Nigerians, African-Americans; Asians: Japanese, Chinese, Koreans; Native Americans: Cherokee, Sioux, Blackfoot; Latinos: Puerto Ricans, Mexicans, Colombians; to name a few.
- Just because a person has the same color of skin or comes from the same ethnic background as another person, it is unfair to assume that they are both alike.
- People from the same racial or ethnic group in the United States may differ from people of that identical group who live in various parts of the world. Depending on geographical locations, individuals may also differ greatly in their lifestyles, choices of food, dress, language, etc.

Good Manners
- Regardless of a person's race, gender, age, etc., always treat the person with dignity and respect.
- For example, when you are standing in line at a hotel or department store, do not step in front of people of color in line because you assume that they are members of the staff.

WHAT IS PLATINUM CORRECT?

Being platinum correct can be both challenging and confusing. What is "in" language one day may be "out" the next day. For example, people of African descent in the

United States at various times in history have been referred to as African-Americans, Blacks, Negroes, and Colored. Try to stay in tune with platinum correct language by listening to how individuals refer to themselves. Bear in mind that platinum correctness can change with the wind and what may be platinum correct to one person in a group may be incorrect to another.

For example, most African-American people would resent being called "colored people." Some prefer to be called African-American and not Black (and vice versa); while certain people from Hispanic backgrounds prefer to be called Latinos, some people from Spain may not like to be referred to as Latinos.

To further complicate the issue, some individuals who have traditionally been called Indians may want to be known as Native Americans. Also, there are individuals with disabilities who do not like to be referred to as handicapped, disabled or invalids.

Question: What is a person to do about all of this?
Answer: Listen to how people refer to themselves and follow their lead.

Think About How You Use the Word "Minority"
You may wish to think about how you use the word minority. When speaking about the people of the world, it is a misnomer to use the word "minorities" to refer to African-Americans, Asians, Latinos, Native Americans and Pacific Islanders. They actually constitute the majority of people in the world. In some areas of the United States (e.g., New York, Los Angeles, Chicago, Washington, D.C.), some people of color have, in fact, become the majority population.

Take Time to Understand History
On November 27, 2003 (Thanksgiving Day), I did something I've always wanted to do—spend that holiday in Plymouth, Massachusetts, the site of the first Thanksgiving in 1621. My family and I learned much on that day about the

50 Pilgrims and 90 Wampanoag Indians who celebrated that first feast together.

That morning we watched the Pilgrims march in their traditional Pilgrim Progress Procession. The afternoon activities with the Native Americans were far more somber as they marched in a rally to signify Thanksgiving as their National Day of Mourning. They do not feel thankful about what the Pilgrims did to them and their land. Sometimes becoming more diverse involves understanding why different groups view the same event or period in history from different perspectives.

Show Me the Money: Consumer Stats About Women that Everyone Should Know

☆ A study by General Electric of its 135,000 professionals found that women quit at a higher rate than men—8% versus 6.5% or 2,025 more women than men each year.

☆ Catalyst research firm found that 26% of professional women not yet in senior level positions say they do not want them.

☆ Women occupy 21% of college presidencies.

☆ 14% each of the U.S. Senate and the House of Representatives is composed of women.

☆ Of the top-level decision-makers in corporate America (that's Executive Vice Presidents and higher) only 8% are women. In addition, there are only 8 female CEOs included in the 2003 *FORTUNE* 500.

☆ A study conducted by Simmons College and the Committee of 200, a woman's group, in 2002 found that of 4,200 teenagers only 9% of girls and 15% of boys want business careers.

☆ Only 36% of MBA students are women, whereas 47% of medical school and 49% of law school students are female.

Source: Sellers, Patricia. "Power: Do Women Really Want It?"
FORTUNE. *October 13, 2003; pp. 86–100*

☆ Equilar, a data analysis firm, compared the paychecks of 2,120 male executives and 112 females. These findings revealed that the median pay for women—$2.1 million—is 24% less than that of the men.

Source: Harrington, Ann and Melanie Shanley.
"The Power 50: 15 Highest Paid." FORTUNE. October 13, 2003; p. 110

About Other Groups

☆ As much as 6% or 7% of the population may be gay or lesbian.

☆ 70% of American workers will be women or racial minorities by 2040.

☆ The buying power of racial and ethnic minorities in the U.S. is expected to grow from just under $2 trillion in 2002 to $2.8 trillion by 2008.

Source: Smith, Lee. "The Business Case for Diversity." FORTUNE, October 13, 2003. p. S8-S12.

U.S. Current Buying Power:
Diversity Constituents and the Bottom Line Impact

Group	# in Population	Buying Power
Hispanic-Americans	38.8 million	$580 billion
Asian-Americans	11.5 million	$253 billion
African-Americans	36.7 million	$645 billion
Gays, Lesbians, Bisexuals, Transexuals	17 million	$450 billion
Disability	50 million	$175 billion

The combined buying power of the aforementioned groups, minus 25% from the cumulative amount allowed for overlap, is equal to the GDP of France!

Sources: Smith, Lee. "The Business Case for Diversity." FORTUNE, October 13, 2003. p. S10. Center for Immigration Studies; Cultural Access Group; Human Rights Campaign; Kang and Lee Advertising; The New York Times; Syracuse University, OpusComm Group, GSociety Study; University at Albany, Lewis Munford Center for Comparative Urban and Regional Research; University of Georgia, Selig Center; U.S. Census Bureau; U.S. Department of Commerce; The Washington Post.

" " Quote Of Note

Martha R. A. Fields, a management consultant based in Cambridge, Mass., singles out another diversity issue that is likely to sneak up on many unsuspecting companies in a few years: mixing generations in the workplace.

As they become senior or near-senior citizens, Baby Boomers will be less likely to retire than their predecessors, because they will be in good health but lack sufficient wealth to quit working. Moreover, companies will be eager to have them stay on the job, says Fields, because the trailing and smaller Generation X will not provide enough labor. "But how will the companies deal with collisions? Younger people will be supervising those old enough to be their parents. Different generations will expect different health and other benefits."

Source: Smith, Lee. "The Diversity Factor." FORTUNE,
October 13, 2003. pp. S2-S4

THE NEXT GENERATION OF DIVERSITY ISSUES

This generation is described as "the first generation to accept mixed races, nontraditional families, and gender-bending sex roles as mainstream." (*American Demographics,* October 1995, p. 22) One third of young Americans are Black, Latino, Asian or Native American. Eighty percent of these have friends not of their race.

Take the hip-hop culture, for instance. Hip-hop is a $1 billion industry. Guess who purchases 60% of rap music? White American teens.

Here are some "next generation" diversity issues that you may face as you try to recruit and retain diverse indispensable employees, including women, people of color, Gen-Xers and matures:

- Shifting workforce demographics
- Building a diverse workforce at ALL levels
- White males as full diversity partners
- Interacting with diverse candidates in multicultural communities
- When MTV meets AARP
- Globalization issues
- Dealing with individuals with a disability
- Communicating and managing across generations
- Socioeconomics (gender and racial pay-scale inequities)

SHIFTING WORKFORCE DEMOGRAPHICS

Organizations that are looking at statistics, such as those published by the U.S. Census Bureau and the Bureau of Labor Statistics, are seeing that the workforce composition is changing. In addition, labor shortages will force organizations to consider a variety of diverse candidates to fill positions due to a shortage of qualified workers. Consider these statistics:

- As predicted by the Hudson Institute (in its landmark research found in the book Workforce 2020), in the late 1980s, 85% of new workforce entrants were women, immigrants and people of color.
- Close to 50 percent of the workforce is women.
- A shortage of qualified workers with adequate technical skills has resulted in millions of jobs going unfilled. Furthermore, population growth is expected not to keep up with the increase of new jobs created by organizations.
- Most future jobs will require more than a high school education. Illiteracy is rapidly becoming a concern.
- The immigrant population is now at its highest level since World War II.
- Not only are the demographics in the workforce changing, but in the general population as well. White Americans represent the smallest-growing racial population in the United States. Factors contributing to this include a decline in births among

Wise Words
George Providakes—Executive Director, MITRE

If you have six clones in a room and ask them a question, you might get the same answer from all of them. If you have a diverse group in that same room, you will get a richer set of solutions. Diversity is a powerful tool for friendly and better outcomes for an organization.

To be successful in today's world, organizations need to identify and develop diverse talent and teams. On those teams, there needs to be different personalities but they must be managed. For example, if an individual is always pounding a table to make a point and another one can't tolerate that, there will be tension. The leader must know how to get team members to contribute ideas. Some people need to listen before giving their response. Others must digest, then provide feedback, while a third group can pop out idea after non-stop idea.

whites and a decline in the number of white immigrants, particularly those of European descent.

As population demographics have shifted, in some areas the minorities have turned into the majority. People of color are or will be the majority in California, Florida and Texas. Those states account for 45 percent of the US population growth. Of this number, Latinos and Asians have had the most rapid growth. Another minority-turned-majority is women.

BUILDING A DIVERSE WORKFORCE AT ALL LEVELS

One of the keys to sustaining a leadership position is attracting and retaining high quality, diverse leaders and growing leadership depth. As the U.S. Census 2000 showed, the demographics of the U.S. population are changing dramatically. These changes may ultimately further diversify an organization, especially in large urban centers.

Currently the Hispanic/Latino and Asian populations are the fastest growing segments of the nation's population. According to the June 11, 2001 issue of *FORTUNE* magazine, "for the first time, non-Hispanic whites are in the minority population in the 100 largest U.S. cities. By 2010 almost half of all the nation's new workers will be individuals traditionally classified as minorities." The city of Boston, with a minority population of 51%, is among those U.S. cities which are referred to as "minority majority" cities.

Fewer new, younger people (approximately 1 percent per year) will be entering the workforce since Baby Boomers had millions of fewer children from the period of 1965 until 1990. In light of this, organizations will need to develop a diversity strategy for dealing with an aging workforce.

Wise Words

Michael F. Rubner, Ph.D.—TDK Professor of Polymer Materials Science and Engineering, Massachusetts Institute of Technology (MIT)

We are all driven by different masters in our bodies. To be successful at loving your work and life, you must learn to accept people who are different from yourself. For example, if you are managing people, a young person should be blended or paired with someone who has gone beyond the point of being driven by hormones and youthful chemistry.

This blend of young and old can be magnificent and can be created through mentorships, partnerships, or collaborations. We need more knowledge-based mentoring where both sides, regardless of age, feel empowered and that they are contributing to the relationship in a meaningful, not superficial way.

Bringing people who are young and old into an organization is good. We face a lot of cultural diversity in this country. There are people in the workplace who have very diverse perspectives.

Ethnic, cultural and age diversity is wonderful if you take advantage of it. We are all hardwired in a specific way. In certain situations, you must step outside of what you are. You should ask yourself: Is the way I grew up making me respond based on the hardwiring I've received, or am I truly taking into account the circumstances of the other individual?

I don't think diversity is a bad thing if it is managed properly. It brings new perspectives and ideas to the table. For diversity to work in organizations, certain things may have to be deprogrammed in individuals. As a leader managing a diverse team, you may need to temper your beliefs with those of others to get the best results.

Since many organizations are diverse in the non-management ranks, but have few diverse leaders in middle and senior management, they will need to consider ways to grow diverse leadership from within and attract talent from outside of their borders.

Challenges for most organizations include not only creating a more diverse employee and management population at all levels of the organization, but making sure that the sales and marketing staff are reflective of the communities they serve. They will be needed to develop and deliver programs, services and products that are reflective of the diverse consumer base in the United States and abroad.

WHITE MALES AS FULL DIVERSITY PARTNERS

People of color are becoming the majority in some parts of the United States. They are already the majority in the world. But does that mean that top jobs are being taken over by women and other minorities? In some instances, yes. In many cases though, the numbers don't support this theory. Unfortunately, as organizations try to enhance the ranks of minorities and women, they sometimes have to deal with a backlash and "reverse discrimination." Decide how you'll deal with such backlash if it occurs in your organization. Texas Instruments offers a good example: It developed a comprehensive diversity program and has conducted workshops in its Attleboro, Massachusetts plant for white males (the group that, for the most part, typically held those top jobs) so they have a platform to discuss their opinions on diversity.

White males make up approximately 39.2% of the population. In the *Forbes 400*, out of those who earned at least $265 million, 82.5% were white males. White males make up approximately 77% of Congress, 92% of state governors and 70% of tenured faculty. They also account for 100% of U.S. presidents. They must be included in the Diversity Dialogue. Paul Chin, Manager of Diversity and EEO Compliance of Raytheon has developed a very useful tool to help white males with their Most Frequently Asked Questions (FAQ) about Diversity.

Wise Words

Timothy Fenstermacher—Associate Director Marketing
Services and Operations, Sepracor

Being a white male, how can I be sure not to be taken advantage of by individuals who leverage their diversity to their advantage?

Responses to Most FAQs (Frequently Asked Questions) About Diversity

Contributed by Paul Chin—Manager of Diversity and EEO Compliance, Raytheon Company

1. **Isn't diversity the same as the Affirmative Action/Equal Employment Opportunity stuff to meet legal compliance?**
    No: Affirmative Action/Equal Employment

Opportunity represents the organization's legal obligation we are under as a federal employer and contractor and was grounded in a vision of the "level playing field" and compels employers to identify and count people on the basis of gender and heredity; whereas diversity represents the organization's aspirations to become an inclusive organization that seeks to optimize all the differences that everyone brings to the workplace to achieve business objectives.

2. **If I don't understand or support diversity does that mean I am a racist, sexist or homophobic?**

No: But there is a chance that you could be an unwitting passive supporter of systemic racism, sexism and homophobia that prevents equity and fairness in the workplace for those who are not in the "majority."

3. **Isn't diversity only for women and minorities?**

No: As you can see from the Raytheon Company's Diversity Wheel—diversity is inclusive of all the differences that people bring into the workplace. Diversity is for all of US!

4. **Does all this diversity mean we must lower our standards so women and minorities can come IN?**

No: Neither diversity or affirmative action require the lowering of standards, it just means that we need to provide equal access to job related opportunities, promotions and benefits. We all want the "most qualified" candidates and will continue to pursue them. We don't want to hire just any female or person of color to meet "quotas," we all want and need the "most qualified" candidate for each position and will continue to pursue them to fill our openings. To hire otherwise would be a disservice to both the candidate and Raytheon.

"Affirmative Action/Equal Employment Opportunity is about counting heads; diversity is about making heads count."
—Thelma Kailiwai

---

5. **Why does it seem that we are focusing on doing this diversity stuff just for women and minorities?**

Again, diversity is inclusive of everyone and because of a long history of being excluded or under-represented in the workplace, initiatives and efforts are being made to enable them to "catch up," thus creating a level playing field on all workplace issues.

6. **How does diversity benefit me and Raytheon?**

It has been proven through many empirical studies (since the mid-1950s) that diversity of perspective/thought has produced better results in groups than similar efforts with strictly homogeneous groups. Therefore, if we (Raytheon and you) want to produce the best products, we need to be open to what others bring to the table and contribute to the outcome/results. If they don't have a place at our table to contribute, they can easily go somewhere else (like our competitors). The goal of diversity is to attract people with an array of talents, experiences, and perspectives and then to empower them to give everything they've got in order to attain business objectives. Diversity seeks to create a WIN–WIN proposition for all parties.

7. **What can I do to be a full partner in Raytheon's diversity initiative?**

By joining an affinity group or starting one (e.g., "White Males for Diversity," Raytheon's Veterans Group) and discussing issues of the "white male culture" and finding how to identify and deal with the mixed emotions that diversity may evoke. ALL Raytheon affinity groups are open to everyone.

8. **Is it true that white males will be the new minority this century?**

Yes: Worldwide demographic trends show that

- Workforce growth in industrialized nations such as the U.S. is very low, while workforce growth in developing nations is quite high—therefore some of the excess workers in those developing nations will be migrating to industrialized nations like the U.S.

- In the U.S. the demand for well-educated "knowledge workers" is high… and is getting ever higher due to sweeping technological advances in many fields.

- In worldwide terms, the proportion of U.S. high school and college graduates is dropping while that of developing nations is rising rapidly. In the year 2000, three-fifths of the world's college students were from developing nations. A related trend is that the academic performance of American high school students is declining relative to that of youth abroad.

- In the U.S. we see that native whites have a lower birthrate while minorities and immigrants have a high birthrate. Consequently, by 2005 native white males (both well and poorly educated) will make up only 38% of the American workforce, not the current 42.5%.

9. **As a white male, am I excluded from any diversity efforts/initiatives?**
No: As previously stated, diversity includes everyone. There are no exclusive programs just for women and minorities. Example: Raytheon programs, such as mentoring, are open to all because everyone can benefit from this type of resource.

10. **Do diversity programs and initiatives create reverse discrimination?**
No: We as an organization/employer, whenever or wherever there is a substantial imbalance found with our programs/resources utilization by our workforce, special efforts will be initiated to correct it (this will be determined by statistical analysis.)

For multicultural work to be successful, we must have the involvement of our white males as full partners for diversity.

Web Browser

www.wmfdp.com (White Males as Full Diversity Partners—Bill Proudman, CEO)

INDIVIDUALS WITH A DISABILITY

According to the March 20, 2002 issue of *Business Week*, the percentage of adult Americans with disabilities who are working age and unemployed is 75 percent. Believe it or not, chronic illness (such as heart disease and strokes) can begin to set in around age 45. With the vast majority of workers in the 35-years-plus category, disability-related issues are rapidly becoming a major concern.

When chronic illness sets in, how can organizations help employees? Some employee benefits could include assisted living, burial benefits, back-to-work programs and grief counseling. Reasonable accommodations and adapting the workplace for those with disabilities could help too.

On Tuesday, March 25, 2003, I had the pleasure of meeting and providing remarks about Coretta Scott King, widow of Dr. Martin Luther King, Jr., at the Linkage Annual Diversity Summit in Atlanta, Georgia. This is an event that I've co-chaired for several years.

I was struck by a statement Mrs. King made in her speech—"Reaching That Mountain Top." She said, in essence, that regarding diversity we still have a "long road to travel" but we can't forget about "how far we've come."

As we continue our journey, in the next chapter we will look at a very important aspect of diversity, managing across generations, as we discuss ways that people who love MTV (Music Television) or the AARP (American Association of Retired Persons) can LwL[2].

Wise Words

David—Sepracor, Inc. Sales Conference, Atlanta, Georgia 5/28/03

Accepting diversity is like the law of physics—whether you like it or not, it's going to happen.

Chapter 15

WHEN MTV MEETS AARP: COMMUNICATING AND MANAGING ACROSS GENERATIONS

COMMUNICATING AND MANAGING ACROSS GENERATIONS

SPECIAL CONCERNS ARE RAISED WHEN Baby Boomers and Matures meet Gen-Xers. I like to think of this as when MTV (Music Television) meets AARP (American Association of Retired Persons). What happens when young people begin to supervise people who are their parents' or grandparents' ages—and vice versa? Think about the dynamics (and sometimes fireworks) that are created by such situations. Age diversity will surely be one of the biggest management challenges in the years ahead.

WHEN MTV MEETS AARP

I grew up with my mom telling me the same stories about her childhood and life over and over again. Yesterday, a friend of mine was reflecting on her mother-in-law who had passed away just five minutes before she called to tell me the horrendous news. "You know, I was the only one in the family who listened to her stories over and over and over again. I actually liked hearing them," she uttered softly, then sighed.

How many of us can remember an older relative, friend of the family or community storyteller who shared their endlessly repetitive stories all the time?

The other day, my 13-year-old daughter caught me using those "When I was a kid…" repetitive statements

and halted me right in my tracks by exclaiming gently but firmly, "Mom, I've heard that story a million times." It's funny how history repeats itself. I vividly remember saying the same thing to my mom when I was about my daughter's age.

One of my mom's stories was about the first time she saw Elvis Presley on TV. She would state with excitement in her voice, "He was swirling, twirling and gyrating those hips around on TV. You know, your grandmother almost made me turn off our black-and-white TV. A lot of the adults back then thought what he was doing was obscene."

Now, when I look into the mirror, I'm sometimes shocked at the reflection of my mother glaring back at me. I often look, act, sound, and talk like her. It's like I've become a middle-aged version of her—who would've ever thought that was possible?

As people are living longer and Baby Boomers, like myself, collide with the values and lifestyles of senior citizens our parents' age and Generations X and Y, some interesting dynamics emerge for those of us who are trying to LwL². In this chapter, we will explore what happens when the MTV generation meets the AARP folks and the implications on LwL².

Here are two emails I received from Monica Calzolari on August 13, 2003. I think they clearly outline the issues faced when MTV meets AARP.

Subject: How Old is Grandma?
(This is an Eye-Opener)

[How old is Grandma? Stay with this—the answer is at the end.]

One evening a grandson was talking to his grandmother about current events. The grandson asked his grandmother what she thought about the shootings at schools, the computer age, and just things in general.

The Grandma replied, "Well, let me think a minute. I was born before television, penicillin, polio shots, frozen foods, Xerox, contact lenses, Frisbees and the pill. There was no radar, credit cards, laser beams or ballpoint pens. Man had not invented pantyhose, air conditioners, dishwashers, clothes dryers, and clothes were hung out to dry in the fresh air, and man hadn't yet walked on the moon.

"Your grandfather and I got married first—and then lived together. Every family had a father and a mother. Until I was 25, I called every man older than me "Sir," and after I turned 25, I still called policemen and every man with a title "Sir." We were before gay rights, computer dating, dual careers, daycare centers and group therapy.

"Our lives were governed by the Ten Commandments, good judgment and common sense. We were taught to know the difference between right and wrong and to stand up and take responsibility for our actions. Serving your country was a privilege; living in this country was a bigger privilege.

"We thought fast food was what people ate during Lent. Having a meaningful relationship meant getting along with your cousins. Draft dodgers were people who closed their front doors when the evening breeze started. Time-sharing meant time the family spent together in the evenings and weekends, not purchasing a condo.

"We never heard of FM radios, tape decks, CDs, electric typewriters, yogurt, or guys wearing earrings. We listened to the Big Bands, Jack Benny, and the President's speeches on our radios. And I don't ever remember any kid blowing his brains out listening to Tommy Dorsey. If you saw anything with "Made in Japan" on it, it was junk. The term "making out" referred to how you did on your school exam. Pizza Hut, McDonald's and instant coffee were unheard of.

"We had 5 & 10 Cent stores where you could actually buy things for 5 and 10 cents. Ice cream cones, phone calls, rides on a streetcar, and a Pepsi were all a nickel. And if you didn't want to splurge, you could spend your nickel on enough stamps to mail one letter and two postcards. You could buy a new Chevy Coupe for $600 but who could afford one? Too bad, because gas was eleven cents a gallon.

"In my day, *grass* was mowed, *coke* was a cold drink, *pot* was something your mother cooked in, and *rock music* was your grandmother's lullaby. *Aides* were helpers in the Principal's office, *chip* meant a piece of wood, *hardware* was found in a hardware store and *software* wasn't even a word.

"And we were the last generation to actually believe that a lady needed a husband to have a baby. No wonder people call us "old and confused" and say there is a generation gap…and how old do you think I am???"

I bet you have this really old lady in mind…you are in for a shock!

Read on to see… This woman would be only *58 years old*!

How things have changed...here's where the Class of 2005 is coming from:

Beloit College's Class of 2005 "Mindset List"

1. Most students starting college this fall (2003) were born in 1983.
2. Ricky Nelson, Marvin Gaye and Laura Ashley have always been dead.
3. The New Kids on the Block are over the hill.
4. They want to be PHAT but not fat.
5. IBM Selectrics are antiques.
6. Thongs no longer come in pairs and slide between the toes.
7. God has never been a "He" in many churches.
8. Hard copy has nothing to do with a TV show; a browser is not someone relaxing in a bookstore; a virus does not make humans sick; and a mouse is not a rodent (and there is no proper plural for it).
9. Moscow has always been opposed to "star wars."
10. Recording TV programs on VCRs became legal the year they were born.
11. The British royal family has always behaved badly.
12. There has always been Diet Coke.
13. Artificial hearts have always been ticking.
14. The Social Security system has always been on the brink.
15. There have always been warnings about second-hand smoke.
16. They have never experienced a real recession.
17. A hacker is not just a kid who won't stop fooling around.
18. Grenada has always been safe for democracy.
19. They were born the same year as the PC and the Mac.
20. The U.S. Senate has always had a daycare program.
21. One earring on a man indicates that he is probably pretty conservative.
22. CDs have always been labeled for explicit content.
23. Lethal Weapon in one form or another has always been "at the movies."
24. Boeing has not built the 727 since they were born.
25. Sarajevo was a war zone, not an Olympic host.
26. They don't remember Janet Jackson when she was cute and chubby.
27. Drug testing of athletes has always been routine.
28. There has always been a hole in the ozone layer.
29. They have always had access to email.
30. The Colts have always been in Indianapolis.
31. The precise location of the Titanic has always been known.
32. When they were born, Madonna was still a radiant woman holding a beatific child.
33. Jimmy Hoffa has always been officially dead.
34. Tylenol has always been impossible for children or adults to open.
35. Volkswagen beetles have always had engines in the front.
36. They do not know what the Selective Service is, but men routinely register for it on their financial aid forms.
37. Ron Howard and Rob Reiner have always been balding, older film directors.
38. Cal Ripken has always been playing baseball.
39. They have probably never used carbon paper and do not know what cc and bcc mean.
40. Lasers have always been marketed as toys.
41. Major newspapers have always been printed in color.
42. Beta is a preview version of software, not a VCR format.
43. They have never known exactly what to call the rock star formerly—and currently—known as Prince.
44. They are the first generation to prefer tanning indoors.
45. Survivor is a TV show not a rock group.
46. They have heard "just say no" since they were toddlers.

47. Most of them know someone who was born with the help of a test tube.
48. It has paid to "Discover" since they were four.
49. Oprah has always been a national institution.
50. With a life expectancy of 77 years, they can anticipate living until about 2060.

Tips to Communicate and Manage Across Generations

1. If you're old, get out of the "they can't teach an old dog new tricks" syndrome.
2. If you're young, get out of the "I'm too young to do that" frame of mind—Alexander the Great was 24 years old when he conquered the world; Martin Luther King, Jr. at 19, graduated from Morehouse College.·
3. If you supervise someone 25 years old and he can do the job better than a 52 year old, let them go for it or vice versa.

In the next chapter, you will gain some valuable tips on how to excel at communicating across generations.

Ray Charles is 72 years old and still going strong!
—*CBS Sunday Morning (9/6/03)*

Chapter 16

SECRET #5: EXCEL AT COMMUNICATIONS. NETWORK. BECOME A CORPORATE CUPID AND PRACTICE THE WALT DISNEY SCHOOL OF MARKETING

Secret #5

Excel at Communications. Network. Become a Corporate Cupid and Practice the Walt Disney School of Marketing.

SINCE THE VAST MAJORITY OF US DO NOT live by ourselves on a deserted tropical island, learning how to communicate effectively with others becomes critical if we are to succeed at LwL[2].

The inability to communicate properly can hamper your ability to accomplish your life's work. In this chapter, we will explore Secret #5: Excel at Communications. Network. Become a Corporate Cupid and Practice the Walt Disney School of Marketing.

EXCEL AT COMMUNICATIONS

If you want to communicate with others about your work or life, and if you want to excel at communication, remember that people take in and process information differently. All of us have preferred ways of procuring information, for example:

- Written
- Oral
- Visual
- Listening

Observe how others receive their information best, and then communicate with them in that manner. A person who prefers face-to-face communication may like to hear from you through a phone call or a voice mail. Email after email that goes unanswered may be a signal that this is not the most effective way to reach out and touch that individual.

If you don't know how people best like to receive their information, what should you do? The simple answer is to ask them. You can say something like, "There are a lot of ways that people like to receive communications, such as via email, face-to-face, or by voicemail. Which way do you prefer?"

Another question you may want to ask is what time(s) of the day are most convenient for them to receive communications. For example, some people describe themselves as early birds. Contacting them at six or seven in the morning may be perfectly fine. Calling at 11 p.m. or midnight, however, wouldn't be acceptable since they'd be disturbed from their slumber.

Reaching people at preferred times helps you to connect with the least amount of irritation. It also prevents those annoying games of telephone or email tag.

USE A VARIETY OF APPROACHES TO COMMUNICATE

Try to distribute important messages through multiple communication vehicles. Consider these mechanisms:

- Memos
- Letters
- Bulletin Boards (Companywide and departmental)
- Newsletters (Hard copy and e-zine)
- Email
- Fax
- Videos
- Staff Meetings
- Individual Meetings
- Formal Performance Evaluations
- Video Conferencing and Teleconferencing

PLANNING YOUR COMMUNICATION APPROACHES

Think about and plan how you want to communicate information related to your life and your work. Explore how you will communicate the message and utilize a variety of approaches such as those previously listed. Consider where you will deliver your communication. Telling a person they no longer have a job in a crowded elevator, for example, would not be a suitable site to communicate such sensitive information. I read once that a rock star let his wife know he wanted a divorce via e-mail. The result? A very nasty and costly, multimillion-dollar divorce settlement with his usually nice and mild-tempered ex-wife.

When you communicate the message is also very important. "Timing is everything" as the old cliché goes. Asking for a raise right after your company has lost its largest account will probably not yield the results you want.

Wise Words

Golden Handcuffs: Management Communications

The number one reason people leave their positions is because of poor management relations.
Good management is a skill and an art…it combines technical skills with the ability to generate confidence in a staff by demonstrating that you know how to control a situation, a project or people. It is the key to retention. As a manager, your job is to be honest and to be clear about your expectations.

Communication is a tool. Communication:

- ❑ Is a medium for consistent messages
- ❑ Demonstrates and spreads the culture
- ❑ Ensures goal alignment
- ❑ Reduces conflict over direction, design, etc.
- ❑ Proactively identifies potential problems

Source: Lois L. Lindauer Searches, Golden Handcuffs Seminar 2002

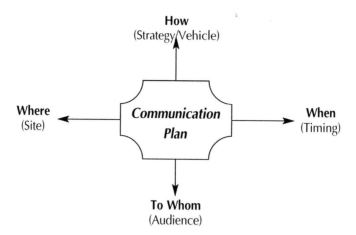

Finally, consider to whom you will deliver your communication. The level of formality or informality will be dictated by the person you are contacting. Think about how news anchors deliver a horrific breaking news story. They tend to be more formal and somber in their approach rather than jovial.

I'm Not Being Communicated To, but I'm All Plugged In

It always amazes me when I hear people complaining that their bosses and/or executives are "not communicating to us." I hear that statement so often that I decided to explore further what they meant by it. Typically, when someone says that to me, I start to ask them these questions:

- Do you get email from them?
- Does your company have an intranet where information is posted?
- Are people using hand-held devices?
- Beepers? Cell phones? Faxes?
- Two-way walkie talkies?
- Newsletters in hard copy and/or e-zine formats?

The answer they generally give to most of these items is "Yes."

"Why then are you feeling that they are not communicating with you?" I finally inquire. At that point the truth starts to rear its head. After probing deeper, I find that it is not that they aren't being communicated to, it's the manner of the communication that is *really* troubling them. "They are not communicating with me" is code for "they are not communicating *face-to-face* with me."

Information technology has been a major agent of change when it comes to communicating with each other at work and in our private lives. Since the birth of the personal computer in 1983, we've watched as snail mail, rotary telephones and busy signals have slowly gone in the direction of the dinosaur. Faxes, then email, cell phones and hand-held devices have all broadened the means by which we can communicate more effectively in our lives and at work.

Old fashioned face-to-face communication may not always occur. I believe that people may be craving for this level of contact when they complain, "I am not being communicated with." In reality, they are receiving information, just not in the face-to-face, eye-ball to eye-ball context.

Electronic means of communication can be most effective in reaching people quickly as well as in disseminating information to large numbers of people. It should not, however, replace face-to-face communication, especially if the news is:

1. Bad or
2. Knowingly bound to cause a negative or emotional response

Delivering Bad News in a Good Way

When I see a parent giving a small child a caffeine-laden soda, I get this gut-wrenching feeling in the pit of my stomach. I think, "Doesn't that person realize the connection between her act and why she won't be able to control the kid shortly thereafter once the caffeine and sugar kicks into that tiny body?"

That same response surfaces deep inside of me when I hear stories about the way some people are choosing to communicate bad news or difficult issues to others these days. Take, for example, a situation that a client faced when one of her young supervisors informed an employee that they were fired via email. That gut-wrenching feeling popped up inside of me again when I learned of that situation as well as the supervisor's reaction to it. The young supervisor had no clue that a severe management faux pas had been committed. Clearly, this individual thought what she did was entirely appropriate. When confronted about this horrendous behavior, the person stated, "I didn't think I did anything wrong. We are an email culture and everybody communicates that way."

During July of 2003, I heard another hair-curling communication horror story. A Nebraska woman, Judy Howell, was notified of her son's untimely death in an unconventional manner. A police officer tried to telephone her but was unable to reach her. He must have needed to check that communication task off his "To Do" list. He accomplished this by doing what obviously at that time seemed like the right thing to do: The police officer left a message *on the answering machine* informing this poor woman that her beloved son was dead.

As in the case of the parent who gave the small child the caffeine- and sugar-laden soda, my thoughts were "Didn't they understand the connection between their acts of communication and the impact it would have on the recipients of that information?" Learning *how to communicate in a way you can be heard and your message will be received* is important if you are to be successful at LwL[2].

Wise Words

Watch how you throw around angry words and/or disparaging remarks in the heat of the moment. Unfortunately, the human brain doesn't contain a Backspace and/or Delete function when it comes to erasing those words.

Wise Words

Monica Ross-Rustici—Cosmetologist and Owner, Monica's Beauty Salon

I like people and love my work. I enjoy other things aside from my job, like gardening, cooking, entertaining family and friends. If I wasn't a cosmetologist, I'd be an interior decorator or landscaper. I like to get along with people and I'm very sensitive to what people say to me. As a hairdresser, I hear all kinds of stories. Sometimes, I feel like I'm a psychologist who also does my patient's hair. I'm also careful about what I say about others. I don't like to upset anyone. People need to think before they say bad things to others. You can't take back those things once they are said.

You need to take one day at a time because tomorrow is not promised to anyone. Whatever God gives you, you should make the best of it. You have to be kind to other people. What you give out is what you get.

Question: *In the absence of information, what do people do?*

Answer: Create their own. Some examples of this include the grapevine and restroom/water cooler conversations, as well as those in elevators, cafeterias and at train/bus stops and airports.

Negative Effects

What happens when the rumor mill works overtime? Often the following will take place: low productivity, lack of trust (who should we really believe?) and unpredictable situations when rumors turn out to be true, regardless if they are good or bad.

Asking for Opinions

Before you ask others for their opinion, make sure you know what you will do with the information. Consider this: If you ask for information and don't use it, how will people respond the next time you request their help?

Answer: They probably will not take you seriously and/or be guarded in their response as they think, "She's going to do what she wants to do anyway, so *why* is she wasting my time by asking me my opinion?" To manage expectations, when you want someone's opinion, think about exactly what advice it is you want from them. You may ask, "I'd like to know what you're thinking about, and I'll take that information and do whatever you tell me" versus "I'm interested in what you have to say so I can think things through before I make my final decision."

In the first situation, the individual's expectation is that you will take what he says verbatim and do exactly what he has recommended. In the second case, you've made it clear that he is only making a recommendation to you, but you, not he, will make the final decision. If for some reason you decide not to go with his direction, he probably won't be upset because you've already managed his expectations regarding what you will do with the information he provides.

Always Be Honest

Instead of masking behind a lie, practice the policy of honesty when it comes to communicating bad or difficult news or information. Use these sayings when different situations arise:

- "I can't give you any information right now, but I will when I can."
- "I don't know, but I will let you know when I know."
- "Here is the real story, and even though you may not like what I'm about to tell you, it's the truth."

Listening

An important aspect of communication is listening. You won't be able to communicate about your life's work if you are not able to hear others' opinions and/or listen to what the voices and silence around you are telling you to do with your work and life.

Here are some tips on active listening as well as some thoughts on silence.

- Ways to practice active listening:
  - Stop talking
  - Stop thinking about what you are going to say next
  - Focus on the exact words the individual is saying, not your interpretation of what you think they mean

- Useful techniques for active listening:
  - Parroting—Repeating what the other person says word-for-word so you know exactly what they are trying to communicate
  - Paraphrasing—Rephrasing what the other person said, putting their meaning into your own words
  - Empathizing—Reflect back what the other person said on the feeling level
  - When paraphrasing and empathizing, check for accuracy. Do this by prefacing your statement with "I imagine that you…" or ending your statement by asking, "Is that right?" or "Did I understand what you were saying?"

Knowing When to Come Unplugged/How to Take a Disconnection Break

The information age has done wonderful things to keep us connected with others. We stay in a constant state of "in-tuneness" through email, cell phones, faxes, the world wide web, hand held devices, telephones with videos and picture sending capabilities, and an array of electronic gizmos. We have become a society that can truly "reach out and touch" someone 24/7, but what affect does all of this constant state of being in touch and in tune do to us? It never allows us the time to come unplugged and spend the necessary quiet moments to reflect on why we must LwL²; what we need to do to LwL²; and who we must have to help us and where they are in their lives.

I am an advocate for taking what I will call "disconnection breaks." These are defined as periods when you put the cell and regular phone, instant messenger, e-mails, two-way pagers, walkie talkies, and beepers on hold and take a break. Literally, you become unplugged.

In the olden days, those disconnection breaks were built into our society and our way of life. Believe it or not, I recall a time before constant communication devices, such as the cell phone, when you could get into your car and concentrate on driving safely and listening to your radio or your brain. Today, many of us are multitasking big time when we drive as we concentrate on the road, the radio, and the conversation we can't wait to have via our cell phone or some other device.

If my memory serves me correctly, there was also a time in my life when Sunday "Blue Laws" allowed you to happily disconnect with chores on Sunday, such as grocery or clothes shopping because the stores were closed. On Sunday mornings you were forced to unplug from activities and perhaps slow down, and smell the coffee at breakfast because you couldn't get into your car and talk on your cell phone on your way to the grocery store.

I can vividly remember the first time the thought entered my mind that sometimes we have to declare that enough is enough and hang up, if only for a short period, our cell phones, the internet, or anything that keeps us plugged in and turned on. It was a Sunday in May of 1998, and I was attending the graduation of a family member from Boston University. As I sat in the stands of Nickerson Field, it was kind of like, as Yogi Berra once said, "déjà vu all over again."

In May of 1975, I had been sitting at that same field—not as an observer, but as a graduate. The 1998 field was crammed with thousands upon thousands of graduates, and their well-wishers looked basically the same as well-wishers did back in the mid-1970s. There were, however, two exceptions that I noticed: First, they didn't have huge afros and they weren't wearing hippie clothes. Second, in 1975, the sound of beeping, pulsating or cutesy-song-ringing cell phones was nowhere to be heard.

I was caught off-guard the first time I heard a cell phone go off at a college graduation. My gut reaction was "I can't believe that person won't disconnect long enough to savor the moments of this graduation and take time to honor the major educational accomplishments of all these graduates!"

I am a firm believer that in life everything has a season, and so it goes with taking disconnection breaks. Leave the cell phone in the car or at home. Allow yourself blocks of time to become unplugged during graduations and special life events. Put away those gizmos and concentrate on what more you can do to better LwL². As has become the craze with some, laptops at the beach should not replace the enjoyment of watching the rhythm of the water as it laps against the shore. Allow yourself time to listen to and hear the voice of your breath as you take a disconnection break and enjoy the season of life you inhabit.

Wise Words
Ecclesiastes 3:2-8

There is an appointed time for everything. And there is a time for every event under heaven:

A time to give birth, and a time to die;
A time to plant, and a time to uproot what is planted;
A time to kill, and a time to heal;
A time to tear down, and a time to build up;
A time to weep, and a time to laugh;
A time to mourn, and a time to dance;
A time to throw stones, and a time to gather stones;
A time to embrace, and a time to shun embracing;
A time to search, and a time to give up as lost;
A time to keep, and a time to throw away;
A time to tear apart, and a time to sew together;
A time to be silent, and a time to speak;
A time to love, and a time to hate;
A time for war, and a time for peace.

MY BEST PROFILE

Each of us has a set of general personality patterns that make up our behavior. These patterns express themselves in our actions and in the way we interact with others. By first understanding how and why we behave as we do, we can then begin to be more positive and productive in our relationships with others.

The BEST Profile is an instrument which helps you determine and understand your general personality patterns. It will help develop

- an awareness about yourself and others
- your ability to resolve conflicts
- better performance on the job
- more productive team building
- a more positive boss-subordinate relationship
- your leadership styles
- a happier family environment

The BEST Profile is easy to take, easy to understand and easy to use. No special training is necessary to interpret this information. Myers Briggs is also an instrument you can use to help understand different types of people.

In the next chapter, you'll learn how to communicate through networking.

Fortune Cookie and Tea Bag Tag Messages

"Every beat of your heart is the rhythm of your soul. The voice of your soul is your breath."

—Yogi Tea Bag Tag 9/14/03 (Sunday)

"What is meditation? When you empty yourself and let the universe come to you."

—Yogi Tea Bag Tag 9/04/03

Wise Words

Suzanne Bates—President, CEO, Bates Communications, Inc.

What people need to do to love their work:

Listen to your intuition. If you are unhappy there is a reason. Find some quiet time and respect that inner voice.

What people need to do to love their life:

Find people who truly care about you; family and friends who truly have your best interest at heart, and love you for who you are. Show them every day how much they matter to you, by your actions as well as your words.

Tips on loving your work or life that have worked for me:

I took a hard look at a dream career and realized I had outgrown it. I went through an arduous process to change directions, but at the end of that process I had new friends, a better life, and more joy than my first "dream career" had given me.

How organizations can help staff to love their work and life:

Let them know you care about them—that what they do is important. People who work for you want to be part of the success story; if they know their role and you support them, they will return your investment a thousand times over.

Wise Words

"Don't open your mouth until your brain kicks into gear."

Chapter 17

WHAT IS NETWORKING? NETWORKING FOR THE I-HATE-TO-NETWORK PERSON

NETWORKING

WHAT IS NETWORKING?

NETWORKING IS MUTUALLY BENEFICIAL relationship building that allows for all parties to support each other in their work and life endeavors. These relationships are built on a foundation of sharing and extend to both individuals and groups.

Good networkers are organized and plan how to utilize and develop contacts to expand and accomplish their work and life goals. Exchanging, acquiring, sharing and receiving information are the tools used to network effectively.

Networking has a *Quid Quo Pro* quality to it. What you give you get back is typically an end product. Successful networkers, however, know that they don't just put out so they'll receive. It's like giving a gift to someone on her birthday. While it might be nice to also receive a gift from that person on your birthday, it should not be a prerequisite for sending a gift from your heart to that individual. You may be disappointed if she doesn't reciprocate on your day of birth, but you wouldn't take your gift back when you don't receive one from your friend.

WHY NETWORK?

For most of us, to make our life's work a reality, it can't be done without a little help from our friends. To bring our life's work into fruition, we will need a village of people to assist us. Networking becomes a tool that can be utilized to accomplish this initiative.

Here are a number of reasons why people network to accomplish their life's work and help them in career goals and their job:

- Builds social, personal, and professional contacts
- Provides support mechanisms
- Helps to procure job information and interviews in and outside the company
- Assists with personal and career development
- Provides a place to receive answers to stupid or personal questions and not feel embarrassed.

TO NETWORK, TAP ALL YOUR RESOURCES!!!

Here are some suggestions of network resources every great networker should tap into:

- Previous employers/co-workers
- Teachers, professors, counselors
- Acquaintances from social, civic, religious, professional and fraternal organizations
- Friends, mentors, neighbors
- People you trust
- Consultants, vendors
- People who know your potential and skills
- Individuals who provide services to you (plumber, hairdresser, waitperson, dry cleaner, etc.)
- Internet, organizations, conferences, social affairs
- Ex-colleagues who are out of work or don't have a job—through their job search, they may be in tune with what is really happening in the job and marketplace.

Your Network Can Help You Define ...

- Your skills and abilities
- Jobs and skills needed by organizations both now and in the future
- How your career plans match up with the jobs and skills needed in the future
- Ways your life's work/purpose fits into your current and future career and personal life
- How to brand yourself so people know what you stand for at work and in life.

In this next article, esteemed communications expert, Janine Fondon, provides some tips on how to excel at communications by creating your professional image.

To Love your work by Loving your Life, Excel at Communication

By Janine Fondon—Publisher and CEO of UnityFirst.com/ African American Newswire

Janine Fondon is publisher and CEO of UnityFirst.com/African American Newswire. She founded these businesses with her husband, Tom. Janine and Tom are the co-authors of The Practice of Power: Finding Success in a Diverse World. *As an accomplished "corporate cupid" and networker par excellence, she shares her thoughts on how you can LwL^2 by excelling at communications and branding yourself.*

LOVING YOUR WORK BY LOVING YOUR LIFE means creating a professional image that reflects the positiveness of your life. Take the time to look at your life and work and create a refreshed image for yourself simply by

- developing or updating your biography
- creating a fact sheet of key events, jobs, or achievements and
- writing a press release that reflects the new story of your success.

Creating these documents is considered "forward thinking" and provides a mechanism for you to move to the next level. If you don't love your life, it will be difficult to love your work.

Most people never take the initiative to write about themselves, think about themselves or vision their purpose. Take the time to create the life and work image that allows you to reach your goals. If you don't have the experience, then find opportunities to get it and write about it.

What Words Represent You

Someone once told me, "You are a reflection of the words that represent you." Think for a moment about the words that express who you are today. What phrases and terms reflect your inner spirit, yet position you in the profession you so love? While some people hire public relations or marketing professionals to craft their image, I suggest that you spend time with yourself to craft the personal message YOU want to send. Believe that others can view you in that way, and then share your findings with them. If they doubt your vision, move on to more positive ground.

You are the author of your success. One of my bosses told me, "Don't wait for your work to define who you are; remember that it is you who defines your work."

Now is the time to paint on your open canvas. Who do you want to be? What do you want to be? How would you like to be remembered? How do you define your profession?

Writing Your Personal Bio and Press Release

Take a fresh look at your bio and write it to fit the new you. Take old jobs and merge them with your current experiences. I knew someone who went from a book publisher to a dancer and now is a teacher. We all have transferable skills. Organize the facts that support who you are. Don't write resumes and bios that aren't really you (and that reflect what others want you to be).

Creating a fact sheet of your activities over the past years helps lay the foundation for your journey to find the balance you need to love your life and work. The fact sheet creates a roadmap that tells you where you have been. It will even give you clues as to where you want and need to go. Take the time to map out your success. You have a better chance of reaching your goals if you are familiar with the roads that will take you to your final destination.

Take the lead to draft a press release about yourself that you would want to send out. Don't fill your press release with hype and false expectations. Fill it with facts that reflect who "you" really want to see. Don't be afraid to dream. Then, begin to put the pieces together and transform yourself—using words—into the work or life you want to have.

All you have to do is put together the "who, what, where, when, why" information about the expectations you have for yourself. Start to chart your new reality, accented by real life goals that you have achieved. Loving your life and work is the right mixture for a passionate new life story that fulfills your life's purpose. Just think, with a powerful bio, fact sheet and press release, every newspaper or magazine on the stands will want to cover the success story that you have just created.

NETWORKING FOR THE I-HATE-TO-NETWORK PERSON

The benefits of networking are numerous and fairly obvious, but what if you **hate** to network? If you're one of those individuals, perhaps you need to think about how you are networking and whether or not there are techniques that you currently aren't utilizing.

I often hear people complaining that they don't like to network because it feels like "selling out and having to kiss up to people you really could care less about." My answer to those individuals is not to compromise your beliefs, values or desire—not to suck up to someone for the sake of networking. Instead, focus on meeting people you have something in common with and build your network from there.

As people progress in their careers, they often find that unless they network with certain people, they are left out of the loop when it comes to advance information, job opportunities and choice assignment. Networking and business are often combined on the golf course or at a lunch or breakfast with a friend, colleague or boss.

I've come across many people who cringe at the thought of networking because they think of it in what I call the "culture vulture" approach to networking. Culture vultures are people who prey on their suspects at cultural, social and job-related events. Like a vulture that can't wait to swoop down and devour a carcass, the minute they spy one, a culture vulture operates in much the same way. These are the people who go to a conference, cocktail party, or professional association meeting with one goal in mind—to prey on and network with as many leads, prospects and important people they can find by "working the room." This culture vulture is the person who can barely keep their eyes on one person. Their eagle eyes are in constant motion surveying the room for the next high ranking person to connect with and network.

If you find the term "culture vulture" (as it applies to networking) repulsive, you are not alone. What other ways can people network without being so overly aggressive and culture vulture-like? Here are some suggestions that I've gathered for the *I-hate-to-network* person.

Networking Tips for the I-Hate-to-Network Person

1. Cultivate a diverse and global network and include people of different age, gender, race, culture, socio-economic and geographical background.
2. Get to know people inside and outside of your industry.
3. Become a corporate cupid/matchmaker. Practice bringing people from different companies or diverse divisions or departments inside your organization together to share best, interesting and radical practices.
4. Make speeches inside your organization or for social, civic, religious, or educational associations.
5. Build personal relationships and remember to recognize significant life events of people in your network via cards, flowers, phone calls, e-mails, gifts, etc.
6. Develop relationships with consultants, vendors and business owners who understand trends in business and can relate information regarding cross-industry best practices.
7. Carry and distribute business cards.
8. Attend professional and trade association meetings. Join a committee or volunteer your services as a means to get to know colleagues better.
9. Write articles and publish them in local and national newspapers, the Internet and magazines.
10. Participate in conferences and seminars and introduce yourself to at least one person. Follow up with people you meet at events.
11. Send FYIs and articles of interest to people in your network.
12. Develop strategic alliances when appropriate. Always operate with the WIFYAM in mind (**W**hat's **I**n It **F**or **Y**ou **A**nd **M**e).
13. Use mentors to open doors. Be a mentor to others. When asking someone to mentor you, carefully consider what you have to offer that person and why someone should spend their precious time on you and not someone else.
14. Keep an updated resume.
15. Employ the "Walt Disney School of Marketing" techniques by constantly letting people know what you are doing, what you've done in the past and where you are taking your life and work interests.
16. Tell others about your career dreams and aspirations and keep track of theirs. Offer any assistance you can to help them and seek their help.
17. Have power lunches, dinners, and breakfasts.
18. Stay in touch with people who leave your organization.
19. Don't burn bridges because what goes around comes around.
20. Become active in politics, schools, or activities within your community.
21. Take courses at adult education centers as a way of connecting with people who share your interests.
22. When you receive an award, or promotion, send out a press release announcing your accomplishments. Some organizations have Public Relations, Communications or Community Relations departments that will do this for you.
23. Forward any news clips on or about you to colleagues and relatives.
24. Submit articles to company newsletters as well as to professional association journals and publications.
25. Maintain a database of contacts in your network and communicate with people about six times a year. This can be achieved through e-mail blasts, cards, letters, or e-zines utilizing your database.
26. When you first establish a relationship, ask that person how they prefer for people to communicate with them—e-mail, voice mail, face-to-face—and what time they prefer to be contacted—morning, afternoon, or late at night.

An effective way to network is to join and participate in professional associations. The benefits of networking in these groups are revealed in our next chapter.

Chapter 18

Why Spend Time Networking in Professional Associations?

Networking by Joining Professional, Voluntary, Social or Civic Organizations and Activities

CONSIDER JOINING PROFESSIONAL ORGANI-zations to help you create a memorable difference in the world and enlarge your network. Find a way to participate fully and devote two days per month to professional-related activities or events.

Don't be a spectator—join a committee or the board. This can help you to gain more visibility with members. They can get to know you and your skills on a personal level and vice versa.

Why Spend Two Days Per Month Attending Professional Association/ Development Activities?

I have been active in many professional associations in my career. I've served on boards and as a president and/or officer of many. Networking in this way has really paid off in more ways than one.

First, it allowed me to become acquainted with people in and outside my industry. For example, when I was a health care executive, I'd go to meetings with colleagues at the Boston Human Resources Association, the Massachusetts and American Health Care Human Resources Associations and programs put on by the American Management Association and the National Association of Corporate Directors. In my case, I got to know a broad section of people this way. I increased my network in my

1. industry (health care)
2. profession (human resources)
3. position (management)
4. social, civic and professional interests (board affiliation)

I received two added benefits by following my rule of taking two days per month to attend a professional development function. For one of my days, I'd attend a meeting of these groups which usually focused on an educational or professional development topic. This allowed me to brush up on and keep up-to-date on issues in my field. An added benefit was that at each meeting, I also met and got to know new people or maintained relationships within my network.

Free benchmarking information was also obtained. At these sessions, the speakers quite often talked about their companies or consultants mentioned best-practices work of their clients. Most of those meetings had a networking component that included breakfast, lunch, dinner or a reception where colleagues chit-chatted and talked about what they were doing in their organization. Some also gossiped about other organizations, and how they were faring in the good or bad economy of the day. I'd leave professional association meetings armed with loads of information to take back to my company about policies, procedures and benefits that we may want to consider because everyone at the meeting talked about the latest and greatest management du jour trends. After hearing my colleagues' stories, I'd often return from those meetings feeling very good about the work I was doing and/or how my company was treating me. After all, the grass is not always greener elsewhere!

The power of professional networking was also revealed to me when I decided in 1994 to start my firm, Fields Associates, Inc. Many of the people that I got to know through my professional association connections were business owners. When I was thinking about starting my business, they more-than-readily provided me with *honest* and practical information about the good, the bad and the ugly of becoming an entrepreneur.

Later, people such as Judy Weil (who owned a Human Resources consulting company and is now the Executive Director of the Northeast Human Resources Association) or Larry Stybel and Ben Morrill (who I networked with after meeting Dr. Stybel) guided and coached me through my early years of establishing Fields Associates, Inc.

I am forever grateful to those people who mentored me and showed me the entrepreneurial path. I don't believe I would have been connected with them had it not been for my work on boards and various professional association events I planned and attended over the years. Many of my clients and referrals in my nine-plus years of business can be directly traced to individuals I've met through my professional association connections!

Today, I am still very active in professional associations. One organization that I have been affiliated with for numerous years is the Northeast Human Resources Association (NEHRA). NEHRA has a membership of 4,000

Human Resource professionals throughout New England. It is also an affiliate of another organization in which I am active—the Society of Human Resource Management (SHRM). SHRM has 170,000 members worldwide.

Here's what the Executive Director of NEHRA, Judy Weil, had to say about LwL².

Wise Words

Judith S. Weil—Executive Director, Northeast Human Resources Association

I've noticed that successful, fulfilled individuals ensure that their work is

☆ Aligned with their personal values
☆ A vehicle for contributing their ideas and talents
☆ A source of energy and pride

Because NEHRA has been such an integral part of my success as a professional, I decided to include the story of its cofounder, Barry Bograd. He and his partner, John Erdlen, founded this organization in 1986. Today, due to their forward thinking and love for this profession, this organization helps thousands of Human Resource professionals and their companies help their staff to love their work.

Profile of Success
Barry Bograd

My life has been a wonderful journey full of ups and downs—successes and failures—recessions and boom times—but through it all I've tried to maintain a positive attitude and perspective by displaying a sense of humor and by not being afraid to take a risk. I believe my signature was doing it out of the box, being both traditional and at times, when applicable, being non-traditional. The fact that I worked in several aspects of Human Resources, from the agency business to corporate Human Resources to several phases of consulting in all kinds of economic times, gave me a terrific opportunity to experience my business from all sides of the desk. I honestly believe that that helped me appreciate the challenges of everyone's world and eventually succeed.

Many years ago, when I was attempting to break into Human Resources, I made a pledge I've tried to keep throughout the years. I interviewed with 27 companies trying to get my first corporate job in Personnel (that's what we called Human Resources back then). You know how interviews go for young people…you are attempting to get a job but have little to no applicable experience—it's the old chicken-and-egg deal—and sometimes interviewers exploit you and really take advantage. At least they did in those days.

Toward the end of the process, I went on an interview at Dewey & Almy in Cambridge, MA, a division of W.R. Grace, and within 15 minutes both the staffing representative and I realized that I really wasn't qualified for the position. However, this special man, a fellow named Bill Bowen, spent two hours with me helping me understand the process and explaining how I should handle ensuing interviews. I was truly blown away by his kindness and caring about my well-being, especially considering how shabbily I had been treated in some of the previous interviews.

At the end, I thanked him and asked what I could do for him. He said, "Some day you'll be sitting in a chair like mine, and all I ask is that you take the time to help people achieve their goals and dreams. One hour of your time and wise counsel, setting them on the right path and course to success, could save them months of frustration." I promised him that I would follow through on his request, and I've tried to live that pledge throughout the years. I honestly don't think I've ever turned down anyone's request for time and advice. I truly still believe that his suggestion is the right thing to do!

Forty years in business creates a lot of stories, both good and bad. I would love to sit on a high stool in the middle of the room sharing all of them with you, but time precludes us doing that. However, if you'll allow me…let me offer a few tips for having a fulfilled, fun-filled and (we hope) successful career:

- **Get involved**—don't just be a member of professional associations, get onto committees and make a difference. It's great for networking and learning more about the variety of people and industries in our business.
- **Continually upgrade** your knowledge about the profession, both technically and tactically.
- **Take risks.** When in doubt just do what's right—and if you have to ask what's right, you're probably in the wrong place or profession.
- **Have fun.** If you are not having fun but are continually stressing, go to another career. This one is too hard not to have fun with. Don't take yourself too seriously.
- **If and when you fail**—and we all do at various times—the successful ones pick themselves up, brush themselves off, and start all over again.

- **Give back and invest** in your profession. If you give to it, it will give back to you. Make it a profession, not just a job.
- **Don't get stuck** sitting behind a computer. Get out and interface with your constituents. We seem to be losing the interrelationships because it's easier to just move that mouse than to physically meet with people. It's becoming a lost art.
- And finally, **take the pledge** as I did. Help and mentor young people in your profession. It is not only rewarding for all concerned, but it truly is an investment into the future of your profession.

Chameleon Barry

I have known Barry Bograd for 15 years. In May of 2003, I had the pleasure of introducing him as he received the John D. Erdlen Five Star Award from the Northeast Human Resource Association. This coveted and distinguished award is given once a year to an individual or organization that has contributed in an exceptional and extraordinary way to the field of Human Resource Management.

When I was preparing my remarks, I had the pleasure of talking at length with Barry about his background and the key to his success. He said something very revealing about himself that is so relevant given the times we're living in now. Barry said, "You have to be a chameleon in our business and have to adjust constantly to things." I'd like to tell you a little about Chameleon Barry.

He was born in New Hampshire and at age four moved to Broadway—his dad was a musician in a big band and appeared in Leonard Bernstein's first show, "On The Town." Then they moved to Hollywood where his father was in big band movies. Then they moved back to New York.

His mother was a proper, well-bred Bostonian. Her six-year-old son came home one day and pronounced the word c-a-l-f as kiff rather than calf! That was it—her boy had to be brought back to the Beantown area where he could regain his Boston accent and say that he could "pahk his cah in the Hahvahd yahd" like any proper Bostonian. They moved to Newton, Massachusetts, where he went to school. His dad continued to be a musician and also became a music teacher.

Barry learned his work ethic from his dad who worked seven nights playing in his band and six days a week teaching kids to play music. Barry was destined to be a business owner because (he will tell you) he grew up thinking everyone worked seven nights and six days a week.

After high school, Barry went to Boston University where he was very involved in ROTC and when he graduated in 1961, he joined the Army. There he became a company commander of a transportation company that handled petroleum in Germany. He'll freely tell you that he went to Germany a boy and left there a man.

As an only child he had been taken extraordinarily good care of by his mother. He had never been away from home and all of a sudden was in a country where he saw the Berlin Wall being erected. The most important lesson he learned was how to wash clothes—he didn't know he was supposed to separate the white clothes from the colors so he put them all together. After his white jockey shorts came out pink and blue—well, let's just say that luckily he had some friends who told him what to do so he wouldn't have to wear pink and blue jockey shorts for the rest of his life.

Before he was to be discharged from the military in March of 1964, Barry the Chameleon was already adjusting and had already had a job lined up at GTE Sylvania. Then, one month before he was to start that job, Chameleon Barry had to adjust again because he received a letter from them rescinding the offer. Barry says he knew from that point, when he was laid off before he even started the job, that he was destined to go into outplacement.

Barry has been in Human Resources for over 40 years now. He says when he started in Human Resources he was 6 foot 2 inches, blonde and gorgeous. In 40 years, he is no longer blonde and 6 foot 2 inches, but he is still gorgeous! He began in the employment agency field with Martin Grant Associates. He moved into the corporate world with the Laboratory for Electronics.

The next step for Chameleon Barry was at Digital Equipment Corporation (DEC). In 10 years he held various positions, but one of the things he is proud about is that in 1975 he became Digital's first dedicated recruiter—the staffing had been done by generalists.

In the 1980s, he reconnected with Jack Erdlen through a professional association called EMA. They later formed the Erdlen-Bograd Group which was eventually renamed Strategic Outsourcing. This was indeed a family affair as Elaine, Barry's wife of 37 years, and Jack's wife Peggy helped them with the business.

I've told you about Chameleon Barry the Human Resources professional and business leader and entrepreneur, but there is also Chameleon Barry the visionary and corporate cupid.

For three days in 1985, Barry, along with Jack Erdlen, took a flipchart and hid out in a room where they were determined to create an innovative new professional Human Resources association. They'd take the best of all the associations and create it into this organization. They decided that their first meeting would be held at the Newton Marriott, even though the organization didn't have a name and had no members. Barry tells of going down to the Newton Marriott to book the room and the lady who he met with thought he had lost it because he couldn't tell her the name of the organization.

On January 21, 1986 Barry and Jack sent out a mailing announcing this meeting of a new group—NEHRA. In June 1986, 260 people attended NEHRA's first meeting. Today, the organization has over 4,000 members throughout New England and is part of the internationally connected Society of Human Resource Management.

On March 4, 1996, Barry and Jack sold Strategic Outsourcing to ROMAC. As if you're not impressed enough with the life of Chameleon Barry, I'm going to close by telling you about another side to this complex man. I couldn't believe this when he told me that he is painfully shy (yeah, right!), but once he meets you he's fine.

This "painfully shy" guy has led a life of service to others and commitment to his family. For six years he has coached the Newton South High School Varsity football team. Barry has also coached baseball. The coach feels he utilizes his Human Resources skills daily in these activities. He's also served on the Personnel Board and as a Parks and Recreation Commissioner and is currently on the Finance Committee for the Town of Framingham. For nine years he's worked on the Channel 2 Auction (a Boston PBS station) and has even helped as a campaign manager for his lifelong friend, Massachusetts State Auditor Joe Denucci.

Although he is in semi-retirement, he has done work for such prestigious companies as Studley and Associates, Gatti and Associates, and King and Bishop. Chameleon Barry is also a devoted husband, father and grandfather.

There is one statement that Barry once made that I think captures the essence of this most accomplished man. He said, "I've gotten as much out of all this as I've given."

Participating on boards and in community organizations is another effective way to network. Our next Profile of Success story, Dr. Ashley Fields (no relation), talks about how his involvement on boards helps him to network and benefits both him and his organization, the Shell Oil Company.

Profile of Success
Dr. Ashley Fields—Senior Consultant, Shell Oil Company

For me, Loving your work by Loving your Life is being able to do what's progressive and beneficial for people around you. It's finding the common element that benefits others at the same time allowing you to do what you want to do. This could be something you're passionate about, something new that you want to learn or experience or an expression of your core values.

For the last five years, I've served on the Board of the African American Theater. It has helped me in the area of the arts, which I hadn't experienced because I'm more business-oriented at work, and the African American culture to which I've never been exposed because I am a white male. Culture has a way of being more open and honest about aspects of difference than we tend to be allowed to be at work. On the job, you have to be more business oriented. Through the theater, plays can be about REAL life and go below that surface and expose more of the wider perspective of what differences entail.

It is most rewarding to see people from a different perspective. This is an example of where I contribute back to the community: The Board can benefit because I use my professional expertise in Human Resources to help them with their personnel issues and my business acumen to assist them with strategy issues. I bring the company I work for, Shell Oil, into the room through philanthropic means and they in turn contribute resources to the arts to sustain the effort of bringing the arts to the public. It's a win–win situation for everyone—for me, for Shell Oil and for the patrons and attendees who enjoy quality productions through these efforts.

I also network to connect people with similar wants and needs. In other words, I serve as a linkage.

My Philosophy
As I reflect back on my life, I have no regrets. I've lived a "fantasy work life." Everything I've done, I've wanted to do—but I haven't done everything I want to do just yet!

Professional associations can help you advance in your career. Becoming a "corporate cupid," and learning how to market yourself are also ways to effectively network. In the next chapter, you'll gain insights on how to do both.

Become a Corporate Cupid and Practice the Walt Disney School of Marketing

BECOME A CORPORATE CUPID

WHEN MOST OF US THINK ABOUT THE concept of networking, we see individuals communicating with each other. It can also involve interactions between corporations and organizations. Years ago, I was searching for a term to describe what happens when corporations come together to network, and devised the term "corporate cupiding."

What is corporate cupiding? Corporate cupiding is defined here:

Definition: Cor•por•ate Cu•pid•ing

 1. Helping organizations love and learn from each other as well as the people within them. **2.** Connecting organizations together to explore best, interesting and radical practices and win–win solutions to issues. **3.** The act of bringing groups and/or individuals in organizations and corporations together to help them expand their businesses and/or relationships.

Source: Martha R. A. Fields

Quite often, I practice corporate cupiding through my work as a consultant and writer. Holding conferences where diverse companies and industries are invited or speaking at professional association meetings and dispensing information about best, interesting and radical business practices are just a few ways that corporate cupiding can be practiced.

Corporate cupiding can also take place inside a corporation. The corporate cupid can be very effective when he shoots his darts and brings together departments or divisions and the individuals within them. Often, organizations have best, interesting and radical practices taking place inside but people are not always aware of them and how they might be utilized effectively in other parts of the company. Here, the corporate cupid will work to bring various entities inside the institution together to share practices, policies and procedures as well as build stronger working relationships.

THE IMPORTANCE OF MAINTAINING YOUR NETWORK

Even the best network can come unplugged if it is not maintained properly. Once you've cultivated your network, it must be maintained. Take time to prune through your list of contacts regularly. Enter business cards into your database and update personal information as it changes. Since people are changing jobs more frequently, this is an essential task if you want to remain connected. Good marketers will tell you that to reach an audience you must stay in touch. Contact people you want to establish strong ties with about six times a year. That may not be as ominous as it seems if you utilize multiple approaches such as email and sending cards to remember special occasions such as birthdays, anniversaries, job promotions, etc.

EMILY POST-ISH THINGS TO REMEMBER

Anyone who has a young child has probably heard the character Barney echo these words: "Good manners are important to everyone in the world." Remember to be like Miss Manners and Emily Post when it comes to your network. Here are some things to keep in mind:

- **RSVPs** (*Répondre s'il vous plaît*) This means you should let people know if you are **or** are not attending their event. If you receive an invitation that says "Regrets only" then you need not let the person know that you will *attend*; only make contact if you *can't* make the occasion.
- **Thank You cards** Remember to send them out when people have given you gifts or done a good deed to or for you.
- **Recognize significant dates for employees** To make this task easy, keep a box of all-occasion cards handy (births, deaths, weddings, birthdays, thank-yous, promotions, get well, encouragement, congratulations, etc.).
- **Practice the Walt Disney School of Marketing** to let people know about your current, future and past interests and activities.

THE WALT DISNEY SCHOOL OF MARKETING

As you maintain your network, you will want to keep people apprised of your personal and professional goals and aspirations. The Walt Disney School of Marketing is one method that accomplishes this activity. You won't find this concept in a marketing or communications textbook. It is a phenomenon that I discovered when my daughter was a little girl and loved watching Walt Disney movies and videos.

One year, I took my daughter to see the latest Walt Disney blockbuster, *The Lion King*. She loved that movie and of course, when the video version came out, the

pressure was on for me to buy it. On playing the video, I discovered something very interesting about how Walt Disney used marketing to tell people about his past, current and future projects.

The *Lion King* video opened by introducing my child and me to Disney's next project after *The Lion King*. In that case, it was *Pocahontas*. The video trailer announced that it was coming to a theater near me that following summer. (I'm always amazed that they know there is a theater near me and everyone else who watches that video!)

In addition to telling you what his next project was, a hit song—"The Colors of the Wind"—from the to-be-released movie was performed. Like many kids, my little darling played that video every chance she got so that by the time *Pocahontas* was ready for release, she had already learned the lyrics to "The Colors of the Wind." Just about every day from November, when we purchased the *Lion King* video, she also inquired about whether it was summer yet because she couldn't wait to see *Pocahontas* at the movies.

The *Lion King* video was spectacularly done. While it was playing in theaters, *Lion King* paraphernalia populated the shelves of toy stores. After the *Lion King* video, there was an added feature. The people at Walt Disney also let the video consumer remember all of the other wonderful Disney products that were available for their consumption. In many Disney videos, they will remind you that for a "limited time" only, you can enjoy the magic of *Snow White and the Seven Dwarfs* or *Pinocchio, Cinderella*, etc. Just as you were delighted by these wonderful stories as a child, the voice on the video encourages you to share such precious moments with your children by purchasing a copy of it for this abbreviated time. I, of course, recalled my joy at watching Pinocchio and his antics and after hearing those words couldn't resist purchasing that video too.

In my opinion, Walt Disney does a superb job at letting people know about his current projects—in this example, *The Lion King*; what he is working on next (*Pocahontas*), and reminding you of what he has successfully produced in the past (like *Pinocchio*). My advice to people who want to stay connected with their network is to practice this Walt Disney School of Marketing. As this construct demonstrates, letting people know about your past, current and future career and life aspirations will help them to better understand where you are taking your life and work and provide information so they know how they might help you in the process.

One person who can either help or hinder you with your past, current and future aspirations is your *BOSS*. In the next chapter, we will explore how to make *BOSS* your favorite 4-Letter Word.

Chapter 20

Secret #6:
Make BOSS Your
Favorite 4-Letter Word
and Don't Believe in
Customer Satisfaction

Secret #6

Make *BOSS* Your Favorite 4-Letter Word and Don't Believe in Customer Satisfaction

WHEN YOU READ THE STATEMENT, "MAKE *BOSS* Your Favorite 4-Letter Word," what did you think I meant by those words? When I ask that question, most people start to laugh or chuckle, then say something like, "I believe a lot of people see the word BOSS as a bad word, as something awful." Usually, a smile or smirk is now plastered across their faces. Quite often, they will follow with "There are a lot of bad bosses in companies." It is not uncommon for them to finally pour out *all* their emotions by stating, "I should know…I work for one."

Make BOSS Your Favorite 4-Letter Word actually means 4 things:

1. The word BOSS literally comprises four letters: B-O-S-S

2. To many people, this statement does have a negative connotation, and images of BOSSes who manage people poorly and who are incompetent and unfair spring to mind. I call this BOSS a **negative (−) 4-Letter Word.**

3. BOSS, however, can be what I call a **positive (+) 4-Letter Word**. Believe it or not, there are people who truly do love their BOSS and enjoy working with him or her.

4. Make BOSS Your Favorite 4-Letter Word also means that you have to become the BOSS of your life and work and must become that CEO of your ME, Inc.

BOSS AS MY FAVORITE 4-LETTER WORD

(–) BOSS = negative (expletive deleted) #&*@%*@!
BOSS = 4 Letters: B-O-S-S
(+) BOSS = positive
(+) BOSS = I am the BOSS of my life and work.
I've established my ME Inc., and I am
CEO of it.

In this chapter, we explore our Secret #6: Make BOSS Your Favorite 4-Letter Word and Don't Believe in Customer Satisfaction. We will delve deeper into *how* to Make BOSS Your Favorite positive (+) 4-Letter Word. Whether you are a BOSS or are BOSSed around, the information presented in this chapter is designed to help you understand the power and influence a BOSS may have on your work and life.

What effect can a boss have on your ability to LwL^2? The answer is simple—lots. Consider these facts:

- The number one reason that people leave an organization to work elsewhere is because of poor management. Translation: The BOSS. Unfortunately, this statement has been validated in far too many studies and surveys.

The position of BOSS is so powerful that it can rule your ability to LwL^2 if you allow it to happen.

- The effect that a negative (–) 4-Letter Word BOSS has on your life during most of your waking hours is staggering. While many individuals work the proverbial 9-to-5 shift or 8 hours a day, in recent years most of us are working considerably more hours. According to a study in *USA Today*, American workers actually work more hours than those in any of the other industrialized nations including Great Britain, France, Japan and Germany.

- Some companies are heavily ruled by the concept of "face time," where to get ahead, your face must be seen as you work around the office at all times of the day and night. In such cases, you may be spending more time at the job with that 4-Letter Word BOSS than with your family and/or significant others, or even by yourself. If you are fortunate to have a (+) 4-Letter Word BOSS, this huge chunk of your day may not seem so horrible. Conversely, if you find yourself under the tyrannical rule of a (–) 4-Letter Word BOSS, those hours can seem endless, grueling and downright unbearable.

- Not only does the (+) or (–) 4-Letter Word BOSS affect the quality of your time on the job, but it can also affect your hours outside of work. While a lot of us try to guard our private time and not let our job interfere with our personal life, often that is more easily said than done. Once we are at home and back in contact with our life, the powerful effect—especially of a (–) 4-Letter Word BOSS—can be felt in several ways. At the dinner table or in a leisurely conversation over the phone with friends, relatives and/or loved ones, a casual icebreaker comment may be made, such as "How was your day?"

Whether our day was great or grueling, when we hear that statement we tend to open up like water rushing from a dam and give blow-by-blow snippets, rehashing the low-point highlights of the day with our (–) 4-Letter Word BOSS. At that point, no thought is given to what we've done during the day in regard to accomplishing our life's work and/or becoming CEO of our ME, Inc. The (–) 4-Letter Word BOSS rules and grabs center stage in our lives again.

Finally you are ready to go to bed and get a good night's sleep so you can wake up refreshed for yet another stressful day. The time has come to retire and put the thoughts of that (–) 4-Letter Word

BOSS to rest as well. Some nights, falling asleep comes quickly—as soon as your head hits the pillow, you close your eyes and *BAM!* dreamland appears instantly. Other nights, you toss and turn before finally dozing off or you fall asleep quickly, only to wake up in the middle of the night, unable to go back to sleep. Of course you awaken because the stress of the day leads to a bad dream about the job and/or that (–) 4-Letter Word BOSS.

LwL² Practical Meaning Moment

Any way you slice or dice it, the power of a (+) or (–) 4-Letter Word BOSS will affect your ability to succeed at LwL².

B-O-S-S is a strong and powerful 4-Letter Word. It stirs up the same type of emotions as its cousins, who are also 4-Letter Words:
L-O-V-E and H-A-T-E. You can either *love* or *hate* your 4-Letter Word BOSS— the choice is up to you!

Characteristics of a (–) 4-Letter Word Boss

Famous director Alfred Hitchcock once claimed, "I never said actors were cattle. I said they should be treated as cattle."

A (–) 4-Letter Word BOSS often follows in the footsteps of Mr. Hitchcock, who was the king of suspense and fright. He may rearrange Mr. Hitchcock's saying and articulate his attitude about staff in this way: "I never said employees were cattle. I said they should be treated as cattle!"

Descriptions of a (–) 4-Letter Word Boss

To understand what you must do to LwL² if you have a (–) 4-Letter Word BOSS, first try to understand the characteristics of such a person. If you can relate to any of the following statements, you're probably working for one.

- A BOSS who has no real relationships with people although he has to be around and manage a lot of them.
- Someone who does a minimum amount of work but takes the maximum amount of glory and never shares the limelight with his staff.
- An individual who refers to her staff as "my people" or "my staff." Rarely does this person refer to the group who works for her as "our team."
- A superior who only wants me to work under him and won't allow me to soar *above* him.
- A person who takes credit for my work, doesn't give me compliments and seems to always put me down—it's as though he thinks I'm after his job, which they couldn't pay me enough to do. He's very insecure.
- A person who tells me I should just be thankful to have a job if I ask for more dollars to compensate me for new duties and the increased workload I've taken on consistently as people have left and/or been laid off.
- An individual who never gives me any feedback on my work. I had my performance review (which of course was late) and was shocked to hear that my boss thought I was not performing well in two of the six areas in which we are evaluated. This is the first time I've heard about these issues.
- My BOSS lives across the country and doesn't really see my performance on a day-to-day basis. She only communicates with me when she catches me doing something wrong but never gives me positive feedback or praise.

- A person who plays favorites and socializes and goes out with two of my colleagues almost daily. Behind his back, these two take advantage of their relationship with him. They are like bullies to the rest of us. So many people have left because of the two of them and our boss knows about this but chooses to do nothing about it.
- My boss won't take care of the "bad apple" disciplinary problems in our department. Everyone knows that he is just avoiding the situation. This rotten apple is spoiling the morale of everyone on our team.

Wise Words
It's not really the job so much as the person you work for. You can make almost any job work if the right person is in charge.

If I Work for a (–) 4-Letter Word BOSS, What Can I Do?

Options for Dealing with a (–) 4-Letter Word BOSS

You may be asking, "What if I have a (–) 4-Letter Word BOSS; what do I need to do?" Well, believe it or not, you *do* have a few options:

- Try to work with that BOSS to change him or her.
- Just accept it and say this is the way it is.
- Resolve that your BOSS will never change so you must change your attitude and approach in dealing with her (if you want to keep your job).
- Do what I call T.T.J.S.: **T**ake **T**his **J**ob and **S**hove it.

I interviewed Jerome Smalls of The TJX Companies for this book. He said this:

> "People whose spirits die at the office door are like the walking dead."

If you are one of those individuals you need to think about whether you should stay or go.

Profile of Success
Marilyn Midyette—Regional Vice President, Sprint

There are many roles that I play in my life. I'm an employee, a parent, daughter, sister, spouse, and community member. I love my family. In addition, I get fulfillment by having an identity that is separate and apart from a familial unit. What I'm seeking in my work is totally different from what I seek in my personal life. As human beings, we are multi-faceted. For most of us, there is a practical side as to why we have to work—clothes to be put on our bodies and a roof over our heads.

We need to take time as human beings to think clearly about who we are. We also should slow down and ask what does goodness and fulfillment look like in my life—would I know it if I saw it? Ask what are your ambitions? What motivates you? What are your talents, preferences and interests? Are you scientific and interested in knowing the "whys" behind the "whats"; are you interested in the process and how you got to the end result versus just knowing you arrived there? Are you inquisitive or not? I'm the type of person who is inquisitive and likes to ask a lot of questions. Other people may not be interested in the details. If I'm dealing with a person who is not into the details, I could be intimidating to that individual.

Once you've done this work and have learned about yourself, you can then pursue a vocation that allows you to deal from a position of strength. You will like what you do because you do it well and you will do it well because you like what you do. As early as high school and certainly in college you can begin to have a sense of awareness and know how you are hardwired. That knowledge can assist you in your choice of mates, where you live and what you do to Love your work by Loving your Life. This is really important for people who don't know themselves or understand why they do what they do and like what they like.

Dealing with a (–) 4-Letter Word BOSS
If you have a (–) 4-Letter Word BOSS, find a way to get along with him or her or find another job. Make sure you are in a work environment in which you are maximizing your strengths and therefore your options. If you're looking for the boss that you want him or her to be, and he/she is not there, you have to find ways to narrow the gap. You can't change the way people are hardwired or the way they think. You have to meet them where they are. If you start to move toward them on a tough issue, they'll usually start to move closer to you.

Profile of Success

Gloria Thompson—Retired Nurse and Real Estate Business Owner

I detested my job. I worked at it for 25 years but was in my profession for 40 years. I did an excellent job.

When I was growing up, I always had to get an A in school, not a C. I graduated *cum laude* in college and graduate school. Everything for me had to be tops.

Why did I work at a job in a racist, toxic environment for 25 years? I did it because the hours were convenient for me and my family. The position paid well, and I got time off during school vacations to be with my kids. But things weren't perfect and they still worked out—my generation knew that.

Sometimes I think this new generation believes everything has to be perfect to work—and it doesn't. While I was working at this horrendous job, I invested wisely and purchased many pieces of real estate. I was living vicariously. I said to myself, "I'm working in this hostile environment, and they don't know I'm slowly building up a nest egg."

At work, I always had a smile on my face and zip in my step. I knew what I was there for and was secure in my life's purpose. My goal, which I achieved, was to pay for my children's college educations so they would have choices I didn't have growing up.

I also was secure because I was financially stable. My property kept appreciating in the hot Cambridge, Massachusetts marketplace, and before I knew it, I could retire and live very comfortably.

The moral of my story is *You can hate your work but still love your life and do a good job at both*.

Sage Advice: Resolving Work Problems that People Cause Each Other

By Laura Avakian—Vice President, Human
Resources, Massachusetts
Institute of Technology (MIT)

THIS ARTICLE PROVIDES TIPS ABOUT RESOLV-
ing problems that people cause each other when
they work together. It is called "Sage Advice"
because the simple wisdom needed in these situations is akin to the idea of natural, uncomplicat-
ed herbal therapies that have withstood the test
of time.

Tip One: Practice the Art of Simpling

Managers dealing with people problems tend
to overcomplicate situations, "over diagnose"
the issue, and look for global answers to local
problems. Solutions are found in empathy,
immediacy of response, and what works. As
the cliché goes, practice the KISS principle:
Keep It Simple, Stupid!

Tip Two: Pain Avoidance Causes Pain

Confronting problems caused by people
almost always means that conflict must surface, that individuals will align themselves
with particular points of view or with those
they believe are allies. Confrontation and disputes are uncomfortable for most of us. Given
the options of fight or flight, managers run for
the metaphorical woods. What they don't realize is that the problem won't disappear and
that pain avoidance causes more pain in the
future.

Tip Three: There Are No Quick Fixes

We're impatient with problems that can't be
readily fixed. We can send a message to 50
people with one flick of a computer key, get
a glass of ice cubes by pressing the refrigerator door, and view our niece's wedding
album on the web. When the VCR or the coffee maker breaks, we throw it away and get a
new one. We are conditioned to get immediate responses to our needs, and when things

don't work, to dispose of them without guilt.
Important people problems can't be quickly
fixed, and disposing of people is against the
law—or ought to be.

Tip Four: The Need to Win Can Be a Losing Proposition

In organizational life, from elementary school
onward, we get rewarded for winning, for
getting better grades or running faster than
the person next to us. We may be taught
about "healthy" competition and "graceful"
losing, but in the end we know that winning
is good and everything short of that, isn't.
When people issues get resolved with the
emergence of winners and losers, the organization suffers. A new definition of victory is
needed, for the need to win can truly be a
losing proposition.

Tip Five: Become a People Person Even if You're Not

Despite a plethora of leadership development
seminars and libraries full of how-to-manage
texts, the folklore persists that one is either a
"people person" or one isn't. In other words,
the ability to get along with others is considered somehow innate. This ability is accompanied by a value judgment that refers to this
capability as "soft skills." Those without them
in organizational life are the tough guys who
make and manage money, who build sky-
scrapers or invent Velcro. Because the ability
to manage and work with people does not
constitute a profit center, it is often devalued.
It is relegated to the status of a nice-to-have
qualification for someone we hire for his
"business savvy." This parochial attitude has
sunk more than one company! Some sage
advice—learn how to become a people person, especially if you are not.

Tip Six: Find the Right Fit

Most managers subscribe to the "star theory" when they make hiring decisions. Filling a vacancy is seen as an opportunity to correct everything that's wrong with the mediocrity or weak performance of the department. While a successful new hire does not make for miracles, it is true that making effective hiring decisions is critical to an organization's long-term success. It is possible to evaluate an applicant's fit with your organization. It is, however, more important to cultivate those aspects of compatibility once an employee is onboard.

Tip Seven: Love Your Work

Studies have shown that a majority of people really do not like the job they go to every day. Given how much of our lives is spent working, or avoiding it, it is important to understand how we can make the work experience positive for ourselves and those around us.

I hope my sage advice—like pinches of herbs and spices tossed into a simmering pot of stew—may provide you with food for thought and give zest, color, and imagination to the otherwise bland conundrums of organizational life.

BOSS AS A (+) 4-LETTER WORD

TIPS IF YOU'RE THE BOSS

Here are some tips you'll want to consider if you want to be a favorite (+) 4-Letter Word BOSS:

1. Remember who your staff talk about over the dinner table—you.
2. Leadership isn't an on-call position. True leaders are always on the job.
3. If you haven't been formally trained recently as a manager, take some courses and do something about your management skills.
4. Don't be a hog! Share the limelight! Give credit where it's due.
5. Avoid performance punishment and giving work to Mikey all the time because he'll get it done. Hold others accountable for their work or you'll burn out—and lose—Mikey.
6. Put diversity on your radar screen, and mentor and look for staff who are not cookie cutters of yourself but different.
7. Know that it's more than just showing your corporate MVPs the money. Take time each day for saying "atta boy or girl" to praise staff for jobs well done. Write letters of congratulations to their personnel files and carbon copy them to your boss.
8. Don't be confused by face time. Respect and help staff to keep time for both work and life on their radar screens.
9. Catch people doing something right—provide ongoing feedback, not when things are wrong or bad. Have a policy of no surprises at performance appraisal time and a zero tolerance for late performance appraisals.
10. Let staff know what you are going to do with that information you request from them. For example, "I'll take it under advisement but I'm going to make the final decision, or whatever you give me is what we'll go with." Unless you inform them up front, people will clam up and won't be "straight" with you if they think you're not going to use something they've done.
11. Don't ask and they won't tell—don't try to guess at what type of rewards, benefits or incentives to give staff—just *ask* them. All too often people are not asked their preferences, and the boss ends up missing the boat when it comes to awards, sometimes expensively.

12. Make your message clear regarding when something is due. Don't use terms that can be open to interpretation, such as *ASAP, when you get around to it* or *STAT.*

13. Lead less like a buffalo and more like a goose. Are you confused by this statement? Read on and see what I mean.

TO BECOME A (+) 4-LETTER WORD BOSS, ACT MORE LIKE A GOOSE AND LESS LIKE A BUFFALO

(+) 4-Letter Word BOSSes lead people less like buffalo and more like geese.

What?

Here's how buffalo lead: A "head" buffalo leads the herd and all of the animals follow blindly behind the Big Kahuna. If the head buffalo is grazing and munching on grass, guess what? The rest of them follow suit. There have been cases where the head buffalo has jumped over a cliff. Yes, the entire herd follows, plunging to their death because they followed blindly behind their leader. 4-Letter Word BOSSes need to lead less like buffalo. They should take some lessons from geese on how to make staff soar.

Geese fly in a "v" formation. As a result of flying in this manner, they fly 71% farther. If one gets out of formation, the updraft is so powerful, it makes the lagging goose want to rejoin the flock. A "lead" goose is at the tip of the "v." The rest of the flock is behind honking ("*honk, honk, honk*"). Like cheerleaders, they are encouraging their leader to keep up the good work. In addition, when that lead goose gets tired, it rotates to the back of the flock and another goose takes its former place.

Whether we manage people or someone manages us, people who LwL² must have the ability to both lead and follow. They have to learn that they don't always have all the answers and that they should recognize when to let someone else take over.

The Facts of Geese and Collaboration

As told by Angeles Arrien, Ph.D.

Fact #1: By flying in a "V," geese can fly 71% farther than a goose flying alone.

Fact #2: Whenever a goose falls out of formation, it immediately feels the drag and gets back as soon as possible to feel the uplift power from other geese.

Fact #3: When the lead goose gets tired, it rotates back into formation and another goose takes over.

Fact #4: The geese in formation honk from behind to encourage those up front to keep up their speed.

Fact #5: When a goose gets sick, wounded or is shot down, two geese fall out of formation to help and protect it. They stay with it until it is healed or dies; then they move out to form a new "V" or catch up with the original "V."

Recommended Reading

Arrien, Angeles, Ph.D. *The Four-Fold Way: Walking the Paths of the Warrior, Teacher, Healer and Visionary.* 1993. Harper, San Francisco, a division of HarperCollinsPublishers

Profile of Success

Steve Hanamura—President, Hanamura Consulting

I feel like I am in a very rare position because my work is my life. My wife, Becky, married me and knew that about me. Work to me is what I stand for. My life's work is bigger than my paid work. My life's work is my calling.

When I write my personal business plan, I include work and life issues because my work is my life. For example, my business plan contains action items to take my kids to the beach.

For many people work is "just" a job for them, and those people are usually looking for meaning to their life. My brother's job was a city official but he defines his life in broader terms—his work was also to play golf and go fishing.

I once visited a NASA Flight Center to do some work for them. I was talking to one of their custodians in Florida. When I asked him, "what do you do?", he responded, "I help people go to the moon." I was impressed that he had attached his life's work to reaching the moon. He understood the larger purpose of his organization and his contribution to the work of NASA. He didn't feel less than anyone else because he was a custodian.

My work is to be good to my children, my life, and church. Celebrate oneness is the mission of my company. A fatal mistake most people make is they work toward something instead of "from" something. The place I work from is "oneness."

In chapter seven of my book, *In Search of Vision,* I talk about oneness and use an illustration from my own life. Before I married Becky, I was a single parent and my son Neil asked to stay overnight at a friend's house. The two of us began a shouting match when I told him, "NO." Finally, I stopped and asked Neil, "What's our mission?"

He replied, "Celebrate oneness," and I explained we were not doing this.

"Let me tell you why I need for you to stay at home," I said. "I will be leaving for a week-long trip and I need to be together with you before I leave—that is oneness." After telling him that, he was more than happy to forget about the overnight at his friend's house. Although I operate from a place of oneness, I'm not always there—I'm human.

Mission statements of organizations have to be to work from something, not towards something. They should be sayable by every employee in the organization, but 98% of companies don't have a properly set up mission statement.

You are in alignment with your job if you have meaning in your life. It doesn't have to come from the employer—that would be nice, but it's not always what happens.

What Leaders Can Do to Help Staff LwL[2]

I've seen some leaders help staff to Love their work by Loving their Lives. Mostly it depends on who the manager is at the time and usually that goes away when the person leaves.

I have a friend that exemplified excellence in leadership. He used an all-purpose staff meeting to get the "baby steps" so his staff could move. Here's what he did:

1. Took care of his people at the place they needed to be.
2. Gave direction and let people know what's expected of them.
3. Grew his people—told them 'here is the path for success and here's what you need to do to get there'— he mentored them.
4. Had fun.

The problem is when he left, that went away. So this form of leadership, to be successful in an organization, must be passed from leader to leader. That doesn't mean that if you are the new manager you have to replace that person, but you have to put your brand on it and continue the process.

Most people go to work to find meaning and their worth, but that isn't necessarily where they'll find it. Just go somewhere and don't talk about what you do and see how far you get. So, here are some hints leaders can take to help their staff LwL[2]:

1. Affirm *who* they are and *what* they bring.
2. Teach, coach, and provide direction.
3. Help them understand the meaning of what they do and why it is important to the organization.

Recommended Reading

Steve Hanamura, *In Search of Vision*, published by Global Insights 2000.

LwL² Lessons Learned from Fan Loyalty and The Curse of the Bambino

In this chapter, we've explained:

1. Why it is important to lead less like buffalo and more like geese;

2. How to manage a (+) and (−) 4-Letter Word BOSS.

To LwL² effectively, you have to learn how to lead as well as follow. It is also about understanding how to be a player as well as a fan. We've learned how geese are successful by honking on their leader. The role we play as a fan is also important as we seek to LwL². Whether you are a BOSS or being bossed, it is important to know how to play the role of a fan and have an "attitude of gratitude" toward the work of others in your life. This attitude of gratitude extends to how you support family, friends and colleagues through the good, bad and the ugly of their lives.

I believe we all can learn how to be a fan by understanding how fans operate in the town that I call home—Boston. Although I wasn't born in Boston, like many other transplants I came to this fabulous city at the age of 18 to pursue my education at Boston University.

I've now called Beantown my home for 32 years and have discovered that, in my humble opinion, there are no fans more loyal to their sports teams than the fans of the "home of the bean and the cod, where the Cabots speak only to the Lowells and the Lowells speak only to God!"

Here's how deeply fan loyalty runs in Boston:

In 1914, a young man by the name of George Hermann Ruth—a.k.a. "Babe" Ruth—started to play baseball for the Boston Red Sox. At that time, they were a rather mediocre team. With the mighty talent of Babe Ruth, by 1918 they were on top of the baseball world. This was after WWI when Woodrow Wilson was President. In 1918, with Babe's strong arm at play, the Red Sox won the World Series.

Fans in Boston went wild! A year later, Babe's 4-Letter Word BOSS did something that surprised and shocked many. To thank Babe for his wonderful hard work in helping the Sox clinch the Pennant, he was rewarded royally—by being traded that next year, 1919, to the New York Yankees.

How many of us know someone who has been in a predicament similar to Babe's? You work yourself into the ground to bring fame, glory and success to a company only to find that you are let go, overlooked for a promotion, or rewarded with no more money but more work after your gallant efforts. Babe Ruth was traded to the Yankees for $100,000. Legend has it that the owner of the Red Sox needed money to fund a business venture—a musical called "No No Nannette."

The Babe, however, didn't take this treatment well. He vowed in his own way not to get mad but get even with the Red Sox. As legend has it, after he was traded, he was furious and decided to put a curse on his former team. Just like many people in organizations who work hard but always see people with lesser skills and talents getting advanced or promoted, Babe Ruth was pretty angry about how he had been treated in his workplace. Regardless of the fabulous job he had done, he lost his job through no fault of his own.

The "curse of the Bambino," as it has come to be known, was cast by the Babe. This spell was that for 100 years, the Red Sox would not win another series. What can we learn from this situation?

First, whether you believe that spells can or cannot be cast, the reality is that at the time that I am writing this information, it is early November 2003, and we have just concluded the baseball season. The Red Sox lost their postseason bid for the Pennant against the New York Yankees. For 85 years, the Sox have not won the World Series. In 1986 and 2003, they came close, but somehow, some people believe that Babe Ruth is smiling peacefully in his grave, knowing that the Sox have at least 15 more years of suffering before his spell will expire.

Imagine you played on a team that for a consecutive 85 years lost its games. Do you think that team would have very many loyal fans? That's what makes the story about Boston fans so amazing. Despite the horrendous records of their sports teams like the Red Sox or the Patriots, who until Super Bowl XXXVI had never won a Super Bowl title, Boston fans are like perennial flowers when it comes to supporting their teams. You know that they will come back every season with more energy and vitality despite the curses and disappointing previous season.

Learning from Boston fans about lessons of loyalty and love, even for a losing team that's been down on its luck for years, is a valuable lesson for anyone who truly wants to LwL[2]. Another valuable lesson is learning when you need to take a job and shove it. Take the following quiz to see if you may be a candidate for such action.

Everything *good* about my week had *nothing* to do with my job.

Quiz: Signs That You Need to Take Your Job and Shove It

Read the following statements and check any that apply to you:

- ❏ A knot, tension, and/or anxiety occurs or persists when I reach the entranceway of my job.

- ❏ I can't wait for any of these to occur:
  - The end of my work day
  - A holiday
  - Vacation time

- ❏ Sunday evenings and/or Monday mornings are painful because I know I've got to go back to work.

- ❏ A week doesn't go by that I don't feel the need to document "for the record" something bad, unjust or unfair that happened to me on the job or was done to me by my boss.

- ❏ This statement resonates with me: "I feel dead-ended and going no where in my job. It is no longer challenging, and I don't see any promotional or advancement opportunities in sight. But I do feel I still have a lot to offer an organization that treats me right."

- ❏ I can definitely relate to this statement: Regarding my job, I believe that "The light at the end of the tunnel has been turned off until further notice."

- ❏ I'd be happier working as a beach bum than I am at this job.

- ❏ I constantly daydream and fantasize about being my own boss and/or working as a consultant or owning my own business where I don't have to answer to anyone but myself.

- ❏ The job and my personal values, ethics and philosophies conflict. I have to be someone at work that I'm not. I feel I put who I am on pause at work, and it doesn't get released until I leave at the end of my work day.

- ❏ I feel like I work for the Wizard of Oz's Wicked Witch of the North, and she will never change.

❏ I can't work in this environment any longer. If I stay, they will get the best out of me without giving anything but stress back to me.

❏ My company believes in and rewards face time. They say that I have to work 40 hours and *no* less, but when I work 50 hours, they don't say "You've worked too many hours—so take the day off."

❏ They told me one thing when I was interviewing, but when I got the job it was something totally different.

❏ When I took my promotion, they embellished the job. Now that I'm doing it, I realize that it's not what they promised.

Interpreting This Quiz

• If you answered yes to any of these statements, my advice to you is to T.T.J.S. (**T**ake **T**his **J**ob and **S**hove it!).

• If you didn't answer yes to any of the questions, *congratulations*! You are well on your way to Loving your work and probably have a (+) 4-Letter Word BOSS.

Not all of us hit the genius jackpot—according to MTV, it took Ozzy Osbourne 6 months to notice he had two cats living in his house instead of one. But don't wait until *you* are totally demoralized and down about your job to notice that you need to take steps to change.

TWENTY TIPS TO RETAIN YOUR CORPORATE MOST VALUABLE PLAYERS AND YOUR MVP WANNABES

As a management consultant, keynote speaker and author, people often ask me to dispense one pill that will solve all of their recruitment and retention woes. Unfortunately, there is no panacea. In my book—*Indispensable Employees: How to Hire Them. How to Keep Them.*—I talk about how to get and keep organizational superstars. Retaining corporate MVPs (cMVPs) in today's competitive marketplace requires a gargantuan amount of blood, sweat, tears, patience and perseverance. The unprecedented changes we all are experiencing—we haven't seen this type of change in the workforce since the Industrial Revolution—require us to look at retention issues through revolutionary and radical lenses. While there isn't one pill that will solve retention woes, here are some tips to help put you on your path to retention wellness. If you're not a BOSS this will provide an insight as to what you should expect from him.

1. **It pays to be nice.**
   Numerous studies point to a connection between positive customer and employee satisfaction. Treat staff well and they will in turn do the same to customers. Remember it pays to be nice.

2. **Address technical management promotions.**
   Don't assume that someone who has excellent technical skills will be a superb manager. Too often people with stellar technical skills are promoted into management roles without the proper training. So, they fail in their new role. Provide all managers with the proper tools and training to improve their management skills.

3. **Take more than a quarter (time and money) approach to retention.**
   It will take more than a quarter (time and money) to retain staff. Know your employee demographics now and what you'll need in the future. Develop a long range strategic retention plan including a labor forecasting plan which outlines how you will

fill jobs in the future and retrain current workers to fill future jobs.

4. **Avoid performance punishment and the give-it-to-Mikey syndrome.**

   Don't always reward top performers with more work. I call this the "Give it to Mikey Syndrome." Mikey is the outstanding employee you count on to always get the job done. He may grow to resent having to always do more than others. Sometimes others, who also want to be challenged and stretched in their jobs, will become upset by never having Mikey's learning and advancement opportunities.

5. **Communicate. Communicate. Communicate.**

   Employees often complain that managers don't communicate well. Use a variety of mechanisms to communicate and ask people how best to communicate with them, e.g.—email, in person, voice mail, etc. Take time to communicate face-to-face with staff. Avoid sending "bad messages," taking disciplinary actions and communicating annual performance appraisals via email. Be specific about timelines and avoid terms that can be open for interpretation like "when you get around to it," "as soon as possible (ASAP)," or STAT.

6. **Say bye bye to my-way-or-the-highway school of management.**

   Get managers to understand that Indispensable Employees are in top demand despite economic downturns. Say bye bye to "my-way-or-the-highway" school of management. Understand that managers, not just Human Resource departments, must take responsibility for recruitment and retention. Many people leave organizations because of poor management.

7. **Remember that bad apples (poor performers) do spoil the morale of others.**

   Address poor performance and bad behavior issues soon after they occur. Don't let them linger and fester because you're afraid of not having anyone to do the work. Consider the impact these bad apples (poor performers) have on the morale and productivity of other staff and whether they are eroding and spoiling morale and causing increased turnover as others leave because of them.

8. **Meet staff where they are in life.**

   When possible, be flexible and meet people where they are in life and survey them regularly about ways you can reward and motivate them. Don't guess at what they desire. Tailor benefits, compensation, training and advancement opportunities to employee wants and needs.

9. **Grow your own employees.**

   Grow your own employees through mentors, succession planning and skills development programs. Encourage staff to create Individual Development Plans so you better understand their career and professional aspirations.

10. **Help staff to keep their eyes on the prize.**

    Keep staff informed on your organization's mission, vision, values, strategic direction and how their job fits into these things. Employees can only keep their eyes on the organization's prize if you tell them what it is and how their accomplishments will help to achieve it.

11. **Be concerned about how staff enter and exit the organization.**

    Be concerned about how you orient new staff (entrance) and let them go (exit). The people left behind, especially after a downsizing, merger or acquisition are scrutinizing your actions and often are thinking when will the next shoe drop, and if that happened to my ex-colleague, could it happen to me?

12. **Help staff mutate regularly.**

    Keep staff informed of career and advancement opportunities in your organization. Don't assume that they know what is available and what they must do to obtain them. Remind staff to learn continuously and mutate regularly.

13. **Practice reciprocal loyalty and WIFYAM (What's In It For You and Me).**

    Practice a new attitude in regard to staff loyalty—reciprocal loyalty. This entails an attitude where employees are not just expected to give loyalty and the organization not give back in regard to job security, advancement and promotional opportunities and resources to adequately perform a job. Reciprocal loyalty is not about the WIFM—What's In It For Me—but the WIFYAM—What's In It For You And Me.

14. **Provide pay for performance.**

    Regularly reward and motivate staff. Take time to explain how and why people receive incentives and pay increases. Pay people based upon their performance and contributions. When possible, avoid across the board increases as the only type of salary increase. Most people are not motivated to work harder if their financial reward is the same as a co-worker who is a slacker.

15. **Give regular performance feedback not just at performance review time.**

    When employees apply for and do not get jobs, explain to them why, especially if an outside candidate will be brought in to fill it. Provide regular performance feedback. Don't let the annual performance review meeting be the only time staff hear from you about their bad or good performance.

16. **Give credit where it's due, catch people doing something right and don't hog the limelight.**

    Let employees and others in and outside the organization know when someone has done something noteworthy. Don't hog the limelight and take credit for your staff's work without recognizing them too.

17. **Examine face time and help staff to keep work and personal lives spinning smoothly.**

    Don't assume that more face time equates with higher productivity. Help staff to keep work and personal lives spinning smoothly. All work and no play does make John and Jane dull boys and girls and also burns them out.

18. **Define your sense of purpose and how you're making a memorable positive difference in the world.**

    Some staff are looking for a sense of purpose to their work. Encourage social enterprise (profitability and responsibility). Let people know what your organization is doing to make a memorable positive difference in the world. Don't assume they know what you're doing and how their efforts are helping your organization accomplish its mission.

19. **Not everyone is a corporate MVP (cMVP)—you may be a hero today and a zero tomorrow.**

    cMVPs must constantly learn and evolve. They have the right skills at the right time. This is a dynamic, not a static concept and people may move from being indispensable to disposable. If a person does not possess the right stuff at the right time, they may be a hero today and a zero tomorrow.

20. **Review the root cause of turnover, and know when to hold 'em, fold 'em, and walk away.**

    Constantly review turnover statistics and the root cause of turnover. Don't just sit on the information, do something about it. Is it cheaper to keep staff or are they eroding the morale of others even if they are high revenue producers? To paraphrase what Kenny Rogers once sang in a song, "You got to know when to hold 'em, fold 'em and walk away."

EMPLOYEES AND CUSTOMER SATISFACTION

There is a direct correlation between satisfied customers and happy and satisfied employees. Positive (+) 4-Letter Word BOSSes understand this concept. They work to make sure that an employee is loving their work and that as the peaks and valleys in their life crop up, they are there to assist them.

DON'T BELIEVE IN CUSTOMER SATISFACTION

Whether you work for a positive (+) or negative (–) 4-Letter Word BOSS, if you want to be successful, don't believe in customer satisfaction!

WHAT?!

You don't want customers to be satisfied: You want them to be *delighted*. Think about it. If I'm just satisfied, I'm just satisfied. If, however, I'm delighted, then I'm going to come back to you for more business and/or tell my friends and other potential customers about you.

PRACTICAL MEANING MOMENT

To Love your work by Loving your Life, practice making your BOSS, customers, family, friends and significant others delighted!

WHAT ARE EMPLOYERS LOOKING FOR IN EMPLOYEES?

As I've surveyed managers, here are some of the things that both positive (+) and negative (–) 4-Letter Word BOSSes are looking for in employees:

1. Can work effectively in teams
2. Has excellent interpersonal and communication skills
3. Has an outstanding customer service attitude
4. Can network with the right type of people so relationships are developed that capture business
5. Is computer literate
6. Practices continuous life-long learning. Is an "out of the box" thinker with thick skin
7. Can keep up with trends in business and their industry/field/profession
8. Multiskilled, flexible and can multitask
9. Not afraid to take on extra work or stuck on "It's not in my job description"
10. Can effectively deal in the global marketplace and with diverse customers and employees
11. Adds value and can do more with less
12. Finds ways to increase revenue
13. Quality and excellence driven
14. Seeks continuous improvement and keeps up skills
15. Understands the business, the industry and how their job fits into the strategic direction of the organization
16. Works effectively as a team member or individual contributor
17. Can work as a contingency worker—consultants, part timers, temporary help
18. Not overly concerned about job security
19. Possesses an "excellence always" work ethic
20. Not into the job just for the money
21. Won't abandon the organization when the chips are down
22. Can bounce back quickly after change or a shift in direction or leadership within the company
23. Knows how to self-manage

Wise Words

She Works Hard for the Money
She/he works hard for the money.
So hard for it honey.
They work hard for the money
So you better treat them right.
*—Adapted from the Donna Summers disco song,
"She Works Hard for the Money"*

Ten Ways to Self-Manage

By Dr. Barbara Addison Reid—Executive Director of Human Resources,
Bentley College

1. Establish positive work relationships with those around you. It's up to you to take the initiative.
2. Know your organization's goals so you can help achieve them.
3. Build your relationship with your boss on genuine mutual interests, abilities, and goals.
4. Establish a reputation for reliability by completing assignments well and on time.
5. Record and communicate your accomplishments. They are the building blocks of your career.
6. Never present a problem without suggesting a constructive solution.
7. Know your strengths. Practice them, build on them, and plan your career around them.
8. Continue your personal and professional growth. Never be without a goal.
9. Recognize the contributions of others.
10. Build a network of positive, constructive, successful people and communicate with them frequently.

Believe it or not, you can learn volumes from both positive (+) and negative (–) 4-Letter Word BOSSes that can help you to LwL². In the next chapter, Henry Ryan, Director of Human Resource Services at Harvard University, gives you an insight into lessons he learned.

Chapter 21

Things I've Learned from Negative (−) and Positive (+) 4-Letter Word BOSSes

Things I've Learned from BOSSes

By Henry Ryan—Director of Human Resource Services at Harvard University. He has contributed in the Human Resources arena in various management capacities for 30 years.

EVERYONE HAS A BOSS. EVEN THE BOSS HAS a boss. Bosses are described in many ways, including tough, fair, competent, nice, smart, dumb, jerk, etc. Bosses can be any gender, race, nationality, personality, disposition or educational level.

Before I became a boss, I used to ponder the purpose of their existence. I thought they were created to torment, aggravate, frustrate, and stonewall both people and organizational progress.

Nevertheless, learning from a boss is important, not only for surviving or thriving in a work environment, but also for establishing a baseline for determining what it takes to be successful (title, compensation, recognition, or whatever motivates you) for future career aspirations.

My first "boss lesson" from my first paying job out of high school was: The boss might not always be right, but the boss is still the boss. I have experienced many boss styles over my professional career and there has been a dramatic evolution ranging from autocratic dictator during the early years to more collaborative partner in recent years.

My most important boss lesson was: Learn how to listen. Early on, I used to take a pad and pen to my boss's office to ensure I documented his or her instructions. When you don't have a photographic memory, it is always wise to write things down and even repeat them.

Next, I learned to ask questions if something was not totally clear. Another boss used to say: "Speak up and don't mumble!" Most bosses value employee perspectives and insights on work issues, but this is not always the case.

Another boss reminded me early in my human resource career, "Timely, competent service (problem solving) is always important, especially if you are not generating revenue." Every customer is important …whether it be the custodian or the president.

Some bosses were mentors or coaches, while others were colleagues and/or friends. Friendship (although nice) is the least important aspect of a boss/staff relationship. Friendship can sometimes get in the way of focus, purpose and responsibility. Bosses are not necessarily collegial. Some of my bosses have been rude and unreasonable; others were competent and personable or some combination of the aforementioned characteristics. One former boss even intimidated all of her direct reports by refusing to speak to us, even to say, "Good morning."

Even so, I always learned something of value from every boss I ever reported to—even if it was simply how not to behave. Unacceptable behavior towards staff or customers includes yelling (or raising your voice), being rude, admonishing staff in front of coworkers and making unprofessional, inappropriate remarks.

In my role as boss, I try to model behavior that favorably represents the institution, as well as the Christian upbringing provided by my mother. Sometimes I am more successful at being a boss than other times. Occasionally, I revisit my Harvard "Leadership in Action" training or other training from previous assignments.

My particular "boss job" is frequently interesting, challenging, and fulfilling. My fundamental, core boss modus operandi is to assume that everyone I interact and collaborate with is an adult. I presume my staff knows their specific jobs better than I do. Few employees like to be micromanaged. As long as employees are enthusiastic about what they are doing, such energy should be channeled into positive, potential outcomes.

Periodically, we all need encouragement to validate that what we do has purpose or value. While most employees strive for excellence, sometimes "stuff" happens and human beings typically respond better to encouragement, rather than browbeating.

I try to be accessible to staff, but this is not always easy because of the numerous meetings I must attend. However, whenever I am in my office, my door is generally open. I remember past frustration about needing direction to resolve issues and being told to make an appointment that required three to four days of waiting in order to meet with a boss. This is not acceptable when urgent issues need to be addressed.

I am an advocate for self-motivation by way of self-development. I see my role as one of project or activity facilitator who strives to be strategic, efficient, resourceful, and adding customer value. Internal and external customers determine the value of services provided, so it is always important to be responsive to customer perceptions. Most days I really do enjoy coming to work and I would hope the majority of my staff would feel similarly. I do not consider myself a motivator per se, but I try to be supportive and encouraging. I learn more from listening than I do talking.

Talent Management: A Proactive Approach to Affect the Bottom Line

By Susan Gordon—Director Talent Management,
National Commercial Financial Services, FleetBoston Financial

I AM RESPONSIBLE FOR PROVIDING STRATEGIC direction as it relates to talent. Talent Management is a proactive, strategic method of managing your human assets. It is focused on results that have an impact on the bottom line. Very few FORTUNE 500 companies are doing this, but those who effectively engage in the process are seeing very positive bottom line growth and revenue results.

Talent Management works best when it is aligned with the business strategy and supported by senior management. For example, if you go through an organizational talent review, you might see gaps in critical skills employees need to reach the goals of your business strategy. Often, businesses do not have effective plans in place to deal with these skill gaps. This problem can be compounded when positions are left vacant unexpectedly.

Companies need to focus on issues like: What if one or two major revenue producers die or leave the company suddenly? How would that impact the corporate bottom line? Talent Management is about proactively identifying a pipeline of candidates who possess the skills needed to fill key positions. It is also about effectively retaining this talent by focusing on their career development to ensure that their careers are fulfilling and that they continue to be an asset to the company. So, Talent Management is a holistic approach to the recruitment, development and retention of all employees with a special emphasis on high potential employees and succession management for key positions. Holding managers accountable is also an important component. All of this is much more effective when properly planned and executed. This takes the burden off managers in that when a person leaves, they don't have the typical burden of trying to decide who will fill the position.

I believe that our employees are our most valuable assets. They are the fuel that makes our organization run. So it makes a lot of sense to provide a high level of focus on them. In addition, employees must also take responsibility for their own careers. Managers can help give guidance and support, but the individual is responsible for what he or she wants to do and what he or she is willing to do to get there. This can be a win-win situation for everyone—the employee, manager and the company. So much depends on employees having confidence about their ability to take on new responsibilities, overcoming obstacles, and asking for help when needed. Employees do well if they take responsibility and remain focused on their career. Life can derail anyone if you haven't taken the time to plan your career.

> Don't be afraid to take charge of your career! You are the
> Chief Navigator; you own it, and you control it.
>
> —Susan Gordon

Wise Words

Alesia Wilson—Director of Organizational Effectiveness, Fidelity Investments

To me, LwL^2 means one accord. There is a unity between living your life purpose and your everyday existence. There is freedom, power, focus, energy—and satisfaction beyond any monetary compensation.

To love their work, people need to like relationships. Sometimes we have to "rekindle the flame" and remember what about working is fulfilling and intrinsically rewarding.

To love their life, people should give up thinking their life is any different than it is. Be grateful for what is. Then and only then will you be able to create something anew.

Once you are clear about the contribution you want to make, any work can be a vehicle to express that contribution. Work is a means for self-expression.

Organizations can help staff to love their work and life by offering aptitude assessments for job fit.

Wise Words

Stop looking for the perfect job! Start looking for the position that gives the best expression to who you are.

—Kevin W. McCarthy, Author

In the pages that follow, we will examine what it takes to be a corporate Most Valuable Player (cMVP).

Chapter 22

What Does It Take to Be a corporate Most Valuable Player (cMVP)?

T O BE ON TOP OF YOUR GAME IN THE workplace, you must become a cMVP. While this acronym does stand for corporate Most Valuable Player, it also stands for the following.

*M*otivated: and learns as much, *if not more*, from the downs as the ups

*V*alue-added: understands how their work adds value to their life and vice-versa

*P*ositive Performance and Perseverance: maintains "Stick-to-itiveness"

"…There is really little difference between people—but that little difference makes a great deal of differences."
—Bruce Wilkinson, *The Prayer of Jabez*

---

cMVPs are motivated and that makes them Indispensable Employees. They practice a philosophy of "excellence always." Whether they win or lose at the job game, they are always looking for the "value-added." This may include looking for ways to add excellence to their work, but also seeing how the job can enhance their ability to LwL^2. Value-added for them is a two-way street: They apply the "WIFYAM" (or What's In It For You *And* Me) concept to the relationships they have with their bosses.

A cMVP also has a positive performance, perseverance and Stick-to-itiveness. No one wants a player who is a loser, slacker or a has-been when it comes to performance. cMVPs must be at the top of their game and exhibit a track record of positive performance through organizational ups, downs, wins and losses. This requires

perseverance and an attitude that says "when the going gets tough, the cMVP gets going."

cMVPs know that many games are won by the individual who can "go the distance" and exhibit Stick-to-itiveness. They understand the parable of "The Tortoise and The Hare." For them, the winner is not always the fastest runner. They understand the need to pace themselves and how to stay on track and stick to their goals when the odds are not in their favor to win the gold.

As we've learned, your time at the office can have a powerful effect on your ability to LwL^2. Now that you know what a BOSS might want from you, I want to explore some ways that you can begin to become a corporate Most Valuable Player (cMVP). To do this, we will look at the following questions:

1. What are the new rules of the workforce?
2. What can you do to become a corporate Most Valuable Player (cMVP)?
3. Are you ready for a job game change?

SAME GAME— DIFFERENT RULES

The rules of the workforce game have changed. If you want to be a cMVP, here's what you need to know about the old workforce game and what the new rules have become:

OLD GAME
　　Cradle-to-grave employment
NEW RULE
　　You're on your own

OLD GAME

Get your education, then you're set for life

NEW RULE

Lifelong learning is the name of the game

OLD GAME

Acting locally

NEW RULE

Acting locally *and* with far away places with strange sounding names

OLD GAME

"I never wanted to be a leader. My boss told me what I had to do and I just did it. I did a good job, then I left things behind and went home."

NEW RULE

"My boss isn't always around and often I have to make decisions on my own. They're making me work in teams where I sometimes have to be a leader."

OLD GAME

"My team is the people I work with in my department."

NEW RULE

"My team is the people in my department and I'm also asked to work on teams outside of my department and with consultants and vendors outside of the organization."

OLD GAME

"My company planned my career for me, told me when and how I would get promoted, then made career opportunities happen for me."

NEW RULE

"I must chart my own destiny. My organization can't necessarily promise me job security or career advancement."

"I must form a ME, Inc. and become its CEO so that I can be gainfully employed in the future in my own organization or elsewhere."

cMVP as an Evolving Term

Not everyone can be a cMVP. It takes hard work, sweat, and determination. A game plan and an ability to graciously accept the agony of defeat are also needed. *MVP* is a dynamic, not static, concept. One can be a hero today and a zero tomorrow.

The key to success in the workforce game is found in the profound words of a song once sung by Kenny Rogers—"You've got to know when to hold'em.; know when to fold'em; know when to walk away; know when to run."

---

cMVPs and Change

When faced with megachanges in the workplace such as downsizings, mergers, acquisitions, and changes in leadership or world changes that affect your ability to LwL^2, a cMVP should ask

- What can I learn from this experience?
- What can I do to add skills to my professional and/or personal portfolio?

Whose Court is the Ball In During Economic Uncertainty?

As we learned previously, economic highs and lows will probably be a permanent part of the workforce game. Whose court is the ball in during downsizings, mergers, acquisitions, and changes in leadership? In many cases, the ball is in the hands of cMVPs who are left behind after the dust settles and the people who have been asked to turn in their jerseys have left—or the new Head Coach or General Manager takes control of the team. Never forget that there was a reason why *your* number was kept on the workforce roster. To restore profitability and/or improve customer delight, the top BOSS will need you to perform at your peak.

I will show you a simple way to remember how to be a cMVP at work and life.

E³MPLOY

E³ VOLVE, ELASTIC, EMOTIONAL INTELLIGENCE

- cMVPs mutate regularly and are constantly refreshing and updating their skill sets so they have the right skills at the perfect time.
- They possess outstanding technical, interpersonal and communication skills (oral and written).
- cMVPs can maneuver and produce effectively, even during organizational change and chaos, and can snap back after challenges. They are elastic and stretch goals, and are ready to pitch in and don't just see things as being "not part of my job description."
- cMVPs have superb technical skills *and* Emotional Intelligence (EQ) which includes, but is not limited to, the ability to effectively manage relationships as well as themselves. They know how to read and understand emotions (theirs and others), and recognize customer needs.

M ANAGE DIVERSITY

- Since 85% of the new entrants to the workforce are women, immigrants, and people of color, cMVPs can work, and if appropriate, manage in a diverse environment of people and customers with different ages, races, genders, sexual orientations, abilities, etc.
- More companies are operating in a global environment and cMVPs can maneuver in international arenas.

P LAN

- cMVPs plan for their career and the work they do in an organization. They understand the mission and vision of their organization and how their job fits into it.

- They know that "if you fail to plan, you plan to fail."

L OYALTY

- cMVPs believe in "reciprocal loyalty"—this is a new attitude of loyalty. They are not just in it for the WIFM (What's In It For Me) but, the WIFYAM (What's In It For You And Me).
- They don't abandon their company at the first sign of trouble or chaos and change. They do a good job for the company and the company in return helps them grow in their careers.

O PTIMISTIC

- cMVPs know where they are going and are eternally optimistic yet realistic.
- They are not part of the "Ain't it awful" crowd. Instead, they motivate others, and serve as mentors and have mentors.

Y IELD RESULTS

cMVPs are results-oriented, have superb technical skills and contribute positively to their organization's bottom line. They possess excellent customer service skills. cMVPs are outstanding individuals and team contributors.

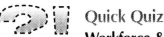

Quick Quiz
Workforce & Marketplace Stats Super Bowl Questions

Here are some stats that every cMVP should know. This information will help you to understand whose court the ball is in and provides insights on where the workforce game is going in the future.

1. This is the number of nursing vacancies that will be created by 2020:

   a. 400,000   b. 40,000   c. 4,000

   Source: USA Today

2. Fifty-three percent of federal employees will qualify for retirement during 2002–2007. How many jobs could that open up?

   a. 9,540   b. 95,400   c. 954,000

   Source: US News and World Report, February 18, 2002, page 37

3. The person who coined the phrase: "The thrill of victory and the agony of defeat."

   a. Alexander the Great—occupation: conqueror

   b. Jim McKay—occupation: sports announcer and voice most closely associated with the Olympics

   c. OJ Simpson—occupation: former NFL player

4. This country with 10.7 million people, always leads the Olympics' Parade of Nations Ceremony:

   a. United States   b. China   c. Greece

5. This school is tops in its league and has an endowment of $18.3 billion. Its closest competitor's endowments are $10.7 billion and $9.4 billion:

   a. University of Texas   b. Yale   c. Harvard

   Source: Business Week, February 18, 2002, page 78

What does this quiz tell you about workforce and marketplace trends that cMVPs should be concerned about?

Answers to Quick Quiz

1. a: 400,000; 2. c: 954,000; 3. b: Jim McKay; 4. c: Greece;

5. c: Harvard

The 7-Step Game Plan on How to Become a cMVP

From our previous chapters, you've learned about many of the skills you need to become a cMVP. To go for the gold, silver or bronze LwL² medal, implement this 7-Step Game Plan on How to Become a cMVP.

1. Visualize yourself as a winner and understand the new rules of the workforce game.
2. Get into the workforce and the LwL² game by linking your life's work and career.
3. To successfully play, create a ME, Inc. Board of Directors and Senior Management Team.

4. For a competitive advantage, don't believe in customer satisfaction, but learn to *delight* the fans.

5. Whether you are the General Manager, team captain, or just a player, learn how to lead more like a goose and less like a buffalo.

6. Manage the coach: *your* 4-Letter Word BOSS.

7. Don't rest on your laurels. Network, become a corporate cupid and have Stick-to-itiveness.

Other Savvy Ways to Bulletproof Your Career and LwL²

1. Recognize that cradle-to-grave employment is dead.

2. Seize educational and development opportunities offered in your organization while you are employed.

3. Develop a continuous learning attitude and become an "outside the box" thinker with thick skin.

4. Be a Jack and Jackie of all trades and master of one. Have a toolbox with many skills inside so you can change your game with the times and be ready to play. Be the master of one trade or skill that, regardless of economic highs or lows, will be in demand and keep you gainfully employed.

5. Be customer-focused and quality-driven.

6. Sharpen your oral and written communication skills.

7. Become an entrepreneur and an *intra*preneur. Act as if you are the CEO of your destiny. Be entrepreneurial and stay on top of lucrative outside connections by networking. Don't forget to do the same inside your organization and become an intrapreneur.

8. Learn how to manage your boss.

9. Be considerate—RSVP (whether or not you plan to attend an event).

10. Avoid sexual harassment by not participating in office romances, especially if you are a supervisor.

11. Become known as a respectable person who possesses integrity, has high morals and values, and is a good corporate and individual citizen.

12. Keep your word—follow up and do things when you say you'll do them.

13. If you can't meet a deadline, call in advance and let the person know why.

14. Don't become an individual who has mentally checked out of her job but physically stayed.

15. Find a mentor. Be a mentor.

In the next chapter on mentoring, you will discover that mentoring takes on many different forms. Traditionally, mentors have been older people who guide, coach and show younger people the way. Increasingly, younger people are mentoring older adults, helping them to understand and maneuver through the information technology age. This next chapter explores new ways that mentor relationships are developing.

Chapter 23

FIND A MENTOR.
BE A MENTOR.

men·tor (men′ tôr, -tər) *n.* A wise and trusted counselor or teacher. **Mentor** *Greek Mythology.* Odysseus' trusted counselor, in whose guise Athena became the guardian and teacher of Telemachus. *v.* Informal **men·tored**, **men·tor·ing**, **men·tors** *v. intr.* To serve as a trusted counselor or teacher, especially in occupational settings. *v. tr.* To serve as a trusted counselor or teacher to (another person).
Source: http://dictionary.reference.com/search?q=mentor

I 'LL ALWAYS REMEMBER THE FIRST TWO mentors in my professional life. The year was 1981, and I had just gotten married the previous year. The happiness of my new marriage was tempered by the sadness brought about by the loss of my job. I had worked for a consulting firm that unfortunately went out of business soon after Jimmy Carter lost the presidential election to Ronald Reagan. The federal contracts that were good and plentiful while Mr. Carter was in office had all but dried up as Mr. Reagan ascended the presidential throne.

I was out pounding the pavement looking for a position when I decided to stop in and see what jobs might be available at Children's Hospital in Boston. As I eyed the job postings board in the Personnel Department (that's what we called Human Resources back then), I saw a position that caught my attention. The listing was for a Manager of Employee Relations. The hiring manager's name listed at the bottom of the job posting read *J. Faklis.*

I had known a Janine Faklis, who had been an advisory board member on a national board I had worked with at my now-defunct consulting firm. Wow, I thought to myself, how many J. Faklises could there be in the world? Could it possibly be the same person? Of course not, I thought; she's all the way out in Chicago, working at the American Hospital Association.

I don't know why, but something told me to ask the receptionist about the J. Faklis who was listed at the bottom of the job posting. I hesitantly approached the receptionist and asked, "Is the hiring manager, J. Faklis, on the bottom of the Employee Relations position *Janine Faklis?*"

To my utter surprise, she replied, "Yes, she's our new Vice President of Human Resources."

I couldn't believe my ears. I asked, "Is she from Chicago?"

"Yes," the receptionist replied with a puzzled tone in her voice.

"Could I leave a note for her?" I asked.

"Sure," the receptionist said warmly.

I scribbled a message to Janine and left with a smile on my face, thinking how ironic it was that Janine was now in Boston and was the hiring manager for a job I thought sounded appealing. The last time I had seen her was when I did some work for her in Chicago at the American Hospital Association and later that year at a Board meeting in Washington, D.C.

That afternoon when I returned home, I received a call from Janine. She was ecstatic that I had dropped her a note. She explained to me that she had just given up her job at the American Hospital Association and moved to Boston to become VP of Human Resources at Boston's Children Hospital. I explained to her how I had been laid off.

To that, she replied, "Why don't you come back and see me, because I'm building my management team—I have a position open for Manager of Employee Relations, and I think you'd be great for it."

I remember vividly my response: "Janine, I'm really honored to think that you'd consider me for a management position on your team, but there are just a few problems. I've never really worked in Personnel except as a consultant, and I don't know anything about Employee Relations!"

I was poised to hear her rejection reply after she recalled my credentials; but, to my surprise, she told me that I did have enough background in Personnel through my consulting work and also had a working knowledge of labor laws through the work I had done assisting organizations throughout the United States to comply with Section 504 of the Rehabilitation Act of 1973. (This legislation was the precursor to the Americans with Disabilities Act, or ADA.)

She totally shocked me when she added, "You're a quick study, and I've seen your work and how you move into action and get things done. I know you'll learn what you don't know fast, and I'm willing to mentor you."

I'll never forget Janine's offer to mentor me, because she kept her word: In the months that followed I got my break to get started in a career and field that, to this day, I totally adore. If Janine hadn't been willing to mentor me and believed in my abilities, perhaps I would never have explored Human Resources, health care, or management as career options.

I started working at Children's Hospital in 1981 as Manager of Employee Relations and later also took on the role of Manager of Training and Development at this Harvard-affiliated teaching hospital that is one of the largest children's hospitals in the United States. My mentoring story, however, doesn't stop there.

Janine left to become Vice President of Human Resources at what was during that time New England's largest health maintenance organization, the Harvard Community Health Plan; and I was put in charge of the entire Human Resources Department at Children's until a new Vice President could be found. Through that experience, I discovered that I had the potential to become the head of a Human Resources department.

When a position as Director of Human Resources became available at a hospital where my mentor, Janine, worked, again I found out first hand the power of a mentor. I consulted with Janine about the opening and wanted to know her honest opinion about my ability to function at that level. She assured me that I was more than ready and capable to take on that next level of management. She opened the door for an interview with the president of that hospital, but she cautioned me that I'd have to get the job on my own.

I interviewed with President Arthur Berarducci of the Harvard Community Health Plan Hospital and was subsequently offered the job as Director of Human Resources. History repeated itself in my mentoring relationship with Art.

Years later, he became the Chief Operating Officer of yet another Harvard-affiliated teaching hospital, the Massachusetts Eye and Ear Infirmary. Just as I had done with Janine, I was in contact with him when a job as Vice President of Human Resources became available at his new hospital. Again, a mentor opened a critical door for me. When I applied for that position, he let me know that he could not simply give me the job and that I would have to go through an extensive and grueling interview process with the senior administrative and medical staff of this prestigious hospital.

"You'll have to convince a lot of people that you are the best person for the job," Art advised me. "I can only make sure that they take your candidacy seriously." At age 33, as an African-American and Native American female professional, I truly needed Art—a white male—as a mentor not to *get* me the job but, as he said, to ensure that my candidacy was taken seriously.

At that time there were no other people with my racial background at a vice-presidential-level position at that hospital or virtually any of the other 10+ Harvard-affiliated teaching hospitals. I didn't want to be taken as an affirmative-action hire who only won the job because of her race. I wanted to be viewed as a competent professional who possessed the skills and credentials to get and keep a high-level job in the Harvard Medical School teaching hospital system. I firmly believe that without Art Berarducci's ensuring that I got the *opportunity* to interview and be taken seriously for that position, it's uncertain whether I'd be where I am today. I believe in the power of mentors.

Just as people like Art and Janine helped me, I believe it is important to give back to others and be a mentor. I've had the privilege of seeing and meeting author, educator, and internationally known poet Maya Angelou on several occasions throughout the years. Frequently she talks about the notion of "Each one reach one" and "Each one teach one." There will always be someone who knows more than you do and that person can serve as a mentor and role model to you. In addition, there are always individuals who possess less knowledge than you do. These are the people to whom you can serve as a mentor. Not only must we have a mentor, but we must also be a mentor.

Ms. Angelou tells a moving story in her speeches about her Uncle Willy. He was an uneducated man with a disability. She attributes this man, who was short on book savvy but tall on street smarts, with having taught her many skills. From him, she learned not only her multiplication tables but lessons of life that have guided her along the path to success. She points out that, although he was uneducated, Uncle Willy's brilliance and genius as a mentor lighted the way for her and others to do memorable and positive things in the world.

The power of mentoring is cumulative. Just as Maya was mentored, so has she mentored others. For example, she has served as a mentor to one of my favorite role models, Oprah Winfrey. Between Oprah and Maya, imagine the millions of lives that have been inspired by their work. Think about the major impact that Uncle Willy's mentoring had on this earth.

Most people who have unlocked the secrets of LwL^2 understand that they can't be successful or achieve their life's work in a vacuum. Having mentors from varied races, genders, backgrounds and perspectives is an essential ingredient in the recipe for LwL^2 success.

In the pages that follow, I'd like you to hear the perspectives of my first two professional mentors, Janine (Faklis) Kilty and Art Berarducci. I hope their words will inspire you as much as they have me. To this day, I am still in contact with them and am forever grateful to them for opening doors of opportunity to me through their mentoring.

Profile of Success

Art Berarducci—Executive Recruiter, Alexander, Wollman and Stark

I think Loving your work and Life all stems back to some people who grow up thinking they can make a difference and some thinking they can't. The inspiration comes from different sources and making a difference is all about your relationships with people, especially when you are in management.

If you're in management and going to make a difference in people's lives, there are different kinds of interfaces. There are the people you work with and the customers. To be really excited about what you do, you have to be ecstatic about serving your customers. This is the same whether your job is making a donut for people to enjoy eating or helping someone get through a major life event like an illness.

There are people who come to work and think they can make a difference. I am on the phone constantly and some assistants answer so pleasantly and are clearly interested in helping me as a customer. Others are downright rude. When a person feels he can make a difference, there is a restlessness. He is anxious to do something that gives back to others.

In my job as an Executive Recruiter, I can treat my clients and candidates nicely and make a difference. To feel fulfilled, I also need to help people less fortunate than me. When I ran hospitals, I put in a Family Care Center so relatives could be with the patient while they were in anesthesia. I felt so good about that accomplishment.

Sometimes you are in a position where you feel you can make a big-scale difference, like being a brain surgeon. Other times, you're not in a job like that, but regardless of your profession, opportunities exist for people to make things better. If you look at people outside of monetary rewards and they are successful, there are usually a lot of people who would say that individual really made a difference in their life. It's the old question about how many people will come to my funeral?

Yogi Bera once said something like "If you don't go to other people's funerals, they won't go to yours." This is an interesting test. So, if you want a lot of people to attend your funeral and celebrate your life as well as mourn you, lead the kind of life where they will want to be there.

I've got to make a difference. I think that is a guidepost and is the sign of a successful life.

Fulfillment in one's personal or professional life is built on personal relationships, not transactions.
Leave no strangers because relationships produce both ongoing dividends and long-term gains,
while transactions produce only short-term gains.

—Art Berarducci

Profile of Success

Janine Kilty—Vice President of Human Resources,
Health Imaging Group, Kodak

When I heard that only 2% of people are loving their jobs and their lives, my first thought was "Is it really that bad?" As a Human Resources Executive, I worry about the prospect that people are so unhappy. I think there is considerable anxiety and pressure in many settings today. I believe this is not as much the product of job mismatches as it is the climate accompanying a sea of change. We are living through the third industrial revolution and it affects people in a variety of ways. Thanks to technology, our work doesn't have boundaries anymore. In almost every setting, we are rubbing shoulders with people who are experiencing change and struggling with the accompanying stress. Often, we are their customers. Sometimes, they are ours. In every day and in every way people are bumping up against it.

Not to pick on the beleaguered airline industry, but it serves as a perfect example of how interconnected our individual stresses have become. I was flying back from Chicago recently, and was struck by this situation. The plane was full of people, many of them visibly stressed with a fretful countenance and busily "multitasking." Several overheard conversations were about the next possible bad event (for their business? for themselves? for the world?). The flight attendants no doubt carrying a full plate of overwork, anxiety and negativity, struggled to maintain a façade of hospitality. So often in service situations these days, the palpable undercurrent is: if you are a recipient of service "Don't complain because it's the best I can do given the circumstances."

I have never taken a job that I haven't been drawn to totally. I have never stayed in a job that I did not, fundamentally, enjoy. Now, into every job a little rain must fall. The context of your work, the economy, the particular challenges might go through hard times, but even if you are feeling really bad, ask yourself, "Do I love my job?" If you can say that you still like what you're doing when the chips are down, that's a good thing. I do believe we are feeling the effects of globalization and having not yet adjusted our habits to the world "socio-economy." If we could resurrect people from the Industrial Revolution of the nineteenth century, I bet we'd find many people who felt then the way we do today.

When you talk about Loving your work by Loving your Life, you can love your life better if you love your work. Sometimes when the pressure is really on, I feel as though I don't move through life, I career. Just taking a moment to slow down for this interview and have a dialogue about this topic is important and it needs to continue.

Sometimes your BOSS can serve as a mentor, and other times you will have to seek mentors on your own. In any case, you will need to consider what type of mentoring you will need. What follows is information on different types of mentoring.

FOUR TYPES OF MENTORING

There are four ways to mentor. A mentoree can be coached on how to increase or improve his or her

1. **Skill Sets:**
   - To enhance skills utilized in a current job. For example, technical skills, communication skills, knowledge needed.

2. **Career and Personal Development:**
   - To focus on an individual's future job and provides skills and/or career advice to help the individual advance to a higher level on the job or within life.

3. **Performance or Behavior:**
   - To improve a person's present job performance and/or behaviors which impede or interfere with performance. For example, the person has ability and skill, but is not working to his full potential and/or is exhibiting poor behavior, like not participating effectively as a team player.

4. **Motivation and Inspiration:**
   - To increase individual and team performance and/or morale. The purpose is to motivate or inspire the person to perform at a higher level.

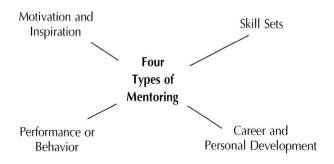

Mentoring relationships take a variety of forms. These include traditional, radical, peer-to-peer and reverse mentoring.

Traditional: This form is what we typically think mentoring is about—an older or seasoned person with experience taking a younger person in and providing much needed advice and tools to succeed.

Radical: Skills typically gained over a period of years must be acquired in a matter of months. Accelerated learning/mentoring must take place immediately for the individual to be successful in the position or situation.

For example, a Generation X manager learning how to manage people her parents' age.

Peer-to-Peer: This type of mentoring involves receiving guidance from individuals who are contemporaries, colleagues and peers. For example, a person who is new to the organization, or when a newly promoted employee is assigned a peer mentor who helps the individual learn the ropes of the organization or job.

Reverse: This involves a non-traditional approach where young people mentor older individuals on skills in which they are more experienced (e.g., computer skills).

MENTOR EXERCISE

These are my current mentors

_____

_____

_____

I would like to find mentors who can help me to

_____

_____

_____

Be a Mentor

The people I currently mentor are

_____

_____

_____

Other people I could mentor are

_____

_____

_____

Sample Mentoring Agreement

Name: _____

Date: _____

Mentor: _____

Mentoree: _____

What are the areas on which we will work?

_____

_____

How often will we meet to work on these issues?

❏ Daily   ❏ Weekly   ❏ Monthly   ❏ Quarterly   ❏ Other

Please explain:

_____

We anticipate that this mentoring work will be completed by _____

My role and responsibilities as a mentor will be _____

_____

_____

My role as a mentoree will be _____

_____

_____

What boundaries around confidentiality must we establish? _____

Final Outcomes

Define what success will look like:

_____

How will we measure and evaluate our success:

_____

When will we measure and evaluate our progress:

_____

Signature indicates that we will both adhere to what has been set forth in this agreement.

_____   _____
            Mentor   Mentoree

210

Profile of Success

Leland Melvin—NASA Astronaut and Co-Program Manager of the Educator Astronaut Program

NASA Astronaut Leland Melvin didn't grow up with dreams of exploring space and becoming an astronaut. His journey to become a NASA astronaut evolved. In fact, his first professional career had nothing to do with NASA. He was drafted by the National Football League's Detroit Lions in 1986 and later spent time with the Dallas Cowboys and the Toronto Argonauts of the Canadian Football League before he retired his cleats. How does a person replace a football jersey with a space suit and go from kickoff to liftoff?

To understand the story behind this complex and multi-talented man, one must start by exploring the origins of his life's journey.

Childhood and Role Models

Leland Melvin was born in February of 1964 in Lynchburg, Virginia, to Deems and Grace Melvin. Both parents were educators at the local middle school and have been his greatest inspiration. He realizes the influence his parents had on their community and the lives of young people and states:

> "Even today, when I go home, people stop me and talk about the impact my parents had on their lives. Some say that if they hadn't been their students and learned right and wrong from my parents, they might possibly be in jail or even dead. I realized that my parents didn't just have an influence on one person— they impacted the entire community."

Melvin has continued in his parents' footprints. He has a strong sense of service to others, especially young people. He was the Co-Manager of NASA's Educator Astronaut Program and works tirelessly to connect space exploration with the classroom, helping inspire the next generation of explorers.

As a child, Melvin's favorite subjects were science and mathematics. He also loved athletics and became an avid football, basketball and tennis player. In addition, he played the clarinet, took piano lessons and tinkered with photography, which today continues to be one of his passions.

Mixing Academics with Athletics

In 1981, Melvin was a senior at Heritage High School in Lynchburg, Virginia. He tells a story about those days when he had been given the chance of a lifetime by his football coach in a Homecoming game. His coach, who really had faith in him, called a play that would require him to run down the sideline and catch a pass that would make him the Homecoming hero. Melvin describes that tense moment:

> "It was a defining moment for me as a young wide receiver because not many passes had been thrown my way. In addition, unbeknownst to me, in the stands was a football talent scout from the University of Richmond. They hiked the ball, and I beat the defender to the end zone where I saw this football spiraling directly into my hands. The whole crowd was screaming at the tops of their lungs for me to catch it. At the moment of impact, the ball slipped out of my fingers and bounced high and far in the end zone."

Melvin could have become a hero, but now he was a zero in the eyes of many in the stadium, including that talent scout. He was dejected as he returned to the huddle.

His coach, however, had faith in Melvin's ability to bounce back and he called the exact same play. "I'm thinking, 'He has faith in me, he believes in me!'" Melvin exclaims. "But the scout is now walking out of the stadium thinking, 'This guy can't play for us if he dropped a game-winning touchdown pass.' I've been told that just as the scout was leaving the stadium, he turned around when he heard the crowd screaming wildly. I'm in the end zone with the football in my hands and the winning touchdown on the scoreboard." As Melvin went from defeat to triumph within that fateful football game, he also did so in his career as he was later offered a football scholarship to play at the University of Richmond.

At college, he again combined academics and athletics. He majored in chemistry and also became a football player who helped his team go to the playoffs his senior year.

From College Chemistry to NFL Football Player

An article in *SPACE.com* details how Melvin took his college degree in chemistry from the University of Richmond and put it to use as an NFL football player[1]:

"With a reputation for being a guy that can turn something around, the pro scouts began to take notice and after graduating from college in 1986, the Lions drafted him in the 11th round to come play ball in Detroit.

It was two weeks into training camp that Melvin's flight path to the NFL Hall of Fame made a major course correction. He pulled a hamstring and became damaged goods. Although he played fairly well in a couple of pre-season games, he was cut from the team just before the season began.

A whirlwind week followed. He remembers being cut from Detroit on a Tuesday, being in Dallas on Wednesday to be looked at by the Cowboys and by Friday was in Toronto, signed with the Argonauts on a practice contract, while waiting for Dallas to make up its mind.

Two weeks passed then Melvin got a call from his agent, telling him to return to Dallas because they want to sign him for the next season. To kill time and make a buck, Melvin started driving as a courier for his agent.

Then one day a friend suggested he stop being a courier and go to work at the University of Virginia. A professor of materials science needed laboratory assistance. Melvin put up resistance, still hoping to attend Dallas mini-camp in the spring.

"My friend said go talk to him anyway," Melvin said. "The professor said 'Why don't you come do some research with me instead of driving a car and delivering packages?'" So he did.

The holidays passed, it was January and his boss suggested Melvin enroll in a masters program for materials science. Dallas was still in the back of Melvin's mind but his professor said sign up anyway.

"My motto has always been to 'listen.' People sometimes know things that you don't know, so listen," Melvin said.

Taking courses via television at night and catching footballs at Dallas by day, Melvin made one final run at joining the ranks of America's Team in April at the Cowboy's mini-camp.

Melvin was stretching on the field with Dallas quarterback Danny White when he suggested Melvin run some half-speed, 10-yard passing plays. Then the Cowboy's legendary head coach Tom Landry appeared.

"Landry walks on the field. Danny sees Tom, I see Tom, and I know what's about to happen. He's about to change it from a 10-yard, half-speed out, to a bomb. Which he does, and I'm running," Melvin recalled.

But on the field, Melvin pulled his hamstring, ending his football career forever.

Melvin believes that things "happen for a reason." He doesn't believe that he would have been in the Astronaut Corps had his football injury not occurred. It was a "blessing in disguise," he states. He also knows that his core of athleticism also helped him become a better astronaut: "Sports are all about teamwork. You can't win a game if you can't work with your team. Working in tight spaces of the shuttle or the station takes teamwork as well. You can't be a good astronaut if you can't get along with the people around you."

After leaving the NFL, Melvin went on to complete his Master of Science degree in Material Science Engineering at the University of Virginia in Charlottesville, Virginia. After graduating, he went to work for NASA's Langley Research Center. There, he helped to develop fiber optics sensors for helping detect hydrogen leaks in aerospace vehicles, like the Space Shuttle. A co-worker thought he would make a great astronaut and in 1995 gave him an application. Melvin didn't fill it out then, but when the next selection cycle came in 1997, he decided to do so.

About 3,000 people applied for the Astronaut Corps that year and only 31 were accepted. Those who applied had less than a one percent chance of making the Astronaut Corps draft in the first round. Melvin was a first-round pick. He recalls: "I got into the 'Penguin' Class of 1998. [Each Astronaut Class has a nickname, and the previous class was called the Sardines.] After I entered the corps, I was trained for 18 months on the shuttle and station systems. I then requested assignments based on my wish list from the areas of Extra-Vehicular Activity (Space Walking), Robotics, and Shuttle or Station Systems."

Melvin explains, "I chose to go to Russia as a member of the support team for the International Space Station Expedition 1 crew—the first crew to live on the space station. It was one of the most enlightening experiences of my life. I became familiar with Russian culture and participated in everyday living in the country. It was a cultural exchange. All the work we are doing in space now is an international effort. I think the beauty of space is that it breaks down the barriers and promotes peace."

He returned from Russia and worked in the Robotics branch at NASA Johnson Space Center. Following this, he moved to NASA Headquarters in Washington, D.C. and was asked by management to support a new initiative. NASA administrator, Sean O'Keefe, wanted to elevate education to another level by creating the Education Enterprise. This program takes space into the classroom. "I travel around the country stimulating interest in our NASA Educator Astronaut Program (EAP). We want to get kids, especially in middle school, inspired and educated about math and science. We see girls' eyes light up when they see women floating in space, working the robotics arm or being a commander of a space shuttle. They see that one of their own can be an astronaut.

"I want students to know that you can study science and not be a nerd. You can be a top-notch athlete and still pursue a career in science or mathematics. You can be an African American and become an astronaut.

"Whenever I talk with children, I pull out goofy pictures of myself when I was their age. I show them that I went through the same things that they are going through growing up, and that there were people along the way that helped me. I let them know they need to have faith and a back-up plan in life. I also stress that sports can be important, but education is the key to success. As mentors, we have to believe in kids and instill in them the knowledge that they can do anything if they just put their minds to it."

About the Risk of Flying in Space After the Columbia

Melvin does not discuss in graphic detail what caused the Columbia explosion and tragedy. In an interview, however, on National Public Radio after the incident, he was asked about the risks of space travel. He is well aware of the dangers and risks of his profession and states that space exploration is "something we have to do to further our civilization."

Melvin also expands upon his thoughts on the risks and dangers of a profession that has a mission to discover unexplored realms:

"We're always on the edge. We push the envelope. That can mean sacrificing personal comfort and safety for the good of one program. When you step into an orbiter, it's not like going to the corner store to get a quart of milk. This is serious stuff. Many times in my life, milliseconds of time have kept me safe. What is going to happen is going to happen. It's a matter of fate, of destiny. I truly believe that whether you are waking up, tripping over a shoe or getting into a shuttle, you shouldn't live life in fear. God knows my time."

Melvin's personal philosophy about Loving your work by Loving your Life can be summed up into these two statements:

"All the things in my life aligned themselves in the right way to put me where I am today. I feel that God has put me here for a reason."

"Life's journey is not always about the destination, but the richness and beauty of the moments you experience along the way."

Profile of Success

Joe Feaster, Esq.—President, Feaster Enterprises

At least 75% of doing what you're doing is liking it. I could not wake up every morning and go into a place where I would rather not be.

How one can reach success? Here are some tips that I have found useful:

1. You must be diligent about the work you do.
2. You have to do your job well.
3. You cannot operate in a vacuum…you cannot be successful on your own. Networking is key.
4. It is critically important to mentor both upward and downward.
5. Team work is paramount. If you build a great team you can accomplish exceedingly more than you can alone.

A quote I believe in is "Pigs get fat, but hogs get slaughtered!" Thus, pigs get fattened up and nurtured while hogs get killed—you do not deal with them, they are not eaten, and they do not become the chosen.

Unfortunately, at the end of the day, pigs are also slaughtered, but before that time, they are taken care of very well. In the years I've been in the workforce (since I was 17), this philosophy has benefited me in my work in academia, the community, politics, lobbying, boards of directors, the legal arena, and my family life.

Furthermore, I believe in helping others. I am a prostate cancer survivor, and I want to educate other males and speak with them about the disease. This is consistent with my mentoring philosophy. I have become evangelical about prostate cancer rather than remaining silent.

Regarding loving my work and life, my professional, organizational and family life have the same thread and consistency in how I approach things.

The key is caring about others and mentoring.

The proverb "When the student is ready, the teacher will appear," often applies to mentor relationships. People who want to be mentored successfully can't be in a state of presenteeism, the topic of our next chapter.

Chapter 24

CURING PRESENTEEISM: EMPLOYEES WHO HAVE CHECKED OUT, ARE NOT ABSENT, BUT HAVE STAYED ON THE JOB

WHAT IS PRESENTEEISM?

ARE YOU PLAGUED BY "PRESENTEEISM"? Presenteeism is a form of absenteeism. It is when you are present, but absent, and it works like this: You are present every day of your life with respect to your physical form, but you're feeling like you "just aren't there." In other words, you are present, but feel absent. Often, your mind wanders. You want to be somewhere else when it comes to doing your job and/or living your life. During this heightened state of negativity, you may often detach from your reality. This may occur in the form of fantasies or day or nighttime dreams about a different life, lifestyle and/or work.

In my last book, *Indispensable Employees: How to Hire Them. How to Keep Them.*, I quoted Larry Gibson who described the problem of presenteeism this way:

> "It's not the people who have checked out and left that I'm concerned about, but those who have checked out and stayed."

If you are exhibiting any signs of presenteeism, it is imperative that you take time to examine the root causes of your condition. What is happening in your life or work that is preventing you from LwL^2? Take steps to change your situation. If the grass appears greener in just about every life pasture other than your own, you are probably a card carrying member of the "presenteeism" club and may want to consider canceling your membership before it's too late.

SEVEN CHARACTERISTICS OF INDISPENSABLE EMPLOYEES (IEs)

To help you cure presenteeism and become an Indispensable Employee, consider working on how you can develop these seven characteristics:

1. Mutate regularly to maintain the right skills.
   - IEs are learning sponges and they upgrade their skills constantly.
   - They develop measurable personal and professional goals and possess the right skills at the appropriate time.
2. Are rubber-band flexible and can maneuver in diverse workplaces and the world.
   - Can go with the flow as their organization changes (e.g., mergers, acquisitions, and downsizes).
   - Do not have an "if it's not in my job description, I'm not doing it" attitude.
   - Can navigate untapped oceans and are enterprising and successfully maneuver in a diverse workplace and world.
3. Give and expect reciprocal loyalty and practice the WIFYAM, not WIFM.
   - Don't practice "What's In It For Me," but "What's In It For You And Me!"

- Know that if their company is loyal to them they shouldn't take carrots that are dangled by competitors.
- Believe that if a company is not giving them the right skills and opportunities, they may need to move out to move up.

4. Won't abandon ship at the first sign of trouble and chaos.
   - IEs weather the storm to collect the pot of gold at the end of the rainbow. They stay with the organization for the long haul because they believe in the direction the organization is taking and in their role to help the organization achieve this direction/mission.
   - Understand that money is not everything; the grass is not always greener on the other work pasture.
   - Help the company to retain and attract staff because they spread the word and are goodwill ambassadors and headhunters who feel honored to let others know about job and career opportunities inside their organization.

5. Practice rotational geese leadership and followship.
   - Can lead or follow as needed.

6. Can talk the talk and walk the walk. They are consummate "corporate cupids."
   - Have stellar technical and interpersonal skills; they can work in teams or groups as well as make individual contributions.
   - Practice Management by Walking Around (MBWA)
   - Serve as corporate cupids who shoot out arrows and bring people and organizations together to form strategic alliances.
   - Are mentors and have mentors.

7. Can see the unknown and know that if you fail to plan, you plan to fail.
   - Know their organization's mission, vision, and values and how their job fits into those concepts.
   - Understand the value of planning and charting a course and direction.
   - Know that part of planning is discovering how to continuously learn.

In the next chapter, you'll discover the importance of continuous and lifelong learning.

Chapter 25

CONTINUOUS LEARNING

CONTINUOUS LEARNING—
A LIFELONG ENDEAVOR

IT HAS BEEN SAID THAT WHEN WE STOP learning, we die. Another cliché adds that the more we learn, the more we understand how much we don't know.

As the world and our careers continue to change, the need to update our skills and knowledge must become a priority. Whether you are an educator or an engineer, in the pharmaceutical or the communications industry, your ability to LwL² will be determined to a large extent by how committed you are to grow your mind by expanding your knowledge base.

In this chapter, you'll hear perspectives from a variety of professionals about the importance of continuous learning.

Wise Words

Kim Cromwell, Principal, Cromwell Consulting

To me, the concept of "Loving your work by Loving your Life" is about integrating our lives, recognizing that "work" and "life" can't be truly separated. I take responsibility for choosing work, a work environment and colleagues that stimulate me and support my learning. My work choices are a subset of my life choices, and I believe we have much more power over both than we sometimes realize.

Profile of Success

Regina DeTore—Vice President, Human Resources, Sepracor

When I heard the phrase "Love your work by Loving your Life" (LwL²), the first thing that popped into my head was passion. To keep motivated in life and work, you must have passion. The key to LwL² is learning. I'm a constant learner and keep up with trends, and emerging issues. I do this by talking with people, getting certifications, such as my Masters Degree, and internet research. The older I get, the more I realize that I've got a lot to learn and that keeps me motivated and fresh.

I like to work at being a good wife to my husband and a wonderful aunt to my nieces and nephews, a great sister and a terrific daughter to my dad. They are my support team, and I feel very lucky to have them in my life. My mom died when I was 23, and I learned from that experience that there isn't anything so bad that you can't surmount it. You get through things and learn that you are not here forever and that there is a bigger purpose. That's on a good day. On a bad day, I feel anxious like everyone else and I go to my spiritual end and understand there is a larger purpose.

I have a strong faith and am very forward-looking—I only look to the past in order to learn from it. When I hit my 40s, it dawned on me I needed to examine how I learned things and what I had done to be where I am. I looked to the past and where I was and it explained where I am today. I also explored what I could learn from the past, what areas I needed to work on to cope with the here and now and what I need to do inside of me in order to deal with the future.

Another great awakening in my 40s was that I'm not perfect and can't do it all. I had to learn to accept myself and others for who I am and who they are. After 16 years of marriage, I've learned to accept my husband for who he is, and he returns the favor.

Sometimes I get frustrated that I'm not doing enough but I've learned with age that to be and do my best, I have to find a balance where and to whom I give of myself, because I give 100%. If I overload at home or in my personal life, then work suffers and vice versa. If I am upset about my work, then my personal life suffers and vice versa. It's about trying to maintain some balance. When I get overloaded I don't take care of myself.

To get out of overload, I stop my world and take extra time to do more for myself and focus on what I need to do that will keep me fresh and open. I have to give special credit to my husband and sister, because they keep me balanced and on track by saying "what about me?"

On most days I feel very happy about what I am doing. I have an analytical brain but I have a desire to help people improve their working life. I take the vocation of Human Resources very seriously. I struggle sometimes when my work isn't taken in the right context, or isn't appreciated.

To me, the key to Loving your work by Loving your Life is for you to know yourself, and if you're able to work in an environment where you can do something good and use your skills, you are very fortunate. Luckily, I have that at Sepracor.

I think anyone can do it. It's just a matter of tapping into your skills and using them in a work or service setting that is right for you.

My final words of wisdom are to adhere to four keys of success:

1. Know who you are.
2. Know your skills and what you can do.
3. Find the right use of your personal and professional skills.
4. Continuously learn and grow.

Ways To Procure Needed Skills

✓ Professional Organizations
✓ On-the-Job Training
✓ Volunteer Work
✓ Reading Business and Trade Publications

✓ Mentoring and Coaching
✓ Training and Certification Programs
✓ College and University Programs
✓ Adult and Vocational Education Programs

 ### Quotes of Note

Contributed by Jessie Shea

Carry the sun inside you, and reach out for the dreams that guide you, You have everything you need to take you where you want to go. You have the abilities and talents and attributes that belong to you alone, And you have what it takes to make your path of success…lead to happiness.

—Douglas Pagels

You have powers you never dreamed of. You can do things you never thought you could do. There are no limitations in what you can do except the limitations in your own mind as to what you cannot do. Don't think you cannot. Think you can.

—Darwin P. Kingsley

[On education] Place yourself among those who carry on their lives with passion, and true learning will take place, no matter how humble or exalted the setting. But no matter what path you follow, do not be ashamed of your learning. In some corner of your life, you know more about something than anyone else on earth. The true measure of your education is not what you know, but how you share what you know with others.

—from *Simple Truths,* Nerburn

Profile of Success

Dr. Richard K. Fields—President, Benjamin Franklin Institute of Technology

Dr. Fields leads the Benjamin Franklin Institute of Technology located in Boston's historic South End. This technical college primarily prepares urban students for careers in Engineering and Industrial Technologies.

When I think about Loving my work by Loving my Life, I believe there are certain aspects of my work that bring me satisfaction and others that I really don't like. I'd just as soon not do certain tasks, but they come with the territory. I wouldn't be able to have the type of life I have compared to other people who were born at the same time and under similar circumstances if it had not been for education.

My life began in poverty in an impoverished neighborhood called Eleven Street Bottom in Winston Salem, North Carolina. No one in my family had ever graduated from high school. At age nine, I went to live with a foster family—two elderly widowed sisters who were ex-school teachers (I called them Aunt Eliza and Aunt Sallie). They had a niece, Lil (Lillian), who lived in New York City but visited frequently.

Their home was filled with books and they instilled in me the value of a good education. I went on to earn a bachelor's degree from North Carolina Central University and two master's degrees from the University of Pittsburgh and Harvard University. Eventually, I received my doctorate in Education from Harvard.

I always believed that one has a moral obligation to give to others when one receives certain kinds of opportunities to progress in life. I wanted to give back as my Aunt Eliza, Aunt Sally and Lil gave back to me. The material deficiencies that I experienced as a child taught me to appreciate opportunities and to be prepared to do the same for others when I obtained the means to do so. I've chosen to give back through my profession as an urban educator.

As a college president, I work with urban students of all races and economic means. Many of them come from backgrounds similar to mine. Some are from homes in the projects while others are first generation immigrants.

It's ironic that my college was founded by money bequeathed from Benjamin Franklin. He was a man from Boston's working class who also believed in giving back and mentoring young, struggling apprentices. When I'm engaged in activities that are not trivial but meaningful, then I am satisfied and love my job. For example, I enjoy presiding over graduations. When you have graduating students and their families and—most importantly—their younger siblings, it underscores to them the importance of what they've accomplished. To me, that confirms that I'm making a meaningful contribution.

In contrast, when I'm engaged in a self-study for an accreditation visit from a regulatory agency, I am not so satisfied. This is a necessary activity, but it is not really related to what I like to do and what makes me happy.

Tips on Continuously Learning

Early in my career, I set a goal to head an educational institution. I knew that to do so, I needed a doctorate in Education. So what drove me was the goal I had in mind and the need to gain respect in that world for which I needed a certain level of degree. It's all about one's goals. You need to have a plan and it should include an awareness of what and who you need to know. It also should include information on what you must do to accomplish your goals and the steps involved. You must constantly ask yourself, "Is this what I really want? Is it what I really need?" You must also do a reality check that says, "Am I progressing in that direction?"

I was 44 years old when I went back to get my doctorate from Harvard University. I worked fulltime when I started and was married with one child. Two years into the process, I had a daughter.

I had to stay focused on my goal to get my doctorate. While it was difficult juggling all those balls, I had a plan in mind and completed my doctorate in four years and continued my full-time job. Some of my colleagues who started with me were full-time students with no job, and it took them ten years to complete their degree, while others never finished. With proper support, I'd recommend this. Otherwise, you probably should not attempt this endeavor. I had support from my wife and my employer. These things are not done alone or in a vacuum.

Continuous Learning Through Intuition and Diversity of Thought

By Dr. Ashley F. Fields—Senior Advisor, Shell Oil Company

Introduction

INTUITION APPEARS TO BE A VAGUE AND undefined process in diversity of thought which provides a competitive edge for some people and is inaccessible to others. Intuition is shown to be a phenomenon arising naturally in individuals using a particular information processing/decision-making method and mode. Intuitive individuals are statistically more likely to be found in certain organizational functions than in others.

There is, however, an inability to articulate just what diversity of thought means. In other words, "something" really exists, but most people cannot agree on just "what" exists or "why" it works as it does. Diversity of thought looks at intuition as "a phenomenon arising naturally from an information processing/decision making method and mode employed by individuals." (Fields, 2001, p. iv).

Background

Attempts to define and harness the mechanism of intuition are as old as recorded history. The popular mind thinks of it as a "sixth sense," while the ancient Chinese "I Ching" used intuition as an interpretive tool.

Intuition can be defined as knowing or sensing something without the use of rational processes. It has also been described as a "perception of reality not known to consciousness in which the intuitive knows, but does not know how he knows." (Clark, 1973)

It seems that some of us have this capacity and some do not.

Managers are likely to use intuition to resolve business issues and that is partially "why" these managers are more successful than peers who remain at the lower rungs of the organizational ladder. For example, imagine heading a soon-to-launch dot-com firm. The only numbers to analyze are derived from hypothetical market research. If you believe market research provides "real" answers, talk with Ford Motor Co. about their 1950s Edsel; massive market research was followed by complete failure in the marketplace. No one has any idea what the "real" demand for your offering will be, so how could a structured analytical approach work for problem solving or decision-making in this instance?

The very nature of high-level organizational problem solving, with its frequent emphasis on as-yet-undefined trends, demands use of unpatterned strategies. With these strategies come behaviors attributed to "intuitive" abilities. In other words, the environment of the senior executive favors unpatterned strategies, and in using such strategies, the executive displays intuitive behaviors.

The functions within organizations require different strategic styles as a path to excellence and demonstrate the value of diversity. "One size fits all" models need to be replaced with specific interventions for specific areas and functions. Just as no one bridge is right for traversing all chasms, no one formula provides optimal management for the diverse functions of modern organizations.

Other areas that might benefit from application of diversity of thought are limited only by one's imagination. For example, Training and Development might use these insights in designing training content. Career developers might use diversity of thought to better guide young people toward positions promising greater personal satisfaction. Senior executives might benefit from designing strategies, policies, and cultures that complement, rather than conflict with, the composition of their workforce.

Bibliography

Agor, Weston (1997). *The measurement, use, and development of intellectual capital to increase public sector productivity.* Public Personnel Management, Summer, 175–186.

Barnard, Chester (1938/1968). *Functions of the executive.* Cambridge: Harvard University Press.

Brown, C. (1993). Intuition and introspection in the advertising decision process. (Doctoral dissertation, Stanford University). UMI Dissertation Services.

Clark, F. (1973). *Exploring intuition: Prospects and possibilities.* The Journal of Transpersonal Psychology, 2, 156–170.

Fields, Ashley F. (2001). *A study of intuition in decision-making using Organizational Engineering methodology.* (Doctoral dissertation, Nova Southeastern University). UMI Dissertation Services.

Hermann, N., (1981). *The creative brain.* Training and Development Journal. October, pp. 11–16.

Jung, Carl G. (1934). *Modern man in search of a soul.* New York: Harcourt Brace.

Kant, Immanuel. (1781/1990). *Critique of pure reason.* Trans. J. M. D. Meiklejohn. Buffalo: Prometheus Books.

Leavitt, H. J. (1975). *Beyond the analytic manager, Part II.* California Management Review, 17, (4), pp. 11–21.

Maslow, Abraham (1954). *Motivation and personality.* New York: Harper & Row.

Parikh, J. (1994). *Intuition: The new frontier of management.* Cambridge, MA: Blackwell Publishers.

Salton, Gary J. (1996). *Organizational Engineering: A new method of creating high performance human structures.* Ann Arbor. MI: Professional Communications.

Salton, Gary J. and Fields, Ashley (1999). "*Understanding and optimizing team learning,*" Applied Management and Entrepreneurship, 5, (1), September, 48-60.

Wise Words

Jeremy Lew—Senior Software Engineer, Mathsoft Engineering & Education, Inc.

The adage "variety is the spice of life" applies to working life as well. Constantly pushing yourself to learn new skills and to improve your old ones makes you a more valuable contributor, whatever the vocation. Choose a line of work which you are passionate about and good at doing. Never become complacent about enriching yourself and others. Organizations should recognize their staff's contributions, even in small ways.

Profile of Success

Jessica McWade—President, McWade Group, Inc.

"In business, it's about money. It's just not all about money."

Loving your work

Loving your work means finding satisfaction in seeing the results of your work. It's about taking what you know from experience and instinct, applying it and seeing it reach fruition and find its place in the world. I'm driven by ideas and inspirations, and much of it is only as good as its application to help organizations and individuals grow and reach their fullest potential.

Loving my work has much to do with the fact I engage my clients, fellow employees and business partners in very deep and meaningful ways—and not without a dose of humor. Too many organizations are humorless today, and that stifles original thinking and creativity. This defies some of the popular wisdom that says "don't get too close to your clients and co-workers and become their friends because you may have to fire them or vice-versa." Well, truly working with mutual respect and trust, and not just mouthing these things, gives you the emotional and intellectual capacity to counsel somebody or even fire them, if that must be done. In war, adversaries dehumanize each other, which we're told makes it more tolerable to kill or wound them. Hmmm. Quite the contrary, our clients and co-workers need to be fully humanized if we are to unleash their potential and our own. Emotional distance creates just one thing—distance!

I particularly like watching my ideas in action as they are spoken by others or seen in acts they perform. Ideas and ideals are my fuel when I work with my clients. In particular, I find such meaning in working with non-profits, religious and military organizations. There's an espirt de corps in these institutions that's often missing in corporate life, much to the detriment of the latter. Their mission is more powerful and pervasive and they have passion about their work. They also recognize that progress, growth, faith and welfare are their currency and their measure, not just money.

I love my work because I love to see it being used or applied in the real world to help people to think and to believe in themselves, to help organizations convey their message and to help leaders learn to lead. My clients know that I am not all about just making money. With a sincere practice of that attitude, guess what? You end up making more money. That's because they trust you and want to work with you. You deliver, and you make them think and laugh.

You can't go wrong if you practice what Immanuel Kant told us: "Live your life as though your every act were to become universal law for all mankind."

Loving your Life

I'm blessed to work with organizations whose mission I believe in—this fuels my love of work. I work a lot, but it is totally integrated into my life—my relationship with my sons, my sublime love of art and my ridiculous love of sport. I crave to keep making new, better leaders and help corporations communicate and my work runs into my personal research, scholarship and, yes, my play.

The worse thing we do as adults is to forget how to play. It's that childlike wonderment
and impish humor that keeps everything so interesting and compelling.
It's fuel for how I think, write, speak and produce.

Boundaries are important. They're important when you work for someone else, but you are still CEO of your own life. When you work for yourself, the risk is that your work is all you do. So you have to work hard at not making that happen.

I have a love affair with life. It's easy to get cynical and down because negativity surrounds us. I like to see the positive and be open to new ways of thinking. When I grew up, I had no knowledge of music or fine arts, and no appreciation for the world of ideas. So I taught myself, and I've become a lifelong learner. It's learning and growing as a lifestyle. I like to make connections (one of my favorite words). For example, I connect literature, sport, film, politics and economics. I like people who connect knowledge and feelings across differing boundaries. It makes you strong and enables you to cross borders more easily and joyously.

Regina Carter, a classically trained violinist, is an example of someone who does this well. She wasn't able to listen to any other type of music growing up. In her 20s, she discovered Jazz, Blues and Motown and combined them with her classical training. She crosses boundaries and the result is a thing of beauty. When you try to express an aptitude in multiple fields, however, these "Renaissance" qualities are often beaten down because people may say that's not the way it's done, but it may become the norm if you persevere. That's what pioneers and brave people have done throughout history. Leonard Bernstein, for example. The critics and purists scolded him for doing *West Side Story* when he was arguably the greatest symphonic orchestral director of his time. He saw the possibilities and, with confidence, crossed the boundary. These are artistic examples, but it can be applied to anyone who is not afraid to explore and take a risk.

We should not lose our connection and desire to be connected to the sound and soul of others, especially those who are not like us—tall to short, men to women, black to white, gay to straight. When you open yourself up, you just have so much fun. Clearly you are anchored in your own roots and your soul and values, but what revolves around that is a world of wonderment that educates and entertains.

As a kid, I ate a lot of canned food. I had to first eat fresh broccoli before I learned I liked it. It was the same with Shakespeare, Jazz and chamber music.

Our diversity is limited to what we open ourselves to in this world of unlimited diversity. It's a problem when diversity is only what the individual is willing to accept or, dare I say, "tolerate." People should get used to a process that reduces their fears and opens them up to understanding. Then you can deal with unwarranted fears.

I need more than just a series of hobbies—I need family and the love of my two sons and my sister. There would still be something missing if there weren't a thirst for knowledge that comes from integrating how we feel with how we think—that brings together the heart and the mind. The emotional affairs of the heart are your family, spouse, friends and the affairs of the mind are things like chess, good books, the work we love and hobbies. Then, there is this mysterious third realm—affairs of the soul. None of us really knows what to make of the soul. I think soul is the spiritual integration of the heart and the mind, and it's the care and feeding of our soul that enables us to love work and love life.

I love life and am deeply engaged in it. It remains an adventure—childlike—the wonderment, curiosity and openness of why the moon is in the sky, why a flower blooms and these all can be addressed from the heart, mind, and then come together in the soul.

Having said all this, I'm still on a path. I have the passion and the preparation, but I'm still searching for the larger purpose. This journey has taken many forms, and all the things I didn't have access to years ago have yet to find a home, but I'm close. I am incredibly purposeful, but like so many of us I am still searching for my unique purpose. I'm unbelievably close. I believe it's about leadership, redefining fear and nurturing my dialogue in a direction that breaks down barriers and eliminates hatred. I'll never have all the answers, but I'm getting closer every day.

Individuals who have a thirst for learning often find that in order to quench it, they must begin to put their knowledge into practice. Implementing your work often involves planning. In this next chapter, you learn that if you fail to plan, you plan to fail.

Wise Words

Wen "Jasmine" Zhao—Senior Analyst, Scotia Bank, Canada

My philosophy on life is to hold on and never give up. For example, my 66-year-old Mom just arrived in Canada from China. She has a zest for life and part of that involves learning. She wants to learn English and went to a store and purchased a children's book so she could understand simple words and phrases. She is determined to learn English, and I have no doubt that she will succeed.

Life is a constant learning experience. You should embrace what it has to offer you and never give up.

Chapter 26

Secret #7:
Plan to Fail.
Learn as Much,
If Not More,
from the Downs
as from the Ups

Secret #7

Plan to Fail. Learn as Much, if Not More, from the Downs as from the Ups

OUR 7TH SECRET IS TO PLAN TO FAIL and Learn as Much, If Not More, from the Downs as from the Ups. We become busy or preoccupied with the business of life and sometimes our LwL² priorities simply fall by the wayside. Planning is an essential component to LwL² successfully. One of my favorite sayings is: "If you fail to plan, you plan to fail." When and how you should plan are concepts that often cause confusion for people who want to LwL². In addition, individuals become confused when they try to understand the concept of planning in relation to the issue of living in the NOW which we previously discussed.

THE CHALLENGES OF LIVING IN THE NOW!

No one said that living in the NOW is easy. I've been reminded of this challenge on several occasions when I was shopping and stores were getting ready for a holiday season. Case in point: On Thursday, August 7, 2003, I was shopping for some decorations for a teenager's birthday party. The summer sun was heating up the pavement outside, but inside a flotilla of store clerks were scurrying around like ants around an anthill. They were busy putting up every Halloween costume imaginable.

As I thought about how much I didn't want the summer to end, it became very difficult at that moment to concentrate in the NOW rather than on my feelings about how utterly absurd it seemed that the store was already pushing a holiday that was a little more than two months away. I remember having that same feeling when I went into a large department store around Labor Day in September one year, and lo and behold I was greeted with fake snow and an artificial Christmas tree decorated with red, blue and silver holiday ornaments as "We Wish You a Merry Christmas" tinkled gently in the background.

Even the most devout living in the NOW practitioner might find it hard to steer a course in the present with that type of interference. If you do succumb to outside pressure luring you to other times and places, take time to reflect on what you can do to get back in step with the moment.

Living in the NOW does not, however, imply that we should not

1. Plan for the future,
   or
2. Reflect on our past.

I am also a firm believer that to know where you're going, you have to know where you've been. By analyzing your history and that of others, you come to know what acts, words, thoughts and deeds should or must never be repeated.

So to live in the NOW, it is necessary to drop in on memories of the past and imagine those of the future, but not dwell on them or spend your entire life camped out there. It is important to spend about 80% of your time being what some people call "in the present." This means that you are focused on what is going on around and inside you as it is occurring. No distractions about what you did in the past or what you'll do in the future should seep in. This concept is about taking the time to smell the roses, inhale the aroma of the coffee as it is brewed or enjoy the scent of homemade bread as it is being baked.

When I think about approaches to help me stay in the NOW, I am reminded of a game that my mother played with me and my brothers and sisters when we were children living in Okinawa.

As you may know, Okinawa was the site of some of the fiercest battles of WWII. We lived there in the early 1960s, and the War had ended in 1945, just 15 years before. As such, there were still grenades, land mines and war paraphernalia hidden in the tropical foliage of my neighborhood on Kadena Air Force Base. As kids, we would play like Tarzan and Jane and run through the bamboo forests, swinging on vines as we thumped with one hand on our heart, yelling out at the top of our lungs a Tarzan-like war cry of *Ah-Ah-Ah-Ah-Ah!*

My mother didn't want to curtail our fun as we romped in the tropical paradise, but she wanted to keep us safe while we'd do the things that kids do when they play. She devised a game and would play it with us at random and unexpected moments. The game went like this: She would say, "Close your eyes real tight—no peeping." As a way of illustrating her technique, let's say that we were at a restaurant when she decided to play her game. After we'd close our eyes, she'd say, "I want you to think about the room we are in today." Then she'd start to ask us a series of questions pertaining to the contents of that room, such as

☆ What color is the tablecloth?
☆ The napkins?
☆ Are there any flowers on the table?
☆ What about the waiters and waitresses? What color are their uniforms?
☆ Are there any pictures on the wall? If yes, what are the pictures about?
☆ What was the name of the last song played on the stereo system?

We were the typical competitive siblings and each of us tried to be the first to answer my mom's questions correctly. After a while, she would ask us to open our eyes and look around the room to see how well we had observed our surroundings. She then reminded us how important it is to always be aware of what is going on around us each moment, especially when we were outside playing our Tarzan and Jane games.

I often think of the wonderful gift of observation and living in the NOW that my mother instilled in me as a child. Perhaps this story will provide you with a technique to help you and your children be more observant of things occurring in the NOW!

To live in the NOW, we must also understand how to plan for the future as well as develop goals to get us there. In this next section, we will focus on a technique that I frequently use and have taught to literally thousands of people who have also found it to be a helpful tool to develop goals that are specific and easy to implement.

You may already be familiar with this technique known as the "SMART Model" of goal setting. It is a popular model used by many people within organizations. I have somewhat altered the model as well as provided a mechanism as to how it can be used to prioritize tasks. I hope that you will indeed fell SMARTER after you have utilized the SMART Model of goal setting.

SMART MODEL AND GOAL SETTING

Many tools exist to help you plan. I'd like to tell you about the five-step process I use to set, prioritize, implement and evaluate goals. They are

Step I: Set SMART model goals

Step II: Construct a *mind map* to identify tasks

Step III: Prioritize tasks so that you know in what order to complete them

Step IV: Complete a project planning worksheet which maps out the who, what, where, when and how to achieve a task at hand

Step V: Mutate regularly and evaluate goals throughout the year.

An explanation of each step follows.

Step I: Set SMART model goals.

The SMART model of goal-setting is a well-known tool. It works whether you are setting professional or personal goals. The beauty of this model is that once a goal is set, it has all of the required elements so it won't be difficult to measure whether or not it has been achieved.

When you develop a goal, use this model to see that it contains all of these elements before you begin to implement it. Here is what the acronym SMART stands for:

S   pecific (will result in a tangible outcome)

M   easurable (basis for evaluation and comparison)

A   ligned, aggressive, and agreed to (aligned to organizational goals, this goal is something you want to be aggressive in attacking, and agreed upon by persons doing the work and their supervisor)

R   ealistic (reasonable, able to achieve even when bad times and/or tragedy occurs in the organization or world)

T   ime-bound (outlines a specific time to achieve the goal)

To illustrate how setting a SMART model goal works, I'm going to take a goal and turn it into one that is SMART:

Regular Goal
I want to go back to school and get a degree.

SMART Goal
By December 31st of this year, I will enroll in two graduate school courses each semester at a prestigious university to work on my master's degree in business administration so I can become a senior manager in my company within three years. I will obtain agreement on this strategy with my family before I begin the application process and maintain a 3.5 grade point average.

In contrast to the regular goal, notice how much more specific this goal is regarding what will be achieved.

S   **pecific:** See how much more specific this goal is versus the regular one.

M   **easurable:** You will be able to measure success by obtaining at least a 3.5 grade-point average, by enrolling in a program by December 31, and by taking at least two courses each semester.

A   **ligned, aggressive and agreed to:** The goal is aggressive given the fact that you are working full-time. It is aligned to the goals of the organization and you are also seeking acceptance from your family so they all agree to participate in this process and they understand what you are committing to do in order to fulfill this goal.

R   **ealistic:** Is it a realistic goal to take two courses per semester given your hectic work schedule? Only you can assess that, but on the surface it seems like a viable option.

T   **ime-bound:** The goal is time-bound because you know that in order to start your degree, you must begin the process before December 31.

Step II: Mind Mapping (to identify task)
I will never forget the day I learned how to do mind mapping. That enlightened moment came at an all-day

standing-room-only seminar in the 1980s given by a man named David Allen. I was so intrigued by the concept that I've taught it to hundreds of people through my consulting and training practice. I also have used it as a personal tool consistently over the last two decades.

Below, I explain how this phenomenal tool works. I hope it will bring you the same clarity to take your professional and personal SMART goals and turn them into reality. This process allows you to think through the tasks needed to implement your goals and the order of priority needed to complete them.

Mind Mapping Technique Illustrated

Begin with a blank piece of paper; in the middle of the page draw a circle and write inside it the goal on which you need to work. Again, this can be a personal or a professional item, as well as a SMART goal. For the sake of this illustration, I am going to go back and use my SMART model goal of going back to school and getting my masters in business administration.

☆   Draw a circle and write inside it what you want to work on.

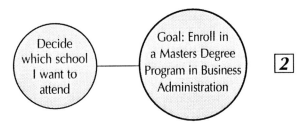

☆   Identify the steps I need to take.

Now I have to think about what steps I must accomplish to fulfill this goal. I do this by drawing lines away from the goal then adding a circle next to the line. Inside that circle I will place my ideas about how to accomplish those tasks. I'll place these ideas around the center circle as they enter my mind. The first thing that pops into my mind about what I must do to enroll is to

decide which school I want to attend. So I've drawn a line to a circle at the end of the line and inserted that thought into the circle.

At this point, I do not need to worry about the order in which the tasks must occur. All I am concerned about is getting on to paper anything that pops into my mind about what I need to do in order to enroll in a program.

☆   I will now take the circle that I previously put on paper and move on to making other lines with circles as I think of additional tasks. My next thought is to get application forms from the desired schools. This idea gets placed on this mind map diagram in yet another circle extended by a line.

☆ The third item that surfaces in my mind is to talk with my family about my decision and make sure they are comfortable with it.

4

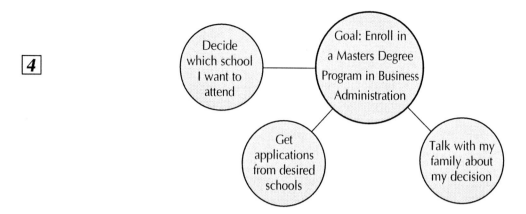

☆ The final step is to complete the applications, get references, and mail them out by September 30th.

5

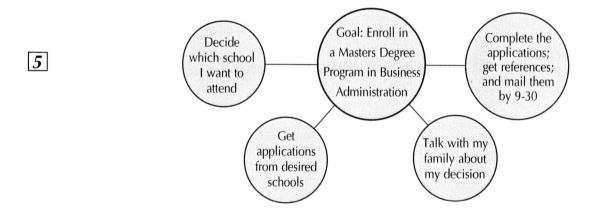

After thinking this issue through, I feel satisfied that these are the tasks that must be completed to enroll myself in a master in business administration program. Now I am ready to move to Step III: Prioritize Tasks.

Step III: Prioritize Tasks

Now I am ready to prioritize the tasks I have identified so I will know the order in which they must be completed.

To complete this step, I simply look at the Mind Map diagram that I created and determine the order in which each circle must occur. I will then rank order them by placing numbers inside each circle indicating which circle must be completed first, second, third, and fourth. In my example, I would probably want to start by talking with my family so I can get them involved with the idea. So, I would place the #1 inside the circle that says "Talk With My Family About My Decision."

Next I need to decide which schools I want to attend. It would be wise for me to do that before I waste my time getting, then filling out a lot of applications for schools I may not want to attend.

The order of my last two tasks are then to get the applications from desired schools (#3); followed by completing the applications; then getting references and mailing them out by September 30th (#4). The final diagram with all of my priorities on tasks looks like this:

Final Mind Map Diagram with Order of Priority Identified

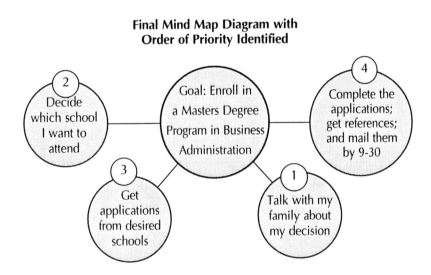

Step IV: Project Planning

In Step IV, I must begin planning how I will get the rest of this project completed. I will now start to identify

- Who will be responsible for completing the task;
- Where it will take place;
- When it will need to be done; and
- How much it will cost.

Listed below is a simple, but extensive, form that I created based on work I did at the Harvard Business School and with several major organizations that I have successfully used with clients, colleagues, family and friends who were interested in implementing their professional and/or personal SMART goals. You can feel free to put this form on your computer and use it as a way of keeping track of work assignments and progress in achieving your goals.

Capturing this information up front will help you better manage all the tasks that must be completed successfully. If my Mind Map involves others who must help to implement it, such as a team, my staff, or my family, it also serves as an invaluable roadmap and communications tool to update all who are involved. Everyone helping out on the project will understand their roles and responsibilities and that of others working on the initiative. They will also understand when their assignments are to be completed.

Step V: Mutate Regularly And Evaluate Goals Throughout The Year

As we have discussed in previous chapters, the world and workplace seem to constantly change these days. To keep on top of things, you will need to mutate regularly

LwL² PROJECT ACTION PLANNING FORM

List your SMART Model Goal: <u>Enroll in a Masters' Degree program in Business Administration</u>

The What	The Who	When		How Much
Specific Tasks	Responsible Person(s)	Start Date	End Date	Cost
1 Talk with family				
2 Decide on schools				
3 Get applications				
4 Complete applications				
5				
6				
7				
8				
9				
10				

and evaluate your goals at various times throughout the year. Here are some tips to help you in your quest to mutate regularly.

Mutate Regularly and Become a Continuous Learning Sponge

- Don't rest on your laurels. If you are static in your learning, you will soon be stagnant in the workforce.
- Continually ask yourself, "Where are the opportunities now and in the future?"
- What skill sets do you need to acquire so you can survive and thrive?

People aren't dogs. You *can* teach them new tricks.

—Martha R. A. Fields

Nina Miller-Browne has developed the following handy form to help you set SMART Model goals in relation to your performance goals. She has provided an example of how the form can be completed.

Using the SMART Model to Set Performance Goals

By Nina Miller-Browne—Senior Business Analyst, FleetBoston Financial

NMB 2004
Performance Goals
(SMART)

Performance Goals: Specific	Measurable	Aligned, Aggressive, Agreed To	Realistic	Time Frame
1 Focus on Team Work	**2** Adhere to Corporate Code of Business Conduct and Ethics and Policy on Workplace Standards	**3** Demonstrate courtesy, respect, honesty, fairness and decency in all relationships with fellow employees.	**4** Communication	**5** Ongoing
	Be aware of what the team has to accomplish; adapt as necessary to help the team accomplish goals.	Review the team's calendar and deliverables, provide assistance and tailor agenda to adapt as practical. For example, if others are working on tasks that take priority, offer to help or acknowledge priority of personal deliverables in relation to team deliverables.	Customer Service, Result Orientation & Team membership	Monthly—Ongoing
	Assist in cross-training of similar graded employees (Other Assets/Liabilities) and (Deposits, Scorecard)	Teach methodologies used in forecasting, describe files and calculations used and share forecasting and input into ePlanning (Balance Sheet). Discuss sources for Scorecard.	Result Orientation, Change Orientation	Quarterly—Ongoing As Needed
	Begin to learn about forecasting/planning of lending products	Learn methodologies used in forecasting, become familiar with files and calculations used and share input of Loans into ePlanning. Develop preliminary understanding of Products and variables impacting revenue.	Continuous Learning,	Quarterly—Ongoing As Needed
	Share helpful information with team	Share information that will help team members (career development etc.)	Team Membership	Monthly—Ongoing

- What obstacles may affect your ability to achieve your goals?
- What resources and support do you need to accomplish the action steps?

The Strength of Strategy

By Anthony Griffin—President, Metro PowerNet, LLC

STRATEGIC PLANNING IS A POPULAR TERM AND IT is well worth its notoriety because there is strength in strategy.

In today's business world, it is standard practice (or should be) to have one or more strategies for your business or life. Here are five strengths that you'll discover if you operate with a strategy:

1. Your perspective is forced to broaden when you think through your strategy. You will catch more problems before they find you, and increase your level of innovation and solutions.
2. Your thinking will enter paths it hasn't gone before or those it hasn't gone far enough or deep into enough times.
3. You will see an increase in your awareness of what's going on that could negatively impact your business or life.
4. Long term momentum is created.
5. Following your strategy will help you to be ready for "your moment."

Creating and implementing a strategy for your business or product/service should boost your productivity even more. It will reveal low-lying areas that have placed a hold on your success. There is an extremely intangible benefit of creating a strategy, pursuing it and sticking to it even when situations occur that could knock you off course. I've done things that align with my strategies, but didn't have an enormous immediate benefit. At an unforeseen time in the future, there was a pay-off that would not have occurred without a strategy in place. On the other side, I've missed out on opportunities because I did not fully implement a strategy that was created.

Strategy is more than planning. Planning is the plotting of the details that bring the strategy to life. Strategy is where you build muscle to succeed at LwL².

Making a Plan of Action

By Thomas C. Matera—Partner, Highland Consulting

EVERY DAY THAT PASSES IT BECOMES MORE and more impossible to separate our personal selves from our corporate selves. The demands of work (globalization, competition, productivity, added responsibilities, better quality, customer satisfaction, leading and inspiring) are enough of a challenge, so that pretending we can do all these things with just our rational, logical, corporate selves is becoming more and more nonsensical.

What we know and must find the courage to show, is that these demands need our full, all out, best-we-have-to-offer selves; our diverse selves within (intuitive, heart-feeling, ambitious, sympathetic

selves) and our diverse selves externally (collaborative, cooperative, committed, accountable and responsible selves).

So starting today, what is YOUR plan?

What people need to do to love their work:
1. Decide you are the one who is responsible for loving your work.
2. Assess your satisfaction and be honest with yourself when doing so.
3. Describe the gap between what you want and what is so.
4. Create strategies to fill the gap.

5. Take action today and everyday.
6. Use people you trust and who care about you to do Steps 2–5. This is the most important step and the most difficult. Avoid avoiding it.

Keep in mind that planning and acting on a good plan are always good things to do for the human spirit if not for the human mind and body. But that's not enough. Daily you have to be it. Loving your work and your Life is as much about finding it daily as it is about making a plan for action. That's just one of life's little paradoxes.

Best, Interesting and Radical Practices
Tom Matera

Since the implied employment contract was broken some 15–20 years ago, a manager's best remedy today is to ensure that he or she knows what the motivation profile of each of his or her people is and acts on it. What is the motivation profile? It's all the answers to the question "What gets you up on Monday morning to come to work?" As a manager, if you are honest with yourself, you already know how well you know your employees' motivation profile and what the work is you need to do on that score.

PLANNING YOUR LIFE'S WORK IS LIKE PLANTING A BEAUTIFUL GARDEN

Planning how to Love your work by Loving your Life is a lot like gardening. You have to start by

1. **Pulling out the weeds**—Discard those things that grow out of control and do nothing to improve the soil of your work or life. These are weeds of mass destruction or distraction that only pull you down and zap nutrients from the positive things you could do.
2. **Tilling the soil**—Once you have pulled the weeds from your work and life soil, proceed to till the soil in advance of preparing it for fertilization. Tilling involves using the right kinds of instruments to turn the soil over. The goal is to break up and aerate the ground so once fertilized, plants will have the right conditions to grow. In your work and life soil, positive growth will not appear until you have pulled out the weeds and aerated your environment properly so your life becomes a space where things will grow.
3. **Preparing the soil**—Your work and life soil must be properly prepared before you proceed with planting. For example, you need to put in the proper configuration of nutrients so that the plants will have a healthy, nutritious environment in which to grow and thrive. Peat moss, cow manure, lime, and fertilizer help strengthen garden soil. Work and life soil require similar ingredients, which, if configured properly, will bring together your mind, body, and soul. To be successful at this, you must work on issues that cloud and obfuscate your harmonious existence. In addition, you must provide the correct amount of nutrients and nutrition to establish an environment inside your body that will be ripe for you to plant your work and life seeds.
4. **Planting a garden**—Have a plan before you start planting so you have an idea where things should be arranged. There are different size plants that need to be grouped together. A tall plant placed in the front border of your garden will overpower its shorter companions that may be of equal beauty but may get hidden by the largeness of the big plants.

The colors and hues of the garden must be considered. Do you want to establish a palette that is more pastel—light yellows, pinks and soft lilacs as opposed to creating one with darker, heavy colors of the burgundy, purple, and mauve shades.

Everything in the garden has a season, so if you want continuous color and blossoms in your life garden, you must know what plants will come to life at which season/cycle—those that bloom in the spring, early and late summer versus those than can survive up to the first frost of fall or winter. Follow these tips as you develop your work life garden for the winter, spring, summer, and fall of your life.

Wise Words

- Give yourself enough time to let things marinate, sauté and simmer before acting upon them.
- Practice the "poor planning on your part doesn't constitute an emergency on mine" approach.
- When you do something ask yourself, "Is every year better than last year? Have I grown more this year than last?"

Wise Words

Michelle Chambers—President, New Tilt

My partner and I are in our fifties and have seen a lot of people die (because of the AIDS epidemic). We've discovered that it is very important to have life. We will all live for a certain amount of time and have to make a living. So we made a plan. That's the reason why I'm feeling good, because I know where I'm headed. We always do a 6-month evaluation to see where we are in meeting the goals of our plan.

Wise Words

Haywood Fennell, Sr.—Author and Playwright

Not only is honesty the best policy. It is the *only* policy.
No job will validate you. Through your work, you will validate the job.
Simple can become difficult when we have an approach instead of a plan.

Chapter 27

LET'S GET
ORGANIZED

LET'S GET ORGANIZED

ARE YOU "STRIVING-YET-NEVER-ARRIVING"?

WE HAVE JUST EXPLORED THE FIRST part of Secret #7: Plan to Fail. Learn as Much, If Not More, from the Downs as from the Ups. In his book, *10 Secrets for Success and Inner Peace*, Dr. Wayne Dyer[1] introduces an important concept—that of "striving-yet-never-arriving." If you can relate to that phrase, could it be that you have not taken the time to truly plan your life and your work? In this section, we will look at tips on how you can get organized. Later, we will examine how you can learn as much, if not more, from the downs as from the ups. This is a concept that may get you out of the striving-yet-never-arriving syndrome.

Many of us spend more time planning a vacation or wedding, doing comparison shopping to purchase a pair of shoes, coffee maker or car than we do in planning our careers or lives.

Once you've done your work planning and setting SMART model goals, you must begin to implement your plan. Most people will not succeed with their goals if their life and work are not organized. I'd like to offer the following ways to straighten up and organize your life.

7 Steps to Straighten Up Your Life

1. Organize your professional and personal life as a package deal and recognize both must be together in order for you to be successful at each one.
2. Acknowledge and analyze your state of disorganization, then take action to correct things.
3. Find a place for everything and put the most frequently used items nearby in a location where they are easily reachable.
4. Once you've found a place for everything, put everything back in its place.
5. Handle things once, stay focused and finish tasks.
6. Develop short and long range plans and make mid-course corrections as needed.
7. Write it down. Then:
   - Act on it.
   - Check your progress and maintain your priorities.
   - Mutate and reinvent yourself regularly to keep up with changes caused by circumstances beyond your control.

WHAT TO DO IF YOU'RE TIME-BANKRUPT AND OVER-SCHEDULED

You may be thinking, "This all sounds great, but my life feels totally over-booked and I'm completely time bankrupt." Do you catch yourself saying any of the following?

Sound Familiar?
- "I feel 'time-bankrupt' and don't have enough hours in the day to accomplish everything at work much less in my life."

---

1 Dyer, Wayne. *10 Secrets for Success and Inner Peace*. Carlsbad, CA: Hay House, 2001.

- "The day just flies by, and at the end of too many, I'm asking myself, 'What have I done? Where has the time gone?'"
- "I have nothing to show for all the time I've put in today."
- "I'm running faster, but not moving farther in my life or work."

The reality is that there are only 24 hours in a day, and you can't create more time in your life. So, what can you do if any of the above apply to you? The answer is that you can learn how to use the time you have more efficiently and, therefore, become more effective in your LwL² journey. What strategies can you use to be better with time? Let's begin by looking at time wasters in your life and work. We will identify where you are losing time, then outline strategies to gain it back. Let's start by completing an exercise to examine your biggest time problem areas.

Quick Quiz
Biggest Time Problem Areas
Check off your three biggest problem areas, then complete the questions on the next page.

1. Always putting out fires so I fall behind on my work	
2. Checking email frequently so they don't pile up	
3. Not enough time to plan	
4. Can't say no and get stuck with too much work	
5. Chit chat and talking with people who drop by	
6. Getting interrupted by people with questions	
7. Inability to get organized at home and/or at work	
8. Can't get motivated	
9. Taking on too much and stretching too far	
10. Lack of communication or direction from my boss	
11. Too many meetings	
12. Paper work and/or filing piles up	
13. Switching from task to task; not finishing things one at a time	
14. Constant telephone interruptions	
15. Direction or goals haven't been established	
16. Unclear about responsibility	
17. Procrastination or waiting until the last minute	
18. Not enough information to do my job properly	
19. Can't easily locate things in my work space	
20. I travel too much so I can't keep organized	
21. Little self discipline	
22. Losing things (keys, glasses, to-do lists)	
23. Inadequate filing systems	
24. People not getting back to me by a deadline	
25. Not getting clear directions	
26. Not giving clear directions	
27. Running out of supplies	
28. Computer too slow or equipment too old to do my job	
29. Having to answer the same questions from customers	
30. Going to meetings I really don't need to attend	
31. Work, telephone calls or email that should be handled by others	
32. Can't find things on my computer easily	
33. Others (please list)	
34.	

Time Problem Areas Analysis

After completing the exercise and identifying your top three problem areas, please answer these questions:

My top three time problem areas in order of worst to least are:

1. _____
2. _____
3. _____

Why are the items I checked a problem?

1. _____
2. _____
3. _____

What steps could I take (if any) to minimize or correct my time problem areas?

1. _____
2. _____
3. _____

Create a To-Do List

To more efficiently organize yourself, create a To-Do List:

- **Write** down what you have to do and review the list daily. This can be done at the beginning, end, or middle of the day. You should select a time that works best for you. So that this activity becomes a routine, preferably you will undertake this task at the same time each day.
- **Prioritize** your tasks each day.
- **Update** your To-Do List regularly. Check periodically throughout the day on your progress and update as needed.
- **Don't be afraid to add to** or **delete from** your list as new items surface and you reassess your priorities.

Create a Personal To-Do List

Creating To-Do Lists should not just be limited to work-related tasks. Remember to compose To-Do Lists for personal tasks that must be completed. This can include a

- Grocery store list
- Medication/Pharmacy list
- Health food store list
- Shopping list
- What to take on vacation list
- Activities related to family, significant others, hobbies, and social, civic and religious activities

---

Creating To-Do Lists destroys/devastates impulse buying.

To-Do List Yearly

Many people find it helpful to develop a yearly To-Do List. If you decide to establish one, make sure you follow these steps:

1. Review the list at least twice a year.
2. Prioritize then re-prioritize it as time progresses.
3. Update and think regularly about what (if anything) you must do now to accomplish things on your list this year.

Times to Review My To-Do List

Commit to review your To-Do List during these four times:

I. To-Do List: DAILY
   Time of day: _____

II. To-Do List: WEEKLY
   Day of the week (circle one):

   Monday   Tuesday   Wednesday   Thursday

   Friday   Saturday   Sunday

III. To-Do List: MONTHLY
   Day of the Month: _____

IV. To-Do List: YEARLY
   Two times a year (circle *two* months):

   January   February   March   April

   May   June   July   August

   September   October   November

   December

Prioritizing Your To-Do List

Once you've thought through the tasks to be done on your To-Do List, you'll need to prioritize them in order to decide in what order and when you will complete them. You may want to use your Mind Map to help you to better identify such tasks. You can also use this form to help you prioritize better. Think about your To-Do List and follow these instructions:

I. List five items on your To-Do List

II. Prioritize each system by selecting a number
1 = Must be done today
2 = Second priority items
3 = Would like to do today, but can wait to complete

III. Rank the list from the highest to lowest priority number one to five

I. To-Do List	*II. Priority* (1 = Must do 2 = Second priority 3 = Can wait)	*III. Rank Order #1–5*
1.		
2.		
3.		
4.	.	
5.		

RECLAIMING YOUR ENERGY BY DISCOVERING YOUR MOST AND LEAST PRODUCTIVE TIMES

I was on a business trip and stopped to pick up some laundry from a dry cleaner near the Smithsonian's National Air and Space Museum and NASA's Headquarters in Washington, D.C. The clerk at that store said something that took my thinking to a place that was out of this world.

I had just finished jogging around the Mall and was picking up the suit that I would be wearing to my business meeting that day at NASA. She commented how nice it must be to have enough energy to jog on a beautiful day in the Nation's Capital. She went on to declare

that she must "reclaim her energy." What a fabulous concept, I thought, as I stared into space.

After understanding what your life's purpose is and what makes your heart smile, begin to think about how you can incorporate more of that "thing" which energizes you, whatever it is, into your life. You will make quicker and longer strides on your To-Do List if you also begin to analyze (if you don't know this already) what are your peak energy times. Then, reclaim your energy by doing tasks you've yearned to accomplish during those peak periods.

For example, you may discover that you are the proverbial night owl and creative juices just start to jump around midnight. For me, 3 A.M. to 6 A.M. is when my creativity flows endlessly. At midnight, however, I typically can't utter a coherent word. Here is an exercise you can use to reclaim your energy by discovering your most and least productive times.

Reclaiming Your Energy Exercise

To reclaim your energy, you must first analyze what are your peak energy times. Take this exercise to help you to understand yours.

Please circle one and/or a range of times that fit the following.

Peak times for me (indicate time of day and A.M. or P.M.):

1. My most creative and productive (work and brain-power-wise) times (circle all relevant times):
(A.M.) 12 1 2 3 4 5 6 7 8 9 10 11
(P.M.) 12 1 2 3 4 5 6 7 8 9 10 11

2. I can tackle most physical/manual work and/or exercise best at (circle all relevant times)

(A.M.) 12 1 2 3 4 5 6 7 8 9 10 11
(P.M.) 12 1 2 3 4 5 6 7 8 9 10 11

3. The best times to relax and/or rest during waking hours are (circle all relevant times):

(A.M.) 12 1 2 3 4 5 6 7 8 9 10 11
(P.M.) 12 1 2 3 4 5 6 7 8 9 10 11

4. My best time to sleep is (circle all relevant times):

(A.M.) 12 1 2 3 4 5 6 7 8 9 10 11
(P.M.) 12 1 2 3 4 5 6 7 8 9 10 11

5. The number of hours of sleep I require to be refreshed enough to start my day and continue it for 14–16 hours before the next period of sleep is needed: _____

6. My best time for romantic interludes are (circle all relevant times):

(A.M.) 12 1 2 3 4 5 6 7 8 9 10 11
(P.M.) 12 1 2 3 4 5 6 7 8 9 10 11

7. My most effective time to meditate/pray/be silent and listen to my inner voice is (circle all relevant times):

(A.M.) 12 1 2 3 4 5 6 7 8 9 10 11
(P.M.) 12 1 2 3 4 5 6 7 8 9 10 11

Once you've analyzed your peak energy times, use the graph below to chart your peak times.

My Most and Least Productive Times

Time Periods	Most Productive (list activities)	Least Productive (list activities)
Early morning 4 A.M.–6 A.M.		
Morning 7 A.M.–9 A.M.		
Mid-morning 10 A.M.–noon		
Early afternoon 1 P.M.–3 P.M.		

Time Periods	Most Productive (check one)	Least Productive (check one)
Late afternoon 4 P.M.–5 P.M.		
Early evening 6 P.M.–8 P.M.		
Mid-evening 9 P.M.–11 P.M.		
Late evening 12 A.M.–3 A.M.		

LET'S GET ORGANIZED—STEPS TO STRAIGHTEN UP YOUR LIFE

If You Fail to Plan, You Plan to Fail

- Schedule time for yourself to do proper short and long range planning
- Invest time in planning to "save" time
- Keep your SMART goals in mind
- Plan for projects by prioritizing tasks and creating To-Do Lists for work and personal chores
- Execute, track and evaluate your progress

Write It Down

Experts say that which is written down is completed. Write down what you need to do to remain organized.

- Act on it
- Check your progress, maintain your order, then mutate regularly

Act On What You Write Down

- Build a contingency plan for worst case scenarios
- Make mid-course corrections
- Schedule clean up days to reorganize your office and/or have space and to purge things from hard copy and/or electronic files.
- Learn as much, if not more, from the downs as the ups.

Chapter 28

LEARNING AS MUCH, IF NOT MORE, FROM THE DOWNS AS FROM THE UPS

TO LwL² WE ALSO HAVE TO REALIZE THAT we can learn as much, if not more, from the downs as from the ups. I learned of this particular issue two weeks before my 40th birthday. Since the age of 33, I had been a Vice President at a Harvard Medical School Affiliated Teaching Hospital. Even though I had been in hospital administration for so many years, I had never personally seen a person die. Of course, people like me were administrators who bossed people around, but didn't necessarily have to participate in seeing such difficult things.

Two weeks before my 40th birthday, I saw my first person die. It was an unbelievably profound experience, and I will never forget it—because that person was my mother.

I learned so much from that situation. I was at a point in my career when I really needed to do something else with my life but I had the golden handcuffs on—six figure salary and bonuses, great benefits, the prestige of working as an executive at a Harvard affiliated hospital—all that sort of stuff. I didn't want to leave the comfort of that situation, but I knew I was ready to move on to a new chapter in my life. I also realized that I was not going to move into a higher position, such as the presidency of a Harvard affiliated hospital. I was the wrong gender, age, and race—and I wasn't a doctor. Instinctively, I knew it wasn't going to happen for me in my lifetime.

So after my mom's death, I began a path of learning as much from the downs as from the ups. I saw my mother die at a young age, and she had dreamed dreams and some of them didn't get realized.

I realized I needed to stop dreaming my dreams and start living them!

From that seemingly horrific experience, I came to understand that life is short. As we are learning to Love our work by Loving our Life, we've got to begin building our dreams and our life's purpose before our time runs out. I often hear my mom's voice telling me one of her favorite sayings, "Make hay while the sun is high."

Tomorrow is promised to no one. I knew that if I truly wanted to live a life like my mom's—such that when she left this earth *so* many people loved her—I needed to change my life. I decided to stop dreaming my dreams and make them materialize.

For a long time I had yearned to start my own business. From that "downer" experience, I gained the courage and insight to make that move. At age 41 in 1994, the year after my mom's death, I established my company, Field's Associates, Inc. I adore my job and often thank the Heavens for making that dream come true.

Wise Words

I've missed more than 9000 shots in my career. I've lost almost 300 games. 26 times, I've been trusted to take the game winning shot and missed. I've failed over and over and over again in my life. And that is why I succeed.

—Michael Jordan

Fortune Cookie/Tea Bag Tag

There are many new opportunities that are being presented to you. Stop dreaming. Start acting.

—Fortune cookie, opened 11/10/03

Wise Words

When you don't like your situation, think about what options you have. My philosophy is "Giving up is NOT an option!" The thought of quitting is so depressing anyway.

—Cecilia Shipley

What must we do to move on after we've experienced some "downs?" We can learn lessons from some people who experienced the Great Summer Blackout of 2003 in New York City.

LEARNING AS MUCH, IF NOT MORE, FROM THE DOWNS AS FROM THE UPS

LESSONS FROM THE GREAT BLACKOUT OF AUGUST 14, 2003 AND SEABISCUIT

The date was Saturday, August 16, 2003. Early that morning, I received a call from Janine Fondon, a colleague and friend who had just returned from what was to have been a routine business trip to New York City. While she *did* arrive in New York City on Thursday morning to prepare for a photo shoot with two other prominent women, Alicia Evans and Gina Russell

Stevens, for their book, *Mosaica*, she left the Big Apple and never got to the photo shoot.

Why? The Great Blackout of August 14, 2003 intervened.

In my conversation that early Saturday morning, Janine filled me in on what it was like to be an active participant in that historic event that left 50 million people without power. After it was over, it was viewed as having a greater effect on the economy—as well as on peoples' lives—than similar blackouts had done in 1965 and 1977.

After speaking with Janine, I took a break from my hectic writing schedule to attend a movie, *Seabiscuit*, with my family. Both the conversation with Janine and the movie *Seabiscuit*, made me think about the second part of our #7 Secret: Learn as Much, If Not More, from the Downs as from the Ups.

In our quest to discover what it means to learn as much, if not more, from the downs as from the ups, I'd like to begin by sharing two stories. The first is written by Janine Fondon, and it is about her reflections on the lessons learned as she was one of the 50 million people who experienced the blackout.

After hearing her story, we'll turn our attention to the summer of 2003's hot and sizzlin' "feel-good" movie, *Seabiscuit*. You'll learn that just because someone is down and broken doesn't mean he should be killed—just because someone is injured and down, regardless of the injury, he can be fixed.

Wise Words

Sometimes stretching is good, even though it might not feel like it when you're going through it.

—Pam Covington, NASA

"Mental hardness forms when you face adversity."

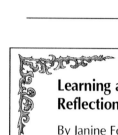

Learning as Much, If Not More, from the Downs as from the Ups: Reflections on How I Survived the NYC 2003 Blackout

By Janine Fondon

TODAY IS SATURDAY, AUGUST 16. IT IS TWO days since the NYC Blackout on Thursday, August 14 and I'm just returning to my home today from my ordeal. I was on a business trip to NYC and had driven there Thursday morning from Massachusetts. I was preparing for a major photo shoot on Friday. I was at a beauty parlor getting my hair done. I was under the hair dryer when my world went dark.

When the lights went out, people kicked into gear from 9-11. One man I'll call the Sergeant, went into leadership mode. He went into the back and brought out candles. He lit them and told everyone they should hit the bathroom before going out and someone volunteered to stand outside the bathroom because we couldn't shut the door because there was no light. Everyone used the bathroom and they placed candles on various locations of the stairway so we could see our way out of the building.

I was with two friends and I hadn't eaten all day so I definitely needed to find food and something to drink quickly before the stores closed. We bombard-ed the first street vendor we saw and purchased some chicken shish kabob sandwiches. We got out into 5th Avenue and there were all these people—no police, but just a sea of people. We found some-one who was selling a $15 flashlight and thank goodness we purchased it.

We started walking to my hotel. I was on 46th and Madison and my hotel was near Times Square on 7th and 53rd. We walked up 5th and 6th Ave. and of course the crowds! That was the most over-whelming piece. As we walked in the sea of people, to my surprise they kept calm and said things like, "We've been through 9-11 and we can get through anything and we'll get through this, we're New Yorkers," they said with gusto. I was amazed at their resiliency. They kept repeating this was the greatest city on earth.

When we got to Rockefeller Center, people in stores were battering down the hatches to secure their businesses. I got to my hotel, the Sheraton, at 7th and 53rd. Luckily, I had my email confirmation because they were only allowing people who could prove that they were guests to enter. They opened their restaurant and gave free food and drinks to everyone. The hotel also made provisions for guests to make phone calls to loved ones—a very nice touch. My husband and daughter were supposed to join me on the trip and at the last moment decided to stay home because she wanted to go to summer camp and he had a lot of work to do. Luckily, I was registered for three people so my two friends who were stranded with me could stay, because they couldn't get to their homes in Long Island by walking.

So the good news was that I had a hotel room and the bad news was that the room was on the 23rd floor. We had to walk 46 flights of stairs, huffing and puffing, to our room that was luckily still cool on that sweltering summer day. Once there, however, we had no communication. Remember it takes electricity to power TVs, radios and computers. The stairwells had been pitch black so our $15 flashlight came in very handy!

You have to count your blessings—we weren't mugged or didn't have to sleep in the street that night—or have to walk to Brooklyn or Long Island in heels.

Lessons Learned re: LwL^2

What does all this mean in regards to LwL^2?

1. Survival is an important thing and when the chips fall you have to pull it together and make sure you survive.

2. We never found an ATM that was working and people weren't taking credit cards. Lesson: Keep some money with you for emergencies.

3. I had driven to NY and didn't fill up with gas before I left Massachusetts so my gas was low and there was traffic everywhere. Lesson: Don't let your gas tank get too low.

4. We couldn't find very many places open for food. We found a pizza place and got six slices of pizza and three sodas, priceless at $35. Lesson: Before you're starved, find reasonably priced food and water if you're in emergency mode.

5. Hotel guests at other properties weren't as fortunate and the establishments closed their doors (some took this measure because they felt they couldn't assure the security of their guests) and left them to sleep on the sidewalk or wherever that night. Do you think those patrons will ever return to those places to stay? In contrast, we were treated so well by the Sheraton I'm sure that they lost a lot of money that night making sure their guests had enough food and beverages and were comfortable. I know they will gain more financially in the future because of those gestures.

6. I was in NYC because of my work and so I was able to do some great brainstorming with my friends.

7. I thought a lot about if I would ever see my husband, daughter and friends again. Although you're in survival mode, your priority becomes concern for those that are nearest and dearest to you. The photo shoot that I was in NYC to do was of no relevance then—how my husband and child were doing *was* important. Work commitments were not physically possible and in the final scheme of things were not even important. A lesson to learn here is that although you have work priorities, ultimately the personal side of your life must be your main focus.

In summary, remember through it all that to LwL^2, reshift your priorities and don't be totally consumed by overwhelming events when they occur.

SEABISCUIT—LEARNING FROM THE DOWNS

After a grueling week of writing and meeting with clients, I needed a break. My family decided to go to the movies and see one of those movies that a number of people had recommended as a "must see."

On the drive to the movies, I told my daughter and her father about the conversation I had with Janine Fondon and her experiences being caught in the Great Blackout of 2003. Imagine that for most of the time on Thursday and Friday (August 14 and 15) she didn't even know what was really going on because New York had no electricity and she couldn't watch TV, listen to the radio or read about it in the newspaper because they couldn't even produce newspapers in NYC!

After paying for our tickets then getting to our seats with popcorn, M&Ms, Starbursts and Gummy Bears in tow, we spent an enjoyable, and as the old song said, "Lazy, hazy, crazy day of summer" relaxing in a cool theater, watching the much talked about movie, *Seabiscuit*. Little did I know at the time that not only would I benefit from the relaxing down time with my family, but that I'd pick up some valuable and insightful thoughts from the flick about learning as much, if not more, from the downs as from the ups.

Seabiscuit, the Story

Seabiscuit is the story of the champion racehorse, Seabiscuit, who in the 1930s and 40s became one of the greatest racing horses who ever lived. Seabiscuit's lineage spelled championship racehorse, as he had been the son of a champion. Based on his background, Seabiscuit was destined to follow in the family's hoof steps. However, due to his early poor and downright pitiful performances in horse racing, Seabiscuit was a nose length away from being sent to the glue factory.

As fate would have it, after a long series of events, a gentleman by the name of Howard and his wife purchased the down and out horse and vowed to turn him into the winner they knew he could become. The cast of characters who were assembled to help Seabiscuit (remember he was a few hoof steps away from being sent to horse heaven at the glue factory) were straight from an episode of a soap opera that would be called The Down and the Restless. This motley crew had been so beaten down by life after the Great Depression that they were crawling around with the snakes and the only place for them to go was up.

The cast of characters included:

The owner—Howard was a self-made man and a poster child for the rags-to-riches story. He was a survivor and rebuilt his fortune after the Depression but still encountered a string of bad luck. His only child, a son, was killed tragically in an automobile accident, and his marriage subsequently collapsed and his wife left him. He remarried into a "May-December" relationship, and his young wife is in the process of teaching him to live again when they purchase Seabiscuit at the rock bottom cost of $2,000.

Seabiscuit—Of course, the star of this down-and-out-then-up, rags-to-riches riches-to-rags-and-back-to-riches story. Whereas Seabiscuit was born with a silver spoon in his mouth and possessed winners circle genes, in his early years, he trotted down a path that was disgracing the family reputation. As opposed to many championship racehorses that were massive in build, Seabiscuit was tiny and puny in comparison.

Seabiscuit appeared to be lazy, so the owner had attempted to beat the laziness out of him by repeatedly striking him, almost mercilessly, on his left side. All of the whacking seemed to build up Seabiscuit's resolve to show them who was in charge by underperforming and losing races despite the beatings.

He was frequently sold as owners grew tired of the horse's temperament and decided to cut their losses as they realized they had acquired the black sheep of the champion racehorse family. Seabiscuit, it seemed, would always be lazy, unmotivated and good for nothing except to lose race after race. To make matters even worse, Seabiscuit cost them more money to feed than some of the horses who *did* win, because although Mr. Seabiscuit was tiny, he could eat double the amount, or more, than the average horse!

The trainer—A trainer working for Howard discovered Seabiscuit and convinced Howard to take a chance on the incorrigible horse. The trainer peered into the eyes and soul of Seabiscuit and felt that in the right environment and with the correct coaching, Seabiscuit could indeed achieve his family's championship legacy.

He was able to convince Howard and his wife to purchase Seabiscuit. In regards to learning as much, if not more, from the downs as from the ups, the trainer firmly believed that just because a horse like Seabiscuit was damaged goods and even injured, he wasn't dead. The trainer felt that with time, perseverance and understanding, the horse could be fixed and turned into a champion.

The jockey—The man who rode Seabiscuit is the last of the main characters. He was angry because his parents had abandoned him after the Great Depression that occurred after the Stock Market crashed in October 1929. Before that time, the jockey had come from a well-to-do family. That same family lost everything after the Depression. With 25% unemployment, the jockey's father, like so many people, couldn't find enough work to make ends even start to come together, much less meet.

The mother and father knew that their son had a gift for riding and training horses. As difficult a decision as it must have been for them, they decided to leave him with a man who owned a stable and could use their son to help him out around the barn. With the tears in their eyes and lumps of sadness in their throats and voices, they bid farewell to their dear son, letting him know that this was the best thing for him even though he wanted to leave with them. In addition, they vowed to keep in contact with him. This was a promise, however, they did not keep.

The man he worked for at the stables also proved to be a slave driver of sorts who beat him up when his horse lost races—which was almost always. He also made him perform the dirtiest of dirty chores around the stable.

As the jockey matured and developed, his anger about his situation was unleashed upon the world. He lashed out by fighting, both figuratively and literally as a boxer. However, life and his opponents in the ring kept knocking him down until he learned how to control and channel all his anger. He would get into fist fights *and* battles where his weapons were words. In both cases, he found himself failing miserably at relationships and in his career as a jockey.

After the owner of his house asked him, at one of those right-times-right-moment times, why he was so angry, he started to reflect on his personal answer to that question. After much soul searching, he came to grips with the anger he harbored towards his parents and what the Depression had done to break up his family—and make his once-stable and happy life come unglued and in need of repair.

Wise Words

When you go through tough and rocky turns on the highway of life, take time to understand what happened to get you down, then what steps you took to bring yourself back up and what you'll do so you never go back over that same bridge or travel through that same road again.

Practical Meaning Moment

The LwL[2] lessons from *Seabiscuit* are many:

1. Just because you've had some injury and/or are hurt, doesn't mean that you should give up on your life.

2. Know that when you've been knocked down, it doesn't mean you've been knocked out for good. You may be down for the count, but a T.K.O. hasn't been called. You may just need to pick yourself up, dust yourself off and start all over again.

3. If you are experiencing a hard time in your life, that is no reason to give up on everything. Focus, instead, on the blessings that you do have and the good things that exist for you even in the midst of the bad times. Also, take the time to analyze why you may be going through the low time and what you can learn from that experience.

4. The evil habits, ghosts and demons of the past that hurt you, caused you to feel abandoned and betrayed and/or caused your heart to harden, sour and not feel positive or happy must be dealt with before you can truly LwL[2].

Seabiscuit was angry because the previous owners had beaten him on his left side. Once his new trainer recognized that that was his blind spot/Achilles heel, he unlocked one of the things that could get in the horse's way of becoming the champion racehorse he was destined to be. The jockey was angry because his parents had left him. The owner had to get over the loss of his son who died and his wife who left him. The trainer first articulated the Seabiscuit theme—that just because something is hurt doesn't mean it has to be killed or that it doesn't have a reason to live and can't be taught to be a productive contributor to life.

Remember this message when you are struggling to LwL[2].

Tea Bag Tag Message

If you can't have the best, make the best of what you have.

—Yogi Tea Bag Tag; 9/28/03 (Sunday)

Wise Words

- What bad habits keep cropping up for you? Why do you let them continue to haunt you?
- What are the things that are destroying the peace, joy, happiness and contentment in your life? Your work?

When faced with a "down" time in your life, and deciding what to do, remember that your options are as follows:

- Continue to wallow in your misery and/or take it out on others.
- Adapt to what's wrong and say, "Que sera sera," it's something I'll never be able to control and I just have to live with it.
- Decide to change the situation and live with the consequences of that decision.

Wise Words

A problem is a chance for you to do your best.

—Duke Ellington, American jazz composer and performer

Breaking Through Your Blocks

By Ken Lizotte—President, Emerson Consulting

WHEN CONFRONTED WITH A BLOCK, MOST people's first impulse is to submit to it. Facing blocks can be overwhelming, as in "What do I do now? How will I ever deal with this one?" Your brain goes numb; no clear direction or strategy comes immediately to mind.

That's just a natural response, of course, designed to create time to process the problem and organize your thoughts toward a solution. The key is not to panic and give up. Instead, be patient and let yourself speculate, ruminate, ponder, and muse. You are working on your problem. Ultimately, your block is your belief that you may never find a solution. It's rarely something external.

Suppose your Personal Balance Statement reads, "I want to have a wonderful married life and a fabulous family." *Initially*, your brain blocks you away from knowing how to achieve this endeavor. Internally, you may even say, "Nice idea, but I don't even have a significant other, let alone a budding family."

First, be patient. Relax. Sit back in a soft chair. Take a load off. Breathe in slowly, then breathe out. Let thoughts or ideas roam freely in your mind and don't worry if they're not practical enough, or whether they're reasonable or logical or "implementable." Begin jotting down notes of whatever comes into your mind, and watch your ideas flow: blind dates, parties, joining a singles club. Some ideas might be downright wacky: interview potential mates in a supermarket, order your future spouse from a catalog, build a mate out of holograms. Write them down! As your ideas flow, strategies emerge. You are moving toward an answer.

Involve friends or colleagues in the process, and watch your ideas and potential solutions mushroom! Just be sure your friends and colleagues are positive. Make certain you and they allow *any* idea to emerge. Idea, idea, idea, bing, bing, bing! Traditionally this has been called brainstorming, though I like the more modern term "freewheeling." Be free, wheel your imagination around. Don't worry about the practicality of your ideas; just keep them flowing. Blocks hold you back, while generating positive ideas gets you moving.

You can always do something about your blocks, no matter how daunting. Not a penny to your name? Find a job, start a business, borrow money from a friend, panhandle on the street. Out of shape, low energy, always tired? See a doctor, join a gym, take vitamins, eat better, get more sleep. Can't stand your job? Children won't behave? There are always answers. (Yes, parents, for you too!) The decision that there aren't, or that you've already thought of everything, is just an excuse to quit looking.

BLOCK PORTRAIT

When you use your blocks in this way—clinging to them, refusing to initiate a blockbusting technique like freewheeling—you create excuses. But when you use your blocks to take you to a next step, they'll point you in a new direction and tell you what's missing. Once you've identified what you don't have but wish you did, you acquire self-knowledge about what you want and how to get it.

So, to effectively break through your blocks, first define them. In the space on the next page, draw a picture of yourself with your blocks around you. Show in your drawing how your blocks exert power over you. (What? You say you can't draw? You haven't picked up a box of crayons since first grade and you sure don't want to go back to picking any up right now? Good work! You've just defined another block. Dust yourself off, tear into those crayons or magic markers, and have fun busting through this too, your most up-to-the-minute block!)

MY BLOCK PORTRAIT

BLOCK WHEEL

Now let's connect your blocks to ideas that could lead to solutions. In each space of the wheel below, write in the name of one of your blocks. Outside the wheel, jot down ideas for breaking through them. Use as much space outside the wheel as you like. If you need to, draw a similar wheel on a larger sheet of paper.

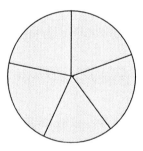

Blocks of some kind will always be with you. Besides, if people didn't have problems and blocks, how would they learn, grow, achieve? Like it or not, life would get pretty boring. In many ways, dealing with blocks is really what life is all about. So always see your blocks as signposts for moving forward while you freewheel down the road.

The Freewheeling Process

- Relax, settle your mind, and breathe slowly.
- Let ideas, thoughts, and pictures float freely into your mind.
- Jot down notes of as many ideas, thoughts, and mental pictures as you can.
- Do not censor yourself. Weed out impractical ideas later.
- After at least ten to fifteen minutes, take a break, and then come back for a fresh look at your list.
- Circle all ideas you find intriguing.
- Next, circle all the ideas you'd like to implement or explore further.
- Make a separate list of the ideas you've circled. What action steps can you take to bring them to life?
- List all your action steps, then set a time frame for implementing them.
- Begin taking action, and watch your blocks melt away!

BLOCKBUSTING MADE EASY

Once you are able to define what your blocks are, breaking them becomes simply a matter of faith and positive thinking. You *can* break through any block, no matter how challenging. To believe otherwise, as we have said, is to harbor an excuse not to try.

I favor a simple three-step method for breaking through your blocks. Although simple may not always mean easy—some blocks are tougher to break than others—this process will get you started (often the hardest part) and move you toward victory.

My three-step process for breaking blocks goes like this:

Step 1: Believe You Can!

Sounds Pollyanna-ish, Norman Vincent Peale-ish, Forrest Gump-ish, we know, but you've really got to start with this one. Try *not* believing you can break through your blocks and see how far you get. Dr. Charles Garfield, a motivation expert and author of a study on peak performers, says that the greatest single characteristic of those who achieve

their goals is the simple "belief that you can do it." Not education, not gender, not age, not strength, not intelligence, not contacts nor anything else, Garfield proclaims. His voluminous research on peak performers is clear: Believing in yourself is paramount.

The terrible anxieties and self-doubt that infect people, the sheer terror of facing some of their blocks, and a deep confusion about which strategy to employ frequently hold people back from giving their blockbreaking efforts the requisite "old college try." So commit yourself to doing whatever you have to by believing in your capacity to follow through successfully. Although you may be clueless about how you will eventually pull it off, you cannot begin this process in an optimal way without believing you can win.

Step 2: Imagine Yourself Doing It!

Even when you find yourself in mortal fear of your block, you still have the power to imagine what life would be like without it. Fantasize that this block is no longer in your life, that you've gained dominion over it. *Wow!* Just imagine! What would things be like otherwise? What would you be like?

Suppose you're scared to death of public speaking. (Surveys show, in fact, that more people fear public speaking than death, anyway!) You want to do something about it; you feel that public speaking skills would advance you professionally and help you grow personally. You've decided that you can overcome your fears (Step 1 accomplished!) but now you've got to figure out how.

Relax in a soft chair or on a couch or sit by a bubbly brook or in your garden. Have a cup of tea with you or a bottle of water, something restful (no drugs or alcohol). Breathe in slowly, breathe out. Take in your surroundings. Let images float into your mind, then float away. Quiet yourself.

Now, observe yourself striding confidently into a Toastmasters' Club meeting at your local library. You shake hands with everyone and smile and take in the camaraderie. Yes, you're a little nervous, that's natural, but you're glad to be there.

You watch yourself volunteer to be the first speaker, then smoothly execute your speech. Gracefully, you accept feedback from your attentive, discerning audience, listening carefully to all comments. This feedback is good; it will help you get better at public speaking. You love being here! You're a public speaker!

That's all you need to do in Step 2—welcome pictures and images into your head, observe yourself acting and living a life you *want*. See yourself handling the gritty details. Hey, the best thing here is that this doesn't cost you anything, and on top of that, nobody can tell you that you didn't do it right! Have some fun! Don't worry about a thing. Just imagine yourself handling this in a completely different way!

Step 3: Act as if You've Already Done It!

Susan Jeffers titled her book about breaking through fears (blocks) this way: *Feel the Fear and Do It Anyway.* The title truly says it all.

Return to our previous example of public speaking. Now it's time to physically *go* to a Toastmasters' Club meeting. You've imagined doing it, but you can't deny that you're still more than a little shaky about it.

While imagining yourself doing this, you sketched out a script to follow. That directs your brain to coordinate your behavior in a particular way. So you drive to the library on the appointed evening and bravely push yourself through the door of the Toastmaster's Club meeting room. Despite how you feel inside ("Whoever's knees are rattling, would they please stop?"), you try playing the part of a calm, and collected novice speaker. You're not trying to put on airs here you just want to convey that you know you can do this and that your nervousness will not defeat you. You're up to the challenge. You're in the right room.

If you keep thinking this way, behaving as though you are more confident than you in fact really feel, one night (maybe the first night!) you'll surprise yourself as you notice how confident you've become. You'll be excited to be there and you'll actually be looking forward to stepping up to the podium (though probably still a little nervous). Somewhere along the way you'll have stopped being terrified. You'll officially be a public speaker and your block will be gone!

BALANCING ACT: ALICE HALE

For more than twenty years, Alice Hale had felt completely secure in her career. A high school history teacher, she'd been appointed head of the department at age 22, an event that would set the tone of her work and life for two decades. She could ignore recessions and job market turmoil and just go to work and do her job. As a divorced single mother, she could raise her son, Tim, and never worry about the outside world.

But after she passed age 40, Alice's life changed. The cutbacks and layoffs and downsizings she'd been dimly hearing about; stories of work and family lives getting torn apart in private industry throughout the 1980's, suddenly came slashing her way. Her town's school board began chopping up its budget and eliminating entire departments. Once sacred cows, these departments had now been rendered obsolete, untenable, a luxury. She got word about her own dismissal from the newspapers: Her safe, secure, comfortable, familiar routine would be over at the end of June.

"I have no connections. I'm too old, I'm not qualified for anything else," she told anyone who would listen. She felt her life beginning to unravel. "I only know teaching. What will I do? What? I'm just terrified!"

Alice worried about other blocks, too, great, lurking internal ones. As she considered moving herself from here to there, she confronted a truth about herself.

"I'm a classic self-saboteur," she confided to me. "Whenever I try to change my life I make sure I don't succeed. I'll do everything I'm supposed to, everything people say you've got to do to make progress, but I keep resisting the process all the way. I refuse to let myself succeed."

Balance Check

- If your own work life faced a sudden end or radical change, how would you react? Would you share Alice's panic? What personal blocks of yours might contribute to your fears?
- What's your vision of where you'd like to go, whether you current work life

continues or not? Refer to your Personal Balance Statement.

- What course of action might you follow to solve a crisis such as Alice encountered? Do you have any specific action steps in mind?
- How might you have advised Alice as she brought her fears and concerns to you?

In the midst of this crisis Alice surprised herself. With my guidance, she began by "de-whelming" herself, breaking down the scary big picture she faced, downsizing it into small, realizable steps. That got her started. With each step she advanced a little further down the path. And each time she stepped off, she automatically left an old place and arrived somewhere new—new vistas, new resources, fresh possibilities.

By taking such beginning steps, Alice got herself into gear, despite her terror. What form did her steps take? She simply began chatting with people. That was all at first, just chatting folks up. Here's my story, sad but true. Everyone she met got an earful—grocers, mailmen, gas station attendants, old friends. Astonishingly, the mere act of reporting her personal crisis to others released many of her blocks. People returned positive feedback to her about all her concerns.

"I'm trying to find out what I want to do next, but I'm not sure what that is," she told anyone and everyone who would listen. "I'm looking for a new opportunity." Alice's openings were short, sweet, and candid. Now lob the ball back.

Balance Check
- If Alice had approached you, how would you have lobbed her ball back? What advice or suggestions might you have given her?
- Would you be able to carry out Alice's plan of action? What blocks might get in your way? What are some ideas for breaking through these blocks?
- Can you imagine another course of action for breaking this crisis down into manageable steps?

Nearly all the people Alice talked to had some kind of idea, suggestion, or tale of their own life turnarounds to offer her. Many truly great conversations ensued, including not a few invaluable ideas from totally unexpected sources. Soon she had so many options to explore there was no time left for panic, self-denigration, or hopelessness. She could make this change, whatever it was going to be. She really could.

All these interactions, all this chit-chat with a purpose, propelled Alice Hale into a new image of herself and of what life could be. She put all the pieces together, including her home life with her son, Tim. She could spend more time with him, help him grow, pay attention. She could feel more creative and confident and personally powerful than she'd ever felt working at the school.

Someone somewhere told her about a man who wanted to sell a profitable home-based newsletter. After speaking with others who ran similar businesses, Alice quickly came to understand, to her amazement, how eminently qualified she was: Her excellent organizing and editing skills would enable her to set up the business easily in her own home, and she also began noticing a knack for coming up with creative ideas for better marketing the business. The ideas just started flowing through her head and she couldn't stop them. The more she thought of herself in this new role, in fact, the more she felt that she could manage this business even better than its present owner!

So she took out a second mortgage on her home, negotiated a fair price for all, and bought herself a new world.

"I'm independent now, in control of my life," she could later report to all those willing contacts and resources she'd met along the way. "Now no one can fire me—I'm running my own show. That forces me to be more creative, energized, and alive than I ever was at the school! It's up to *me* to keep making things happen now. That's still a scary thought at times, but not so scary as the idea that I couldn't make my life work out the way I want to."

Balancing Check
- Could you have taken the risk Alice took? Would a home-based business appeal to you? What positive attributes and talents could you bring to such a work life?

- If a home-based business does not appeal to you, what opportunity would you rather have stumbled upon? What talents and skills could you bring to such an opportunity?
- Are there any particular aspects of your home life or your personal goals that might be affected by a work-change crisis such as this one? How could your personal life and goals be advanced positively by such a crisis? What blocks would get in the way of your turning this crisis into an opportunity for healthy growth?

As so often transpires when people break through blocks and start taking command of their lives, Alice's universe turned around completely as a result of her decisions. In the midst of all this remarkable personal change, in fact, her school reinstated her department and offered her her old job back. Immediately she thought, "How dare they! They just got me used to the idea that they don't want me anymore, and I finally came to accept that. Now they want to drag me back. The arrogance!" My, how the lady had changed!

But Alice reframed the dilemma as a window of opportunity, a challenge to her new assertiveness. What if she could shape this into something that worked for her? Sure, I'll come back, she decided to tell the school principal, but first I want you to release my accumulated retirement funds to me, then hire me on a part-time basis only, and at hours of my own choosing. The old Alice would never have even thought of doing this negotiation.

So Alice Hale now works mornings as a teacher, the profession she carefully crafted throughout most of her adult life, and the rest of her day as a successful desktop publisher. She spends much time with her son, takes classes in areas of other interest, and runs her own life.

Do blocks and old doubts still rumble around in her head, taunting her, pushing at her? Sure, they keep trying to creep back in, she acknowledges, but they're no longer welcome, nor do they visit for very long. Whatever blocks come her way now, whatever terrors spring forward, she faces

them down. She's worked out her own definition of balance, and she's made it a reality.

Balance Check

- How prepared are you for a similar crisis in your work life? What action steps must you take to be fully prepared? What personal blocks hold you back from getting fully prepared?
- What if a similar crisis hit your home life? Do you do all you can to prevent it? Do you give full attention to your loved ones, keeping communication with them strong? Does your Personal Balance Statement reflect your desires for your personal life?
- What does our discussion of blocks imply for your overall thinking about behavior? Which blocks do you need to work on first? Which blocks do you eradicate completely? Which blocks get in your way the most?

BLOCKS WE HAVE KNOWN AND LOVED

Whether in our own lives, in the lives of our clients, or just kicking around the universe, we've encountered many of the same blocks over and over. They're listed in the accompanying worksheet. Some of these may be one of yours at the moment. Or, have you concocted a few that are unique to you? (If so, good work! Always acknowledge your creative achievements!)

MY OWN PET BLOCKS

Please check off all blocks in the following list that you recognize as your own. Then circle the top three blocks you've checked, those that are now holding you back the most. Finally, place a star beside the block most holding you back among your top three.

- ❏ Fear of failure
- ❏ Fear of success
- ❏ Procrastination
- ❏ Perfectionism
- ❏ Low self-confidence
- ❏ Negative thinking
- ❏ Lack of spontaneity
- ❏ Not a risk taker
- ❏ Too shy
- ❏ Not enough time
- ❏ Not enough money
- ❏ Not good-looking enough

- ❏ Fear of authority
- ❏ Always seeking approval
- ❏ Giving up too soon
- ❏ Thinking I'm not smart enough
- ❏ Regretting the past
- ❏ Laziness
- ❏ Concoctions of my own:

  _____

  _____

  _____

  _____

  _____

Once you've designated your Top Block, try out my three-step process. Then after you've vanquished this block from your life, or while you're still chipping away at it, get started on block 2. Gradually work your way down your whole list. Note: I said gradually. Don't take on all your blocks at once!

Recommended Reading

Laura Avakian, Vice President of Human Resources at the Massachusetts Institute of Technology, highly recommends this children's book that contains a very adult message: *Oh The Places You'll Go!* by Dr. Seuss.

Sometimes when people are in bad spots in their lives, they can make foolish decisions because they're driven by fear—not by opportunity.
—Robin Pedrelli, Vice President Program Director, Linkage Inc.

Wise Words
On Facing Failure

We put so much emphasis on success that the people who don't reach it think they are a failure.

—Robert Browne, Systems Engineer, Cisco Systems

The number 27 has great significance to me. There is a known writer who was turned down 27 times by publishers. His name was Dr. Seuss. What I've learned from his story is you should never give up. If there is something you want to do, never give up.

—Carl Wooten, Sales Training Manager, Sepracor

Wise Words

"There is no reward without risk. When you are faced with making a risky decision, ask yourself: Am I ready to drive my ship to the next destination?"

—Sarah Ducharme, President and CEO, New England Group

When faced with a down, consider these wise words:

"Absence can make the heart grow fonder of the things you've left or of those with which you've replaced it."

—Martha R. A. Fields

"When things start out bad for me and I get out of that proverbial 'wrong side of bed,' I know that I have to stop and ask myself—what must I do so I don't have just another downhill day?"

—Martha R. A. Fields

"It doesn't happen all at once, you become. It takes a long time. That's why it doesn't often happen to people who break easily, or have sharp edges, or who have to be carefully kept."

—Margery Williams, *The Velveteen Rabbit*

Recommended Reading

Susan Taylor, *Lessons in Living*. New York: Anchor Books, a division of Random House, 1998.

Quotes of Note

"Every day take the time and count your blessings."

—Patricia Whelchel, H.Q. Global Workplaces

"I approach one day at a time."

—Laura Melville, H.Q. Global Workplaces

"Little with content is great gain. For example, if you work and only get paid 50¢, it is more than you had before. That means if you get a little bit out of anything you do, you've gained a lot. That goes for whatever you do in life."

—Lisa Roberts

Chapter 29

Turning Tragedy into Triumph: Stories of Courage

IN WRITING THIS BOOK, I RAN ACROSS A number of people who relayed stories, inspirational messages, and quotes about turning tragedy into triumph. I'd like to share with you some of those insights in the pages that follow.

Keeping Your Faith as You Go Through the Downs— A Message from Gandhi

I first heard the following quote watching the movie *Gandhi*, which detailed the life of India's Mahatma Gandhi. After purchasing the videotape, whenever I got to the scene where Gandhi uttered this quote, I always went into a daze as I contemplated the profound words. This is a message I've run back to so many times in my life when the downs just seem so insurmountable and closing in for the kill. I hear these words and am reminded of how hope does spring eternal if you are just patient and focused.

Quote from the movie "Gandhi"

"When I despair, I remember that throughout history, the way of truth and light has always won. There have been tyrants and murderers and for a time they seem invincible. But, in the end they always fall. Think of this always."

—Mahatma Gandhi

Profile of Success

Francine Achbar—Principal, High Impact Marketing and Media

I had a career in television in a company that is a FORTUNE 500 company—CBS. I was a product of the women's movement, one of the first to get a professional job and move up. For women of my age, 57, that was a very heady time. We all got excited wearing our power suits and going to seminars on how to think like a man in business. We tried to model ourselves by copying aspects set by men.

I was Executive Producer of the News and Director of Programming and Client Marketing. That was exciting. A lot of us were into that whole Super-woman genre and wanted to have the career and the kids, but were tired often and felt time-bankrupt. I had no time to be a friend or go to lunch with my husband. We made a lot of money together, but were always over spent.

I thought about leaving my job, then looked into our pension plan. I only had to stay for eight more years to reap its benefits. I couldn't hang in there. The same-old, same-old and the aggressive corporate culture were too much. After 27 years, I left my high-powered job at CBS affiliate WBZ-TV in Boston.

I took a job in public TV in my early 50's and thought it would be less stressful and more cerebral. I really HATED it! I've developed a life philosophy—You learn more from the bad ones than the good ones. I obtained much knowledge from that experience. Aside from disliking my job, some major events occurred in my life. My husband was sick due to alcoholism, my two kids were transitioning from elementary to high school and I got breast cancer. Luckily, it hadn't spread and was fixable. Everything in my life was out of whack, but I was determined to get it back on track. In two years, I dumped my husband and filed for a divorce, went through breast cancer treatment and sold my house. I took a deep look into my life. I found that what resonated with me in my work were the community focused events and the power of TV to do good in the community.

I did some career counseling. One day, a woman said to me that I belonged in the non-profit fundraising world. She said, "You want to work in something beneficial and the non-profit world won't say to a woman in her 50's that you don't belong here." I took her word to heart and started a business with a colleague. We began a business marketing for non-profits where our primary focus was development people (fundraisers in non-profits). I took what I loved—writing, producing, marketing, getting to the emotional essence and selling—and put it into a business.

About one year after I completed radiation for breast cancer, I started my business when another life altering experience occurred. I was in the process of a divorce from my severely alcoholic husband when he died suddenly from a heart attack that was provoked by his drinking. Now, I was a single parent with two teenage daughters and the show had to go on. I had to get on with my life.

As I moved from tragedy to triumph, I became a much more compassionate person through it all. I think each stage of life has a different agenda. In my 20's, 30's and 40's, I wanted to play the corporate game and be a women's success story. In my 50's, I've learned life is too short to be doing something you don't like to do. I could never hang in a job just for the money. I'm coming to a point where I might do something different.

To Love your work and Life, you need to listen to yourself. Think hard if you're miserable about what needs to change. Lots of people are trapped and locked into financial commitments. If you give the job everything you have and still HATE it, that's usually a signal you need to think about doing something else. Sometimes it is easier for high-level women to walk away from corporate life than it is for men. They are not willing to pay the corporate price and give up Loving their Life. The process of realistically evaluating your financial obligations and trying to think constructively and creatively about finding a job that can reignite you can be difficult. So, get some help and explore what you can do realistically, aside from going to Vermont to ski or becoming a beach bum.

Wise Words

Dima Berdiev—Credit Analyst, Cambridge Trust

Someone once said that everybody falls, but not everybody gets up and moves on. Anyone in the professional environment can learn from this. We are all going to fall, but what do we do about getting up? What do we learn from it and how can it give us the energy and inspiration to succeed in the future?

Dr. Bruce Bonnevier—Vice President Human Resources, Shipley Company, L.L.C.

As Meatloaf says in one of his songs, "If the thrill is gone, then you gotta take it back." There are often many more things in my life, including my work life, that are in my control than I realize or am willing to readily admit. When I am stuck or dissatisfied, I stop and ask myself, "What am I doing to contribute to the problem?" Then, "What can I do to make it better?"

Wise Words

Rod Flakes—AIT Director, Commonwealth of Massachusetts for the Department of Mental Health
    Central Massachusetts Area

There are a few things I have learned about Loving your work by Loving your Life. You have to check out or validate your assumptions. Your assumptions will dictate how you behave. When you don't do this, you may operate in ways that may not be appreciated or be beneficial to you. Maintain a sense of humor. Challenges are always going to be there. In order to get through the most severe or daunting challenges, you must keep this sense of humor. It becomes your coping mechanism.

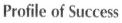

Profile of Success
Wendy Allen Williams

In 1991, I walked into my house in California late at night and ran into an intruder. He shot me in the head and left me for dead. I was in a coma for three months.

My mother, Jackie Benson Jones, flew from Boston to be with me. The neurologist told her that I would never be able to talk, walk, or see again in my life. My poor mother didn't know what I was going to do. A lot of people asked her what they could do to help. She has a strong belief in God and told them to just pray for me. It worked. God is so good. Prayer is so powerful. Today, I can walk, see and have the use of one hand. I've learned that sometimes, doctors aren't always right.

My mom and my brother took care of me and helped me to raise my son, Moses Williams, III. Today, he is 6'3", 21 years old and in college at the University of Massachusetts-Amherst. I am so proud of him.

I feel lucky to be alive and to have such a wonderful and supportive family. Now, I just want to help people who have problems. I want to show them that if I can do it, they can too!

Profile of Success

Marnee Walsh—Director of Human Resources, Archdiocese of Boston

Loving your work and Loving your Life is intertwined. My behaviors and attitudes are similar in my private and my business life.

People look like their job. For example, you have a mental picture of what people who are auditors look like, and they don't look like Human Resources people. A bookkeeper doesn't look like a Public Relations person. It is probably as much the behavior as what they look like—the reaching out versus the inward approach.

The key to LwL² revolves a lot around one's comfort level with his or herself. When you start playing to agendas that are not your own and trying to be someone you're not, your character changes and you are not as happy. If you force fit your values into a culture, then the conflict level impacts on your efficiency. You spend a lot of time figuring out what hats you should wear. That can also happen if there is a job that is above you in terms of your skill level. If you're not in the right job and you manage people, it can squeeze the life out of everyone around you. Some managers get into this when they can't delegate and are too controlling.

Personal Success

My success is due in part to my first job. My boss gave me responsibility. I was 23 and worked as an assistant buyer at Filene's department store, and she let me be a buyer and gave me a piece of the business and held me accountable. I'm sure I made some mistakes, but she let me do that and I didn't have to clear everything with her. That kind of mentoring I still remember today.

I am a strong believer in taking chances and trying something new. I've changed jobs and gone back thousands of dollars to start over—I took a chance and it worked.

What have I learned from my experiences?

The big highlight was being thrown away from a job and becoming unemployed. The process began when some colleagues and I were put into non-meaningful jobs for 30 days and then offered an early retirement benefit.

After 18 years on that job, I was now unemployed. At 55 years old, not knowing what I was going to do with the rest of my life was frightening. I turned that situation into a positive thing. I started putting out feelers and doing volunteer work.

Some individuals were so grateful for my help they put me in contact with people who gave me a job. I worked as a consultant for a year and learned many things about Boston politics and health care. Then I started a small consulting business and got a call from a friend who told me about help in a temporary position in Human Resources with the Archdiocese of Boston.

In looking back over my career, did I ever think I'd work at some of the jobs I did? NEVER! But the years since I was laid off have been the best, and I'm so happy that I went through that experience and learned from it. None of this would have happened if it hadn't been for adversity.

A Tip on How to Deliver Downbeat Information in an Upbeat Way

In 1982, Richard, my husband at the time, provided me with a valuable lifelong lesson on how to deliver bad news in a good way.

I worked at Children's Hospital Boston as the manager of Employee Relations and was waiting in the lobby of Vanderbilt Hall to have lunch with a colleague. Vanderbilt Hall was a popular eating establishment for Harvard medical students and Longwood-area hospital workers and was known for elegant food at reasonable costs.

I arrived before my colleague and waited amidst the bustling crowded throng of people waiting to feed their tummies.

Before working at Children's, I had worked for a consulting firm that had gone out of business. After experiencing a layoff, I was ecstatic to be gainfully employed again. After the layoff, one of the employees I had worked with committed suicide. Her job at the consulting firm had literally been her life. A lot of us who worked with this young woman had speculated that when her job ended she must have decided that her life was over as well.

I knew that the colleague I was meeting had known this woman, whom I will call Melinda (not her real name). When my colleague arrived, we shook hands, hugged and gave the obligatory, "How are you doing?" followed by

"It's *so* good to see you." I couldn't wait to ask her about Melinda's suicide and said without even thinking, "Wasn't it awful about Melinda committing suicide?"

My colleague with the look of utter shock across her face replied, "What do you mean Melinda committed suicide?"

Only until that moment did I have a clue that my colleague was indeed clueless about Melinda's tragic fate. I replied, "You didn't know that she was dead?"

In hindsight, I think it was the "dead" word that struck a cord in my colleague, who proceeded to cry uncontrollably. The vestibule where we were standing was teaming with Harvard medical students, residents and healthcare workers who, of course, stopped what they were doing to focus their attention on me and my colleague. I was embarrassed *beyond* words for her and for me.

Out of that situation, however, I learned an invaluable lesson about delivering bad news. After that event, I had a hard time concentrating for the rest of the day. Not only had it been a terrible scene at Vanderbilt Hall, but more importantly, I felt *awful* that I had been the bearer of bad news and had delivered the message in such a devastating way.

I went home that evening and talked about what had transpired with my husband, Richard. He provided me with some insight about delivering bad news, and I always follow his advice when confronted with that task.

Richard told me that whenever you are going to tell someone something that you know is bad news or you speculate that they may take what you say badly, take some time to prepare them for what you will be telling them. This could be in a situation where you have to relate information about a death, an illness, a tragedy, loss of a job—anything that is of a terrible or devastating nature.

He went on to say that you can prepare what you are about to say by using such things as

- "I've got some bad news to tell you."
- "What I am going to say might shock you or make you sad."
- "I'm sorry that I have to tell you this bad (or terrible) news."
- "I'm not sure you know about this (bad or awful) thing that has happened."

Telling people up front in this manner will help to brace them, and in many cases you, for the difficult message you'll deliver. Richard also warned me not to just assume that someone has heard the bad news. Yes, bad news, as the cliché goes, does travel fast, but in the case of my colleague, even though it had been about a month since Melinda's sad and untimely death, the news hadn't reached everyone in Boston.

So, the next time you are the bearer of bad news, think about softening the blow to others by using this technique. In the next chapter, we will focus our attention on how to effectively juggle all the balls in our work and life without having any of them fall.

IT'S ABOUT
SPINNING PLATES, NOT
WORK/LIFE BALANCE

Balancing Work/Life—Reflections from a Distant Era

YEARS AGO, I RECEIVED A COPY OF SOME text taken from a 1950s high school home economics textbook. The words in that book were absolutely astounding, yet so distantly familiar to me.

I had taken home economics at Thorpe Junior High School in Hampton, Virginia in 1965 and vividly remember the domestic diva era described in that retro book. I recalled living in a time when a woman's place literally and figuratively was in the home. TV had glamorized the lives of stay-at-home moms. Harriet Nelson of *The Ozzie and Harriet Show*, Donna Reed of *The Donna Reed Show*, Jane Wyman of *Father Knows Best*, and Barbara Billingsley—"June Cleaver"—of *Leave It to Beaver* all personified the women who were depicted in that 1950s home economics book.

After reading the pages from that book, I was so struck by what it had to say that I vowed to put it where I would definitely not forget it. My plan was to someday use it in a speech or training session. After a year or so, the right opportunity arose, but then I couldn't find where I'd put it "so I absolutely wouldn't lose it."

The 1990s passed and from time to time I'd think about that home economics textbook. If only I had done a good job of keeping up with it. On July 29, 2003, I was doing some serious merging and purging of hard copy files and low and behold—there it was—staring me in my eyeballs.

What better timing could I have had to find it? I'd be able to share it with people in the context of what they need to do to LwL², I thought. For some who read this home economics text, I'm sure their response will be, as the old Virginia Slims commercial used to say, "We've come a long way, baby." Others, however, will read it and lament, "If only we could return to those good ole days!" Regardless of which sentiment you feel, one thing I'm sure you will agree with—integrating work and life balance today is rarely like it was depicted in this 1950s home economics book.

How to Be a Good Wife

1. **Have dinner ready.** Plan ahead, even the night before, to have a delicious meal on time. This is a way of letting him know that you have been thinking about him and are concerned about his needs. Most men are hungry when they come home and the prospect of a good meal is part of the warm welcome needed.

2. **Prepare yourself.** Take 15 minutes to rest so that you'll be refreshed when he arrives. Touch up your makeup, put a ribbon in your hair and be fresh looking. He has just been with a lot of work-weary people. Be a little gay and a little more interesting. His boring day may need a lift.

3. **Clear away the clutter.** Make one last trip through the main part of the house just before your husband arrives, gathering up school books, toys, and paper. Then, run a

dust cloth over the tables. Your husband will feel he has reached a haven of rest and order, and it will give you a lift too.

4. **Prepare the children.** Take a few minutes to wash the children's hands and faces (if they are small). Comb their hair, and if necessary, change their clothes. They are little treasures and he would like to see them playing the part.

5. **Minimize all noise.** At the time of his arrival, eliminate all noise of the washer, dryer, dishwasher or vacuum. Try to encourage the children to be quiet. Be happy to see him. Greet him with a warm smile.

6. **Some don'ts:** Don't greet him with problems or complaints. Don't complain if he's late for dinner. Count this as minor compared with what he might have gone through that day. Make him comfortable. Have him lean back in a comfortable chair or suggest he lie down in the bedroom. Have a cool or warm drink ready for him. Arrange his pillow and offer to take off his shoes. Speak in a low, soft, soothing and pleasant voice. Allow him to relax and unwind.

7. **Listen to him.** You may have a dozen things to tell him, but the moment of his arrival is not the time. Let him talk first.

8. **Make the evening his.** Never complain if he does not take you out to dinner or to other places of entertainment. Instead, try to understand his world of strain and pressure, his need to be home and relax.

The goal: To try to make your home a place of peace and order where your husband can renew himself in body and spirit.

The world of people who lived the life depicted in this 1950s home economics book was oh so different from ours. Most women stayed at home full-time. The workforce today has a population of about as many women as men. Although women still maintain the bulk of parenting responsibilities, increasingly men are participating more in those endeavors. Nevertheless, some men do not always feel comfortable asking their boss for time off to chaperone their child's kindergarten trip to the local zoo.

The phenomenon of men staying at home to care for the children, while mothers go out and bring home the bacon, has spawned the term "stay-at-home dad." The cover of the May 12, 2003 issue of *Newsweek* magazine read, "She Works, He Doesn't." The article went on to say that some "thirty percent of working women now earn more than their husbands."

As we've moved from families in the 1950s headed by people like Ozzie Nelson to those commanded by Ozzy Osbourne types, we've also noticed other domestic shifts in the family structure that may affect our ability to LwL[2]. With 50% of marriages ending in divorce, many people find challenges to LwL[2] when the nuclear family comes unglued. Single parent, blended families comprised of children from different marriages living together, and adopted and foster families all populate today's familial landscape.

As our society ages and people are living longer, issues of elder care also sometimes challenge one's ability to LwL[2]. A PBS series entitled "Thou Shalt Honor," which aired August 18, 2003, stated that "one in four Americans is a caregiver" and that "80% of care-giving takes place in the home."

More and more, people also find themselves part of what has been termed the "sandwich generation." This is used to describe the phenomenon where mostly middle-aged people find themselves in the dilemma of having to take care of their children on one hand, and their parents on another. The individuals' lives are "sandwiched" between childcare issues on one hand, and elder care issues on the other.

More recently, another term, the "club sandwich generation," has evolved to depict an ever-increasing population whose lives are club-sandwiched between issues that involve taking care of their children, elderly parents/relatives and their children's children—their own grandchildren.

A new term, Boomerang Children/Kids, has also entered our vocabulary and rearranges our LwL[2] vision.

On August 25, 2003, radio talk show host Sean Hannity offered this insight on raising kids and its impact on LwL[2]. He said that when you mature and have kids, you realize that "Life isn't always about you."

Boomerang Kids

On August 25, 2003 I was driving in my car along the perimeter of Fenway Park and heard this quote on a radio news program, the Eagen and Broudie Show. They were doing a segment on Boomerang Children/Kids, those adult children who are increasingly leaving their parents' nest only to boomerang and come back to live.

I heard an interesting quote that I believe was attributed to Mark Twain, and it went something like this: "When I went off to school, I couldn't believe how stupid my parents were. When I graduated, I couldn't believe how much they had learned."

It's About Spinning Plates, Not Work/Life Balance

To help staff deal with the rigors of raising a family, many organizations have developed work/life balance or work/life integration programs. These initiatives are designed to help staff more fully balance or integrate the "day jobs" with their lives outside of work. Often when I hear people talk about the need to "balance" their life, I want to stop and scratch my head. Think about it. How often are our lives truly balanced to the point where like the scales of justice, every aspect is equal, even, and in tune?

While balance in our lives does happen on occasion, mostly our lives don't operate in that manner. Frequently, one aspect of our lives tends to demand our attention. When that occurs, work takes precedence over personal matters and vice-versa.

Instead of thinking about work and life as something to be balanced, I like to think of them as plates that have to be spun.

Spinning Plates and "The Ed Sullivan Show"

When I was young, I watched "The Ed Sullivan Show." One of my favorite acts was a man who would spin plates on long thin poles. My family was glued to our black-and-white TV as we watched this man work his magic with these plates. He'd begin on a stage where poles were strategically placed and then proceed to first balance then spin plates on the poles.

He'd place the first plate gingerly atop the first pole and spin it until it was whirling around. He would then move to the second pole and complete the same routine until he topped off the last pole with the last plate. By the time he got to the last pole and plate, guess what was happening to the first plate? Of course it was wobbling a bit as if it were ready to crash. So the man would scurry over and take care of that falling plate by giving it yet another spin. Once that first plate was fine, the man would hold up both arms in a victory-like "V" pose and bow gracefully as if to say, "*Ta-dah*—look what I've accomplished." Of course the audience was very impressed with this man's feat and the crowd clapped and cheered wildly.

I often feel like our lives are much like those spinning plates. We juggle lots of plates in our lives—mother, wife, business person, daughter, friend, and car pool carrier. Most of these items aren't always spinning smoothly on our life poles. Often, just as we get through a situation at work, another unanticipated issue crops up in our personal lives. Sometimes work issues need more of our spinning plate time. This may happen, for example, if an important contract for a big client is due. During the days before school begins, purchasing back to school items may take center stage in our plate spinning lives. During those times, the plates we spin may be more about home and the heart than the workplace and our career.

So the next time you are scurrying and trying to balance everything in your life, take a deep breath and smell the roses growing or the coffee brewing as you're spinning your work/life plates. Susan Hancox, our next Profile of Success tells a story about how she evaluated all of the plates in her life and reached the conclusion that what she wanted to do when she got older was to be a hospital executive at one of the world's most prestigious Children's Hospitals as well as a farm owner who raises llamas.

Profile of Success

Susan Hancox—Vice President, Administration and Human Resources, Children's Hospital-Boston

I am a lucky person who has always loved my work—whether a summer job during school years or my growing career in Human Resources. But at the age of 40, I began to question my life. A lot was happening. Among other things, I got divorced and I was beginning to feel like my job was becoming too repetitive—and, although it was very time-consuming, it was not enormously challenging. Home life was equally repetitive, because it was mostly chores and getting myself ready again to head out to executive existence. All of my energy was in my 80-hour/week job. The job was defining me. That didn't feel right. I wanted to be self-defined and bring that person to the job instead.

Solving the work front issues was easy. I simply kept offering to take on more—starting with responsibility for the executive oversight of the service departments so that I could be more involved with the pulse of the organization, which was in operations. I also wasn't sure I could do this well—and it was time to be a little "scared." That brought new energy and relevance to my human resources work.

As I thought about my personal life, I had to admit to myself I had always had an unexplainable desire to own a farm and to raise livestock—llamas, being a key interest. I worried that I was a single woman with a demanding job as a hospital administrator. Was the farm dream impossible? But I also knew that most busy people could take on more and more because they tend to be highly organized. I knew I'd never know if I didn't try. I figured I would find a way to fit everything in, so I took the leap.

Now I have 13 llamas and 4 pygmy goats that count on me every day. Some days I am putting together PowerPoint presentations for the Board or studying the next twist or complicated regulation in pension law. Other days, I'm off competing at agricultural fairs, attending a session on controlling parasites at a llama conference, or packing up llamas to head out and do a Harvard Hasty Pudding Club parade. The llamas opened up many new worlds and new and interesting people for me as I began showing, breeding, selling animals and learning how to spin their silky fiber. They also brought me instant serenity after a day in the city.

Each of my worlds has its demands and rewards. My executive colleagues are amused by my other life and my agricultural friends find it equally interesting that I also live in a power suit world. The two worlds are very separate—although I did have one humorous morning when I was racing in to a Board meeting and a colleague pulled me aside to let me know that hay was dragging from my heels! My schizophrenic life allows me to have two fulfilled lives, where I am loving my work *and* loving my personal life.

Slowing Down the Spinning Plates: Taking Time to Smell The Boston Baked Beans Baking

I had been so busy completing my book—working simultaneously with the editor and graphic artist/typesetter while preparing and beginning to implement the marketing plan and putting the finishing touches on the writing; preparing a motivational speech (can't forget about my business); nursing my foot back to health after major foot surgery; and taking care of my daughter—that I lost track of time in the world. All the while, the Boston Red Sox had played the pivotal game against the New York Yankees in their quest for a trip to the World Series—the seventh and deciding game in the seven-game Championship Series. Had they cracked the Curse of the Bambino? Would they go on, despite that evil spell cast by Babe Ruth back in 1918, or would we have to wait another 15 years for the curse to be lifted? (I have heard some say that the curse is only good for 100 years, making 2018 the year for the Sox.)

Well, the day after that crucial game was played, I had been so busy that I hadn't had time to find out the fate of the boys of summer who wore the Red Sox. You've got to slow down and smell the Boston baked beans baking, I reminded myself.

It wasn't until 9:03 that next morning—October 17, 2003—that my forlorn, die-hard Red Sox fan and Executive Assistant, Jessie, told me that the Sox had lost and wouldn't be going on to play the Florida Marlins in the World Series. In the midst of the craze that we had been working through to complete the finishing touches on this book, with my blessing, she made the time to slow down her spinning plates and go to Game 6 of the Championships with her sister—little did she know it would be the last game of an unbelievable 2003 season played at Fenway Park.

As fate would have it, her ticket to Game 5—scheduled for 7:30 P.M. on a Sunday—had been transferred to the following Tuesday at 4:00 P.M. due to a rain delay. How could I say no she couldn't leave work early? She had made the time to spend endless hours (at least three hours for each series offered) simultaneously spinning her plates on the Internet, her cell phone and house phone trying to get the golden tickets.

Well, she had somehow managed to get the ungettable when she got through on the phone that day and struck gold. Despite the disappointing loss at Fenway, she never gave up on her Boston boys. Two days later she took the time to cheer for her home team (or at least watch the Sox with an undying faith and palpitating heart), down to that heartbreaking homerun hit by Aaron Boone in the 11th inning to seal the Yankees' Championship win and trip to

---

Profile of Success

Renée M. Landers, Esq.—Associate Professor of Law, Suffolk University Law School and President of the Boston Bar Association

I consider life to be a series of trade-offs. Every opportunity has a cost. If you pursue one thing, there may be something else in your life that you are unable to do at the same time because of the decision you've made. In this regard, flexibility and being open to opportunities that present themselves are really important.

In the United States, we tend to measure and evaluate people by their careers, by what their jobs are. Career development is important to me, but career is not the only thing in life I value. Right now, the most important thing for me is to help my son become a happy and productive adult. At the end of my career and life, I alone will be the judge of how successful I have been in meeting my personal expectations and reflecting my personal values without regard to the expectations of society.

the World Series. With no regrets for watching and believing in her team, only those for the upsetting outcome, Jessie was able to get right back into the spin of things and continue on our journey to finish this book—while helping me with my foot, my business and even the care of my cats!

The moral of this story: If you can't take the time to slow down your spinning plates, don't let another's crash because of your choice not to do so.

FAMILY FIRST

"Reader's Digest announced the findings of its first biannual Family Well-Being Survey, designed to measure how families are doing. The overall findings indicated the emergence of an "American Paradox," in which many families are positive about their health, emotional well-being, and finances, yet they acknowledge suffering from weight problems, depression and anxiety, and debt. *Reader's Digest* discovered interesting contradictions within the core index categories, correlated to race, income, religion, and the cost of health care. African-Americans rate their family well-being significantly lower than do whites or Hispanics. This perception holds, regardless of income. Yet, African-Americans are more optimistic about their children's financial future than white families. Hispanics have significantly higher ratings of their financial situation as measured by the Financial Index than either whites or African-Americans."

Source: UnityFirst.com/African American Newswire

In the next chapter, we'll review how some companies are helping staff to spin their work/life plates and to LwL[2].

Chapter 31

COMPANIES HELPING STAFF TO LwL²

COMPANIES HELPING STAFF TO LwL²

MORE AND MORE ORGANIZATIONS have also come to better understand the new family structures and the impact that pressures of parenting, grandparenting and elder care concerns have on their employees' ability to LwL². In this chapter, I'd like to highlight the programs of companies and their work to help their staff with work/life issues.

Through my work as a management consultant and keynote/motivational speaker, I've been blessed with the opportunity of working with and/or coming in contact with some of the nation's top for-profit companies as well as non-profit and charitable organizations. I'm often asked, "What organizations are doing *everything* right when it comes to helping their staff to LwL²?"

Since *everything* is a hard standard to achieve, I typically respond by saying, "It's hard to think of companies that are a perfect 10 in *everything*, but there are many companies who are 10s in a variety of areas that help their employees to LwL²."

I'm going to start by introducing you to some best, interesting and radical practices as they relate to organizations helping staff to LwL². Some of these organizations win high honors and accolades for their work by receiving awards such as *FORTUNE* magazine's 100 Best Companies to Work For or *Working Mother's* 100 Best Companies. It wouldn't surprise me if there are some people reading this book who say or think something like, "Well, I know so-and-so who works at that company and they certainly don't think they're so great at helping people to LwL²." Organizations are not without their faults, but in my opinion as I've surveyed hundreds of organizations, I believe that these companies are making a gallant effort to at least begin to address the issue of how to assist their most precious resources and assets—their Human Resources—to LwL². I will highlight some of the programs, activities and events that these top organizations offer in several areas. I've also included interviews and statements from staff within those organizations so you can hear in their own words what they are doing to push the LwL² agenda forward in their organizations.

COMPANIES WHO EXCEL AT WORK/LIFE BALANCE AND INTEGRATION

Imagine this scenario:

You've been working every evening and weekend for the last month coaching your painfully shy six-year-old daughter, Jessica. She needed help to learn the two sentences she must deliver in her first class play. Finally, she's got the lines down and is confident and ready to deliver them. You're so proud of her progress and can't wait to see your little one shine in the school production. Two days before the big event, the Senior Vice President of your division calls an important meeting that you are asked to attend.

This meeting time, coincidentally, is from 8 to 10 A.M.—the exact time of your daughter's school performance. Obviously you can't be in two places at one time. Which event would you attend?

How many of us have been faced with this dilemma throughout our careers? How often do we select attending that business meeting because we fear the repercussions of having to tell our boss that a family or personal issue needs to take precedence over a work obligation? Having to select between an issue of importance at work versus one in your life can be a gut-wrenching experience.

I've got to go to work because it pays the bills, but what price will I pay if I'm not there for the special moments in my child's life? How will my decision to forego a meeting with my Senior Vice President to attend my child's school event affect my ability to advance in the organization? Will I be viewed as a slacker or not dedicated enough to my job? What about others who put in plenty of extra face time, but don't really care how those actions affect their lives outside of work?

The psychological torture we often put ourselves through trying to balance Loving our work and Life can be grueling. I ask you again: How would you handle the dilemma that little Jessica's parent faced when he had to decide between this difficult work and life balance situation?

If you worked at Blue Cross Blue Shield of Massachusetts (BCBSMA), as an employee of that company who relayed a similar situation to me did, you'd go to your child's special event *with* the full blessing *and* encouragement of your BOSS!

Having worked with and seen first hand how many of the senior leaders at BCBSMA work to help staff integrate work and life priorities, I wasn't totally shocked that the Senior Vice President in that scenario was so supportive of his employee's family commitment. This is an organization that has won such prestigious awards as the *Working Mother's* 100 Best Companies for their work/life efforts.

All of us have heard countless war stories of companies who do an atrocious and horrific job at helping staff integrate their work and life. But, believe it or not, there are some companies who have made it part of their corporate culture to help staff in their efforts to LwL².

I'd like to highlight the accomplishments of a number of companies that I've personally known over the years. You'll learn about some of the efforts that these LwL² and family-friendly organizations have undertaken.

The pages ahead provide you with information on some of the stellar and novel programs and services they offer staff. In addition, you'll read about how regular employees, as well as executives, from some of these organizations are using unique approaches to address work, family and personal life integration.

You might be thinking, "That's great that those companies have the money and resources to do those things, but cash is tight in our organization or we are too small or too large for that to happen." I ask you to keep an open mind as you read what these organizations and people have to say. Many have provided "low-cost" or "no-cost" suggestions. Others have articulated an attitude or way of operating that helps them to better juggle work and life balls simultaneously. Yes, there are some examples of programs and benefits that do cost money, but as these employers will attest, an investment in the work *and* life of an employee does have a positive impact on their bottom line. They also know that there is a positive correlation between delighted customers and happy employees who are not distracted from their work by family and personal issues.

Over the past few years, many organizations have come to understand the powerful connection between how a person's home life can positively or negatively shape an individual's performance on the job and vice versa. They realize that helping staff better integrate work and personal/family life is a win/win situation for all involved.

My hope is that this chapter will inspire both individuals and companies to see the range of positive things others are doing to help staff to LwL². I also suspect that many people will read about what these top companies are doing and be surprised because their organizations offer the same type of best practice programs. We will begin our look into these prestigious organizations by examining how Fredi Shonkoff—Senior Vice President of Corporate Relations for Blue Cross Blue Shield of Massachusetts—helps her staff to handle work/life challenges.

Profile of Success

Fredi Shonkoff—Senior Vice President of Corporate Relations,
Blue Cross Blue Shield of Massachusetts

I guard time for both work and life outside work, and I bring what I love about my life into work. Our families and important personal milestones and events are part of what we share at work.

Recently, I was in a Senior Management meeting with a full business agenda and our President began by asking about the health of a colleague's husband who had recently undergone bypass surgery. After that, I thought, what a wonderful place to work where we are invited to speak about ourselves in a business setting and can express the sadness and joy in our lives. At Blue Cross, we are encouraged to talk about other very important aspects of our life away from work.

I had an employee whose mom was dying of cancer. She and I worked out a plan for her to go home one afternoon a week for about six months so that she could take emotional care of herself and spend time with her mom. I never felt for a moment that this wasn't the right thing for our company to do. It allowed her to be a whole person. It makes me feel good that we were able to do that for her.

When Blue Cross needed to turn its culture around—to become more service-focused—we had some interesting conversations encouraging all of us to bring who we are from home to work. We talked about putting our members (customers) first and began to clarify that we don't want our associates to come to the office and feel they must put on a stern face and not be the same caring person they are at their child's PTA meeting or backyard barbecue. We want them to bring that caring compassionate person to the workplace and be that same way with co-workers, their boss and our customers.

People must be allowed to be authentic and natural at work. I'm extremely friendly with my staff and though clear about professional expectations, I also encourage personal conversation. I think you need to let who you are come through and allow people to be relaxed and let their natural selves come out. All that "stuff" in our life affects our performance.

Tips on How to LwL[2]

I put my children, husband, the ocean and house in Maine in my office. (Our Maine house is actually my screen-saver on my desktop.) I see the direct connection between my outside life and my job. Coming to work allows me to do this.

People need to be connected to the values of their work. We need to understand what those values are and what we need in a job to live them.

You should do what you do naturally well. If you force yourself to do work that is not natural or does not connect with your values, you probably won't be successful or fulfilled.

If you are not in the right job get out, network and talk to people. Just keep your eyes open and meet people. Opportunities come from the most unexpected places.

I job shared for ten years and had four different jobs with a friend and neighbor. We both had sons in the same nursery school and wanted time with our families while enjoying the rewards of a professional career. We moved together through these four positions and mastered the art of thorough communication. We used a tape recorder to tell each other what was accomplished during our shift. I worked Monday, Thursday and a half-day on Wednesday. She worked Tuesday, Friday and a half-day on Wednesday. As a job share team we learned to share all the accomplishments and failures, essentially merging our egos. But most important, we performed well and had the opportunity to enjoy important years with our young families while moving ahead with our professional development.

Whether it is job sharing, working with colleagues or staff, it's all about open communication.

Profiles of Success

Darryl and Juliette Mayers

I sat down with Darryl and Juliette Mayers on their twelfth wedding anniversary (August 31, 2003) to discuss their thoughts on LwL[2] and the family. Both hold prestigious, high-powered jobs. She is Director of Sales Planning at Blue Cross Blue Shield of Massachusetts. Darryl is a procurement manager for a multinational corporation. He is also an attorney specializing in contracts and public construction law. They are the parents of two children, ages five and eight.

Darryl: One of the main themes in our family is to always focus on being flexible in terms of work and family. We have always tried to complement each other's work schedule, acknowledging that meeting family and work needs means constantly changing our priorities on a daily basis.

Juliette: It's also about supporting each other. There is always some challenge that comes up, like working late or the children getting sick. For me, it's a tremendous gift to work for an employer who truly values family, so I do what I need to do for my family without the guilt.

Darryl: Yes, keeping our communication open in terms of work issues has also been quite important. Although Juliette may not have a background in construction issues, the management issues that we deal with on a daily basis tend to have similar themes.

Juliette: I think a sense of humor is important. When things get too tough, I try to not take things too seriously. If you put it in the context of life and the family and what's really important, it may not be as overwhelming.

Darryl: Leaving work at work is often a difficult task. This is true especially when starting a new job because there are so many issues that have to be resolved. But when you enjoy the challenges at work and realize that you are part of a project that will shape the destiny of Boston and Massachusetts for years to come, finding time for these issues is made easier. This has made focusing on our children and family matters, scheduling and planning, as well as communicating amongst ourselves so much more important.

Juliette: Yes, you have to compartmentalize. It's also about spirituality. Our home is very spiritually centered and our lives are guided by ethical morals and principles. God is the center of our life and everything flows from there. Even if times are difficult, our belief is that God will take us through it.

You definitely need a good support system of family and friends and a dependable outside child care resource. My parents, especially when the kids were younger, were of tremendous support to us. My in-laws live one-half mile away and are also very supportive in helping us with the kids.

Darryl: You need multiple layers of support. For example, in the early days we had people watch our kids. We also relied heavily on Juliette's mother and sisters. You have to feel comfortable with your child care situation, the 1st layer, 2nd layer and so on or that can interfere with LwL[2].

Juliette: You also must feel comfortable with the people looking after your children. There are so many moving systems and they all have to be managed, so excellent organizational skills are critical. There is home stuff, finances, school plays, community commitments, church commitments and of course, play dates. It's also very important for us to have fun as a family. For example, we like to take family vacations to nice places and do things as a couple.

Darryl: It's important not to see yourself as the focal point. Education and career help to make your family whole. Juliette had aspirations to go back to school and receive her MBA. She probably would have been resentful if she hadn't gone back to school because it was so important to her. I realized the significance of this goal and knew that we had to reshape our priorities.

Juliette: I view the career and educational aspirations as benefiting the family. I always wanted to go back to school, and even though it was difficult the year I took off and got my MBA, in the end it made us stronger because it stretched our capacity as a family. We really had to dig deep because it was a one year intensive experience. It stretched us in managing our family, raising the children and maintaining our relationship. Darryl got closer to the children and managing the household and the finances. He now has a better appreciation for those things and I have a better appreciation for him. I also recognize that he had to sacrifice. In the end, we all increased our "comfort zone" and that was a good thing.

290

Profile of Success

Danny Best—Director of Corporate Diversity, FleetBoston Financial

Danny is responsible for setting the strategic direction for all FleetBoston's corporate diversity initiatives in partnership with the senior executive team. He provides leadership to a team of professionals, who collaborates with Human Resources, business line directors and several groups spread throughout the organization to develop innovative programs, support business directed diversity goals and ensure effective education/communication of the corporation's diversity and business objectives. These groups represent Fleet's 45,000 employees and are in the form of diversity resource groups, business line diversity leadership councils and Fleet management. Danny's office acts as the liaison to all these groups. The Corporate Diversity Office also provides a budget to each group for administrative purposes and to support causes that are important to them. Their charitable giving arm, FleetBoston Financial Foundation, also provides grants. The company has a Corporate Diversity Council made up of executives from different lines of business. They act as an advisory panel to him. FleetBoston has won the "Working Mother's 100 Best Companies" award.

At FleetBoston Financial, we recognize that our employees are central to the company's success—that talented, experienced and diverse individuals are necessary to move the corporation forward in an increasingly complex society. We are concerned about the entire life cycle of our employees. This includes recruiting, orientation, training and development, and career management/progression. Our programs are designed to give all employees the opportunity to reach their full potential. As a Human Resources and diversity professional, I get great satisfaction knowing that I can influence the leaders in the corporation to implement programs and policies that get the most out of a diverse workforce. For me, loving your work is having a positive impact on the lives and/or careers of others, which in turn, creates better companies, enhanced customer loyalty and ultimately better returns for the shareholders. In order to love your work you really have to love what you do. It's important to find the right fit—a role that complements your style, skills, experience, interests and value system. For example, it would be difficult for me to work for a company that manufactures cigarettes because it would go against my value of promoting health and well being. I know people who have what some would consider to be great jobs, but because their day-to-day responsibilities conflict with their value system, they hate what they do. I'm engaged in helping people to make their lives and careers better and that gives me satisfaction.

My wife, Condase, works at a competing bank in Human Resources and surprisingly we don't talk much about business—we have so many other things that are important to us; family, friends, church, traveling and having fun, which is why things go so well between us. As a two-career couple, the "carve out" time for ourselves, and our families, is sacred. The only thing that could get in the way of our precious family time is a complete disaster—we don't break it. For example, we've gone to Turks and Caicos, Aruba, and on a cruise this past year. But even if it's just a walk in the park or a trip to the zoo, we make sure we have some quality time just for us—it keeps us grounded and connected and reinforces that the most important thing in our lives is family and friends. Condase and I like to pretend we're still dating—the two of us will go out to dinner or a movie. The "carve out" time is really beneficial to keeping our marriage and friendship strong.

We have four children, ages 22, 19, 4 and 2, as well as two nephews, ages 18 and 19 that have moved in with us. We have a very busy household—during the week we hardly see each other. Everybody has to pitch in to keep things running smoothly—each of us has several assignments—most of them are around ensuring that the little ones get their needs taken care of. Someone prepares breakfast, another gets clothes, backpacks and lunches ready for school, someone else gets pick-up and drop-off duty. The key is to develop a plan and a system. It helps us to stay on track with what we need to do.

What Companies Are Doing

At Fleet, we firmly believe in the service profit chain. If your employees are happy, they'll in turn make customers satisfied—and if customers are satisfied, they'll do more business with you and possibly bring you more customers, which will keep the company growing and thriving. It's a very simple principle, but it is very important in a business like ours where customers look to us to help them make smarter financial decisions. We have an employee listening initiative whereby we survey employees to learn what's on their minds, how they feel about working at Fleet and generally how satisfied they are with the company. After each survey, Employee Action Teams (EAT's) are set up to delve deeper into the issues, pinpoint the root causes, develop ideas and solutions, and work with business line management to implement programs that address areas where there is opportunity to increase employee satisfaction. For example, in one division, upward communication was an issue—after a couple of months of looking into the issue, the EAT had a number of ideas like setting up an electronic mailbox where questions could be directed to the leadership; enhancing the division's Intranet page; conducting conference calls or brown bag lunches on critical issues; and enhancing the accessibility of management by having them become more visible on the floor by walking around and engaging staff. All of these ideas were implemented and overall employee satisfaction scores went up.

We have a lot of work/life programs and have won numerous awards for creating a work environment in which our diverse employees can thrive. A few examples include: Adoption Assistance, Paid Volunteer Days, Backup Childcare, Flexible Work Arrangements, Benefits for Part-time Workers, Partner Health Benefits that are available to gay, lesbian and unmarried partners, Paid Paternity Leave, Fitness Centers, Health Initiatives and many, many others. Fleet's work/life and diversity initiatives create an environment that values people and helps them Love their work by Loving their Life!

Profiles of Success

Robert Browne—Systems Engineer, Cisco Systems
and
Nina Miller-Browne—Senior Business Analyst, FleetBoston Financial

Nina: There is never a perfect balance. One person will have to do a little more than the other at times in a relationship and there will come a time when the other will do more. So, it never balances out on a day-to-day basis, but in the long run it does. With the children, we make sure they do a variety of activities depending on the season—bike riding, swimming, rollerblading in the summer, skiing in the winter—whatever the season, we make sure they are active. We put activities with the children on our To-Do Lists and schedule them in just like any chore—grocery shopping, cleaning the house or doing laundry. But it's not a chore. The kids need stimulation and we make sure we do something with them regularly.

The fact that I grew up outside in Jamaica, I love to see them outside doing things and not just watching TV all the time.

Rob: We have two children who express themselves in many different ways and one thing they love to do is draw. We look at their pictures and it tells us about their emotional state. For example, are their drawings happy or sad? Is the family included? If we see something negative in the pictures, we know we have to spend more time investigating things. The pictures are worth a million words and can tell us what's going on in their lives.

We also see trends in school, work and in interactions with other kids and people in them. This gives us an idea whether or not they are happy in their environment or if something is bothering them. If the kids aren't satisfied, then their life is not happy and that could potentially affect your life and ability to Love your work by Loving your Life.

Kids don't necessarily have a job, but they do have work to do. We have to create an environment to help them to love their work just like an employer has to set an environment to foster productivity. How many times have you seen a negative work environment that produces a lot of work, but the quality is poor?

Nina: We study our children and figure out what we can do to calm them down. You really need to understand your child so you can get the best out of them. When we understand how our children are, it helps us to expend less energy on negative activities.

Rob: For example, our five year old is extremely active and we travel a lot and take many trips out of the country so she has to sit for hours. We've studied her and learned that music and drawing calm her down. So we pack a CD player with her favorite music and she is perfect and the calmest little angel for any amount of time with her CDs. We've traveled to Italy and Switzerland with her and her music—no problem whatsoever.

Nina: I would call it organization. The reason we are able to have our careers (Nina is a Senior Business Analyst with FleetBoston Financial and Robert is a Systems Engineer with Cisco Systems) is we are organized. We organize their clothes a week at a time, not every day. On Sundays, I may iron their clothes and mine for the week. That allows me to use my morning time more efficiently.

Profiles of Success

Polly Price—Associate Vice President of Human Resources, Harvard University
and
Henry Ryan—Director of Human Resource Services, Harvard University (Harvard University is a recipient of the *Working Mother*'s 100 Best Companies award.)

Loving work

Henry: I love my work because there is never any one day that is exactly the same—I happen to like variety in my work and don't like continually doing the same thing over and over again.

Polly: The advice I'd give to people is to go to an employer where you can reinvent yourself regularly. I've been at Harvard a long time—18 years—but have had three different assignments. I feel like every year I need a new mountain to climb and Harvard lets me do that. If you're in the same job, figure out ways to make it challenging and different. You can learn different things from different bosses. A friend of mine said never work for a jerk. In higher education, we are in a place where we are constantly learning from peers, our boss, our boss' boss, and employees.

Henry: At Harvard there is always something of interest going on. On any given day you might see President Bush, Bruce Willis, or some other celebrity walking around campus. We have museums and performing arts events that employees may attend…some for free. There are many things that make Harvard Square unique, including the street musicians and pan handlers.

Polly: It's very important to me that the people I work with are smart, creative and competent.

Henry: Enthusiastic colleagues with energy are important to me—you can either feed off others' energy or their negativity. I am most productive and engaged when I am around positive people with focused energy.

Harvard has excellent work-life programs and resources. We offer childcare scholarships, adoption assistance, and personal improvement programs. Many employees work flexible work schedules. Outings and Innings Programs offer discounts for entertainment and cultural events. We also provide resource information for elder care. Harvard truly is a great place to work.

Loving your Life

Polly: To love your life, live with someone you love. I'm very lucky my husband taught me a wonderful way to approach life—no matter what happens we're going to have a good time. For example, if we're on a trip and we run out of gas, or if our plane is delayed, he reminds me to have that positive attitude—it's going to be all right.

Henry: I think loving your life is about having flexibility and independence to do the things one enjoys doing. My mom just turned 80 this year and having her in my life for so many years as a role model has had a positive impact on my life. I still learn from her—she's been successful in many ways, both professionally and personally. However, she's been most successful as a human being. She has given more to life than she has taken from it. She is active in her church and helps family and strangers alike.

Polly: My mom just turned 81 and never worked outside of the house for pay but she is a very active volunteer. She has shown that there is a lot more to life. She's made a difference by working in food pantries, hospice care, hospitals, nursing homes, and tutoring at an elementary school.

Helpful Hints

Polly: People should take vacations—even if you just stay home and sit on the couch—get your head into something else.

Henry: Don't take yourself too seriously—relax. Do things outside of your job that will enable you to relax.

Love your work by Loving your Life

Polly: I do think that people are better able to love their work and have a good time if they love what they are doing, if there is a balance. Every time when I am about to go on vacation, there comes a moment—usually the day before I go away—that I say I don't have to finish everything, and yesterday it seemed like an insurmountable problem. Have something that pulls you to stop thinking about work so when you come back to it you are relaxed.

For many artists, their work is their art—writers, painters, dancers—and that vocation isn't work to them. For people like that, I'd say they don't have to separate their work and life. For others who work because it's for the money or to pay for their house, it's a different concept.

Henry: Work at something you enjoy. There is no amount of money in the world that will complete you or make you happy if you are doing something you don't enjoy.

I am a believer in experiential living. I don't want to read about it. I prefer to experience it. Part of living is doing things that take you out of your comfort zone—things that let you utilize your natural curiosity.

Polly: I read a lot of novels—60 to 70 a year—because I like to experience worlds that are not my own or those that are similar to my own but experience it differently. It's about seeing life through someone else's eyes. It's the way I get out of my life and into something else.

Henry: Hobbies provide a means of relaxation to achieve a balance to offset work stress. My hobbies include collecting R&B or jazz CD's and classic movies, playing tennis, painting, and creating small hanging wall quilts (which I have framed).

Best, Interesting or Radical Practices

Carolyn Everette—Assistant Dean for Human Resources, Harvard School of Public Health

Things Employers do to Help People LwL[2]

I was watching TV one evening and saw a story about S.A.S.—a wonderful place to work. It was portrayed as having ethics, great systems and spaces and competitive salaries to make people successful in their jobs. They offer the basics that many professionals need to live. This includes providing staff with access to fitness centers, cleaning services and child care. Their entire company is involved. Employees can enjoy their work and their life without feeling they have to give up one or the other. Their CEO seems to think that this is a basic reality. S.A.S. has low turnover and thousands of employees with the same perspective and vision. They have people knocking down their doors to work there.

S.A.S. is the ideal model of a company that helps people to integrate work and life. This company is interested in getting the most talented staff and they'll make sure that they are fully committed to them. Most companies say these things cost too much. The reality is that the initial outlay will more than pay for itself in time and I believe their CEO believes in that concept.

One of the things that started years ago at the Harvard School of Public Health is we provide a health and fitness benefit for all faculty and staff. Based on seniority, they get an account. Every July 1, if they've been at the school at least five years, they're eligible for the benefit. There are a list of things that qualify for reimbursement such as the latest in fitness equipment, courses in Tae Bo, Tai Chi, stress management and massages. We also bring some of those programs in-house and they cost staff nothing or are low cost—$5 or $10.

Some of our faculty, who are world renowned health and nutrition experts and physicians, serve on an advisory committee to review our program and tell us about the latest trends and how the program may need to be expanded or altered.

Wise Words

Laura Avakian—Vice President for Human Resources, Massachusetts Institute of Technology (MIT)

What people need to do to Love their work:

When looking for a job, pick your boss, not the work.

What people need to do to Love their Life:

Find some quiet time in each day. Trust someone with your joys and sorrows.

What people need to do to Love their work by Loving their Life:

Bring trust, caring, love into the workplace. All businesses are people-businesses; if you care about humanity you will care about your work.

How organizations can help staff to Love their work and Life:

They can emphasize the value of the "whole person" to the job; those things that make each person unique should be celebrated. MIT has an office for "Work, Family and Personal Life." It is a wonderful resource for staff and its very existence makes a statement about what the organization values.

Profile of Success

Paula Hammond Cunningham—Associate Professor in Chemical Engineering, Massachusetts Institute of Technology (MIT)

The Massachusetts Institute of Technology is a "Working Mother's 100 Best Companies" award winner. Here's how one of its tenured professors successfully juggles a demanding career with motherhood.

One of the major things that has helped me to accomplish what I want is to eliminate negative thoughts and pathways in my life. Even in school, you start to assume that others are smarter than you. This is especially true if you are part of a minority group or a woman. You have to eliminate negative self images and allow yourself to assess other people's capabilities. You must not assume that they are more capable than you. To move forward, you need to feel very positive and strong in what you do. A person can get that from several places, but especially from God and family. The first source of power for me is from God, a spiritual place. I also receive it from those I love, especially my husband, Carmon, and my pre-teen daughter, Therese. Family in all forms—my parents, brothers, in-laws, close friends—contribute to the positive influences that keep me going.

I believe we all have skills and that they can be used by others who will benefit from them; through my belief in God, I know this is true. When I see other people, I don't have to perceive them as better or worse than me. I look at how I can benefit from what they are doing, and how to contribute in a way that gives back. This process is enabling and frees you from a mindset that there has to be this variation in who can attain success. It allows you to understand that we all have the capability of succeeding.

In high school or college you may have experienced someone who was smart in a classroom situation. Later, you discover there are always others who are even more intelligent or gifted or talented in a certain area. You must keep the perspective that, while they are bright, there is a reason why God led you to that situation. If you can explore that, it allows you to put yourself out on a limb and take some risks, and that is a freeing concept. I've encountered situations where I thought I wouldn't achieve a certain level of success, then I reflect on it and say, "Why am I thinking like this—am I holding back or afraid to take a risk?" Once you are able to take a second assessment, you will realize that you are at least as bright and capable as your peers. I have learned this so many times in life—trust in your own abilities, and you will often exceed all expectations. This concept of applying your gifts applies to work, but even more importantly to building a family. You work together as a family to glean from each other's gifts.

[I asked Paula how she, at age 38, became tenured at MIT. She is on the faculty as an Associate Professor of Chemical Engineering. Her specialty is in Polymers (plastics).]

I enjoy the ability to take my own ideas and turn them into substantial things. I like doing this through the interactions with students who work with me in my research group. They continue to transform my ideas and blend them with their own. It's energizing. What they come up with is a different and new perspective that complements your own; the combination results in new and promising possibilities. I love seeing students get excited about research then transform it. That process is so exhilarating. In the beginning, as a professor, you face the real fear of being a Jr. faculty member. These and other fears must eventually be faced, although in reality they never entirely go away. Any concerns are diminished, however, by the wonderful things that happen in your work. If you submit for a grant to fund your students, it may fall through, but the likelihood is that if you can convey your excitement, then someone else will become appreciative of your idea and fund it. You have to hang in there and remain positive and assess yourself. If you feel confident and able to clearly assess the value of your work in society, then one way or another you're going to succeed!

Paula's husband, Carmon Cunningham, also works for a company that values family life.

Profile of Success

Carmon Cunningham—Vice President Technology and Communications, Jobs for the Future

In today's world, work consumes so much of our lives. Through the magic of technology, we are always accessible—through computers, cell phones, pagers—and that makes it very easy to work—almost all the time. Given that so much of our life is consumed and influenced by what we do, it is really important that we make certain that if we are going to spend a lot of time doing something, it reflects who we are as people. Your work should be consistent with what gives you joy and satisfaction, and fulfills you as a person.

Loving your work by Loving your Life means understanding who you are in this life and doing something in your work that is complementary to your life's purpose. It means fulfilling your dreams and aspirations and actualizing your best self.

Family

It is very important, when faced with the challenges of a career and raising children, that as a family, and as husband and wife, you are on the same page. This involves sharing the same values and finding a commonality where your spirits and philosophies are in sync with each other. Having such a bond influences your priorities and prepares you to better deal with the challenges of a growing, inquisitive child.

Although our careers are important and consume a lot of our time, our love for God, our love and support of each other and our family must take priority over our careers. Keeping things in the right perspective is critical because God blessed us with the opportunities in the first place. God is responsible for the blessings we receive in life and keeping Him as our number one priority is most important to us.

Advice to Other Professionals of Color

- People are always looking for what they can get. My advice is to be willing to give to others without the expectation of getting something in return. You will be rewarded in ways you could never anticipate. By helping others, at the same time you build a wealth of resources such as friendships and an awareness of new opportunities and networks. However, the simple satisfaction of knowing you helped someone, makes it all worth it.
- Surround yourself with positive people and influences. It is important to maintain the support and love of your family and friends—it keeps you grounded and focused.
- Commit yourself to God's will. Let His divine guidance lead and direct you. This will help you hone into your life's purpose and keep you on track in fulfilling your goals.
- Pursue excellence in everything that you do! Accept nothing less than your best effort from yourself.

Loving work

I work for a not-for-profit organization whose mission is to make life better for low income youth and adults by improving their educational and career advancement opportunities. This is a far cry from where I started. I was trained in business and spent years in the corporate world and as an administrator at MIT and I have found that my level of job satisfaction now far exceeds the joy I received in the corporate world or at an Ivy-league school.

You feel a validation when you can apply the gifts and skills you have to the workplace. If your work is consistent with your personal values, your satisfaction increases tenfold. What motivates me is to do what I feel is very important work every day.

Best, Interesting or Radical Practices
Bright Horizons Family Solutions (BFAM)

Bright Horizons is an organization that wins the hearts of parents around the world for helping them to integrate work and family. It is also a company that practices what it preaches. Bright Horizons has a family feel and a FORTUNE 100 reputation. By having respect for diversity and honoring differences with children and families, as well as faculty and staff, the senior leadership demonstrates its commitment to diversity. The work they do helps companies with work/life solutions. They also "walk the walk and talk the talk" by providing top innovative work and family solutions to their staff. They offer quality benefits and programs to support their diverse staff and their salaries are among the highest in their industry according to *FORTUNE* and *Business Week*. "98% of Bright Horizons' parents say they're satisfied with the care their kids are receiving." (*Business Week*)

Staff, regardless of where they are in their life or career—whether they are handling issues in their own lives related to child care or elder care—BFAM will find benefits and career opportunities to suit them. They offer career enhancement and succession planning regardless of an individual's position, age, and gender. Tuition reimbursement, onsite training and career opportunities exist. BFAM grows and develops current and future leaders through leadership development opportunities. Some professions in the company even have career ladders so staff know what's expected of them to succeed and move their careers forward.

Employee Involvement and Giving Back to the Community and World
BFAM is a company that believes in giving back to the communities it serves and making a difference in the world and wants to help staff do the same. This is accomplished through volunteer activities and foundation work, plus work they do around child and elder care solutions with their clients.

Employee involvement is encouraged. They are constantly surveying staff to gain their opinions on work/life issues. Staff can also participate on a variety of committees to help make work/life better, such as the Diversity Council, Retention Committee, Employee Events, etc. Staff has the satisfaction of knowing they help to shape the lives of children, our future. Individuals are encouraged to participate in volunteer activities to make their communities and children they serve in the world better places for families to live.

"To help children grow and reach their potential, we must create an environment in which our staff can do the same. As we nurture each child's unique qualities and potential in our centers, we strive to do the same with our staff."

Bright Horizons cares about the lives of its employees and offers benefits to help them balance their work and life. These benefits are unmatched in the child care and early education industry and are competitive with many large organizations! They are indeed a family-friendly organization.

- Dependent Care Assistance Program—This allows for employees to pay for the cost of child care or other dependent care on a pre-tax basis.
- Adoption Assistance Program—This program helps to defray the costly expenses associated with adoption.
- Stock Options
- Back-Up Child Care—This gives all employees back-up child care when the regular child care is not available and provides peace of mind about their child care during times such as school vacation days, holidays or ill providers.
- Domestic Partner Benefits
- 401(k) Plan—Designed to help staff save for retirement. Employees over 50 years of age may defer additional before-tax savings.
- Child Care Discount—BFAM is committed to supporting the children and families of its staff by offering a child care discount.
- Employee Assistance Program—The Life Balance Program is offered free to full-time employees and their families. It provides 24-hour telephone consultation for issues such as stress reduction, mental health, substance abuse and day-to-day living concerns.
- Elder Care Program—Designed to help staff as they deal with issues related to the aging of a parent or other family member. Its program is run by one of the country's premier providers of elder care solutions.
- Discounts to such things as movies, rental cars and theme parks such as Universal Studios in Florida.

Profile of Success

Andrina Buffong—Diversity/Work Life Specialist, MITRE

MITRE is a company that is highly regarded for its work with staff and their families. It is among "FORTUNE's 100 Best Companies to Work For;" a recipient of the "Working Mother's 100 Best Companies" and has also been honored for its work with older workers by the American Association of Retired Persons (AARP).

Corporations and managers need to see people as individuals and find out what motivates and excites them. It doesn't have to be every minute, but they can find out what I like, what my strengths are and what I am doing with them.

You have to create an environment where people feel they are happy and are playing to their strengths. Employees should be able to say, "This is what I'm doing now, and this is what I'm better at." For example, if you're a great individual contributor, that doesn't make you a great manager. So, if a person is promoted into that role and can't do it, they should be comfortable saying that to the hiring manager.

For some people, it doesn't have to be that the manager gives them a big award. It can be something as simple as a "Thank you, job well done!" A note, e-mail or just a chat are also welcomed. It's the simple things that most people appreciate.

Our company, MITRE, made the *FORTUNE* "100 Best Companies to Work For" and we gave people a nice, sincere note from the CEO and a lapel pin. It was amazing how many people appreciated that gesture. So, thanks do not have to be huge stock options. It could also be something like finding out the areas the person wants to grow in and giving him the tools and resources to do what he needs to do to accomplish those things.

My Vice President of Human Resources always asks me, "Do you have what you need to get your job done and do you need any help?" If I do, she will try to get me what I need. That is something I REALLY appreciate.

Things Companies Can Do To Help People LwL²

At MITRE, we did a whole push to help support the families of our employees who were serving in the military especially during the Iraq conflict. We sent notes to spouses from the CEO letting them know that we were there for them and who was the point of contact for benefit questions. We also sent a note to managers asking them to stay in touch with the spouses left behind. We invited the spouses to events we were having, like "Take Your Child to Work Day" and the company picnic.

We provide staff with all-occasion greeting cards as a way for them to acknowledge significant events in a colleague's life. This is a great, easy and efficient way to let people know you're thinking about them. The cards include such things as: having a baby/adding to a family (adoption), sympathy, get well, retirement, thank you, job well done, getting married, welcome to MITRE, and a whole host of other occasions. Our new employees seem to appreciate a card that says "Welcome, we're glad to have you."

Another program we have is a leave sharing program. This is for people who have used up all of their time off and now have a hardship, such as a family member who is sick or a spouse, or a child who has cancer or a major operation. How it works is an employee submits something to our Vice President of Human Resources describing his or her situation and it is reviewed and may get approved. The program started with our Vice President's submitting time to the cause. People can donate as little time as an hour.

My final tip is if you are not loving what you're doing, maybe you need to move on, or take a look at the situation and see if there is one more thing you could add to make your work life more enjoyable, what would it be? Then work to add that into your life.

Working with Older Workers

One of the more innovative programs for mature workers is Reserves at the Ready Program. MITRE's Reserves at the Ready are recently retired MITRE technical staff with the skills and corporate memory needed to provide dynamic, short-term support to critical MITRE projects. As part of the Reserves at the Ready program, they are Part-Time-On-Call (PTOC) employees. Candidates for Reserves at the Ready fill out an online resume, and their skills are entered into a database that project leaders may search when they need to fulfill specific program requirements.

As a member of our highly proficient reserve workforce, they may be called upon to quickly contribute to short-term surges in our work program. Reserve (PTOC) staff can work on a short-term assignment(s) or occasionally throughout the year, but cannot exceed 1,000 hours per calendar year.

MITRE retirees benefit by continuing their association with MITRE as a member of this highly dynamic and flexible group of reserve staff. This vast knowledge base and corporate wisdom may be called upon to quickly contribute and help us meet our challenges, as well as to mentor our current full-time staff.

With a reserve workforce, MITRE benefits by uniting project leaders with the expertise and experts they require to get the job done. This helps us to meet and exceed the requirements of our sponsors in both the short and long term.

Wise Words

Ted Roome, Executive Director, MITRE

Organizations must be adaptive and build new relationships all the time. Only then can they go and deal with the complex and diverse outside world in a more effective fashion.

The business we are in is about managing change. We must create a flexible and diverse environment internally so we can better work externally.

As a leader, what you do in setting an example for using the dimensions of diversity can really impact how staff approaches their work.

The following is information contributed by MITRE that explains how they help their staff to LwL[2].

MITRE Quality of Work Life

Focusing on the needs of our employees

For nearly half a century, MITRE has worked to build an environment in which our people can make a difference and help shape the future. MITRE employees have access to the most advanced technologies and are recognized for achievement and innovation. The company values diversity and strives to offer all individuals the opportunity to learn and be challenged.

We realize employees value their time in and out of the office. Through corporate initiatives, the company focuses on the things that are important to our people:

Innovative technologies: MITRE's technical fingerprint is on literally thousands of Department of Defense, Federal Aviation Administration and Internal Revenue Service programs. Our employees have access to the most advanced and sophisticated tools and technologies.

A learning environment: At MITRE, it's easy to earn advanced degrees in relevant fields from an accredited college or university courtesy of the company's tuition reimbursement program. Employees may be eligible to participate in our Accelerated Degree Program in which one-fifth of the work week can be spent pursuing an advanced degree. In addition, MITRE's well-regarded MITRE Institute offers a wide variety of in-house technical, non-technical and management training courses. Employees are also able to learn from each other by collaborating on interesting and innovative projects and, with many in-house opportunities at MITRE, employees can change jobs or careers without changing employers.

Flexible work and telecommuting schedules: Flexible work schedules and telecommuting schedules can help ensure successful and continuing work/life navigation.

Benefits that provide financial protection and security: MITRE's exceptional benefits programs includes top-notch health, dental, disability, vision care and dependent life insurance; pre-paid legal services; and paid time off benefits. Our retirement program, especially the generous company match, may be one of the best in America; employees often build substantial retirement nest eggs while working at MITRE.

Here are some of the programs that MITRE offers its staff:

MITRE's Quality of Work Life Benefits

- **Paid Time Off Bank:** As a new employee, you accrue 23 days of paid time off each year (pro-rated for part-time employees). You can use your paid time off for vacation, sick days, or personal business that requires time away from work.
- **Leave Sharing:** You can donate unused paid time off hours to help other employees in need. You can also request additional leave from the leave sharing pool to help with a family hardship or other extenuating circumstance.
- **Medical Leave:** MITRE's generous medical leave, which is used for short term disability and maternity leave, can provide regular full- and part-time employees with income protection for up to 180 days in the event an employee has a serious illness or injury. Medical leave is first paid at 100% of pay, then at a gradually reduced rate based on length of the illness.
- **Pre-tax Spending Account:** If you have out-of-pocket dependent care or health care expenses (limitations apply), you can set aside a portion of your salary on a pre-tax

basis to cover these expenses, thereby reducing your taxable income.

- **Integrated EAP & Family Resource Service:** Free, confidential counseling support and referral services are available to help with problems associated with work and personal lives—including marriage and family problems, substance abuse and stress-related issues. In addition, child care, elder care, college planning, and summer camp referrals are available. Employees can also get financial advice and attorney referrals.
- **Adoption assistance:** If you are legally adopting a child, MITRE will pay for a portion of qualified expenses.
- **Civic Leave:** MITRE will pay for up to 40 hours per year for approved volunteer work during traditional work hours.
- **Investment Counseling/Retirement Planning Services:** Trained financial representatives from Fidelity and TIAA-CREF can work with you to create a customized retirement savings portfolio.
- **Health Services:** On-site nurses are available to help you maintain your health and make informed decisions regarding your care. The nursing staff coordinates a variety of health and wellness programs, including blood pressure monitoring, annual flu shots and community blood drives.
- **Prenatal/Lactation Support Program:** Nursing equipment is available for use in a private area. Maternity-related publications and videos are also available.
- **Smoking Cessation:** Health Services periodically offers a variety of in-house programs and information on external programs. The company also participates annually in the Great American Smoke Out.

- **Fitness Center:** On-site fitness centers with a host of aerobic and muscle-conditioning equipment and programs are available.
- **Massage Therapy:** Sore muscles? Aching back? You can receive a seated massage.
- **Physical Therapy/Chiropractic Services:** You have access to a free evaluation with a physical therapist. With a physician's authorization, you can schedule sessions with a physical therapist right here at MITRE. You also can benefit from discounted on-site chiropractic services.
- **Lunch-Time Seminars:** Topics related to healthcare, wellness, retirement, financial security, dependent care and more are provided by the company during lunch-hour sessions.
- **Sundry Shop:** Visit our on-site "convenience store," which carries personal care items, magazines, greeting cards and snacks; dry cleaning services available, too.
- **Social/Recreation Programs:** Enjoy discount tickets to movies, theaters and theme parks. In addition, employees can use discount purchase programs from United Buying Service and Mass Buying Power.
- **Vision Care:** Employees and their family members who wear glasses or contact lenses have access to a comprehensive vision plan.
- **Pre-Paid Legal Services:** Employees who choose to enroll in this program can have access to an attorney to assist with a variety of legal needs, from developing a will to court appearances, to real estate transactions.
- **Dependent Life Insurance:** Employees have the opportunity to provide additional insurance for their spouse and children.

In the next chapter, you will learn about more companies with best, interesting or radical practices to help their staff Love their work by Loving their Life.

COMPANIES WITH BEST, INTERESTING OR RADICAL WORK/LIFE PRACTICES

IN THIS CHAPTER, YOU WILL FIND INFORMATION ON A VARIETY OF ORGANIZATIONS WITH

best, interesting or radical work/life practices. You'll also hear from the employees who work within them.

Profile of Success

Lisa Jarvis—Manager of Planning and Analysis Retail Division, Clarks Companies, NA

I'm finally at a place where I really love where I am and what I'm doing. In my career, I've worked in all types of industries—law, consulting, hospitality, manufacturing, and even a dot-com. I have done everything from paralegal work, to restaurant management, systems implementation, training, consulting, tailoring, and finance. Most people are amazed at the diversity and range of positions that I have held, and cannot see how they are related. The key is to concentrate on your "skills," not the positions. By doing this you will find that your skill sets are transferable to other industries, many of which you may have never even considered. This opens up a whole new world of possibilities and career options.

Sometimes the most basic things bring the greatest growth and reward. I find that the more you get involved—just roll up your sleeves and do it—the more you can personally gain, learn, grow, experience and acquire. I am always willing to get involved with new projects, regardless of the scope, which has allowed me to leverage some of my other skills and make meaningful contributions to the company of a non-financial nature. This can also open the doors to other opportunities.

I love where I am currently working, especially the environment and culture. Communication, collaboration, and teamwork are all company core values and have definitely contributed to the success and growth of the company. Personal development and training for all employees is mandatory, and an open door policy fosters creative problem solving. They also understand the importance of "giving back to the community," and encourage us to get involved with community organizations, not only individually, but as a company as well. They value the importance of people, both internal and external, and they take the time to show appreciation. After all, it's the little things that matter most.

Profile of Success

Kelly Shea—Director of Human Resources, Couto Management Group, LLC

Loving your work by Loving your Life starts with assessing your own values and interests then generating a career that caters to both. From a very young age, I knew I wanted to be in business; undoubtedly this stemmed from the strong example set by my mother, the major breadwinner in our family. Once in business school, I signed up for one class in each discipline to help me decide on a major. Ultimately, I decided on Management, specifically Human Resources Management, an area where I can have a direct positive effect on the lives of others.

In my current role as Director of Human Resources for Couto Management Group, a small company that manages operations for 42 Dunkin' Donuts locations, I enjoy the type of influence and authority many must work years to achieve. After graduation, I was fortunate enough to be hired by a small company where I could begin my career with that level of authority.

Loving work

Undoubtedly, the most rewarding aspect of my job is the time I am able to spend serving our employees through training, motivating and resolving disputes. What gets me to work every day is knowing I have a direct impact on our company and the people who work for us. If I felt I wasn't contributing, I would move on.

At the same time, however, I do not romanticize work so much so that I forget the importance of completing the everyday administrative tasks necessary to run a business. I choose to view this more mundane work as something that enables me to stay afloat so I can get to the more rewarding work.

Another part of loving my work is being able to constantly learn and develop myself. When I started with the company right out of college, it was my responsibility to develop and grow the Human Resources Department. So far, my entire job has been a learn-as-you-go process.

My advice to others: Decide what is important to you, both personally and professionally, and be strong enough to carve out a job that suits both. Oftentimes it is not the job itself that is rewarding but how you view your contribution.

Loving Life

How do I love my life? My dad does my laundry (she laughs). I am able to separate my work life from my personal life, most days anyway. This helps me to achieve a sense of balance. It is important to make time for yourself, your health, family, and friends. Do the things you love—reading, shopping, whatever or you will not be a very happy and productive worker. Spend time with your family and friends, people who are important to you; everyone needs to debrief and gain perspective on what is truly important in life.

Right now, if my entire life were just my work, I probably wouldn't love my life. I think about some people, like many entrepreneurs, who tend to let work take over their life because their work is their life. It is their passion and that's how they love their life. For me, a woman in her mid-20's, my work is not my life. I still value spending time with my friends and family and having "me-time."

Tips for Organizations to Help Their Staff Love Their Work and Life

The biggest and most supportive thing we do is to communicate openly to our employees the value we place on promotion from within. We seek and identify employees that might want training and development for managerial positions. I tell all the managers to explain to their employees that if they are interested in moving up in the company, the opportunities are there for them. The employees are then free to approach their manager when they are ready to grow their career.

Profile of Success

Clara Ooyama—Chief Operating Officer, Global Diversity Office, Kodak

My life is my life and my work is a part of my life. Work is not in competition with my life; it is a part of my life. My life includes my family, putting food on the table, and a large chunk of that is work. In order for something to be a part of my life—it has to be a part of my life's goals.

If I am useful and make a difference to a larger picture, and in this case it is Kodak, I am okay. I don't worry about how much money I make. I am not working for the money. Why I work is for the intrinsic value of what I do.

My seven year old daughter, Rachel, asked, "Mommy, What do you do?" and I said, "Are you asking what are my daily activities or what is the purpose of my work?" and she replied, "Both." I responded, "In my daily activities I go to meetings and talk with people. The purpose of my work is to make Kodak a great place to work for employees so they try their best and every day when they come into work they want to give 100%." That's what it boils down to—I need a higher purpose.

My work is on inclusion and diversity and that carries into all parts of my life. For example, I work with the Boy Scouts. I work with the younger kids and they remember when an adult takes them under their wings and helps them. The boys who make it to the high level of Eagle—I see the impact on them. I go on all the campouts with them and talk to the older boys about inclusion of the younger children. I use as an example of how when they were younger and came into the troop, how the older boys treated them and they were made to feel useful and included. So I tell them that when they're working with the new little kids to remember how they felt when they were in their position. This is all the same whether I'm working with kids or at Kodak, where I am more strategic and organizational in my focus.

In all my jobs, I've been able to go beyond my realm of influence. It's about making a difference and not just being a cog in the wheel. I'm not very traditional—I'm the one that goes camping and builds the garden, and my husband takes care of the kids and the house.

Tips to LwL[2]

Be like "Pooh Bear." Winnie the Pooh is a very happy-go-lucky bear and whatever challenge he faces he takes it on full force and accepts what is in front of his path. I find that so many people complain about and bemoan "what is." If I'm not willing to invest energy about doing something about it, why would I invest energy in complaining about it? My philosophy is that—if I'm not going to do something to change the situation, then, I don't complain about it. If I can't or won't take time to work on correcting it, I'm not going to dwell on it and spend a whole lot of time not moving on. When my son complains, I say, "Well if you don't like it, what are you going to do about it?" That is empowering and he can make the choice.

Another tip to LwL² is to have conversations with yourself. I have them with myself when I drive. They take on the tone of a conversation where I take both sides—maybe it's the lawyer in me—as a lawyer you can argue anything. When I have a "me and myself" conversation rather than just complaining or gnawing at it, I take time to examine it from different perspectives. I find that it just works and in the end, I answer my own questions.

Thoughts on Diversity

From a globalization perspective, every human being is the same in that they are different. We keep searching for how people are the same, but we're not. We don't have the same values and that can make it difficult for us to go outside ourselves or connect with others. My brother and I come from the same parents but we are very different. When you meet someone, don't make assumptions. Anything you think about a culture, ask yourself why you think you know that rather than assuming it is the truth.

Profile of Success

Melissa Klinkhamer—Human Resources Project Director, Sepracor

I have always found a lot of satisfaction in my job and I really enjoy the challenge of working for a growing organization. With a new child in my life, my priorities are different and therefore balancing work and my family is essential to me. Because I have the opportunity to work a flexible schedule, I feel that I have a good balance between family life as well as meeting the demands of my job. It is very important for me to continue to develop my career. I want to make a contribution to the growth and development of Sepracor but also feel good about the time I devote to my childrearing responsibilities. At this point in my life, the opportunity for both my husband and I to have a flexible vs. a traditional work week is what really has made the difference.

If you looked up the words *compassion* and *caring* in the corporate dictionary, The TJX Companies would be used as an example. How a company treats its staff is a direct reflection of its senior leadership. President, Ted English, makes it a priority to treat his staff well. Here are some further insights into this great company from two of its management staff.

Profile of Success

Virginia Nelson—Assistant Vice President, Manager of Community Relations, The TJX Companies (Marshalls, T.J. Maxx, HomeGoods & A.J. Wright)

For me, family is a critical bond. Loving our children is about being there for them. From kindergarten to college, when they had special school activities and extracurricular activities, my husband and I were always there for them. As a dual income family, both of us worked to keep the lifestyle we wanted. For us, education is the key and we wanted our kids to have the best. It was *understood* that they WOULD go to college. My kids are 26 and 30 and they still have minds of their own. They had a good foundation.

My parents also instilled education in me. I've learned through the years that education comes in many forms, not just book knowledge. They taught me about religion and interactions with other people.

I also learned about work. My parents were both domestics and we were as poor as church rats, but I was smothered in love and brought up on middle-class values. Since I was three years old, I wanted to be a kindergarten teacher, and that was my first real job after college. I made $7,000 a year.

Then, I got my masters degree and became a librarian. I was a business librarian for a *FORTUNE* 500 company, American Cyanamid, a major chemical company. I was promoted to a position at Prudential Insurance in Boston. From there, I went to work at Filene's Department Store and then to TJX. I've always had jobs that help people.

My final pearls of wisdom are

- Don't take "No" personally.
- Remember that "When Opportunity Knocks, Ability Unlocks and Determination Kicks the Door In!!"

Profile of Success

Jerome Smalls—Manager of Diversity Staffing, The TJX Companies (Marshalls, T.J. Maxx, HomeGoods, A.J. Wright)

Loving your work by Loving your Life is about making a life, not just a living. At this stage of my life, I'm more in touch with my motto, which is 'Making a life, not just a living.' At one point, money and prestige were my drivers. Now my goals drive and motivate me and my core values sustain me.

What's important to me is spontaneity, integrity, leading with a vision, giving back to the community and mutual respect. I need to find work that reflects my values and if I can tie them to my organization's values then that's where there is a very strong marriage. If an organization values something that is not a part of your values, then you should rethink if you want to be a part of it.

When I wake up in the morning and put my feet on the floor I am happy. It's not a chore. It's not about me, but about what I do. It's the intrinsic stuff inside of me.

My daily job at TJX, a *FORTUNE* 200 company, is to provide strategic leadership and direction around diversity, especially around talent acquisition.

How do you tap into talent? I do it through relationships with schools, networking, the internet (websites) and agencies. I use multiple resources to achieve these goals.

In the concentric circles of life, you look at what's most important to you. My work and life's work are inextricably bound together. For some, they are separate but mine are intertwined. So work and play are together. That can be a liability because I could just work and so I have to watch and be cognizant of not becoming so absorbed that I don't know when to stop.

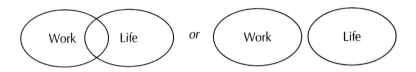

Some Tips I Have to Love your work by Loving your Life

- Identify what it is that motivates you and why it motivates you.
- Know what a good job looks like. To be successful, you have to have a vision of what success looks like for you. For some it's money, for others it may be volunteerism.

    For example, for the past year in Boston, I've taught at Dorchester High School in the Economics and Business Academy. I teach goal setting, problem solving and how to make a life, not just a living. You must be clear on what success looks like for you, not others.

- As a strong believer in the work of the noted author of situational leadership, Ken Blanchard, I've learned no matter what station in life you are in, know about your points of power. My points of power are

    - relationship power
    - personal power
    - positional power
    - task power
    - knowledge power

Here's how these points of power work.

Relationship power is the power of being able to build relationships and have the skill and the ability to maintain them. I learned to build relationships better when I was a training manager in the Southeast. I'd travel and almost always had to change planes in Atlanta. I'd buy cards and fill them out. I must have about $500 in cards now. After a meeting, I'd write a card to the person I had just met with while waiting for my plane then send it to them. I would be specific in the card. For example, I would write something like, "It was a powerful discussion when we talked about mentoring." I try to look at relationships before tasks, or "R" before "T."

The second point of power is personal power and we all have this in some way, shape or form. For example, communications, writing skills, visionary thinking, being a good strategist and also knowing how to tap into it are all personal power traits.

Another point of power is positional power. For example, as a CEO of a company and by virtue of the position, you can achieve things, but you will not be successful in that position if you don't know how to use the power, when to use it and how not to abuse it.

The fourth point of power is task power. I work around people all day who have task power. We created a MetroWest Resource Guide so people who are diverse relative to race, gender and sexual orientation can find their way around our community. The guide was also created for individuals newly relocated to our community. I utilized a lot of people to help with this task. I tapped into community resources and asked people who were newly relocated about what help they needed when they arrived to our community.

My strongest power point is in relationships—bringing people together. When you can identify what task power you have, people will find you. You have to know what you're good at and what others do. People who don't have goals will be used by people who do have them.

The last point of power is knowledge power. I need to know what type of knowledge power I have. For example, I know quite a lot about dogs, philosophy and music. It is important for you to know what knowledge you possess and how you can utilize it to build your personal life as well as your professional career. If I don't know how to do it, do I know where to go to find someone who does? It's about knowing where you can go to get knowledge.

I believe you can diagnose your own skill level on a task, project or new assignment fairly easily. Determine your competence and motivation. Classic enthusiastic beginners are excited but have low confidence. For example, when I started as a stand up speaker, I didn't know what I didn't know and I blacked out and didn't know what to say. My motivation and enthusiasm were strong but my confidence was low and I needed some kind of direction and support. Eventually, I made it to a stage where I really knew I could do it and all I needed was coaching—my confidence, competence and motivation became strong.

Later, as I advanced I became close to a self-reliant achiever. I didn't need a lot of direction or a lot of support. I have stronger confidence and competence levels because I've gone through all these stages. Now I only need to be clear about my objectives and how I'm going to deliver my speech.

People go through the same stages in life. It's not just about announcing the destination in life, it's preparing for the journey. For example, you may want to be a Senior VP or CEO, but what are you going to do to get there?

Some Tips to Love your work and Life

To LwL[2], have a clear sense of purpose and be willing to take a risk in the hopes of finding something better in life. It's about having spiritual and mental contentment. I don't worry about other people's stuff, but I believe in a power bigger than myself. Life isn't just a bed of roses and I know what I need to do when life gets rough. Usually, I need to go inward and focus on what I need to do to get out of the slump. Sometimes you have to do it yourself. I find myself turning inwardly and identifying what I need to do to move on.

I'm very careful about the gifts I've been given and not turning them into over-used skills. For example, a great orator can't just talk all the time. I try to use my skills wisely so they are helpful to me and others.

I am also fortunate and have two excellent mentors. They tell me how I'm perceived by others. My mentors help to remind me of those things. They have been there before and they prepare me for the pitfalls in the road ahead. My mentors may hit me back with stuff like, 'What did you do wrong and what are you going to do to change?' Having good mentors and maintaining good relationships are so very important.

Recommended Reading

To help you better LwL², I recommend two books. The first is Ken Blanchard and Sheldon Bowles' *Gung Ho!* I admire many of Ken Blanchard's principles. He has three secrets in this book:

1. The spirit of the squirrel or doing worthwhile work.
2. The way of the beaver. Beavers build dams together and usually are in control of achieving their goal by working together as a team.
3. The gift of the goose and knowing that success is about honking each other on. This is cheering each other on and saying, "You're doing a good job and keep up the good work."

On Speaking Well by Peggy Noonan is my second pick. This book will help you to understand how clarity of voice can be such a powerful message. It also teaches you how to paint visual pictures for people to see and how the smallest word can be used to move a nation, organization or relationship.

Best, Interesting or Radical Practices

Fidelity Capital Companies: The Seaport Hotel, World Trade Center Boston, Sebastian's Catering and Boston Coach

The Seaport Hotel, World Trade Center Boston, Sebastian's Catering and Boston Coach are four Fidelity Capital companies who invest wisely in their employees. Lisa Wholey, Training Manager, and her Head of Human Resources, Pat Murphy, work to ensure that their diverse employee population receives training that helps them in their job and life. The employee population of The Seaport Hotel, Sebastian's Catering and the World Trade Center Boston looks like a mini-United Nations. Staff from locations around the world service the organization's international clientele. Management, training and leadership programs which cover a variety of areas to improve work and life skills are offered. This includes diversity programs where issues are discussed such as tips on:

- managing a diverse and international staff
- managing across generations
- ways to help staff integrate work and life and
- time management skills

Boston Coach, another Fidelity Company, also does a stellar job of helping its diverse and international staff with life and work skills. Mary Aceto, Vice President of Human Resources, and her staff are often found at airports around the country meeting and greeting Boston Coach employees, who provide sedan services to executives and business travelers, on their turf. The information Aceto gains by meeting staff on their own territory helps her to improve and better tailor programs suited to a mobile workforce who is literally always on the go.

Best, Interesting or Radical Practices
The Dana–Farber Cancer Institute (DFCI)

Anyone who has ever had cancer or experienced a family member who has suffered through this devastating disease can appreciate the work that is done around cancer at hospitals and teaching research centers. DFCI is one of the nation's premier organizations for cancer research, teaching and patient care. Chief Operating Officer, James "Jim" Conway, is an executive who "gets the connection" between how staff are treated and, in turn, how they treat the customer—that is, the patient. Conway makes it a point to become involved in understanding the work/life needs of staff at all levels—physicians, nurses, researchers, managers and staff. Management by walking around and keeping up with the latest management and Human Resource trends help him to better help staff LwL[2].

In the next chapter, we will investigate how some families are successfully integrating work, life and time to enjoy each other.

Chapter 33

Making Your Career and Family Life Work: Lessons from Families Who Get It

O FTEN, COUPLES WITH YOUNG CHILDREN HAVE TO PULL TOGETHER TO KEEP THEIR family's work/life plates spinning in harmony. Here are profiles of some couples who have found a way to successfully manage the rigors of high powered careers while raising a young family.

Profiles of Success

Wayne Martin and Laura Stone

Wayne is the President and Laura is the Executive Producer of Stream Productions, an award winning video and multimedia company.

Wayne: We like what we do and that is important. When we started dating, Laura and I had a lot of philosophies that we agreed upon, and that is why we got married. We wanted to be hard workers, solve problems and deal with people in a positive, rather than negative manner. Frequently, we take that philosophy to our work. We've been together for 16 years and have been running a business together for eight of those years.

Laura: Before, I was working a job out on the road and both our priorities were at odds, but now they are not.

Wayne: Prior to starting my business, I was working as a videographer. I decided to make a change and went out on some job interviews. On one interview I was asked, "Where do you see yourself in three years?" I answered, "Running my own business." At that moment, a light went on. I thought "If I want to be running my own business in three years, I'd better get started now." So I took business courses at Northeastern University and then at Boston College's SBDC—Small Business Development Center. I knew I wanted to start a business, but I didn't know what kind of business.

At the SBDC they said the best way to succeed in starting a business is to choose a field you know well. What I knew how to do best was video production. When Laura said she would do it with me and kicked in some of her savings, we were ready to go.

We created a business plan and have fulfilled it. We found it rewarding to plan goals and achieve them. We also included personal goals in our plan. We decided to get ourselves out of financial debt and to buy a house. We also set financial goals for the business as well as goals about having personnel. We both had a clear idea of what we wanted.

To quote Mark Twain
"I can teach anybody how to get what they want out of life.
The problem is that I can't find anybody who can tell me what they want."

The goals have helped us to get where we want to be and understand how we can accomplish them together.

Our goals are also about family. I read somewhere that kids who are hugged daily and touched in a loving way by their parents grow up to be more secure. I make it a point every day to hug my two kids and tell them I love them. As a result, I have a 15-year-old boy who can come up to me and give me a hug and tell me he loves me. Except for a goodnight kiss, my dad never gave me a hug. As adults, my dad and I learned to greet each other with a hug and a kiss and to end each telephone conversation with "I love you." It meant a lot to me.

Laura: Starting our business was also about a lifestyle change. When my son was a child, I dragged him off to day care at 8 A.M. I rushed to pick him up when day care closed at 6:00 P.M. I'd usually arrive just in the knick of time, so I didn't have to pay the $10-for-every-five-minutes late fee. When we had our second child, our daughter, we didn't want that and starting the business helped us to spend more quality time with the kids.

When my daughter was an infant, we ran the business out of our apartment (which we did for the first four years). I now have control over my schedule. It doesn't make it any easier. Sometimes I am still frustrated because when I'm working, I want to be with the kids and vice-versa. I want to give so much to both.

Wayne: We believe it's very important to be there when our kids get home from school.

Laura: I *now* have the flexibility to work when I want to. It doesn't always work that way. Sometimes we have to bring the kids in to work.

We also like to have that same philosophy with our employees. Our bookkeeper works part-time hours so she can be home in the afternoons with her kids. One employee wanted to arrange his schedule to take banjo lessons. Another wanted to go to Greece and we let him take off the time he needed to take his dream vacation. We try to make it a nice place at work for our staff. We really want our employees to be treated the way we would want to be treated.

To us, flexibility is important and we want that to extend down through our organization. We do not want to create policies that are stagnant because life is ever-changing.

Profiles of Success
Robin and Mark Pedrelli

Robin Pedrelli—Vice President, Program Director, Linkage, Inc.

As far as trends about LwL[2], I'm coming across more women who are pursuing careers while their husbands stay at home to care for the children. I have had the fortune of speaking with several women who were working mothers before this was the norm. It was comforting to learn that these women shared many of my feelings of doubt—feelings that I am not a good mother, not giving enough to my job or my family. It is encouraging to learn that their grown children are a testament to their mothering skills. By working, these mothers instilled in their children a sense that women have much to contribute to the world and provided a positive role model for their daughters.

Trying to balance work and family is not without its challenges. The biggest success factor for Mark and I is that it really is a full partnership. We contribute 50/50 to the family life and we both have made sacrifices in our careers. A relationship with our children was equally important to the both of us. We each work four days a week so our kids get to see more of us. When a "daycare situation" arises we each look at our workload to determine whose schedule can better accommodate a day at home. When I was pregnant, people told Mark that fathers can't have the same bond with their kids as mothers. Refusing to believe this, he worked to develop a strong relationship with our two sons by putting a lot of time and energy into it. As a result, our children have a powerful relationship with their mother and father.

Making this situation work requires discipline and planning. With two small children at home, I have learned to plan for the unexpected. Every night before leaving the office, I pack a bag with all the materials I will need to work from home the following day. As long as I have the necessary materials with me, I can usually manage to get things done. Both my husband and I make a concerted effort to be home for dinner or at least to put the children to bed. This may mean finishing work between the hours of 9:00 pm and 2:00 am. Finally, it is important in this balancing act to let some things go. This can be hard because we are both Type A personalities. It takes discipline. Some times you lose it (she laughs), but you have to just keep it in perspective.

Mark Pedrelli—Art Director, Arnold Worldwide

Off the top of my head, what companies can do is to allow an employee the freedom to be able to take care of their family and work life. It is important for an organization to set a standard to let people balance their work and personal life. I've made arrangements with my company, in which I spend one day at home with my kids. Companies have to be able to assume that the employee will put in the needed time to perform his/her necessary duties. This is, of course, not a given, but must be looked at on a case-by-case basis. The burden of proof is on the employee, not the company, to assure that a flexible work schedule will work. However, the importance of the organization standing behind their flexible schedule policies cannot be understated.

I was home all day today, and although never completely out of touch with my office, the focus was on my kids. This is opposed to having one arm in work and one at home by trying to work and parent simultaneously. There is a stigma that if you only work four days per week, you simply work less. People tend to resent it back in the office, as they wonder why someone receives such "special treatment" simply because they're a parent. People who work five days sometimes think they are putting in more effort, whereas most people don't understand that many nights it is 9:30 p.m. and I'm just starting to work as my kids go to sleep. My wife and I have to sometimes sacrifice our personal time. We have to adjust our personal lives based on the fact that a workday may continue well into the evening, or consume a weekend.

Sometimes managers too think that if you're not putting in "face time," you're not loyal. People may say that a person is just doing it to avoid working 40 hours, when in reality, it's because their family is a priority. I'll put in whatever kind of effort I need to get the job done.

Companies need to understand that there are people who want this type of work/life relationship. They want time with their family and they're committed to their work and are willing to balance both. I think this works well for me, and my organization. I do think that one of the downsides of having this relationship can be that it puts a strain on the employee/boss relationship as well as the peer relationship if all the parties don't understand the arrangement.

Tips

Some tips I'd give to people, especially fathers, is to seek out an organization to support you and your work and life as a father, an organization that will give you the opportunity to be with your kids more. If possible, look internally, and ask a manager if there's a possibility to adjust your work situation to better suit your needs as a parent.

We work hard to include our kids and not rush around all the time. If someone is working from home, they will definitely have to put in the extra time and effort. There will be times when they may need to give a little more than they want to establish a trusting relationship with others with whom they work. They should make sure they are equipped to work at home, like they would be in the office. Have all the equipment necessary to function and communicate properly. Get in the habit of carrying materials back and forth with you from the office. A flexible work schedule is a commitment both of yourself, and of your company. Give a little now and then, stick to your priorities, and communicate.

Best, Interesting or Radical Practices

Arnold Worldwide is a *Working Mother's* 100 Best Company. Here are some of the benefits that make them such a good company:

- One Winter Wellness day per month for October, November, December, January, February, March and April is given to staff to help keep them healthy and wise.
- Every other Friday off can be taken by employees from Memorial Day through Labor Day.
- Christmas Eve, Christmas Day and the day after Christmas; New Year's Day and the day after New Year's are times to be with loved ones—not at work—for Arnold employees.
- Chair massage and chiropractic services help staff to align their bodies, be healthy and better LwL[2].

Source: Robin Pedrelli

Sometimes couples find themselves having to battle the rigors of demanding jobs and finding time for each other. In the case of Darrell Brown, a police officer with the Durham, North Carolina police force and Tedra Brown, M.D., they also have to factor in time to help their award-winning teenage daughter and gymnast, Taylor, pursue her career dreams which may include the Olympics. Here is the story of this impressive family.

Profile of Success

Darrell Brown—Master Officer, Durham, North Carolina Police Department

One of the biggest things for me is that it takes two to make a marriage and family successful. I've come to realize that it's tough on one person to handle all that goes on with kids and work and family.

I have a wife who is a physician, and she has more prestige than I do as a police officer. A situation where the woman has a higher paying job than the man may cause problems in a relationship. Sometimes, the individual making less money is made to feel like they should do more around the house because their income is less. For us, the roles are reversed and she does make more money than me, but she doesn't let that go to her head. We both make decisions about our family and finances.

We've been together for 19 years. I've seen her go through medical school, her residency and her fellowship. I supported her during those times and she's been there for me as I've climbed the ladder as a police officer in special investigations at the Durham, North Carolina Police Department.

We both share the same priorities about life. God is first in our life. Our kids are top priority, and work is our third priority. I also like to golf whenever I can. You have to have some fun in your life.

Looking back at how I was raised, I wanted to make sure that my kids would have things I didn't have and opportunities that weren't granted to me. If, as a parent, you aren't there for your child, they can stray and will find someone out in the street that will be there for them. This could be a positive or negative influence, but nine times out of ten, it is negative.

As a police officer, I see this a lot. Working in different areas, you are actually involved in the communities and you watch kids as they grow up. I've seen the parents, grandparents and the kids follow in the same patterns as their mother and grandmother. It has been my role as a police officer to break that pattern and get the kids away from bad habits. In a lot of the low income and poorly developed neighborhoods, often these children are from single parent female headed households. If kids see their moms drinking, hanging out with a lot of men, unfortunately, they often grow up and repeat that pattern.

The programs that my department implements help to break this cycle. This includes educational and computer programs. These are also activities that they can be involved in after school and summer programs to connect them with the university students as Big Sisters and Big Brothers. All these efforts help to keep them out of trouble. In the schools, we also participate in the Drug Awareness DARE program.

I can relate to children because I have a three year old and a thirteen year old. My thirteen year old is a gymnast, and maybe some day she'll compete in college and Olympic gymnastics. My wife and I, in addition to our jobs, have another full time job with her career as a gymnast. She attends a special school for children who aspire to be professional gymnasts. Her schedule is very rigorous. She goes to school, and must practice at a gym six days a week. She must watch her diet and always be in top form. We take her to gymnastic meets all around the country. My wife and I trade off driving her to and from practice so she can achieve her dream.

I feel so fortunate. God has placed me in a position to do all the things I love to do. It also helps to have a loving and committed wife.

Recommended Reading
Ken Lizotte and Barbara A. Litwak. *Balancing Work and Family*. New York: AMACOM, 1995.

Recommended Reading
Maria Hinojosa. *Raising Raul*. New York, NY: Penguin Books, 2000.

Chapter 34

FINANCES AND FAMILY PLANNING

FINANCES AND FAMILY PLANNING

FINANCIAL PLANNING CAN HELP OR HINDER A PERSON AND OR HIS FAMILY TO LwL². CPA Jeffrey Rose, banking executive Sal Sagarese and business owners Steven and Ellie Kleinberg provide some practical advice on how to LwL² by planning for your financial success.

Profile of Success
Jeffrey V. Rose—CPA

You must have a plan in life and stick to it no matter what. However, you must leave yourself open and flexible to your plan because unexpected situations in life happen, making it necessary to adjust your plan. Do what is necessary to resolve the situation then get back on track with your overall plan. Also, you must constantly assess the specifics of your plan because they will change over time. Make adjustments when necessary and continue to move forward in meeting the objectives of your plan.

Finances are very important in everyone's life and should be part of your life's plan. They govern your lifestyle and can have a major impact on your goals. Without the proper finances or adequate financial planning, you may not be able to achieve your ultimate goals. It is essential that you assess your finances and make sure that they are in line with your goals and objectives in life and at work.

Profile of Success
Sal Sagarese—Lending Officer, Vice President of Cambridge Trust

The first thing you have to do to Love your work by Loving your Life is set a goal for yourself. Be accepting of the good and the bad. Try to find the good in a different situation and learn from it. Sometimes, when people run into difficulty they try to run away or avoid it instead of staying on top of it. If you put it aside, it will become more difficult. If you go at it right away, it might not be as overwhelming as you think. The world and workplace are always changing and things are not going away so you might as well embrace change. You have to change to move forward. If you truly want to succeed, you have to be motivated to attack and go after problem issues and not put them aside for a few days.

When you run into a challenge, ask yourself, "What do they want? What are they asking for?" Some people think if you look for help, there is something wrong, but really there is something right. Asking for help is key.

I have always lived by the motto, "Keep everything small because at the end of the day things add up. If you don't do so, they become bigger than they need to be." Keep it the right size. If you're in a bad situation and the customer is in front of you, you have to make them trust you. If I freaked out every time something went wrong in my job then I wouldn't be here. Also, don't take things personally. If you listen to what goes wrong and solve it, the next time you will have experience at it. You need to take things in steps. Eventually, the baby steps lead to bigger things.

Every year you should set yourself a goal. The company has to also help you to set goals; it is a partnership. They give you the tools and products and if you're motivated you should be okay. The more you do these things, the better you get at them. This develops with experience. The more experience you get, the more you know your limitations. You are building bases. Then you get smarter and become more confident. The more confidence you have, the more creative you become at what you do. It shouldn't all be about profits. It also has to be about helping people in the community. The short-term is profits and the long-term is developing customers and a base. Once you have a satisfied customer, they will stay with you and tell their friends. The business will follow.

As a banker, I have to be in it for the long and short haul. I have to cultivate relationships with a broad base of people. Whether a person is from a different background, or is wealthy or middle class, they all have problems. If you understand their situation, they will respect you. If you are a performer on Broadway, every day the curtain goes up the audience expects a great performance. This is the same in any job. If you really want to succeed and be an MVP or All-Star player, you have to be hungry, not complacent.

You have to live and breathe success. If things go wrong in your life or job, you must figure out why those things happened. It's easier to be a whiner and not a doer. If you want to be successful, you must put in the necessary work. It is not always very easy to come in and perform at a level of excellence every day. Sometimes you need a day off, especially when it feels like everything is coming down on you. You may need to take time off and get some things done so they remain small. Sometimes you need to be away and say to yourself, "I am not that important and the only way I can be clear is to take some time away from the day-to-day-grind." Then you can come back refreshed.

This isn't a formula for everyone. What's good for me may not be good for someone else. As long as you're getting results and it works, then stay with your style.

Basically, things are not always fair, but that's life. Believe you're going to have more good times than bad. Look to deals that really help people. For example, I get a huge satisfaction from people buying their first house.

My final words of advice: Feel you're making a difference in someone's life and make it a part of your business mantra.

Recommended Reading

The Five Minute Mutual Fund Investor by Dana V. C. Mervin. 1995 M Systems Publishing Group Los Alamitos, California.

Order through Amazon.com

Steven and Ellie Kleinberg run a very successful accounting firm. Sometimes families are forced into situations that make sense and cents from a financial point of view. In the case of this awesome couple, they found how to integrate work, life and help each other make and save money at doing something they both love.

Profile of Success

Steven and Ellie Kleinberg—Owners, S.D.K. Financial

Steven and Ellie Kleinberg run a successful family-owned accounting firm—they were first forced into entrepreneurship after Steven lost his job. Here's how Steven describes what happened to him:

Immediately after I left my job, I was already thinking about what I could do. The best and worst job I had was at the same place. I realized that if I felt sorry for myself and angry, I wouldn't have been able to survive so I could be successful—I put the animosity behind me! I took all those energies that I could have used to be angry and channeled them towards my success.

I knew I couldn't get a job in a corporation at my age. I was in my late forties. I decided that I had to work on my own. I had a network of accountants, but was shy and timid and had to learn how to get out there and motivate myself to get work. Now knowing what I know, I would have done it earlier. I built one client at a time.

In the 11 years I've been in the business, I've never missed a paycheck—that's made me proud and given me confidence in everything I do—that has spilled over into my life. I can now talk to anyone—doctors, lawyers, and professional people. I realized that when I started to talk with other accountants that I am as good as, or better than, many of them.

Ellie, Steve's wife, describes how she ended up working for her husband in their accounting firm:

I lost my job after 36 years and had no computer training, so where was I going to go? There were limitations in terms of what I could do. When I worked, it was my tiny corner of the world where I wasn't a wife or mother. I knew what I had to do—I liked it.

Steven and I don't always work well together—I do things my way and Steven has his way of doing things and the rules and standards are different and sometimes it can be too much togetherness.

I don't always have another outlet and the challenge is not to become boring to other people. I work with him side-by-side. In our personal time, if we are always talking about business, clients, and what we have to do, I want to get back to the marriage part. So we balance each other out. There is a time when you have to leave work behind.

It is very different for many people who are older workers right now. We have good friends and his job was taken over by robots and now he has to stock shelves. His wife's company went under and they had to sell their house. This was an enormous transition because they had to go and live out of state near their kids. Other friends have moved to senior citizen housing. Another friend's husband was forced out—she still works. Another friend is a doctor and he decided to enlarge his practice. He could semi-retire, but doesn't want to. However, he has vowed to slow down and spend more time with the grandkids.

A lot of it comes down to money and many people didn't think that they had to work as hard as they do later in life.

Steven and Ellie's Advice on LwL[2]

Accept change and understand change and then work with it. You have to accept that things are changing and that can be fun too. You have to constantly update yourself or you get stale quickly.

We have to learn how to adapt to change—change of jobs, careers, and life. You have to accept change. Once you do, you'll want to learn.

—Steven

I don't think for the average person there's any real spiritual soul searching that they do in relation to their job. To be successful you must go through that exercise.

—Ellie

Everybody's job is important—where would we be without people who pick up garbage? They probably don't go home at night and think about what picking up garbage did for other people. They are probably doing what they feel they have to do. And there is meaning in this—they are bringing home an income and helping people keep things clean.

If you love your work, you're happy to go and be there and it will be reflected in your life. It's the best way to get through the day.

—Steven

Family structures vary greatly. Sometimes members of a family take a position to support their family or not be a burden on their mothers or fathers. The military, for generations, has provided an outlet for young men and women to do both. Next, we will look at family life and the military.

Chapter 35

FAMILY LIFE
AND THE MILITARY

FAMILY LIFE AND THE MILITARY

I GREW UP IN A MILITARY FAMILY. UNTIL I reached 18 years old and left home for college, my entire life was greatly influenced by the United States Air Force. As you learned when I talked about growing up in Okinawa and returning to the United States in 1964, that experience helped to shape my outlook as an adult and my career choice as a consultant and expert on diversity and global workforce issues.

I remember when I was a seventh grader at Thorpe Junior High School in Hampton, Virginia. The Hampton area had numerous military installations in its back yard, including Langley Air Force Base, and many of my classmates were from families whose fathers were stationed at Langley and part of the Tactical Air Command (TAC). While Thorpe was a public school, the influence of the military was felt. Our school song was sung to the lyrics of the Air Force Anthem. You may recall that tune whose lyrics begin:

"Off we go into the wild blue yonder." The final refrain to the song proclaims that in essence since you are part of an organization that climbs and soars high, "Nothing can stop the U.S. Air Force." As an Air Force "brat" (I really do hate when people call me that!), the message was that if you worked hard and reached for the sky and the stars, nothing could stop you.

At school pep rallies, we'd sing our mighty school song and when we got to the part about "nothing can stop," we'd all yell it at the top of our lungs. Did our school teams always win the games after we sang our song? Absolutely not! When we lost, our teachers reminded us that losing

gracefully is all part of the game, and that if we worked a little harder we'd get back on track and win the next game. They told us that whether we won or lost, it was how we played the game that mattered. They also let us know that if you have a winning attitude, whether in sports or in life, nothing can stop you from succeeding if you work hard and put your mind to it.

While my teachers enforced this unstoppable winning attitude and hard work ethic at school, my parents reinforced it at home. My mom always stressed the value of an education and that regardless of the fact that I am a female and my skin color is black that I can be successful in life. She taught me to work hard, get a good education, be respectful and always try to find the beauty in everyone, despite how good or bad, rich or poor that individual is in life.

In this chapter, I wanted to share with you some stories about how military experience can influence not just the military person's work and life, but also that of his or her family members. We will begin by examining a profile of a three-star general. Lt. General David Ohle, retired U.S. Army, is an individual I have come to know, respect and admire for his tremendous accomplishments.

He worked for 32 years in the Army, ultimately as head of Human Resources, and responsible for 1.1 million people. After retiring, he became Vice President of Human Resources for Shell Oil Company. You may remember my story about getting stranded at Shell Oil on September 11, 2001. As fate would have it, Lt. General Ohle was a participant at my seminar and book signing that day. My seminar was on my last book, *Indispensable Employees: How to Hire Them. How To Keep Them.* In that book, I discussed some top organizations that had best practices around getting and keeping employees. One of the organizations I wrote about was the U.S. Army. When I think about how I met Lt. General Ohle, I can hear my Mom's voice in my head saying, "God moves in mysterious ways."

As it turned out, the best practices that I had written about and was speaking about on September 11, 2001 happened to be the programs that had been implemented under Lt. General Ohle's direction when he was in the U.S. Army! Since September 11, I've stayed in touch with him and his lovely and oh-so-brilliant wife, Susan. I hope you will find his insights refreshing and uplifting.

Profile of Success

Lt. General David Ohle—US Army Retired; retired after 32 years of service

Loving my work by Loving my Life is 100% my philosophy.

Back in 1983, the Army got into Organizational Development (OD) before I went into Battalion combat. I had to put together a command philosophy, and I solidified this so it was not just a document.

I was the Deputy Chief of State for Personnel, US Army and was in charge of all aspects of the Human Resource functions for the 1.1 million active soldiers and National Guard and Reserve. The three things I believed in regarding my work then were to:

- maintain combat effectiveness (goals, tasks and mission)
- take care of my employees (soldiers)
- be satisfied and have fun

That goes right into Loving your work and Life; that's what it is all about. Every day is not a fun day, but at the end of the day, week and month if you can't step back and say I'm satisfied and having fun, it's time to move on, especially if you're in the military.

In business, just as in the military, in order to become successful, you must balance achieving goals with taking care of employees. If the equation is out of sync, either the business or the well-being of the employees will fail. To ensure that failure does not occur, every leader must demonstrate in a genuine, believable, and enthusiastic manner that he/she loves life. This is done in three ways:

- by loving the job and accomplishing the goals
- by loving the employees and providing for their well-being
- most importantly by loving and demonstrating a passion for non-work activities centered around family, church and friends

Well Being

At one time, I put together a program to take care of soldiers. You need to know what you're doing and judge how well you're doing it, then tweak your actions based on what you've found. In the Army this is called an AAR, or After Action Review. This allows you to accomplish your mission and take care of your employees (soldiers).

As a general, I had to have fun in my life and really like what I was doing to motivate my troops to accomplish our mission. As a leader, Loving your work by Loving your Life means you have to love the employees, the mission and making the bottom line. Next, you must love your life by creating an environment where you can succeed. You can't go to work every day and say, "I hate my job." The leader has to know how to gauge things. You can drive people at work but you must let them take a break—get a beer, spend time with family.

Loving your Life is about creating an environment you really like and that will spill over into the workforce. Ten years ago, Susan, my wife, was a teacher and taught Spanish and English and wanted to continue to do so and she did that. It wasn't accepted back then. A General's wife was not supposed to work. It was believed that they had too many responsibilities as the General's wife. However, she felt she could do it all— raise a family, be a General's wife and a teacher, and have fun. So we decided it was fine for her to work. She set a new example for what was expected of a General's wife. Today, it is not uncommon for women in that situation to be a wife and have a career.

In business, less than in the Army, leaders don't always do a good job at leading. Sometimes they get so wrapped around their task of getting things done, they don't have fun.

The transition of moving out of the Army and into civilian life was easy for me. I left the Pentagon one day and went to work for Shell Oil as the Vice President of Human Resources. The change wasn't difficult because I had a command philosophy. I knew how to approach work and life and balance everything. One of the first things I did at Shell Oil was to get people together, and instead of doing things in militaryese, I did them in corporatese. I gave my philosophy and let people know I could do the work in a large multinational corporation, not just the military. When you're new, you have to prove your competence and then prove you are a real guy in the corporation. I know at first some people looked at me like I was General George Patten. They had to realize I was a real guy who laughed and talked with people, not a command and control type.

You have to have this philosophy intact within yourself before you can articulate it to others. A lot of people have a problem putting together their command philosophy because they really don't understand what they are all about.

It's about Loving your work and all the things you do to take care of your staff and not just providing them with an EEO opportunity to work. You have to talk to them and sometimes put your arms around them. You need to know what their problems are because, whether you like it or not, their problems become your problems. All of this gets you a positive work environment.

Some people never love life and they really aren't good leaders, but they are good business men and they drive people into the ground. In accomplishing what they need, they become successful business men at the expense of other employees, the corporation, and probably their private lives. When you couple this business approach with loving your life, you can have a life that is overly satisfying and fun. I have no problem going to work because I am fulfilled and the way I approach life is the way I approach business—you're not a Dr. Jekyll and Mr. Hyde. You are the same at work as you are in your personal life. If you have a terrible work life, you will only drive yourself to failure. If you do Love your work and Life, that will spill over and you will accomplish goals and take care of the employees.

My final advice: To Love their work, people need to contribute and be part of the vision. They need to love, be satisfied and have fun. Organizations can help staff to Love their work and Life by making it their bottom line to participate in goal development, giving constant feedback and creating well-being programs.

For many people, like my father, the military offered an avenue to escape from the humble beginnings and travel down roads which would influence the lives and work paths of generations. The military has, for generations, provided young men with an opportunity to mature, increase their status in life and continue their education.

In this next segment, U.S. Marines recruit Mark Browne shares his passion for why he joined the Marines. We also hear the life story of Leonard Mervin, Sr., retired U.S. Air Force. His is a story of a family where two generations committed their lives to serve their country. You'll also discover how the career decision of the father, Leonard Mervin Sr., affected the lives of his sons and daughters. His life is a testament to the power that military life can have on generations to come.

Profile of Success
Mark Browne—U.S. Marines

I spoke to Mark Browne on Sunday, September 20, 2003, one day before he was to ship out to begin basic training as a Marine in Paris Island, South Carolina and become PFC Browne. Here's what he had to say about LwL[2].

Before I shipped out to become a Marine, I was in a program called D.E.P., Delayed Enlistment Program. There were a lot of guys in that program from college or high school. Most came to the program to become a Marine.

On Tuesdays, Thursdays, and every other Saturday we had P.T.—Physical Training—and it was *grueling*. Many guys would get thrashed and come home covered in mud and dripping from sweat.

The one thing the recruiters would ask us was, "Why would you put yourself through all of this?"

All of us would reply, "Because we want to be put through it." We knew that if we wanted to be a Marine, we had to go through P.T. and, as difficult as it was, all of us wanted to be Marines, even more than we wanted life itself.

People have told me that I'm crazy to go into the Marines. I don't believe I am. In fact, I tell them if going into the Marines is crazy, then I'm psychotic.

Profile of Success
Leonard Alexander Mervin, Sr.—U.S. Air Force, Retired

I was just out of High School and 18 years old when I joined the U.S. Air Force in the 1950's. I couldn't afford to go to college. Although my dream was to go to a university and play basketball, given my circumstances, I knew that wasn't going to happen for me and I did not want to be a financial burden to my family. I also did not want to get stuck working at one of the local furniture companies in my North Carolina town located at the foothills of the Blue Ridge Mountains.

I made the decision to join the Air Force. I thought I could save some money and with the GI Bill I would go to college afterwards. It wasn't a big thought process but I had to earn an honest living doing something and that seemed to be the best way. In the military, I would be able to support myself and my family. Living around the world came with the profession. I lived and traveled in many parts of the United States, Japan, The Philippines, Hong Kong, Okinawa and Korea.

The military also allowed me an opportunity to raise my children in a decent, wholesome environment. By living around the world, I also believe that my children gained a sense of who they were as citizens of the world. Diversity and understanding people from different backgrounds are important these days. My children didn't have to learn how to operate in a global environment or deal with foreigners at some company; they were taught how to do this through their experiences of living in so many places in and outside this country. My oldest daughter often thanks me for selecting the career I chose. She believes that it allowed her to grow up thinking globally and being comfortable with all people and in all places.

Regarding "Loving your work by Loving your Life," my work gave me the means to provide for my family, which was my life. My work afforded me the opportunity to live in a diverse environment and mingle with all cultures. I've always thought that you should treat people the way you would like to be treated. I try not to mistreat people. That's one of the most important things in my philosophy.

I've raised 10 children (7 biological and 3 step-children) and believe you should have two chances to raise children. You have raised them once and it would be nice to be able to raise them again, after you've learned from experience how to do it right or better. Sometimes in life you find that perhaps you could have done certain things differently, but you don't have that second chance. You only have one go round in bringing up your children. Your children grow up so quickly, and they have their life and you have a continuation of yours.

Once my kids grew up, I felt that there was a certain appreciation that I had for them that I didn't have when they were younger. You realize they are grown up and you can appreciate them for their adulthood. You look at them and see that they turned out all right. Maybe that's because of you or in spite of you. I would hope that some things I did made a difference to them, but I guess I have to leave that up to them to determine.

After 20 years of service to my country, I retired from the military as a Master Sergeant. While I was a noncommissioned officer, I was so proud when my son, Leonard Mervin, Jr., went into the military. Unlike me, he was able to go to college after high school, and therefore became an officer in the US Army. A few years ago, he retired after 20 years of service. My stepson, Chris Sutton, also followed in my footsteps and recently retired from the U.S. Air Force after 20 years of service. I guess history really does repeat itself.

As I had promised to do at age 18 when I went into the military, I did use the GI Bill after I retired to go to college. I have always been a big believer in education. My wife, Cira, who is on the staff at a large university, also shares that view.

All of my seven biological children and three step-children went to college. Because they obtained a good education, all of our children were able to get great jobs.
They became:

- A rocket scientist and aeronautical engineer who designed airplanes and rockets for such companies as Boeing and McDonald-Douglas
- An Army officer who also got his MBA while in the service
- A manager at a major airline who is responsible for budgets and operations at an airport in New York City
- A senior bank teller at Wachovia
- A manager at a chain of retail stores

- A financial center manager at Wachovia
- A retired Technical Master Sergeant in the U.S. Air Force who also received his MBA while in service
- A supervisor at a large furniture manufacturer
- A consultant, poet, author and publisher
- A vice-president at a Harvard medical school-affiliated teaching hospital, entrepreneur, expert in the workforce and the author of this book, my daughter, Martha R. A. Fields

I believe that my life shows that a parent's career choice can have a significant impact on the lives of generations to come!

What follows is a look at Leonard Mervin's children's views on the topic of LwL[2].

Profile of Success

Dana V. C. Mervin—Full-Time Dad; Former Rocket Scientist and author of *The Five Minute Mutual Fund Investor*

I went from being a rocket scientist and aeronautical engineer to retiring at age 39 and taking care of my daughter. I had the opportunity to try other positions but started to look at the impact that my job and others had in my life. I realized that people had more influence on those things than I wanted.

Sometimes you look around and see people who don't work as hard as you do. Often, they are less inclined to do their job well but get promoted. At times, the people who did well were those who screamed the loudest and worked the least.

I wanted other options in my life. I can find failure or success on my own. I had to ask myself which one I wanted. I decided to go and take a look at this whole world. I didn't want to chase jobs just to have a career. I couldn't have the tail wagging the dog. I had to get my life back in perspective and to test the skills I had developed against the universe. The thing I've learned most is how to survive. This is the tenth year that I haven't worked for someone. I've saved and invested wisely, so I've always paid my bills and have good credit. We don't have the best of everything, but we're not doing badly either. Each day we wake up, I know the sun will shine brightly on me and my family. I have always felt that if I had to go back to work for someone, I'd never fear being laid off. I know I will make it. That's the lesson I've learned through this journey from rocket scientist to full-time Dad.

Profile of Success

Leonard "Bud" Mervin, Jr.—Retired Army Officer

Leonard Mervin, Jr. (Bud) is a second-generation military career man. As you read, his father, Leonard Mervin, Sr., retired after 20 years in the Air Force. In his forties, Bud retired from the Army to start a second career in Orlando, Florida. Here are his thoughts about the years he spent in the military:

In hindsight—as I look back, part of my life strategy has been relatively safe and easy. My goal was to live a good life, have a stable job and maintain good relationships with my loved ones and raise my children. My strategy worked for me. I don't think it's the most lucrative way you can use your life, and you won't get rich, but you will be relatively safe and won't starve.

For example, my career choice was to be in the military. As an officer in the Army, I devoted myself to defending my country. I knew that my job could put me in a combat situation where I could lose my life. That's not usually the case in a job within a corporation.

In the military, the enemy could be looking for you. Your job could kill you, harm you, or severely handicap you, as opposed to going to work for a giant corporation. There you go to do a job and if you don't go to work or don't want to do something required, you can just leave or they will fire you. In the military when you don't go to work, you go to jail because you're AWOL, and you risk your future with a discharge that could haunt you for the rest of your life because it is a dishonorable discharge. If, however, you do what they tell you to do, you will have a good and stable job.

I see jobs such as firefighters, teachers and public officials in much this same way. They allow you to make a good and honorable living and provide good pension benefits. In the end, you can also feel good about the fact that you are helping others and, in a small way, making the world a better place.

Profile of Success

Michael Mervin—Manager of Administration and Environmental Coordinator for a large airline. He works at John F. Kennedy Airport in NYC.

Remember that your happiness is where you are and it is influenced by your attitude. No matter what's going on in your personal life, you can choose by way of your attitude to find happiness at work. You can think negatively all day, but that's going to bring you down. If you have problems at home, leave them there. Don't let it affect your job. I choose to use my time at work positively rather than let any personal problems affect how I feel and how I'm happy at work. We work and interact sometimes more with people on the job than we do with our families. So, do you want to exist in a bad environment where you spend so many of your waking hours? Life is about being happy.

Profiles of Success

Betty Graves—Financial Center Manager, Wachovia Bank

You can be dealt all the wrong cards, but it is up to you how you play them. If you allow it to be your downfall, it will get the best of you. If, however, you take the hand you were dealt and do something with it, you'd be surprised at what the outcome could be.

Looking back over life, sometimes things were difficult, but it was all of those hard times and struggles that made me appreciate what I have today. With God, all things are possible. None of the things I've accomplished in my life would have been possible without Him. Many times, I sat down and cried and couldn't see how things were going to work, but he gave me the tools and all I had to do was use them. He made me quit the whining.

On my Mom's grave is inscribed, "With God, all things are possible, you light the way." I truly believe in that saying. Your life should be a reflection of God's work and nothing is duplicated; it's all original.

Profile of Success

Sharon Brown—Senior Bank Teller, Wachovia and Full-Time Mother

I think it is interesting what the military does to your family. Part of that lifestyle is that you have to learn how to adapt to change. I was at a social event in New Jersey and was listening to a conversation where some people were talking about that concept. The woman in the conversation had lived in New York all her life and she didn't like the fact that she had to adapt to people. She felt that others should adapt to her. By hearing this conversation, I was reminded of how military life helps you to deal with change and diversity. You also have to come out of the box and realize that the world does not just revolve around you. A lot of this is because you have to move around to different military bases and adapt to other people.

Balance and spirituality are important in my life. My husband, Nat, and I believe that we must always provide for our children in terms of their physical, emotional and spiritual needs. The proper order is from spiritual and emotional, then physical needs. Why is it in this order? Because it works for our family. I have kids ages 24, 19, 18 and 3. I definitely see a difference in how they were raised and the issues they face today.

I sometimes think about the two ends of the spectrum—my 24-year-old and my 3-year-old. As an older parent raising kids, I have more knowledge and wisdom, but not necessarily more energy. How does this translate?

It used to be that the issue with time was more quality vs. quantity with my oldest. Today, the youngest gets both. She needs not just one or the other. That is because when I look at the problems kids face these days, they are far more intense than they were 24 years ago.

I have the mindset that when kids were in the formative stages, they needed me more. Now I see that they need me throughout their lives, not just when they are young. That is one reason why I work part-time. My husband and I decided that because we believe they need supervision and guidance at home. Our family is willing to sacrifice certain luxuries so they can benefit from the added attention they receive when I'm not working fulltime.

Profile of Success

Chris Mervin—Manager, Party City of Raleigh

I believe in the philosophy of work hard and play hard. It is paramount when you're at work to give 110% and during your time off to play 110%. This gives me some way to level everything off. It also helps me to put things into perspective.

I am able to have fun when I have fun, and work when I have to work. My extended family has always been athletic and we multitask well, so having this philosophy of 110% is key.

For me, my wife, Della, and the kids, we've come to the realization that it takes effort to work and play. You have to do all of this with the same tenacity. When it comes to parenting, I have sons aged 4, 11 and 21. I've decided not to let anything stop me from working, having a career *and* raising my kids properly. I think that a parent's #1 job, even beyond what they get paid to do at work, is to raise their kids. You have to do what it takes to make sure they do their homework and learn the lessons of life.

Above all, you have to have a personal resolve to do the best you can to teach them morals, values and the difference between right and wrong. Most of us strive to do our best at work, but we also have to maintain that same attitude at home and in our personal lives.

Profile of Success

Pat Schultz

Schultz holds a B.S. in Business Administration (concentration in Economics and Marketing) from The University of North Carolina at Greensboro and has over fourteen years of management experience, and seven years experience as a Technical Trainer. She is also a graduate of Charlotte's Focus on Leadership Program. A true advocate of Total Quality Management, Schultz is a certified Quality Administrator and received the Quality Leadership Award from a former FORTUNE 500 employer, as well as numerous Team Excellence Awards for application results.

In 1996, Schultz established ENHEART Publishing. The name, ENHEART (meaning from the heart) distinctly defines the creative work of Ms. Schultz. Her writing talent and style is lauded by all for its honesty, sincerity and ability to challenge readers to look beyond the surface. ENHEART Publishing was established with the sole purpose of bringing her book, *Metamorphosis—A Life Journey* into existence.

Today ENHEART Publishing exists to bring forth motivational, inspirational and educational literature. ENHEART books are being delivered to the hearts and minds of readers throughout the United States. *Metamorphosis* is featured in the best-selling novel *If This World Were Mine*, by renowned author E. Lynn Harris. Schultz's work is also featured on *The Sound Of Poetry* audio series by The National Library of Poetry and in several anthologies. Ms. Schultz has a distinguished readership that includes poet Nikki Giovanni, authors E. Lynn Harris, Leslie Lewis, Stedman Graham and Jewel Diamond Taylor.

Recommended Reading

ENHEART Publishing has produced the following titles:

Metamorphosis: A Life Journey (1996)
 Author: Pat J. Schultz
Marzetta Stood In For Mama (1999, 2001, 2003)
 Author: Glenda Horton Manning
Saved? (2000)
 Author: Evangelist F. C. Fisher
Daddy Was a Big Man (2002)
 Author: Glenda Horton Manning

Web Brower

"Enhancing Lives Through Messages From the Heart" at www.enheartpublishing.com

Success

By Pat J. Schultz

Success is relative based upon each
Individual's starting point of reference.

It is not measured by the amount of
Treasures in one's safe.
But, how safe one keeps his treasures.
Do not compromise your treasures,
Or you will lose them.

Do not compare yourself to others,
Or you will lose sight of that
Which makes you special.

Measure your success by the test
Of perseverance, and
The barometer of determination.

You will know when you have arrived.
And when you do,
You will not have to tell one soul.

—Copyright © 2002 Pat J. Schultz

Wise Words

John Dixon—Shipping and Transportation Supervisor, Ferguson Copeland Ltd.

"Most of my life is centered around my wife, Chrissy, and son. I'm putting him through college and I look at that as what I have to do as a parent. It's what keeps me working all the time. Every morning that is what gets me up.

I always try to be there for my family. If they need me, I'll be there. I think most of my family members know that about me. My son also knows that if he calls, I'll be there for him."

Wise Words

Chris Sutton—MBA, Technical Master Sergeant, Retired U.S. Air Force

"To LwL[2], I think you have to be really happy and centered and have a good foundation in your home life. This allows you the strength to go back to work and regroup each day. When you know you have something good to go home to, a loving family and support system, it makes it easier to deal with whatever the job throws your way. At the end of the day, family is what it is all about."

"We are family. I've got all my sisters with me. We are family. Get up everybody and sing."
—Song by The Pointer Sisters

As we have seen, the military has helped to shape the work and life of many soldiers and their families as well as young people. Our next chapter, Let's RAP! Young People Speak out about LwL[2], explores the views of LwL[2] by some individuals ages 12–25 years old.

Chapter 36

Let's Rap!
Young People
Speak Out
about LwL²

LET'S RAP! YOUNG PEOPLE SPEAK OUT ABOUT LwL²

IN THE 1960'S AND 1970'S, PEOPLE USED THE WORD "RAP" TO DESCRIBE CONVERSATIONS and dialogues that generally were of a controversial, out of the box, groovy or deep/heavy nature. Today, rap is a form of music that often expresses similar sentiments. In this section, people 12–25 years old rap about their perspectives on LwL².

Wise Words

Feeling good about sharing work experiences with friends and sharing personal experiences with work colleagues tells me I am in a good place.

—Kristen Kennedy—23 years old; Event Coordinator, Network World

---

In this next section, you'll read about how young and older people are teaming up and partnering to learn from each other. You'll also learn about the views of college students and professionals. Their contemporary insights into how they LwL² are refreshing and reflect the views of people who will run and inhabit the world and workplace in the not so distant future.

On the *Road* to Success

By Maureen Tacito—Civil Engineer,
23 years old

AS A 23-YEAR-OLD WOMAN WHO IS ONE class away from a Master's degree in Civil Engineering, I feel that I have an edge over most of my peers for beginning professional life. Looking back on my childhood, I remember the reason I decided to become a civil engineer. As a child, my family went on many road trip vacations where I was always in the backseat with my sister peering out the window staring at the highway in amazement (one of the only times on vacation when I would keep my mouth shut!).

When it was time to attend college, I personally wanted some kind of direction and did not want to enter a field completely clueless. With my combined interests in roadway design and over achievements in mathematics, I chose the civil engineering path and have not looked back since. After completing my undergraduate degree at the University of New Hampshire, I decided to pursue my Master's degree immediately despite much discouragement from professors and friends who didn't have complete confidence that I could excel in the vigorous program at Northeastern University. For me, this was the best time to accomplish the first big step of my career while still highly motivated and young, without many responsibilities. I have finished in only one year which is basically unheard of in my program. Now, fully confident, I am prepared to enter the male dominated world of engineering and leave my mark behind.

A Journey Worth Waiting For: Why I Want to be a Chef

By Yolanda Brown—Student,
New England Culinary Institute

I graduated from high school in June of 1997. I wanted to go to college but wasn't quite sure about what I wanted to do. I also felt that spending a lot of money to go to school when I wasn't sure about where I was going wasn't a good idea.

Since I had no work experience, I decided to wait for a year and work in the meantime. That turned into two years of working. I decided to visit my aunt and uncle in Cambridge, Massachusetts since I had lived all my life in Virginia and North Carolina. To my surprise, I found I was a natural-born city slicker.

After talking with my aunt and uncle, I decided to pursue my education. I narrowed down the fields; applied for college and got accepted into Bentley College. During my year there, I discovered that a career in business wasn't what I wanted to do. After exploring other career possibilities, I sat down and contemplated what I wanted to do and discovered my career by watching the food network. I loved looking at culinary competitions and actually was moved to tears when I realized that I could see myself doing that ten years down the road. In the jobs I had pursued before, I couldn't see myself doing them for many years.

I applied to various culinary schools and visited a few. The New England Culinary Institute was the one that caught my interest and attention. When I applied to the school, I had to write an essay about my life and what made me want to attend culinary school. I think it might have been in my DNA to want to cook. I used to cook in the

kitchen with my mom. We would be in the kitchen, just the two of us, making fried chicken. I have a picture of us cooking when I was a little girl. In it, I have the batter all over my little hands. I was making a "high five" to the camera and a BIG toothy smile was across my face.

When I went to the library as a kid, other children would get Judy Blume books, but I was checking out cookbooks. I'd search for whichever one I hadn't already read. While other kids were watching cartoons like the Looney Toons and Bugs Bunny, I was watching Justin Wilson Louisiana Cooking, the Frugal Gourmet and Yan Can Cook. I used to pretend that I had my own TV show while I was cooking in the kitchen.

My dad was a chef in the military. I would go to his mess hall at Fort Bragg, North Carolina, and look through all of his recipes that he prepared for the soldiers.

It may have taken me awhile to find what I want to do with my life, but the journey has been worth it and I look forward to becoming the next Julia Child.

Taste-Testing the Job Market

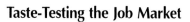

By Justin Lynch-Colameta—Executive Assistant, Fields Associates, Inc. and Student at Fisher College

WOULD I LIKE TO LOVE MY WORK? OF COURSE I would. It is inevitable that I am going to have to work because I wasn't born into wealth. If I want to have even some of the material items I like and if I want to survive, then I have no choice but to work.

It's obvious that people who are making an attempt to survive will work every day—that is, if no one is helping them out. Work happens every day. If you must go to work every single day and it takes up a good part of your life, it could drive you absolutely insane. Obviously you better find something you like to do!

I say this because I could see myself absolutely snapping if I went into a career that I didn't like. I know that I couldn't pretend to like something that I didn't really enjoy.

How am I going to avoid snapping? I'm going to go and get a job I like to go to every day. Is that going to be easy? No, not at all! I have one plan to make this happen. I'm going to taste test as much as I possibly can. I'll try eating just about anything because the stuff that doesn't look too appealing might actually taste good. Even if you are sure about what you want to do with your life, I'd still suggest the taste test approach.

Not all people who think they have it figured out do—sometimes it's because they've been conditioned. Some parents are pretty slick and have instilled certain things in them for one reason or another. There are parents who choose an occupation for their child and drive that into them, like being a doctor or lawyer. They keep pushing their kids, but there may come a point where as a young adult they may want to be something else.

I think it is important to keep your options open. You have to go out there and explore those options. A lot of this takes place in school. I'm a student and working right now. Although I'm tall and slim, I plan to get very fat in my brain by tasting all the options that school and work have to offer me. I know that one day I will truly Love my work by Loving my Life. The alternative is not an option.

Tips for Dealing with Urban Students of Color and Immigrants in the Workplace

By Dr. Richard Fields—President, Benjamin Franklin Institute of Technology

MANY OF THE STUDENTS I WORK WITH AT the high school or college level are urban-based students of color. In most instances, they are the first generation of college students—the first ones to complete high school—as was my case. This poses significant challenges for the educator and employer. Why? The "mainstream" process, where students go to college then assume a role in the economy, doesn't always work for first generation college educated people of color or immigrants. Traditionally, a young person connected to this mainstream process who aspired for a role or occupation in the workplace, quite often knew someone in their family and/or community who was already engaged in that occupation. Students often select an occupation where they know someone who has done that job. In some instances, the job has been performed by generations of family members. For example, it is not uncommon to find two or three generations of doctors, lawyers, auto mechanics or teachers in one family. This helps students not only select an occupation, but it also helps them to know in advance what to expect if they enter that profession or occupation. They know something about it before they go into it. For a variety of reasons, the students we are seeing today, especially the urban students of color and immigrants, don't have that connection with the mainstream economy.

Our first challenge as educators in the urban environment is to educate them about their professional or occupational options. For example, I ran Madison Park Technological Vocational High School in Boston where there were 28 skill occupations that students could enter. They had to select one that they would study for three years. There were two that were most popular—the boys would choose automotive and the girls would select cosmetology. In addition, we found that most students were not as prepared for the workplace as those who had family members or relationships with others in similar occupations.

There are subtleties that you learn about the workplace that aren't a part of the formal curricula. Much learning occurs in an extracurricular fashion. Take school for example, you may learn what the teacher teaches, but you also have learning that takes place through school clubs, sports activities, in the dorms, etc. This is very important for building good citizens and workers. What I've learned is that there are many immigrants from parts of the world who live in neighborhoods that have been disconnected from the American "mainstream" economy, as we know it. To be successful with these students, we have to be intentional and build certain elements in the curricula. This may not be necessary in schools that are in more "mainstream" American communities. As employers experience the increase of workers from other parts of the world and disconnected neighborhoods, they will also have to face these issues. To give such workers an opportunity to advance, the employer may need to train workers about things like networking and employability skills, such as the presentation of yourself at work and appropriate workplace behavior.

At Benjamin Franklin Institute of Technology, where I serve as President, our students go through a series of workshops that include:

- Proper dress and behavior in the interview and on the job
- Resume preparation and
- How to interview, etc.

They have to be certified by our placement office before they can participate in our Employment Placement Program with potential employers. The ultimate remedy for this is for students to be exposed to workplace culture as early in their educational process as possible—certainly by their junior year in high school. Students need to learn early on about what the world is like for a radiologist, doctor, nurse, engineer, etc.

Schools cannot replicate the workplace environment. They can teach students certain skills for the job but they can't teach them how they'll perform those skills in the workplace environment. This argues for changing the relationship between the workplace and the college and will enable the employer to expose students to the workforce via workplace based activities such as internships and cooperative programs.

Through this approach, students spend some time in the workplace as part of their training and education. The increasingly diverse workforce has very little connection or exposure to the workplace or various occupations and would benefit highly from such internships as part of their education and training.

Profile of Success

Dr. Barbara Addison Reid—Executive Director of Human Resources, Bentley College

My own personal philosophy goes back to W.E.B. Dubois' notion of "The Talented Tenth." Dubois used this term to refer to the people of African American decent who were blessed with intelligence and he said we have a responsibility to help lift our race. I have often asked myself how I could help other people to be successful and I decided long ago that I could help others by being a mentor.

I make time in my life to mentor. As a single parent, when my son was growing up, he would often have his friends come over to our house and visit. I became the adult that the youngsters could talk to about girlfriend/boyfriend relationships, school and social issues. They wouldn't raise many of these topics with their own parents. I have always been present and available for children and teenagers. Sometimes you get more information from your youngster's friends than you do from your child. My house has always been a hangout for kids, so I knew where my children were and who they were with most of the time.

Professionally, I've spent most of my career working in colleges and universities with faculty and staff; however, the students who go to school at Bentley find their way to my office. I have mentored freshmen and we have continued the mentoring relationship until they graduated. When young people go to college, they often test out new behaviors and it is also a time when they personally begin dealing with ethical and moral issues. I'm there as an adult to help them deal with these situations and to provide guidance. I can have what is called a "no harm, no foul" conversation with them. They know they can take risks with me. I'm not going to hold it against them, punish them or try and stop them from what they really want to do—unless it's dangerous. They ask things like, "How do I balance my studies with having an active social life?"

A student I was mentoring approached me about investing his money in a product and it was clear to me from his description that this was a pyramid scheme. The student said that this way of making money almost seemed to be "too good to be true" but he just wasn't sure. By the time he confided in me, he had already made a significant cash investment but with my encouragement he was wise enough not to make any further investments. It takes time to build trust in a mentoring relationship so the communication is open and honest.

I wonder if today's generation has a passion for what they do. If you feel passionately about your work and you care about other people, then your values will become a part of your work life. There is an old adage, "Do what you love and the money will follow." I absolutely live by this philosophy. I can remember when I made a personal connection between helping others and Human Resources work. Back then, Human Resources was called Personnel. I have worked in this profession for more than 25 years. I made the connection that I could help people of color by opening the door for them to be interviewed for jobs. I felt energized by the work, and I felt passionate about my ability to serve others, and that's why today I love my work and my life.

Another aspect of mentoring that I am passionate about is working with women of color who are in doctoral programs. Everyone chooses a dissertation topic that is different and of interest to them. In fact, the process of getting through a doctoral program is often very similar. I offer a forum for doctoral students to talk about their experiences and feelings as they engage in their studies, as well as talk about the content of their topic. When you meet with someone every two weeks for several years, you get to know them pretty well. That's the mentoring support that I have offered to several doctoral candidates. Recently, I attended the doctoral defense of a woman I have been mentoring for several years. It was a joy to spend time with her and her committee as she defended her research. When you can see the results of all of your efforts—oh, it's a wonderful feeling!

Mentoring is something that I enjoy and it clearly is a part of who I am and how I live my life.

Profile of Success

Cira S. Mervin—Office Manager for Student Government Office, North Carolina State University

My job is my philosophy of life. I work at NC State University in the Student Government Office. I left my home in the mountains of North Carolina, a job in the corporate arena and moved to Eastern North Carolina in the 1980's. I took a job at the university on a temporary basis to help out for a couple months and have been here for 16 years. Every day I have an opportunity to make someone's day, to add a different outlook on to his or her life, to help someone make a decision. Fortunately, my job allows me to work with exceptional students doing great jobs. I take care of their day-to-day office affairs, order paper, make sure their computers are working, reserve meeting rooms, keep calendars, pay bills, and pay them, but my work also allows me to get a glimpse at who will be running the world one day very soon. I am close enough to them daily to discover who they are, how they think and what their philosophy of life is all about.

These are the future leaders of the country and I hope that my presence with them daily will have some impact on their decision-making as they get into their positions in life. These young people will be making policies and decisions on issues such as Social Security and health care that will affect millions of older adults, whether they are in positions of power or voters. I hope they will think of the conversations we have had from time-to-time and put my face to so many nameless people when they make these tough decisions. We discuss everything from the War in Iraq to the O List (things Oprah Winfrey thinks are great). Acquaintance rape, breast cancer and tattoos have also been among the list of topics of desk side discussions. I have listened to how they would be affected by tuition and fee increases, budget cuts, and the divorce of their parents. I appreciate these gifted student leaders and I value their opinions and their outlook in life. I feel fortunate to be let into their world, and I am honored to be where I can give a challenging and sometimes different point of view to some of the conversations we have had over the years.

These students have been my extended family. I have learned a lot from them. I have heard their life stories and they have heard mine. They have taught me more than just how to do little short cuts on my computer and how to set the alarm on my PDA. It is my dream that they will remember these heart-to-heart talks we have shared over the years and remember me fondly as I cherish my thoughts of them.

Ever so often, I get a telephone call or an email from one of the former officers from Singapore, Washington DC, New York, England, Florida, Ireland, and they tell me that they remember the chair by my desk, the Smartees in the dish on my desk, and the little talks we have had, the crises we have been through together, the secrets they have shared.

Love my work? You bet I do. It adds another element of meaning to my life.

BRIDGING THE GENERATION GAP

Bridging the Generation Gap can be helped through storytelling. If you are a parent, why not tell younger people stories from your life's photo album. Cira Mervin, my loving stepmother, told me the following stories, and they provided me with a wonderful insight into the world in which she grew up. I asked her to write them down for this book. Her tales of old are treasures buried deep in my soul. I hope you can leave some golden nuggets someday about your life to your children or other special people in your life.

Diamonds: Coal Under Pressure

By Cira S. Mervin

I RELATE THINGS THAT HAPPENED IN MY younger life that made me who I am today. I remember my favorite Aunt who helped me bury a piece of coal under a rock so it would turn into a diamond. She worked with me all afternoon. I convinced her to do it after watching a Superman show on TV. The story line was to put a piece of coal under pressure for a very long time and eventually it would turn into a diamond. (Of course, Superman just squeezed the coal with one hand, smoke billowed out between his fingers and there was a huge diamond.) My aunt stopped what she was doing and spent all afternoon listening to my story and then helped me to find the perfect coal and bury it under a rock in the front yard so I could have a diamond one day. The rock is still there, the coal is still under the rock and I still have my precious memory of that afternoon. I want the hundreds of students that I have worked with daily to have memories of me when they look back over their college years and I want those memories to be so special that they will smile and remember the times that we spent together.

I also remember sitting in the backyard under a tree with my older cousin and asking him questions about our family's New Year's tradition. That's also a very fond memory. I woke up very early on New Year's morning and heard Mr. Bud's voice downstairs. He came in the front door and went out the back door. My Grandmother just opened the door, he walked in, she spoke to him as if she was expecting him, he nodded, she opened the back door and he walked out.

Later that day, while the adults started preparing the same foods that we had for New Year's Day dinner every year, I asked my cousin about the Mr. Bud's early-morning visit. He explained to me the southern tradition that: A man must enter your house on New Year's Day through the front door before anyone in the house leaves to ensure that there will not be a death in the house that year. It can't be a female, and the man *must* go out the back. (I had a little problem with the female part.)

Mr. Bud did that every year for the whole neighborhood. I did not understand how this started, why it worked, or who discovered that it worked. But my cousin told me and our family did it, so it must be true. I accepted it. That day is etched in my mind and in my heart forever. Sitting with an older cousin, listening to the family traditions made me feel so grown up and loved.

Recommended Reading

Dr. Mary-Frances Winters. *Only Wet Babies Like Change: Workforce Wisdom for Baby Boomers.* Renaissance Books, June, 2002.

Profile of Success

Patricia Rose—Social Worker

I feel that it is important to have a balance in one's life, both personally and professionally. As a social worker, I enjoy my career, which involves working with children and families. Professionally, on one hand, I work for a large urban school system and see how different it is to keep children focused and how hard it is to keep families together. Many of these children have no incentive to complete their education or to move forward in their lives. I see many children who start off as truants and advance through the juvenile system and beyond, even death, unfortunately. In many cases, these children have no role models at home and/or found the wrong role models. Working in this area is usually confrontational and stressful. On the other end of the spectrum, I work in the area of adoption and see the difficulty that parents have in being able to start a family. In this area, prospective parents have to go through a rigid training and screening process prior to being approved to be parents. This gives them the opportunity to think some things through and to be prepared to address some of the issues which may lie ahead. Working in this area is usually pleasant and upbeat.

In both areas, I work with both single-parent and two-parent families and I also have an opportunity to see how they interact in their homes. I've also observed that whether they are single-parent families or two-parent families, they can raise successful children when they invest time in their children, teach their children good values and if they are good role models for their children.

I find balance in my life by working in a field that I enjoy and by taking the time to also enjoy being with my family. Even though my children are now ages seventeen and twenty-one, we still enjoy going on vacations as a family, whenever possible.

LwL² PERSPECTIVES FROM GENERATION Y

I wanted to include the perspectives of Generation Y, young teens, in this book.

One sunny fall Saturday, I enticed my daughter and several of her friends to watch a video of me talking about LwL². Their reward was that I'd cook all of them their favorite foods that evening if they wrote down their thoughts.

They were asked to respond to these questions:

1. After watching the video, what does Loving your work by Loving your Life mean to you?
2. What advice would you give to other kids your age about what they should do to Love their Life?
3. What tips would you give to adults about what they should do to Love their work and Life, or what they should not do if they want to love their work and Life?
4. When you are grown up and a mother, what will you make sure you do so you can Love your work and Life?

The following are their mature insights into the questions posed.

Let's RAP: Young People Speak Out About LwL²
Vanessa DeCampos—14, Watertown High School, Filipino and Brazilian

After watching the video, what does Loving your work by Loving your Life mean to you?
It means that in order to understand and get to know your workplace then you have to have a great attitude and actually like what you do. I believe in the maxim, "You have to love yourself before you love anything else." I truly think it's true, you have to be happy with yourself or else you're going to spread your bad attitude to your co-workers.

What advice would you give to other kids your age on what they should do to Love their Life?
People my age should make friends, join clubs, participate in school activities.

What tips would you give to adults about what they should do to Love their work and Life or what they should not do if they want to Love their work and their Life?
When they are stressed out then they should take 15 minutes to just clear their minds of everything and close their eyes and think of a place that's relaxing like the beach. That's what I do and it works. I also talk to my friends and family.

When you are grown up and a mother, what will you make sure you do so you can Love your work and Life?
I would spend time with my children whenever I had time to and I would make sure I actually like the job I'm doing.

Let's RAP: Young People Speak Out About LwL²
Shaina DiGiacomo—12, Watertown Middle School, Italian, Irish, Portuguese

After watching the video, what does Loving your work by Loving your Life mean to you?
I think it means that to love life, you are doing something that you enjoy doing that makes you happy with your life.

What advice would you give to other kids your age on what they should do to Love their Life?
They should keep living their lives happily and do things that they love to do, which makes them love their lives.

What tips would you give to adults about what they should do to Love their work and Life or what they should not do if they want to Love their work and their Life?
If they want to love their work they shouldn't give up on it on the first try if they want to do something they like.

When you are grown up and a mother, what will you make sure you do so you can Love your work and Life?
That I choose something that I like and that I will be happy with, and I'll love life by being happy with what I'm doing in it. I'll also love it by being able to achieve my goals and being successful in life.

Let's RAP: Young People Speak Out About LwL²
Shawna Fields—13, Concord Middle School, Peabody building, African-American and Native American

After watching the video, what does loving your work by Loving your Life mean to you?
Loving your work by Loving your Life means liking what you do and having a good outlook on your life.

What advice would you give to other kids your age on what they should do to Love their Life?
I think kids my age should think less about the stereotypes that we should fill and more about having fun with our childhood in order to Love their Life.

What tips would you give to adults about what they should do to Love their work and Life or what they should not do if they want to Love their work and their Life?
I think adults should think about the positive things in their life instead of the negative things, in order to love their work and life.

When you are grown up and a mother, what will you make sure you do so you can love your work and life?

I would always wake up with a smile and live my life to the fullest.

Let's RAP: Young People Speak Out About LwL[2]

Jennifer Le—14, Watertown High School, Vietnamese & Chinese

After watching the video, what does Loving your work by Loving your Life mean to you?

Loving your work by Loving your Life means that you have to enjoy what you do in order to enjoy what you have.

What advice would you give to other kids your age on what they should do to Love their Life?

My advice to other kids my age on what they should do to love their life is get involved and try out new things, because if you try out new things you may get to experience different things. Experiencing different things could allow you to be able to find out what you love. When you love what you do in life, then you just start to love your life in a new perspective.

What tips would you give to adults about what they should do to Love their work and Life or what they should not do if they want to Love their work and their Life?

Well, I think they have to try to make the best of life including work, because not everyone has a job they can be happy with, because of choices that came from the past. They should make the best of what they do because "You make a living by what you get, and you make a life by what you give." I heard that quote from somewhere, and I like it.

When you are grown up and a mother, what will you make sure you do so you can Love your work and Life?

I will make sure that I accept all choices my children will want to make and to support them. I will have a good job (hopefully) but my life would have me happy, because I will have my children to take care of. If they are happy, then so am I.

Let's RAP: Young People Speak Out About LwL[2]

Shanice Wilson—14, Watertown High School, African-American

After watching the video, what does Loving your work by Loving your Life mean to you?

It means doing what you want and loving your life as you please without hurting anyone.

What advice would you give to other kids your age on what they should do to Love their Life?

I would say to not let anyone bring you down, and have good friends that you can trust and open up to.

What tips would you give to adults about what they should do to Love their work and Life or what they should not do if they want to Love their work and their Life?

Make free time for yourself so you can think about what's going on in your life and how your life's going and make the best of it.

When you are grown up and a mother, what will you make sure you do so you can Love your work and Life?

I will make sure I am married to a person I can see myself with forever. Also, I would have a nice job and one that I love.

Recommended Reading

Stedman Graham. *Teens Can Make It Happen: A Nine-Step Plan for Success.* New York: Simon & Schuster, September, 2000. www.stedmangraham.com.

POST SCRIPT

After watching the video and eating dinner, the girls convinced me to let them sleep over so they could take their time completing the answers to the questions. At one point in the evening, they became fun loving, crazy 12, 13 and 14 year olds and started singing and dancing to these catchy songs, "Cinderella," "Girl Power," and "Cheetah Sisters" from a Disney movie. The song entitled "Girl Power" gave me a real insight into how the women's movement that I participated in during the 1970s had reshaped the thinking of girls today. In addition, "Cheetah Sisters" speaks to the issues of diversity and globalization that the younger generations are facing in their everyday lives.

Cinderella

When I was just a little girl
My momma used to tuck me into bed
and she'd read me a story
It always was about a Princess in distress
And how a guy would save her and end up with the glory
I'd lie in bed and think about the person that I want to be
Then one day I realized the fairy tale life wasn't for me

[Chorus]

I don't wanna be like Cinderella
Sittin' in a dark old dusty cellar
Waiting for somebody, to come and set me free
I don't wanna be like Snow White waiting
For a handsome prince to come and save me
On a horse of white, unless we're riding side by side
Don't want to depend on no one else
I'd rather rescue myself

Someday I'm gonna find someone who wants my soul, heart, and mind
Who's not afraid to show that he loves me
Somebody who will understand I'm happy just the way I am
Don't need nobody taking care of me
I will be there for him just as strong as he will be there for me
When I give myself then it has to got to be, an equal thing

[Chorus]

I can slay, my own dragons
I can dream, my own dreams
My knight in shining armour is me
So I'm gonna set me free

[Chorus × 3]

http://www.anysonglyrics.com/lyrics/c/cheetah-girls/cinderella.htm
"Cinderella" by the Cheetah Girls (a made-for-Disney movie group)

Girl Power

Put your hands up if you know that you're a star
You better stand up if you know just who you are
Never give up never stay down
Girl Power Girl Power!!

Put your hands up if you know that you're a star
You better stand up if you know just who you are
Never give up never come too far
Girl Power Girl Power!!

I made mistakes before but I know I'm not perfect
It's okay 'cause who could ever be
As long as I give my best
It don't matter what no one says

'Cause down in my heart I got the power to make it all
happen
Put your hands up if you know that you're a star
You better stand up if you know just who you are
Never give up never stay down
Girl Power Girl Power!!
At times I may just feel like
Backin' through the wall
I hold my head up high
Keep on standin' tall
I know my back is covered
Because we have each other
We could do whatever
If you hear me put your hands up

Put your hands up if you know that you're a star
You better stand up if you know just who you are
Never give up never stay down
Girl Power Girl Power!!

Sometimes life may get you down
But you better hold your ground
Nobody can live your life but you
Stay true to who you are
And always follow your heart
Your heart, your heart

Put your hands up if you know that you're a star
You better stand up if you know just who you are
Never give up never stay down
Girl Power Girl Power!!

http://www.anysonglyrics.com/lyrics/c/cheetah-girls/girl-power.htm
"Girl Power" by the Cheetah Girls (a made-for-Disney movie group)

Cheetah Sisters

We're Cheetah Girls, Cheetah Sisters
Gotta do what we gotta do
Got the brains, got the power and we speak the truth
We're from everywhere around the world
So you best respect the Cheetah Girls
Dancing, singing from our birth
Working hard for what we deserve
Trying hard not to break the rules
Cause mama didn't raise no fools
It may seem we're only dreaming
And we need help to carry on
It's to good to know we're not alone
Cause we are sisters
We stand together
We make up one big family
Though we don't look the same
Our spots are different
Different colors
We make each other stronger
That ain't ever gonna change
OK, just listen
We're Cheetah Girls, Cheetah Sisters
Someone's always there behind
To catch us if we fall
Cause we are sisters
We stand together
We make up one big family
Though we don't look the same
Our spots are different
Different Colors
We make each other stronger
That ain't ever gonna change
OK, just listen
We're Cheetah Girls, Cheetah Sisters

http://www.anysonglyrics.com/lyrics/c/cheetah-girls/
cheetah-sisters.htm
"Cheetah Sisters" by the Cheetah Girls
(a made-for-Disney movie group)

Chapter 37

ALIGNING MIND, BODY AND SOUL

ALIGNING YOUR MIND, BODY AND SOUL

WHILE COMPANIES CAN DO MUCH TO help individuals and their families to better LwL[2], they can't do it alone. Just like only YOU can form yourself into a ME, Inc. and become the CEO of your work and life destiny, only YOU have the power to line up your mind, body and soul so they are in harmony with each other. This, of course, is far more easily uttered than accomplished. In this chapter, I'd like to share with you some tips, insights and thoughts about ways to position your mind, body and soul to be at one with your work and life.

There are many reasons as to why you should eliminate stress and achieve balance in your life. Experts tell us that too much stress can lead to debilitating diseases and can negatively impact our health and overall wellbeing. Excessive stress can lead to serious medical conditions such as high blood pressure, ulcers, sleep disorders, and weight gain or loss. A mind which is out of alignment can cause a person to suffer from certain mental illnesses and can cause them to color their world with a dark palette of negativity. That can push them into the "If I coulda, woulda, shoulda" syndrome or straight into the arms of the "Ain't it awful" crowd at work. Membership in either one of these groups almost guarantees a negative outcome to one's ability to LwL[2].

Anne Volante of the MITRE Corporation, Michelle LaBrosse of Cheetah Learning and Phyllis Barajas of Barajas and Associates offer other important reasons why we should consider balance of brain, body and soul in our lives.

Profile of Success

Michelle LaBrosse—PMP, Chief Cheetah, Cheetah Learning

I believe in spiritual money. To love your work and life you should be at peace with abundance and welcome it into your life. Last fall, I got very sick and had to turn my business over to others. That was the best thing that I could ever have done. I learned to not control everything and that I am the puppeteer who helps rejuvenate things so my cast of employees can perform. You have to learn how to turn things over to others if you are going to be successful at work and life. I believe in work/life integration. Saturday and Sunday are family days and I'm with the kids. When do I have time to relax? When I travel.

Here is a quote that captures what I feel "Love your work by Loving your Life" means: "Do what you love—the money and success will follow."

What people need to do to Love their work:

Do work that is an expression of your core essence—which does change as one grows and evolves.

What people need to do to Love their Life:

Be happy with who they were, who they are, and who they are becoming.

Tips on Loving your work and Life that have worked for me:

Have five full belly laughs every day, develop a deep sense of gratitude and appreciation for the little things in life, and be "in love" with many different aspects of life—instead of saving it all up for that one special someone.

Be the person you'd love to spend the rest of your life with.

Move through life joyfully and with a spirit of lightness because nothing is ever really as bad as it initially appears to be. Situations just exist—we put our own spin on whether they are positive or negative experiences. When evaluating situations, I think about how I would perceive them if I were absolutely in love with them the way I was at the birth of my two daughters—which for me was the deepest and most unconditional love I've ever experienced. See the good in other people and they will always rise to the occasion.

How organizations can help staff to Love their work and Life:

Create an environment where people are appreciated (not simply tolerated) for their unique characteristics and contributions. Enable people to grow and evolve in ways that are right for them—which I have found ultimately helps my company grow in ways that I could never have imagined had I tried to control people's development. Be supportive and be a cheerleader when people take risks—even if those risks don't pan out.

RECHARGING YOUR BATTERIES THROUGH RECREATION, HOBBIES, MINI-RETREATS, WEEKEND GETAWAYS AND VACATIONS

Recharging your batteries and reclaiming your energy are essential steps to align your mind, body and soul. Think about the word *recreate*. It is about re-creating yourself. In other words, we all need to reinvent who we are in our life and at work. What better way to "re-cre-ate" yourself than to participate in activities that help you reclaim your energy. Some people find this through a variety of outlets such as

- Recreational individual sports and exercises such as tennis, golf, walking, hiking, jogging, swimming, dance, surfing, etc.
- Organized team sports such as baseball, softball, football, soccer, etc.
- Martial arts such as Tae kwan do and karate

- Meditation, yoga, attending and participating in religious activities
- Hobbies such as gardening, listening to music, arts and crafts, collecting, wood working, jewelry making, and restoring cars.

TAKING TIME TO GET AWAY FROM IT ALL

The importance of taking time to get away from it all can't be emphasized enough. People who put in the countless hours of face time with no down time cannot keep up that grueling pace without experiencing defeat in aligning mind, body and soul and LwL². Working 24/7 without breaks has devastating consequences. How can someone who is glued to a desk or computer from morning to night be practicing a holistic, healthy lifestyle? Think about it. If that person is constantly working, when does she have time to concentrate in her mind—on anything other than the work at hand? The individual is probably doing next to nothing about planning her life's work or how to be CEO of ME, Inc. That person's body is probably not being nurtured properly—no time for nutritional meals or a workout at the gym or a walk in the park to smell the roses. Eventually that individual's soul will also succumb to the rigors of stress, sleep deprivation, lack of contact with significant others and/or family and lack of a personal life. Listening to the messages that the power of silence brings or taking time to practice an attitude of gratitude is probably also kicked to the curb.

Dr. Carol Bates is a renowned physician at the prestigious Beth Israel Deaconess Hospital. She treats patients with hypertension, obesity and a number of other illnesses that sometimes are caused or aggravated by the conditions previously described. Dr. Bates also helps her patients to prevent falling into this negative health spiral. She offers this prescription for people interested in obtaining or maintaining a healthy, happy and well-balanced life:

Wise Words
Carol Bates, M.D.

It's incredibly important to take time away from work for renewal. Too many people don't take vacations. Americans have less vacation time than most Europeans—take what you have and get away! Preparing to leave for vacation and catching up upon return aren't easy, but the battery recharge and opportunities for personal growth make departure and reentry worthwhile.

RECREATIONAL ACTIVITIES, HOBBIES, MINI-RETREATS, WEEKEND GETAWAYS AND VACATIONS TO KEEP YOU GROUNDED

"This all sounds great," you think, "but the reality is that at this point in time, my company is really busy and I'm under the gun to produce and/or complete this project or perish." Many of us face this reality in our jobs and/or lives. What's a person to do about getting away from it all? Some suggestions may include not taking that two week dream vacation to an exotic location, but why not try

- a mini-retreat
- weekend getaway
- day, afternoon or hour of beauty
- afternoon of golf or exercise
- a romantic interlude with the love of your life

The reality is that "crunch period, high pressure to perform and can't get away at all times" do happen. There must, however, be some point in time that your personal To-Do List is not cluttered with work-related activities. This is a time where the activities on that list only include things that will help you relax, eliminate stress and reclaim your energy. During crunch periods, why not schedule (for a later date when things slow down) a nice vacation to a favorite spot or a place you've always dreamed of visiting. Sometimes knowing that you're working hard now so you can enjoy time off and a great vacation later, helps you to get through that difficult and trying time. It may also assist you to keep things in perspective and know that the light at the end of the tunnel hasn't been turned off until further notice.

WHAT NOT TO DO DURING YOUR PRECIOUS TIME OFF

Earlier, we discussed the need to take disconnection breaks and literally unplug yourself from the computer, phone, fax, beeper, walkie talkie, etc. Taking a laptop to the beach so you can check your messages or connect with staff or the office is a big NO-NO. Allow yourself a moment to breathe, listen to the wind, touch the water and feel the sand between your toes. Your mind, body and soul will thank you later. Your colleagues at work and significant people in your life will as well when they experience the refreshed and realigned YOU in their lives.

ESTABLISHING PARAMETERS AROUND YOUR "FREE/LEISURE" TIME

More and more, people find it necessary to establish some fairly strict parameters in order to guard and keep sacred the free/leisure time needed to re-create themselves. Here are some examples of "hard, no bend rules and boundaries" that people are negotiating with themselves, significant others and the organizations with whom they work:

- Letting your boss know when you will and won't work at home
- Informing people (friends, colleagues and extended family) when you will and won't accept calls at home (e.g., I don't take calls after 10 p.m. or before 7 a.m.)
- Establishing a zero-tolerance policy (except in the case of an emergency) for canceling vacations and/or visits to your child's school, dates with your spouse or significant other and attendance at family, civic, religious and certain social events.

Rosaline Lowe, owner of a popular Brookline, Massachusetts spa and expert on skin care, provides some insights into other ways we can rejuvenate ourselves. She also shares with us a recipe for a Home Spa that she concocted to help people renew and refresh their minds, bodies and souls.

Wise Words

Rosaline Lowe—President, Rosaline's SkinCare & Spa

In order to love work, you need to love what you do. Find your passion in life and focus on improving your skills. When you feel in a rut about your work, take a refresher's course or simply take a class that might be of interest to you. Getting away is always good therapy and makes you feel better about yourself.

Life can be a challenge on a daily basis, and I think people need to find the simple things in life that they enjoy. It is important to have a positive mental attitude about life. Having good friends and family is always a comforting feeling that enhances the quality of life.

After 17 years in business, there are certain aspects of my work that I still enjoy. I love meeting different people on a daily basis. That allows me to have interesting conversations.

Other parts of my work have become very routine, but when I get into a rut, I take a short vacation, or attend seminars that make me feel rejuvenated. I try to find balance in my life by doing interesting things with friends. I enjoy cooking so I take cooking classes. I love to travel, so I plan get-aways. There are so many simple things that one can do to break the routine of that everyday grind. Simple treats are the most enjoyable. For example, take a yoga class, or get a facial or massage for relaxation. Walk, exercise, or create a home spa to enhance your mental and physical well-being. A healthy lifestyle creates a healthy body and a happy person.

Corporate Cupid
Website: *www.rosalinesspa.com* • Email: sales@rosalinesspa.com

Recipe for a Home Spa: Seven Tips To Renew Your Body and Soul

By Rosaline Lowe—President of Rosaline's
SkinCare & Spa

TAKING TIME FOR YOURSELF IS SO IMPORTANT in the high-tech and stressful world in which we live. There are occasions when we have to take time for ourselves and renew our body and soul.

Some of us book a day at our favorite spa, but others simply cannot find the time nor have the funds to spend on spa services. I've assembled some valuable tips that you can post on your refrigerator or in your bathroom as a reminder to be good to yourself. Why not take a night to nurture and pamper your body and soul? Pick an evening when you can devote at least one hour to create your home spa for total relaxation. Here's a simple recipe you can follow.

Creating a Relaxing Atmosphere

Begin to create a relaxing atmosphere to invigorate your body and soul by taking these seven simple steps:

1. Take 15 minutes to loosen muscles and stimulate circulation by doing some stretches. If you practice yoga, this is the best time to do some of the movements that are so good for the body.

2. Light your favorite scented candle in the bathroom. Assemble all the spa products that you need. Check off any of the following that you choose to use:

   - ❏ cleanser
   - ❏ toner
   - ❏ eye cream
   - ❏ night cream
   - ❏ face mask
   - ❏ body scrub
   - ❏ loofah
   - ❏ body lotion
   - ❏ bath salts

3. Fill your largest pot with water and add a handful of lavender, rosemary or sage leaves. (You should keep all these herbs handy in your kitchen cabinet.) Bring water to a boil. While the water is boiling, wash your face with cleanser and exfoliate your entire face and neck.

4. Shut off stove. Apply a large towel over your face, and steam skin *carefully* over the hot water for 15 minutes. This method helps increase circulation, open pores, and release toxins. Blot face and apply a mask on entire face (avoid the eye area).

5. Fill tub and apply either bath salts or pour the scented water from the pot into the tub. These salts or herbs really help to relax the muscles.

6. Before getting into the tub, brush the body with a loofah using upward movements toward the heart, then apply a body scrub to exfoliate the body. This technique will help circulation and rid the skin of dead cells. It also helps to smooth the texture of your skin. Relax in the tub for 15–30 minutes. Keep face mask on for the entire duration.

7. Remove mask and follow up with a toner. Apply eye cream, face cream and body lotion onto damp skin. It's always best to use this technique because the dampness helps to seal the moisture into the skin for a softer, more supple effect.

If you give yourself a treatment periodically, your body will love you for it. You will also feel better mentally and spiritually and ready to Love your work and your Life!

Holistic Approaches to LwL²

For more than 26 years, I have worked and/or lived in Cambridge, Massachusetts near Harvard Square. Needless to say, holistic approaches to LwL² are alive and well in the place that some people refer to as the People's Republic of Cambridge. Given my background, I can not write a book about LwL² without providing some additional, more holistic and alternative approaches that some have found useful in their quest to align mind, body and soul. I believe these methods may be of use to those who seek different ways to connect their work and life. Others may find them a bit too "touchie-feelie" for their tastes but may want to keep an open mind and try some of the techniques before reaching a final conclusion about their utility.

Psychotherapist, Trainer, and Enneagram Specialist Herb Pearce has a practice in which he utilizes some popular holistic approaches. Here are some of the holistic approaches that he recommends in his practice:

Herb's "Self-Caretaking" Tips[1]

1. Go to sleep when you are tired—take a nap on occasion
2. Eat when you are hungry, but don't overeat because you will get a tummy ache
3. Eat little or no junk food; eat real food like fresh vegetables, grains, fruits, salads
4. Drink plenty of water
5. Go for a walk each day in a natural setting or at least in the neighborhood
6. Cut down on excess stimulation (loud music, too much TV, addictions) and have more quiet time, read more, have stimulating conversations with interesting people
7. Get help when you need it—no one can manage life alone
8. Have a hobby or interest that inspires or satisfies you
9. Always have something to look forward to—a trip, time with a friend, a movie, etc.
10. Always be aware of the child part of you—excited, exploring, curious, open

Here are some of the holistic techniques that Herb recommends:

Anger Management
Have you had a hard time managing your anger, whether with your internal feelings or how to express it to others? Learn many important tools to deal with anger inside as well as constructive ways to express it. Get the support you need to have a better relationship to anger! This is also good for those who have a hard time feeling anger, yet it's likely coming out in other ways.

Basics of Astrology
Learn the basic structure of astrology—differences within planets, signs and houses and how your birth chart affects your personality. Have you always felt a little foggy about astrology? Skeptical? Discover another valuable system for understanding yourself and others.

Enneagram
Herb acts out the types, interviews each person for correct core type and points out growth and relationship tips unique to each type. If you haven't done an Enneagram workshop yet, this is essential for understanding types and it's an entertaining and insightful experience.

Relationship Dynamics Between the Types
Learn the ins and outs of how the types tend to relate to each other, tips on how to relate to any Enneagram type and your patterns of attraction and reaction to different types.

---

1 Source: Herb Life Tips Email, October 16, 2003

How to Read Body Language

People respond much more to non-verbal language than the word content, yet most people don't read others well. This includes reading non-verbals, body language, gestures, voice tone, mismatches between words and conflicting body language. Learn to trust seeing when someone likes you, is attracted to you or is turned off in some way to what you do. Learn how to respond verbally and non-verbally to others' body language.

Men's Group

Some men find participating in men's groups therapeutic. Topics in small and large group sharing may include male friendship, gender differences and communication, self-nurturing, spirituality, sexuality, men and feelings, anger management, values clarification, goal setting, communication development, and personality differences.

Myers–Briggs

Learn the Basics of Introversion-Extraversion, Sensing-Intuition, Thinking-Feeling, and Perceiving-Judging. Discover your type and how to relate to other types. The Myers-Briggs system explains differences in a totally different way than the Enneagram and is an essential tool to understand yourself and others.

Personal Life Coaching

- Structured process to clarify and accomplish your personal growth/life and work goals
- Initial session to evaluate your personal life and/or work goals
- Phone consultations (or contact in person) weekly to support action steps, stay accountable and free up fears/blocks regarding completion of goals.

SOUL SEARCHING

The feeding of your soul through prayer, meditation, silence and reflection, yoga or attending a religious service can work wonders to help you LwL[2]. Tending to matters of the soul is a very private and unique experience. No one but you can decide what works best for you. As Joel Osteen, Pastor of the Lakewood Church, in a message entitled "Be Happy with Who You Are," stated:

Wise Words

Just because something works for someone else doesn't necessarily mean it is going to work for you. You've got to run your race.

—Joel Osteen, 11/02/03

Web Brower

www.joelosteen.com

For some, the alignment of mind and body with spiritual self takes on importance when looking for a way to leave a legacy. Dr. Charles Stanley of In Touch Ministries in his message—We Riches of the Grace of God—provided a final compelling reason why people may want to align their mind, body and soul.

Corporate Cupid

http://www.herbpearce.com

Wise Words

Do you realize that no matter what you have, when you die you're not going to be able to take one single copper penny with you? In fact, they may dress you in your finest suit or dress possible. You know what? You're going to have to leave it. You're not going to take anything with you. Watch this carefully. The only thing you are going with is your soul. Your spirit.

—*Dr. Charles Stanley, In Touch Ministries, 11/2/03*

Web Brower

www.intouch.org

Wise Words

When I see all of the people in the world who are hurting, it just motivates me to do more.

—*Creflo A. Dollar, President and CEO, World Changers Ministries*
(an organization of 24,000 members in College Park, Georgia)

With a name like "Dollar," does Creflo A. Dollar teach about anything other than money? Yes. Although Dr. Dollar's ground-breaking revelation of prosperity is what he is best known for, Dr. Dollar makes it a point to teach on a variety of topics because his calling is to teach total life prosperity—spiritual, physical, mental, emotional and financial well-being.

Source: www.creflodollarministries.com

66 99 Quote of Note

When the light of the sun goes down, the light of the moon takes over.

 Tools and Resources

Anthony "Tony" Robbins, "Breakthrough to Vital Health" and "The Body You Deserve." ©1992. Anthony Robbins and Associates.

Order through: Robbins Research Institute, 9191 Towne Center Drive Suite 600, San Diego, CA 92122 or call 1-800-445-8183

Sure Signs You Need to Slow Down

✓ You're standing in front of a microwave, warming up a roll or pizza and pacing in front of it telling it to hurry up.

✓ Tension always penetrates your body just before you get to a stop light; it turns yellow and you step hard onto the accelerator to get through it so you won't have to sit still.

✓ You can't sleep, or you toss and turn and wake up in the middle of the night, dreading that the sun will rise before you're sufficiently rested.

✓ You don't look or feel anything like Billy Crystal's—*Marvelous!*

 Recommended Reading
Unlimited Power by Anthony Robbins. Fawcett. Columbia, New York. 1986.
www.anthonyrobbins.com

Aligning your mind, body and soul can help you to approach a larger, more lasting aspect of LwL^2. When you are at peace with who you are, you put yourself in a better position to help others realize their potentials. In the end, when our mind, body and soul have left this earth, what endures is our legacy. In the pages which follow, we will explore how you can begin to weave, and then leave your legacy by understanding what you stand for regarding your work and life. We'll take a look at people who decided to get up and stand up for their rights.

Chapter 38

Get Up, Stand Up. Stand Up for Your Rights!

GET UP, STAND UP.
STAND UP FOR YOUR RIGHTS!

A COMMON THEME ECHOED BY PEOPLE who Love their work by Loving their Life is that in order to achieve that peaceful state, you have to dramatically change your life by taking a stance about something or someone. For them, this often involved a situation where they knew it would lead to an unpopular outcome. They were fully aware that friends, family members, and colleagues could be lost behind their decision. Still, they had to march forward.

Have you ever reached the boiling point where a situation, person, issue, or event drives you to a place where you need to declare: "I won't take it anymore and I have to change my life around _____?" Many of us can fill in the blank—for example, a rude, crude, or nasty boss or senior leader in your company who is always berating someone in front of others. One day your number is up, and he does it to you in front of your peers. He perceives you've done something when, in reality, someone else was responsible. The Reggae song immortalized many moons ago rises in your brain:

"You can fool some people some time, but you can't fool all the people all the time. Now you see the light. You better stand up for your rights. Get up, stand up. Stand up for your rights. Get up, stand up. Don't give up the fight."
—*Bob Marley*

Like David, you confront this corporate Goliath—right there on the spot, knowing the *moment* you say what you're about to that your death sentence in the company will be issued. You'll be out of there—history—the second you get up and stand up. But somehow instinctively you know that you "can't let this one go." He has crossed the line and more importantly, in doing so, has severed the arteries that carry your integrity, life's philosophy, morals, and values through your veins. You've tried and are not going to take it anymore. Your job is dead, over, when you say what you say. The process may be quick (you get fired on the spot), or a long and painful one. The torture may include

- making your life a living Hades
- providing daily dosages of misery to your work life until you are compelled to resign
- documenting enough of your bad deeds to Human Resources that you are let go later through a layoff or an involuntary termination

You are fully aware of all these consequences, yet you still decide to get up and stand up.

In this chapter, you learn about the lives of four outstanding people who at some point in their lives made the decision to get up and stand up for their beliefs. You'll hear the story of Edie Fraser, a woman who decided to take a stand to help women and people less fortunate after hearing, in the early 1960's, these famous words:

Edie wanted women business owners to be heard, and she established national organizations to do so.

Paul Guzzi is a prominent figure in the Boston political, business, social and civic scene. His ability to bring together seemingly diverse groups to improve the quality of life and business in Boston is legendary. He is profiled after Edie Frasier. I will also introduce you to a man whose name is TURTLE. He got that name because he decided to get up and stand up for the right to let adults be called by whatever name they wanted.

Like Edie Fraser and Paul Guzzi, lifelong civil rights activist, educator and former aide to Martin Luther King, Jr., Reverend CT Vivian has established a movement that has helped so many of us in this country. Esteemed diplomat and former mayor of Atlanta, Andrew Young, credits Reverend Vivian's actions as one of the reasons that the 1964 Voting Rights Act was finally enacted. You'll hear about Reverend Vivian's journey and how his son, Al Vivian, is helping his father to keep the vision of civil rights, equality and justice for all alive.

Edie Fraser, Paul Guzzi, TURTLE and Reverend CT Vivian have worked to weave and leave legacies that will continue long after their souls have left this universe. I hope that you will find through their stories, some ideas to help you in your quest to weave then leave a legacy that will make a memorable positive difference in the world.

Wise Words

Never doubt that a small group of thoughtful, committed citizens can change the world; indeed, it's the only thing that ever does.

—*Margaret Mead*

Wise Words

(This quote was on the Medford High School Bulletin Board referring to the Gay–Straight Alliance 5/18/03—12:55 p.m.)

In Germany, they first came for the Communists, and I didn't speak up because I wasn't a Communist. Then they came for the Jews, and I didn't speak up because I wasn't a Jew. Then they came for the Trade Unionists, and I didn't speak up because I wasn't a Trade Unionist. They came for the Catholics, and I didn't speak up because I was Protestant. Then they came for me—and by that time, no one was left to speak up.

—*Pastor Martin Niemoller*

Profile of Success

Edie Fraser—President, Business Women's Network (BWN) and Diversity Best Practices

I'm always trying to help women, minorities, and young people in different ways. I've probably had about 160 interns in my life and working with young people is a high priority for me. Living your legacy means you don't wait until you die to practice what is important to you.

My dream was to live a life of philanthropy and give back to the world. In the 1960's, I was moved by President John F. Kennedy's call to action when I heard him say those famous words, "Ask not what your country can do for you, but what you can do for your country." The first stop on my philanthropic and service-to-my-country journey was to spend six years in the Peace Corps as staff and then as a desk officer.

I worked tirelessly to help the less fortunate in migrant worker camps and inner city ghettos. I just wanted to make the world a better place for everyone. Later, I went to work for a public relations firm. In 1975, I started my own business. I came from a long line of entrepreneurs. My mom and dad were business owners and started the retail clothing store, Casual Corner.

My philosophy is that whatever the issues of the day are, I try to stay ahead of them. This is imperative if you want to love your work and life. In the early 1990's, few companies were focusing on women's issues and diversity. They weren't even calling it diversity back then. I felt that issues related to women and diversity in the workplace were so important given the changing marketplace and world.

I recognized that a new workplace was emerging. Corporations would need to embrace women and diversity, as well as understand how those issues impact their bottom lines and the return on their investments. I built my company around helping people to understand best practices that relate to women and diversity at work and in the marketplace.

Building a legacy can be accomplished if you look at who does something the best and learn how to share best practices with others.

Loving your work by Loving your Life

Passion for change leadership and relationship building means you must be on the cutting edge and love your work. Loving your life goes back to those relationships, as nothing is more important than that building process, the bridges and pieces of the puzzles. Family, friends, clients and relationships make it all work.

Ways People Can Love Their Work:

- Feel energized in the mission and vision and go for goals and achieve them.
- Know that loving the customer is key with going 150% to exceed every expectation and goal.
- Be appreciative for the unique talents and skills and bring the diverse, inclusive team together, inside and out.
- Be persistent and passionate.
- Be recognized for what you do and how your contributions assist in growing your organization.

To Love Your Life

Have positive relationships with friends and family. Gain their counsel and be there ahead of time for both.

Tips on Loving Your Work and Life That Have Worked for Me:

- Have passion and enthusiasm.
- Practice best practices and constant learning and role modeling.
- Be persistent.
- Create long-term relationships in both work and life. Live the words of the old song: "Make new friends, but keep the old; the first are silver and the other gold."
- Practice appreciation.

How Organizations Can Help Staff to Love Their Work and Life

Be clear on your mission and understand the unique talents of staff as they relate to the goals. Create an atmosphere where people share and exhibit passion and appreciation.

Edie's 14 Daily Adages

Here are my own Daily Adages. (I acknowledge Investor Business Daily (IBD) and its 10 Secrets to Success.)

1. Positive, Energetic and Passionate. How you think is everything. Always be positive. Think Success, not Failure. Beware of a negative environment and surround yourself with a can do, go get them attitude and encourage others to be positive about what they are doing. Yes, be passionate about what you are doing.
2. Keep the vision high. Decide upon your true dreams and goals. If there is one step back, stop and take two steps ahead but keep moving toward measurable goals and achieve them. Go for the day, the week, the month, quantitative and qualitative. (Be growth oriented.)
3. TAKE Action. Goals are nothing without action. Don't be afraid to get started. JUST DO IT with focus, precision and focus, focus, focus.
4. Be PERSISTENT, productive and work hard. Success is a marathon, not a sprint. Never give up.
5. Focus your time. Focus your money. Don't let distractions occur. Again, focus, focus, focus.
6. Be innovative. Don't be afraid to be different and also stay ahead of the curve. Following the herd is a sure way to mediocrity. Leaders are different. Leaders are not afraid to be unique and to push hard for what they believe, to take issues (such as women and diversity) and be the best you can be, ahead of your time.
7. Never stop learning. Read, think, and generate ideas from what you learn. Get training and acquire new skills. Apply them and teach others. Learn something new each day.
8. Network and realize that we are only as good as our many friends, supporters and "buddies." Build with others and mentor and help young people. Give back with mentoring and support. Be helpful. Give of your time and if you can, your money.
9. Be honest and ethical. Be loyal, dedicated, committed and foster pride.
10. Be customer-driven.
11. Laugh a little at yourself and with others; and enjoy what you do.
12. Be grateful for family and find the time to celebrate them. Be grateful for friends and give to them.
13. Be the best you can be.
14. Say thank you 30 times a day.

Profile of Success

Paul Guzzi—President & Chief Executive Officer,
  Greater Boston Chamber of Commerce

Paul Guzzi is president and chief executive officer of the Greater Boston Chamber of Commerce, one of the region's leading business associations. He is a consummate corporate cupid, bringing together many diverse businesses and community leaders. His efforts have helped to make Boston one of the best cities to live and conduct business in within the United States.

Paul brings extensive experience in both business and government to his work at the Chamber. A former Massachusetts secretary of state and chief secretary to the Governor, as well as a member of the management teams of two FORTUNE 500 companies, he is a leading advocate for economic development and job creation.

Before leading the Chamber, he was vice president of state and community affairs for Boston College. Previously, he was a consultant for Heidrick & Struggles, an international recruitment and consulting firm. Paul also served as a vice president at Data General Corporation and as a senior vice president at Wang Laboratories. During his tenure at Wang, he worked closely with Dr. An Wang to oversee the restoration and transformation of what is now the Wang Center for the Performing Arts.

Paul began his public service career as a state representative from Newton in 1970. He was elected Massachusetts secretary of state in 1974. He has served as a chief of staff for Governor Edward King and chief administrator of the Board of Regents of Public Higher Education.

A graduate of Harvard University, he holds a Bachelor of Arts degree in government. He completed the Harvard Business School Management Development Program and was also an officer in the U.S. Marine Corps Reserve.

Among his civic activities, Paul serves as a trustee of the Wang Center for the Performing Arts; is a director on the boards of the Boston Foundation, The Partnership, and Blue Cross Blue Shield of Massachusetts; is a member of the Partners HealthCare Corporation and The Boston Club's Corporate Advisory Boards; and serves as a director of the Host Committee for the 2004 Democratic National Convention. He lives in Newton, Massachusetts, with his wife, Joanne, and has three children.

Here's what Paul had to say about LwL[2]:

A fulfilling profession has been essential to my life. No matter where I have taken my career, or ultimately, where it has taken me, I have followed one simple credo: "Follow your passion." When you listen to your instincts and let your passion inform your decisions, you welcome your own fulfillment, both professionally and personally.
—Paul Guzzi

"C Suite" Checks In
Bennie Wiley—President and CEO, The Partnership, Inc.

A career is merely a collection of experiences. If you are willing to take risks, do what "feels right" for you at each stage of your life, and give 100% to whatever you pursue—it all comes together in the end.

Profile of Success
TURTLE—Sales Associate, Staples

I first met TURTLE in February, 2003. I had written a musical for my 50th birthday called "GenX-BOOM: Generation X to Baby Boomers—50 Years in Song, Words and Dance." TURTLE and his associate, Elizabeth McMannus, had been extraordinarily helpful to me when I was purchasing supplies for the musical at the Staples in the Fresh Pond area of Cambridge, Massachusetts.

I am as curious as a cat, and when I saw that his name badge read TURTLE, I asked him if TURTLE was a first name or last name. His reply was a short, "It's my only name."

I replied, "I know it's your name, but is it your last name?"

Again, he replied in a slightly louder, firmer voice, "It is my only name!"

"Oh," I said, "Is it kind of like Cher? You don't have a last name?"

"Yes!" he commented. He went on to tell me the fascinating story behind his name.

On November 3 of that same year, I hobbled into Staples on crutches (I was still recovering from major foot surgery) to get some supplies to finish this book. TURTLE was standing happily at his cash register that early morning and the store was virtually empty. "Hi TURTLE," I said. Surprised, he turned around and replied, "Oh, hi."

I reminded him who I was and how I had talked to him back in February when he had been so helpful. "TURTLE," I said, "Can you tell me that story again, about how you got your name? I'm writing this book and I think people could benefit from hearing your story." What follows is his account:

TURTLE was born and formerly known as Stanley E. Dickie. He asks, "if you had the last name 'Dickie,' wouldn't you think about changing it?" TURTLE has eight children and when his daughter was born in March of 1976, he decided he didn't want her to go through life with the last name of Dickie. He wanted to change her last name to Färna. He went to the City of Worcester to see city clerk O'Keefe to petition to give his daughter, Anna Stina, the last name Färna instead of Dickie.

To his surprise, O'Keefe denied his request stating that Färna was not an English sounding name and "we can't do that." TURTLE was outraged and decided to pursue legal action. Eventually, he teamed up with others who had issues with their names. Their suit went before the U.S. Supreme Court, and they won the right for adults to change their names. After the trial, some Native Americans had adopted him and gave him the name TURLTE, so he is now legally called TURTLE.

To show me how official his name is, TURTLE pulled out his driver's license. Sure enough, it contains only one word—TURTLE. TURTLE told me on that November 3rd morning that not even his co-workers knew that he was formerly known as Stanley E. Dickie. "It's been 20 years since I've told anyone my past name," he told me.

I was honored that he revealed it to me and asked him if I could mention it in the book and he said, "Yes, just as long as you say I was *formerly* known as, *not* A.K.A. (also known as)."

I assured him that I would honor his wishes. He thanked me and with a twinkle in his eye stated that the thing he was most proud about regarding "his" Supreme Court case was that any adult in Massachusetts can now change their name legally, and they don't have to go to court to do so.

Wise Words

To be an effective leader you have to care passionately about achieving the objective.

—*Bob Eubank, President, Swift Murdock*

Bob Eubank offers some of his favorite quotes about leaders and their power to impact change and leave a legacy:

"Leadership is the capacity to get things done through others by changing people's mindsets and energizing them to action. Successful leadership must accomplish this through ideas and values, not through coercion or Machiavellian manipulation....There is nothing more difficult to take in hand, more perilous to conduct, or more uncertain in its success than to take the lead in the introduction of a new order of things."

—Niccolo Machiavelli

"A leader has the ability to create infectious enthusiasm."

—Ted Turner

"There's a big difference between being interested and being committed. When you're interested in doing something, you do it when it's convenient. When you're committed to something, you accept no excuses—only results."

—Ken Blanchard

"To be an effective leader today you must trust subordinates, develop an inspiring vision, manage by example, practice visible management, listen, delegate, create a sense of urgency, invite dissent, and encourage risk. In a company seeking rapid growth, the chief job of the leader is to prepare people and the organization to deal with change."

—Unknown

Profile of Success

Al and Reverend CT Vivian—Atlanta, Georgia

I sat down with a civil rights legend, the Reverend CT Vivian, who was also a close aide to Dr. Martin Luther King, Jr., at his home in Atlanta, Georgia. We were joined by his son, Al Vivian. Here's what they had to say about LwL[2]:

I am a big tennis fan and love to play the game. What I've observed is that if a tennis player messes up and can't let the mistake go, quite often he loses his concentration and confidence and he'll miss even more points.
— *Reverend CT Vivian*

Reverend CT Vivian: I want to start this interview by making sure you understand that you are talking to a minister. I was called to my work and that's different than the norm. Before I was called, I had two or three things that I wanted to do with my life. In grade school, I wanted to be a doctor, but by high school I realized I didn't want to do what they did as a black doctor. I'd be fixing people up from gunshot wounds, etc. after the weekend. That wouldn't do—I'd be patching them up to send them into an imperfect society. So, I decided to become a doctor for society. I wanted to prevent that from happening.

I went to teachers college because it was there and available. I told myself that whatever I was going to do—I was going to do it well. For many people, life has taken over them even though they think they are in control of their lives. I wanted to get rid of social conditions that were causing people to be destroyed—I didn't want people to be destroyed by social ills.

When I reflected upon my past (he laughs), I think about fourth grade. At my school, there was this famous painting of a man with a hoe and he is a French peasant out in a field. Beside the picture is a poem that says: "Who made this man into what he is versus what he should have been?" To me, that meant how did society create this man? Who made it so those peasants were never educated and couldn't elevate their life? There was something about that poem and picture that resonated with me.

It's about the meaning of my life and if I am not living my life with meaning, the whole thing can be destroyed. At that point, I knew that people were destroying each other for an entirely different reason. Later, I became a literature major in college. We were in the middle of the Depression and that made social issues more important and literature took on a new meaning. When the Depression hit in 1929, there were more people going to the library to find out what had happened in the roaring 20s from hilarity to calamity with the 1929 stock market collapse. People lost everything and everyone's life was changed. If you don't see work connected to your life then you're throwing your life away.

A famous man pulled out of the stock market before the Depression when he heard his shoe shine boy talk about how he was investing and buying stock. This man thought that when the common man can have access to what I have then something is wrong with the stock market. In that case, he was right.

Everyone in the nation wanted to know how the market collapsed. Tremendous numbers of people weren't employed and they didn't know what to do. You begin to understand the world in which you live when you see your life in relationship to the larger issue and the greater society.

People walk around wearing their name, rank and serial number. What do they do for work and how much salary do they make; that's what's out front for people. Some have become no more than that and have lost meaning in their life. When we ask people, "What do you do?" we're really asking, "What do you make and are you lower, middle, or upper class?"

Al Vivian: Years ago, African Americans didn't first ask, "What do you do?" They first asked, "Whose boy are you—who is your mama? What church do you go to?" They were first asking about what kind of a person you are. We are getting away from our sense of ourselves and are just concerned about what people do.

Reverend CT Vivian: The real question we should be asking is "Who are you?" I saw Matrix 2 and the guy with the French accent, he said something like, 'Choices are something that people with power let you think you have.'

Individualism is what seems to drive Americans, but it really is team work that works. There is always team work at the top.

I look at how some Asian and Indian families operate. Everyone brings money to the head of the household and they plan from there. Everyone's income becomes the family income.

As long as we break off and all of us are doing our own thing, we won't be as successful. We need to pool our resources and talk and plan with our family members to be successful.

It's important for all of us to know how we see ourselves in relationship to the total society and our family structure. How do we see ourselves in relationship to them? Life is about relationships.

Al Vivian: Your entire life is a sequence of relationships. Even people that you may not think you need now will become some of the most significant people later in life. This is not because they will help you make money, but will help you make better decisions to reach your goals. You cannot fully love your job unless you love yourself.

Reverend CT Vivian: You won't truly love your job unless it is part of your real life—to be off on one is to be off on the other. There's a difference between a job, a profession, and a calling. When you are doing your calling you are working all the time, but it's not really work.

Al Vivian: You just wake up doing it because it's your passion.

Reverend CT Vivian: My wife tells a story about a welfare mother who called herself a social worker, but she was not educated and didn't have a formal degree as a social worker. This was her title because she helped people.

What always bothers me, is people who go through college and even obtain a graduate degree and in three to four years hate the job and hate people. They are burned out and can't help others or themselves. They go into the profession for the wrong reasons—the money, or mom or dad always wanted them to be in that line of work.

What's missing for people is they don't do what they love to do in life, but what they do is just to pay the bills.

Two great lines that stand out for me—"You do well by doing good," and a great man once said, "You balance the spiritual and the material." You need to have balance of the material so you don't mar the spiritual.

About Leaving and Weaving Your Legacy

Al Vivian: When I first moved back to Atlanta, I visited a college buddy—a doctor in a *beautiful* house. He is in obstetrics and gynecology. This doctor used to be so excited about bringing life into the world. The man now sees his job as just another day in the office. I asked him, "What happened? You always wanted to be a doctor, man." He replied that he was expected to be a doctor because he came from a long line of doctors. "I am now searching for what I can do so I can no longer be a doctor. Now the medical field is so legalized and HMOs require a lot of paper work to be reimbursed and there is the fear of lawsuits and malpractice. It's no longer enjoyable." Thinking about my friend made me realize that why I love my job is that I have never been forced into it.

I was in the Army when I saw my dad on the Oprah show. I told myself, "that's what I want to do." The moment I saw my dad on Oprah I knew I wanted to do what my dad did. I would do more in society than what I was doing for Uncle Sam, although that was fulfilling. I was preprogrammed into serving others and this was who I was. To love my job was to love myself and to do something that had meaning. When I joined the Army my dad said, "You didn't land on Plymouth rock, it landed on you."

There are six kids in my family and five have been entrepreneurs at one point or another. This was never pushed in the family, but we learned by watching my dad stand up for his beliefs.

For example, people like Andrew Young credit an act that my dad committed as being instrumental to the passing of the Voting Rights Act. There was a famous picture of my dad who was hit brutally by the fist of Sheriff Clark in Selma, Alabama at a voting rights demonstration. This picture was beamed around the country and the world. As the saying goes, a picture *is* worth a thousand—or in this case—a *million* words. Once people saw the injustice taking place in this picture, just because a man wanted the simple right to vote, Andy Young said if my dad had acted violently when the camera captured Sheriff Clark's violent deed, then the Voting Rights Act may not have occurred.

Knowing that my dad fought for me and others to vote, in 1984, when I got into the military, as an officer one of my duties was the voting registration officer. It was an election year and I had to get everyone in the installation registered to vote. I had to get an absentee ballot into every one of the 22,000 soldiers' hands. I came home to visit and I wasn't going to be in town on Election Day so I had to vote in Atlanta while there. I had sent my absentee ballot in but my town said it wasn't there. I went to my town hall and I wasn't going to leave the building because they said I couldn't vote.

I took my right to vote seriously because my dad had fought for the right to vote and I knew people had died so I could vote. I pursued this and eventually they called me back and told me I could vote.

When I asked my dad to join his business, dad said he had to think about it and make sure I could do the job. He told me that just because I was his son, didn't mean I had a job. The values of my dad were being imbedded inside us. He told us children, 'I don't care what you become, just be a good person.'

We always are an unconscious model for people. For example, if you are a child of a person who lived for a purpose that is not considered normal and they are doing it all the time, because mom and dad did it, you picked it up. Your children pick up the patterns that go with the commitment to your calling. It's not what you say, it's what you do and what you are that is most likely what they will become.

We have a spiritual imprint that tells us the kind of persons we are supposed to be, but we also have society telling us what we should be. If a huge amount of money was dropped into my lap—I would spend time imparting to children that you can do whatever you want to do and have nothing blocking you from that goal. Whatever you are meant to do and be or become, you have an open door for it. What you start out wanting to do may change in your life as you grow, as other things may open a wider door for you. If you still want to be the same thing at 40 as you did at 10, the chances are you haven't grown.

Money can get in the way of your doing what you are destined to do—you need to work on being free from that trap.

The Calling

each of us
has been given a gift
that we are expected to share.
it is our responsibility
to recognize the gift;
it is our choice to use it.

it is not always easy to know
just what that gift might be.
so many times,
it lies undiscovered
or perhaps
cleverly disguised…

often,
our gift
brings us
heartache and disappointment,
taking us to heights and depths
we do not want to go.

our gift is our calling…
it is the voice of God
that whispers
softly from the heavens
requesting, ever so gently,
our total obedience.

our calling
may not always be what we like to do
or what we feel we are successful at doing…
it is
what He desires us to do
because He knows we are able.

in our private moments
we each must search
our souls,
bending close our hearts
to hear His chosen
calling for our lives.

—Adrienne Rumi White

As the Reverend CT Vivian and Adrienne Rumi White have mentioned, some of us have a calling in life. Whether you feel you have discovered yours or not, some day you WILL no longer exist in a physical form on this earth. Whether we want to or not, each of us will, however, leave a legacy. The choice is up to you if you leave a positive or negative footprint. In the next chapter, you will discover ways that you can weave—then leave—your legacy.

Chapter 39

WEAVING—THEN LEAVING—YOUR LEGACY

Quote of Note

The essence of your existence lies in the hearts and memories of those you touch.

—*Robert Browne; September 15, 2003*

In loving memory of his mother

DISCOVERING YOUR FAMILY ROOTS: LEAVING A LEGACY FOR YOUR CHILDREN AND GENERATIONS TO COME

NOT ALL OF US WILL BECOME AS FAMOUS AS Edie Fraser, Paul Guzzi or the Reverend CT Vivian for the work that we leave behind. Each of us, however, has the capacity to weave—then leave—a legacy for others. At the beginning of this book, you read one of my favorite poems, "Success," which is attributed by some to Ralph Waldo Emerson (others question whether he was the author).

Success

To laugh often and much;
To win the respect of intelligent people
and the affection of children;
To earn the appreciation of honest critics
and endure the betrayal of false friends;
To appreciate beauty;
To find the best in others;
To leave the world a bit better,
whether by a healthy child,
a garden patch or a redeemed social condition;
To know even one life has breathed easier
because you have lived.
That is to have succeeded.

—Ralph Waldo Emerson

As the poem points out, one's legacy can be as large as being known for changing the course of history to changing your life so that your heirs or others you have met along life's journey "breathed easier because you have lived."

Whether you are married, single, widowed or divorced, taking the time to discover who you are is critical if you want to LwL². Equally important, is what you do with the information about yourself once it is unearthed. I am a firm believer in the cliché that in order to know where you're going, you must understand where you've been. An added benefit to understanding your past is that it helps you to know where you might end up and also what pitfalls you may encounter because of family genes and DNA or patterns of behavior you may need to avoid. Knowledge about incidents of family diseases, such as cancer or alcoholism, can be an indication to you about things you need to do to keep yourself cancer and alcohol-free. If you know you come from a long line of entrepreneurs, you may somehow find yourself not able to hold down a regular job effectively because what you *really* want to do is be your own boss and start a business. Knowing about your family's entrepreneurial connection may help you stop fighting your urge to be a business owner and do something about starting a business.

Sharing information about your past and ancestors with your children and others in your life is also helpful.

Disseminating such information may help them to gain a broader insight into you and your life, as well as help them with their efforts to LwL².

If you are adopted and don't know about your biological parents or relatives, don't have living relatives or are estranged from your family, try tackling this issue from another perspective. Think about what you do know and do have access to regarding your past and make sure you share that information with significant others who NOW inhabit your life.

My father is an avid genealogist and has catalogued over 13,000 of our relatives and related individuals. I didn't know anything about why he started on his genealogy journey until I was writing this book and asked him to put together an article that I could include about practical tips to discover your family roots. He told me that I had started him on this trek when I told him that I knew quite a bit about the history of my mother's side of the family, but very little about his ancestors. I hope you find his insights helpful on how you can learn more about from whence you came.

Tips on How to Discover Your Family Roots

By Leonard A. Mervin, Sr.

Leonard Mervin is an avid genealogist and has traced his roots back to the 1700's and ancestors, Brutus Mervin and James Hippard. He constantly shares his research and findings with his children, grandchildren and other relatives and friends.

THE FEDERAL CENSUS IS ONE OF THE BEST tools you can use to research family histories. It is a compilation of the family and their neighbors. It generally shows you who the people were that lived in a neighborhood. Often those neighbors were also relatives, as parents gave land to their children and/or the children purchased land. The Census brings everything together and it also tells you about everyone who lived in a house and often their relationship to the head of the house.

There are public records (usually maintained in the Court House in the county where the event took place). Sometimes people would prefer that you not look into their family circumstances. Be careful not to antagonize these people if they don't want you to know about them. All citizens, however, have the right to review pubic records.

Check out birth, death and marriage records. These records contain a lot of information. For example, a death record may show parents' names and may indicate spouses and other family members, like the person who provided the information about the death to the County officials—they may give their relationship to the deceased—son, daughter, aunt, uncle, etc. There is a lot of information available on these records to help you set the record straight.

Marriage records generally reflect names of those married, their ages, and their parents. Also, they may indicate whether or not the parents of the bride and groom were alive at the time of the marriage, their residence and the date the wedding took place. This information can assist you with your further research.

Birth certificates, marriage certificates and death certificates before 1913 were not regulated. A law, as of January 1914, required that all jurisdictions within the U.S. had to maintain records of birth, death and marriage. Some places did have these documents before that date and others were maintained haphazardly. Records for people of color (African Americans, Asians, Hispanics/Latinos and Native Americans) have been kept sporadically over the years and sometimes not at all.

Sometimes births and marriages were recorded in a family Bible. Some people, however, struggled through life and worried more about having food to eat and a place to stay rather than writing down information about a birth or death. Other people couldn't read or write so that information was not recorded.

The Federal Census has been taken every ten years since 1790. The main reason was for the apportionment for representatives to the lower house of Congress. An entry in the first Census schedule shows the name of the head of household and the number of

- free white males ages 16 and older in the household
- free white males under the age of 16
- free white females
- all other free persons
- slaves

The first listing of all blacks, by name, was in the 1870 Census, in the first Federal Census taken after the Civil War. Free Blacks who were heads of households were enumerated by name in the Censuses from 1790 to 1840 and the names of all free household members were included in the Censuses of 1850 and 1860. So, researching Black family histories prior to 1890 can require more in-depth research.

In 1880, a very important addition was made to the Census format. Each household's head was named and everyone listed within that household was given a relationship indicator to that head (wife, son, daughter, mother, father, grandmother, cousin, aunt, etc., and unrelated individuals were listed as boarders or renters). Information about households and individuals was collected by door-to-door canvass by Census Takers.

Web Browser

There are many websites that could be helpful. A basic one you might want to check out is www.rootsweb.com.

I've thanked my dad countless times for the invaluable sacred gift he has given to me, my children and the generations to come about our ancestors. I urge you to spend some time finding out about your roots then sharing your results with loved ones. Perhaps that information will help them to better LwL[2].

Tea Bag Tag
To be grateful is to be great and full.

—Yogi Tea Bag Tag, 8/21/03

HOW OLD DO YOU HAVE TO BE TO LEAVE A LEGACY?

Have you ever stopped to ponder your answers to that question. Do you have to live to 100 in order to establish your immortal footprints on the universe's landscape? What were the ages of some legends in our generation who, for better or worse, have left an indelible impression on this earth? Let's have some fun with this question. Take a moment to answer the questions regarding the life spans of some of today's legends:

Legacy Quick Quiz

1. In July 2003, Bob Hope, legendary comedian, died at this age.
   a. 50   b. 75   c. 100

2. John F. Kennedy had spent this many years as the President of the United States when he was shot in Dallas.
   a. 3   b. 4   c. 7

3. Martin Luther King, Jr. was this age when he was assassinated.
   a. 29   b. 39   c. 49

4. Mary Kay Ash, Cosmetics Queen Bee, was this age when she started her cosmetics empire in 1963.
   a. 25   b. 35   c. 45

5. Alexander the Great conquered the world at this age.
   a. 18   b. 24   c. 30

6. Marilyn Monroe died tragically, of what appears to have been a drug overdose in 1962, at this age.
   a. 31   b. 41   c. 51

7. Elvis Presley was the King of Rock n' Roll and didn't like for people to call him the King. He was laid to rest, August 16, 1977 in Graceland at this age.
   a. 32   b. 42   c. 52

8. Like Elvis, Johnny Cash recorded some of his legendary records on the Sun Record label. He was this age when he died.
   a. 51   b. 71   c. 81

9. Althea Gibson grew up poor when tennis was a country club sport. She learned how to play by hitting balls against a brick wall. She died in 2003 at this age.
   a. 56   b. 76   c. 100

10. Robert McCloskey was the author of *Make Way for Ducklings*. According to CNN (7/7/03), he claimed that he learned how to draw the ducks by taking them home and giving them wine to sip, then watched as they fluttered around.* He died at this age.
    a. 58   b. 68   c. 88

11. Legendary TV anchor, David Brinkley, was employed by NBC for ___ years before he left to work for ABC.
    a. 18   b. 28   c. 38   *Source: CNN Aaron Brown*

12. This individual was very superstitious and feared the number 13 and Friday the 13th. Ironically, this person died at 11:50 P.M. on Thursday, April 12. If he had died the next day—that is to say, 10 minutes later—he would have passed away on a day he feared most.
    a. President Franklin D. Roosevelt   b. Howard Hughes   c. Sammy Davis, Jr.

13. Which Mickey is older, child actor Mickey Rooney or Mickey Mouse? In 2003, one was 83 years old and the other 75 years old.
    a. Rooney   b. Mouse

---

*We do NOT endorse or recommend this practice!

Wise Words

On How She Became Successful

I was middle aged, had varicose veins and didn't have time to fool around.

—*Mary Kay Ash, Founder, Mary Kay Cosmetics (died 11/23/01)*

At the age of 45 with 3 kids to support, she turned a $5,000 investment into a $2 billion empire.

—*NBC News 11/24/01*

What can we take away from this quiz regarding *what age* someone on this earth needs to start doing something in their life in order for it to "stick" and make a lasting positive impression? The answer to that question is simple—any age. People like Elvis Presley, Marilyn Monroe, Martin Luther King, Jr., and John F. Kennedy never saw their 50th birthdays, but what they accomplished in their brief lives has affected the world forever—and since their presence graced this earth, the universe has never been the same. Individuals such as Bob Hope, Katherine Hepburn, Frank Lloyd Wright and Mary Kay Ash lived into "old age" and, in some cases, started their legacy-building work late in life.

Practical Meaning Moment

It is never too late or too early in your life to pursue those things that you've always wanted to do to make the world a better place and to leave your checkmark on the earth. Remember to eliminate the negative head chatter that we discussed. Stop focusing on the "If I coulda, woulda, shoulda" when it comes to achieving certain accomplishments in your life. Decide what you want to be remembered for then "Go for the Gusto." Shape your words, thoughts and deeds in such a way that you are working to weave—then leave—your legacy and personal footprints behind.

Wise Words

Might Makes Right

Martha McNeil, Social Studies Teacher and a 38-year teaching veteran at the Concord Middle School, Peabody Building, at her Parent Teachers Open House on September 18, 2003 said something profound: "We're teaching the kids an important concept—power and the rule of law versus the rule of man—or, might makes right. It doesn't mean exactly what you think. Yes, it's about muscle might, but it's also about brain might."

As I was sitting on the edge of my seat waiting for an example, she went on to say, "Look at Hitler. He was a rather puny guy and probably didn't have a lot of muscle might. In a period of about 12 years, look at what the might of his mind did to change the course of history and lives of so many men, women and children for generations."

I still have to pause when I think about the might of Martha McNeil's words that night.

One individual who left a powerful legacy is former Prime Minister of India, Indira Gandhi. One of Prime Minister Gandhi's former aides, Mangalam Srinivasan—educator, scientist, researcher and advisor to heads of state and CEOs—gives us some of her thoughts about working for Mrs. Gandhi. We will also learn about the incredible legacy that Mangalam is weaving with her own life.

Profile of Success

Dr. Mangalam Srinivasan—Special Advisor at Harvard's John F. Kennedy School of Government and Associate, Center for International Affairs

Dr. Mangalam Srinivasan is the personification of a Renaissance woman. She possesses highly inter-disciplinary training and skills ranging from international management and finance to classics and literature, mathematics, physics and philosophy to indigenous art and culture, government and business studies to fine arts, law and ecology. Her degrees include a doctorate in technology assessment, advanced special scholar in astronomy, MBA in management, MA in English Literature and BA in mathematics and physics.

Mangalam's most recent positions are Special Advisor at Harvard's Kennedy School of Government and Associate for the Center for International Affairs. Her teaching and research focuses include: Cybernetics, Science, Technology and Society, Technology Assessment and Management, Judicial Activism and Environmental Justice. She has held a variety of international management teaching appointments, invited professorships and seminars at Harvard, MIT, Northeastern University, University of California at Berkeley, University of Madras, and several international universities in Asia, Europe and Latin America. She also served as the chair of a U.N. panel which included Mother Theresa. "She sat next to me and held my hand," Mangalam recalls, "I felt that she was an illumined soul."

An expert on climate change and energy issues, she has served as a resource person on the corporate responsibilities initiatives of the U.N. Secretary General, technology sector issue. Her consultancies include: U.S. Department of Energy, U.S. National Science Foundation, National Academy of Sciences, the European Union, the Smithsonian Institution, U.N. and its Specialized Agencies, and the Organization of the American States. She also advises several overseas organizations, governments, and in some, directly advises the heads of governments and apex bodies.

She has served on many boards including the Board of Directors for Satyam Computer Services. When that company went public, Mangalam rang the opening bell at the New York Stock Exchange.

In the 1980's, Mangalam was an aide to India's famous former Prime Minister, the late Indira Gandhi. Here are Mangalam's reflections on this legendary woman, as well as her thoughts about the legacy she herself is leaving the world.

Reflections on Prime Minister Indira Gandhi

By Dr. Mangalam Srinivasan—Special Advisor at Harvard's John F. Kennedy School of Government

I FIRST MET PRIME MINISTER INDIRA GANDHI in 1975 when she had imposed an emergency order in India. I worked for her in 1982 and 1983 at her invitation. She asked me to join her team. At that time, I had a congenial conversation with her. I told her I wouldn't play on her team if I had a philosophical difference on issues with her, such as war.

She was one of the most powerful persons, not just women, in the entire world at that time. Prime Minister Gandhi believed that we came from and lived in a free country and we had the best of both worlds in India. She totally agreed with my idealism. Once I came home and was staying in the house of one of Mrs. Gandhi's ministers, I sat on my bed for seven hours after talking with her. I was so impressed and felt like I had been in the presence of deity. I do not distinguish people in terms of power. She had filled my mind and heart by her grace, strength and extraordinary good looks. She had incredible power as a woman.

I left after a year and at a later date she invited me to lunch at the Presidential Palace. It was a luncheon with the heads of state from governments around the world. I appeared on a three wheel scooter (which I hoped no one would see). There were 16 heads of state and I was the only woman invited. Mrs. Gandhi gave me exposure like this as a growth opportunity.

She was absolutely the most intellectually vibrant person I knew. She was also shrewd, self-serving, didn't take anyone at their word and would check people out thoroughly. She was very different from other world leaders. Everything went into her brain, she took no notes; she wore silk or simple cotton saris. She always looked you straight into your eyes. She often just listened to you without any questions and after you finished talking, she'd ask, "Is there anything else?" But because she did her homework, she knew all about what you were doing.

I believe she had absolute trust in me. This is who she was. Unfortunately, the way she died was so sad. The day after she was assassinated, I was interviewed by CBS and the McNeil Lehrer Report on PBS. I said that she was an extraordinary person and it was a great loss. She was such an idol and role model.

Today, Indians are in a driver's seat in regard to information technology. Our people are educated and serve an important part of the world's workforce. Mrs. Gandhi, like her father, built India to be the citadel of technology. She thought this was our heritage. Within India, she inspired many people to work.

Women in the Work Place

By Dr. Mangalam Srinivasan—Special Advisor at Harvard's John F. Kennedy School of Government

DREAMING ALONE WILL NOT BE A SUFFICIENT condition for the achievement of any goal. Great aspirations require great beliefs, discipline and work and even greater commitments to setting them in motion toward the path of achievement. Since we live in a community of other workers, families, communities and nations, it becomes mandatory to communicate these dreams so they take shape. In an interview, the famed film producer/director Ismail Merchant offered the following opinion:

In order to get anywhere in life you have to make everybody believe in your dreams.

Sounds simple enough. The art, science and business of selling dreams require unique sensibilities and stamina. Those who have progressed will remain at high noon with light shining on them, while many others will simply stay by the wayside as shadows. The new-to-power-and-influence folks, who had cleared the track and had removed the debris, have responsibilities to cover the tracks for those yet to come.

Today, women are in a preferred place from where they can see not only how far they have traveled, but also all others who can be helped to achieve their full potential. In a 1999 interview for *Praxis,* of the Hindu Business Line, Reena Ramachandran, the head of Hindustan Organic Chemicals said, "A woman manager ten years ago was operating in an environment very different from today where there are a lot more women in the workplace. So the psychology, environment and lifestyles have changed. Therefore, her style of functioning has also changed."

This means that the woman has come to her own in the work place as well as to every other place and hopefully, with confidence, will stand up to what really matters and what truly defines her as a woman, namely, her humanity.

When the chains have been shattered and a new reality of what is possible is no longer caged in ideologies of man versus woman, the manager versus worker, the old versus young and the affluent versus the deprived, the achieved woman is more than a mentor. She is a powerful change agent. Lest we might forget, Nobel Laureate Amartya Sen would remind us to take "the plural view of gender inequalities" because the "effects of such inequalities impoverish women as well as men." The special responsibility then involves that the women leaders create "a critical mass of leaders to usher in change."

While the great strides have taken us leaps and bounds beyond our dreams, a vast majority of us remain not far from where we had started and some even on retrograde. Women, in many cases, are still being viewed as dinner companions. Personal issues against women still show up in work-related evaluations. Just a few years ago, a woman entrepreneur was told that she should be starting a restaurant rather than going around trying to raise venture capital for her start-up company. The woman recovered and went on to win big but not before breaking down.

Many of us have known great support from our families and we face our second shifts at home with a lot of help either from our families or by contracting hired help. The higher order of concern for our children, aging parents, familial tranquility and community obligations, no doubt, suffer with women trying to perform high-wire acts. But, should this not be the concern of the couple and not just the sacred duty set aside for women alone? Should not society owe women the opportunity to excel in whatever their choice of vocation, whether as a home maker or out there in the wide world?

It is tempting to theorize that the new ideologies can dismantle, deconstruct and destroy a past so unequal, unfair and unjust and reconstruct a glorious present which will make a thousand lotuses bloom in every pond. A technical resurrection will not do here and there are no neat algebraic equations that can tell us how to balance life. Much has been expected of the new momentum in women's leadership and hopefully, the qualitative changes brought on by newer and more nurturing insights might modify, perhaps even change, the vision of "machines making more machines."

I was privileged, in the early eighties, to host in my home the world's first woman cosmonaut Valentina Tershkova, scientist and the highest-ranking woman member of the Polit Bureau of the erstwhile Soviet Union. As she sat in my kitchen savoring my culinary productions, she was telling us about her space travel:

> "From my *Soyuz* I watched the little blue planet floating in the Cosmos and I was overcome with motherly instincts. I looked at our Earth as a mother looks at her tiny baby, helpless, but completely trusting that the Mother would protect and nurture. Compassion and love overwhelmed me. When I returned to the Earth, I touched the Siberian soil with love and gratitude!"

Just imagine!

One of India's strongest advocates for women's freedom and progress in every aspect of life including religion is Swami Rangathananda, the President of Ramakrishna Mission. He is repository of knowledge—scientific, sacred and secular. His analytical and rational approaches to knowledge make him one of the greatest thinkers of our times. He finds time to read feminist literature, analyzes the concepts, and translates them into universal language to inspire the foot soldiers engaged in the fight to achieve equality and excellence. He admires pioneers such as Betty Friedan and is ready to publicize her thinking, especially in her book *The Second Stage*. Swamiji quotes the following passage in his book *The Indian Vision of God As Mother:*

> "The second stage has to transcend the battle for equal power in institutions. The second stage will restructure institutions and transform the nature of power itself."

Those of us who have struggled against prejudices of various kinds know that new clothes on old skeletons do not render institutions efficient in delivering equity and fairness.

Our Prime Minister has said that he was not interested in knowing that we are super achievers, or we are super rich and powerful. He said, "Tell me that all our girl children are going to school."

As mothers and nurturers, and now with our emerging roles in the wealth and power sectors, we can make the biggest difference long awaited. The arrivals of women in the global corporations are, in the words of Peter Drucker, "clearly the most important economic instrument *[my addition: social instrument as well]*," again quoting Drucker, "…requires new structures, new methods of integration and new relationships."

Sri. Amma once gave instructions that we think constructively, so we go to work on the positive outcomes we take from here. In that spirit, I offer two challenges, which I hope you will consider.

The first challenge is self-directed to us women: Even while we grieve and rage over past injustices we must recognize that the blame game does not get us anywhere.

The first order of business then is to have the strength and stamina, acquire knowledge and seek wisdom and know our work by its purpose. After all, "it is not know-how but know-what" by which we determine the purpose behind why we do what we do. We have been chart-makers, researchers, paper presenters, but we know how to conceptualize and therefore, we are the manipulators of better human futures.

The second challenge is to CEOs and other leaders to take seriously the ideas of women so they can participate fully and help in the creation of great human futures. Of course we will turn down no good ideas just because they come from men! As Swami Ranganathaji would exclaim, "What a beautiful idea it is!"

The revolutionary poet Subramania Bharati anticipated the new women of India and envisioned that the women and men of India would

Harness the floods of Bengal
To raise crops elsewhere
Unearth gold and deep mine raw material
Make umbrellas—also ploughs
Weave burlap and draw wires
Assemble carts, coaches and flying machines
Build mighty ships tall and proud
Measure the high heavens and also the ocean's depth

And he was emphatic when he declared that the women and men of India

Shall reach the Moon
Research and traverse the Cosmos.
(Free translation by Mangalam Srinivasan)

In closing, I'd like to leave you with the words I once heard quoted by John Dobson, a distinguished astronomer and founder of the San Francisco Side Walk Astronomers:

"The silver haze across the night
is a billion Suns
And one amongst the haze is ours,
One belongs to you and me, one
belongs to you and me."

(Source: Joanie Johnson, Untitled Poem, quoted by John Dobson in Astronomy for Children Under Eighty*)*

Legacies Are Similar Yet Different

leg·a·cy (leg′ ə sē) *n. pl.* **leg·a·cies** 1. Money or property bequeathed to another by will. 2. Something handed down from an ancestor or a predecessor or from the past: *a legacy of religious freedom.*

Source:
http://dictionary.reference.com/search?q=legacy

Legacies can be similar yet different. A case in point is what occurred during the week of June 23, 2003 in regard to the legacies of three mighty men who died—Maynard Jackson, Lester Maddox and Senator Strom Thurman. Each of these legendary individuals was known for his stance on civil rights and championing rights for their constituencies. All of these men left a legacy for the work they did in the civil rights arena and from that perspective, their legacies are similar. The work

they did and how they approached this issue of civil rights during their lifetimes, however, couldn't be more different.

At the age of 35, Maynard Jackson, former Mayor of Atlanta, Georgia, became the first African-American mayor in any major southern city in the United States. Lester Maddox had been the Governor of Mississippi in the 1960s. He was a staunch segregationist and led civil rights campaigns against integrating schools and other civil rights issues. Senator Strom Thurman—who at the time of his death was 100 years old—had in his lifetime gone from leading movements to prevent blacks and others from sharing fully in the American dream to in his later years reconciling with some of the very people he had detested and campaigned against in the early part of his life. After his death, many were shocked to learn in December 2003, that he had fathered a 78-year-old daughter, Essie Mae Washington Williams, with a 16-year-old black servant girl.

Not all of us will leave legacies that have the magnitude of changing the minds of millions as these men did, but regardless of our lot in life, we can work while we are on this earth to weave a legacy that leaves the world a little better off because we lived. Take some time to think about the type of legacy you want and how you can begin through your actions today to make it real tomorrow.

Wise Words

Anita Rowe—Ph.D., Partner, Gardenswartz & Rowe

All work is autobiographical. It is an expression of who we are and a way to share our unique gifts with others.

To Love your work

Find your passion and gifts so that you do what you love and do well.

To Love your Life

Make intentional choices about how to spend precious time. Do what you want, know why you did it, and have no resentment.

Tips

Before committing to something, I ask myself, "If I say yes, will I resent it later?" Work in environments and with people where you blossom, and that bring out the best in you. Avoid toxic people and situations.

How Organizations Can Help Staff

Allow autonomy and creativity and encourage risk and responsibility. Allow people to learn from experience, both good and bad, successful and unsuccessful. Help people find and express their passions and gifts at work.

Reach for the moon—even if you miss it,
you may just land on a star.

As you begin your legacy trek, I'd like to provide you with some tips that may be helpful to you as you jog down the path of life.

Here are some of the pearls of wisdom I enforce in my life. Perhaps some of them will guide your thinking around your life and the legacy you can create, regardless of your age.

My Quotes to Live By

☆ Expect excellence always.

☆ Find the beauty and unique qualities in everyone.

☆ Don't be afraid to be the only one.

☆ Know your roots and those of others.

☆ Keep the world in your address book.

☆ Not everyone has vision and can do strategic planning and implementation.

☆ Practice plate spinning—always prioritize.

☆ It's lonely at the top and even more lonely if you're an entrepreneur.

☆ Discover your life's work and how your job and career fit into it.

☆ Recognize your life's work, and your career and job will make sense.

☆ Do a good job for the company and yourself.

☆ Make hay while the sun is high.

☆ To understand what's in front of you, you must know what you've left behind.

☆ Walk in someone else's moccasins.

☆ Treat everyone with dignity and respect.

☆ The human spirit cries out to be bigger than the "me." It longs to connect to the "we."

☆ Leaving your legacy has everything to do with me and we.

☆ It's easier to be bad than good and harder to think positive than negative thoughts.

☆ My life's work is about connecting humans and businesses in such a way that they can make a memorable positive difference in the world.

☆ I help seemingly diverse groups come together so they can better understand and appreciate each other.

☆ Put up, shut up, or move on.

☆ Now that I've found my life's purpose my chest feels less hard and I can breathe easier.

☆ You can be what you might have been.

☆ It's amazing how when people die young, their youthful picture becomes cemented in your brain. On September 23, 2003, had he lived, John F. Kennedy would have been 86 years old. The image of J.F.K. as an old wrinkled man will never surface in my head or memories.

☆ John F. Kennedy only served as President of the United States for 3 years, but the legend of Camelot will endure forever.

☆ Whether you are working in an organization that is thriving or one that feels like it is one step from conducting a going-out-of-business sale, take the time to LwL[2].

Wise Words

He who wishes to secure the good of others has already secured his own.

—Confucius

One can never consent to creep when one feels the impulse to soar.

—Helen Keller

The future belongs to those that believe in the beauty of their dreams.

—Eleanor Roosevelt

Fortune Cookie and Tea Bag Tag Messages

The job of the human being is to radiate through the finite self the infinite light.

—Yogi Tea Bag Tag; 9/16/03 (Tuesday)

The purpose of life is to do something that will live forever.

—Yogi Tea Bag Tag; 8/19/03 (Tuesday)

If you are remembered, leave nothing behind but goodness.

—Yogi Tea Bag Tag; 9/6/03 (Saturday)

Chapter 40

Redirecting Your Life After Retirement, Death and When Water Is No Longer Available

ONE MORNING, AS I WAS IN THE PROCESS of making my Yogi Green Tea (with Energy) and decaf coffee, don't ask me why, but I started to reflect on what it would be like if I didn't have the water to make these two beverages that I love to consume in the morning. As the water ran from my white porcelain whistling tea kettle and onto the French Roast decaf coffee in the silver Krups aroma control coffee pot, my thoughts went deeper. I reflected on the times that water was not available to me in my life.

My mind went back to the time when I was a child on the island of Okinawa, located off the coast of Japan. We had just experienced a typhoon. My entire family of me and my five brothers and sisters and my father and mother had to move into a typhoon-and-waterproof shelter on the base with all our neighbors. Days later when we returned home, there was no water.

The true value of water was made apparent to all residents of Kadena Air Force Base for what seemed like an eternity, but my dad tells me it was only weeks. Boy, what the rust of time can do to distort your memory! We had to do everything without running water. Our teeth, bodies, clothes, hair, and dirty dishes had to be washed with miniscule amounts of potable water that were provided to us courtesy of the U.S. Government.

When we finally were able to access that precious liquid commodity, I recall that for an extended period, we couldn't drink it directly from the tap. Of course the notion of going to the store to buy bottled water would have been a laughable thought back in the 1960's—after

all, some things in life, like water and air, will always be free, we thought at the time. So, for weeks and weeks we had to purify the water we drank by boiling it or putting special tablets into it.

Other occasions when I have been without water included times when I've traveled to Jamaica, and for some reason the hotel and/or city I was staying in had a temporary electric and/or water outage. Not being able to shower during those tropical waterless times wasn't so bad—you simply took a dip into the delicious turquoise blue Caribbean Sea and dried off under the warmth of a dazzling sun. Although beverages other than water were available, I still understood that the true value of water is not known until it is no longer available. Sometimes, nothing but a tall cold glass of clear water is the only thing that truly quenches your thirst in a tropical heat wave!

It's almost time for me to exercise and get off to an important meeting, and I can't help but think about how much this value of water topic is relevant to other situations we face as we try to LwL[2]. The loss of a job or loved one; the sense of despair we feel when our worldly possessions are washed away by a flood or destroyed by a tornado or fire are all on my mind. It's funny that for many of us, once we have gone through such tragic events and have processed our grief and are ready to face a new reality, something important happens inside us if we truly have learned from those downs.

There were lessons to be learned when the water came back on after the typhoon in Okinawa or the job I lost when I was a young professional and had to live through unemployment. I learned to better appreciate that water, and the next job I took after my first layoff had to be the right one and not just a means to collect a paycheck to pay my bills. I had learned a lesson that I'd use over and over again in life. The death of my mother, as I've explained, showed me how truly short life is and to make the most of it.

By going through those experiences, I learned to better appreciate those things in life that God has blessed me with having. I also learned not to take even something as simple, and in my world as plentiful, as water for granted. I now understand the meaning of the phrases

---

Approach each day with an attitude of gratitude

---

and

The true value of water is not known until it is no longer available!

Wise Words

Sometimes we have to make a mental attitude adjustment in bad times to cope with life and move on. Here is how Dr. Torri Griffin explains one of her coping mechanisms:

"I don't think the bad things in my life have changed, but I've changed my attitude towards those things that were getting me down."

—*Dr. Torri Griffin*

RETIREMENT OR REDIRECTING OUR LIVES

As 53 million Baby Boomers prepare to retire over the coming years, many of us will find the need to redirect our lives if we want to LwL[2]. Statistics regarding the aging population are astounding. According to the *AIRS RecruitNews,*[1]

> "Over the next ten years [2003–2013]…leaders will have a challenge to attract and retain the best talent. A key to organizational success will be the ability to transfer knowledge from retiring workers…"

Leaders inside organizations will be plagued by issues of managing an increasingly older workforce. We are all temporarily able bodied. Age and the wear and tear of time on the body cause things to break down in people, so there will be more individuals with disabilities within our aging population. Employers and the society at large will need to better adapt to the needs of individuals with disabilities.

During the final phase of writing this book, I had to have major foot surgery and needed to limit my walking for months. I had never undergone major surgery and my eyes were opened to the challenges that individuals with disabilities face daily. Simple tasks, like bathing, going to the bathroom, driving, and getting medication and food became difficult chores in my state of immobility.

To my utter surprise, I found that many stores are wheelchair- and crutches-unfriendly. Getting from point A to point B for business meetings was a challenge. My most eye-opening experience was having to do a keynote, motivational speech on crutches and in a wheelchair. Learning how to absorb the stares and whispers from people wondering about how and why I got in to the state I was in was certainly a revealing experience.

---

1 AIR RecruitNews, Boomers to Become Mentors—Job Market at a Crossroads, Email Newsletter, October 28, 2003

During the time my foot was healing, I had a lot of time to reflect about the multiple challenges we will face shortly as so many of us head into the December of our lives.

CHOOSING NOT TO RETIRE

As we age, the vast majority of us will be faced with the dilemma of if we should retire from the workforce. Some of us, however, will choose not to retire. Whether we retire or not, as we enter the December of our existence on earth, we have to learn how to redirect, not necessarily retire, our lives. Redirecting our lives after retirement, or if you choose to work after the normal retirement ages of the 60s or 70s, may prove difficult and challenging but not impossible.

Mrs. Gloria Battle and Joyce Frith, both dear family friends and adopted grandmothers for my child, are both in their seventies and are going strong. Mrs. Battle can barely remember a time when she wasn't a family day care provider and foster mother. She continues to redirect her life as her foster children come into and go out of it.

Joyce Frith retired years ago from her job, then opened a family day care center to take care of children out of her home. After 30 years of babysitting and taking care of children, she redirected her life on many occasions as a school crossing guard and worker for a local school in their cafeteria. She absolutely loves serving hot dogs and french fries to the young people, and interacting with them keeps her young. Both of these ladies, who truly LwL[2], exemplify the power we all have to redirect our lives in a meaningful direction as we grow older.

Katie Booker, President, CEO and owner of Booker's Rest Homes in North Carolina, is almost 69 years old and is a shining example of how we can work for years beyond the traditional retirement age.

Profile of Success
Katie A. Booker—President, CEO and owner
Booker's Rest Homes

I will be 69 years old next month and it's hard to believe. Everything in life has been an experience. The most difficult thing is that today in America it is very difficult to say at what age a person should retire. People are taking better care of themselves—physically, mentally, socially and financially. They are doing a great job of preparing themselves to live out their later years.

I know other people who are my age and have to work. They can't afford medicine, housing or food if they don't have a job. Sometimes elderly people have to keep working because they can't afford to retire! There are a lot of grandparents who are taking care of their grandchildren and doing it on their retirement savings or pension money. I know a man and woman who are 78 and 80 years old and raising their 3-year-old grandchild because the child's mother died.

I think I am an example of the transition generation that is older but not ready to retire. I don't think about retiring—I eat properly and take my vitamins and don't have any major diseases or illnesses. I believe that working has really contributed to my well-being and outlook on life.

The older people who aren't healthy get the most press. You read more about people who are sick, but not all of us are that way. When I went through menopause, I sat down with myself and told myself, "Body, we're going to go through an adventure together," and we went through it successfully! I think you can tell yourself what you're going to do and how you're going to do it and be successful at it. Or, you can defeat yourself with negative words, thoughts and actions.

The strongest thing in my life is my religion. Without Jesus Christ in my life, I don't think I would have ever been successful. Getting old has been an experience of joy and happiness. You can be whatever your mind tells you that you want to be. You can be a healthy, strong older person who walks daily or even jogs in a marathon. On the other hand, you can be on a walker or in a wheelchair or bed-ridden.

I believe that you start to retire at 18 and 21. At those young ages, you begin to get old. By that, I mean the choices you make when you are young in your teens and 20s will determine how your senior years will be structured. What you do in your 20s and 30s may affect you in your 50s and 60s.

I believe Sachel Paige, the baseball legend, said something like, "Age is nothing but a number. How old would you be if you didn't know how old you are?" America has a fixation on youth. When you watch sports, they'll talk about a 30 year old athlete as being "too old" to play basketball or football.

Don't let anyone else define you: Decide for yourself who you want to be, how you want to be and for how long you want to do it. I also believe that you have to plan for old age. You shouldn't squander, but nurture your resources. That way you'll have them in your old age when you'll need them. Sometimes that choice can be taken from you when you least expect it. So to be healthy, wealthy and wise and LwL^2, you need to use your wisdom to plan for the unexpected.

WHAT SHOULD ORGANIZATIONS DO TO HELP OLDER PEOPLE?

To LwL^2, individuals as well as organizations must begin to prepare for the hoards of people who will be faced with redirecting themselves as they reach the December of their lives. Linkage, Inc.'s Center for Organizational Research has conducted some powerful research in a March 2002 white paper entitled, "Holding On: How the Mass Exodus of Retiring Baby Boomers Could Deplete the Workforce, How Employers Can Stem the Tide." Findings of this important study reveal some of the challenges employers and individuals will face in the future as they try to LwL^2. Here are some highlights of this research:

1. "America is rapidly approaching a crisis in its workforce, triggered by the convergence of two demographic trends: the growing number of aging Baby Boomers in the population and the much smaller number of younger people who follow behind them."

2. "The 'Age Bubble' is the balloon effect created by the Baby Boom generation (people born between 1946 and 1964) whenever it does anything en masse—whether it's starting school (which led to overcrowded classrooms and double-sessions, followed by a building boom in new schools), becoming teenagers, going to college (another spell of professor-hirings and expanded campuses), becoming parents, turning 50 (the AARP reinvented itself to become more attractive to 'young elders'), or retiring (the focus of this article). The sheer number of Baby Boomers who will become eligible for retirement between now and 2015, coupled with the much smaller pool of younger workers who can take their place, make the Age Bubble a critical human resource issue for employers."

3. "But the growing ranks of older workers is not the only shift that will be taking place in the workforce. The proportion of younger workers is also shrinking. According to the Bureau of Labor Statistics (BLS), workers age 25-44 will decline by 3 million, dropping to 51% of the labor force in 1998 to 44% in 2008, while over the same period, workers age 45+ will increase from 33% to 40% of the

workforce, an additional 17 million workers."
(Dohm, 2000)

4. "The graying of the U.S. workforce is not just a cosmetic change. In some sectors of the economy, it will bring a serious shortage of workers. According to a recent report from the Employment Policy Foundation, more than 61 million Americans will retire during the next 30 years. Within five years, the U.S. workforce will begin to dwindle."

5. "How severe could the impact be? If the present trend continues, the Foundation projects, the U.S. will face a labor shortage of 4.8 million workers in 10 years, 19.7 million in 20 years and 35.8 million in 30 years. College-educated, highly skilled workers will be in particularly short supply. Unless these shortages can be averted, the country's gross domestic product, the output of goods and services produced by labor and property located in the United States, could drop 3% in 10 years and 17% or more in 30 years. For workers, that would translate into a significant drop in average per capita income (Employment Policy Foundation, 2001)."

6. "BLS projects that five industries will be most affected by retirements in multiple occasions:
   - manufacturing
   - public administration
   - educational services
   - transportation
   - health services (especially hospitals)"
   (Dohm, 2000)

7. "Certain clusters of occupational groups will see a dramatic increase in vacancies (called "replacement needs") due to employee retirements, according to the BLS. The greatest turnover is expected to be in the executive, administrative and managerial occupations. Workers now 45 and older make up 41% of this group, and 42% of them are expected to retire by 2008." (Dohm, 2000)

8. The table below illustrates the top ten replacement needs of the most affected occupations suffering from Baby Boomer retirements, provided by the BLS.[2]

Occupation	Replacements Needed in Occupation Percent change 1993–98 to 2003–08
Total, all employees	25.2
1. Airline pilots and navigators	172.7
2. Management analysts	152.0
3. Teachers, special education	135.4
4. Photographers	94.8
5. Teacher aides	91.8
6. Industrial engineers	87.6
7. Eligibility clerks, social welfare	85.0
8. Personnel & labor relations managers	83.6
9. Postal clerks, except mail carriers	81.0
10. Supervisors, police and detectives	80.2

2 Dohm, 2000 and Bureau of Labor Statistics.

Other professions affected include[3]
- Plumbers, pipefitters, and steamfitters
- Financial managers
- Psychologists
- Social workers
- Lawyers
- Teachers, elementary school
- Administrators, education & related fields
- Registered nurses
- Administrators, officials, public admin.
- Chemists

Moving on after a loss is often difficult. Staying on track as we cross life's hurdles in our quest to LwL^2 can also be equally as challenging. As we face the loss of someone who has completed their LwL^2 journey on this earth, it is important to remember the road traveled by that individual. Take time to analyze how you can gain insight from that person's life that can help you to better LwL^2.

" " Quotes of Note

"I'm not afraid to die, I just don't want to be there when it happens."

—*Woody Allen*

She Is Gone

*You can shed tears that she is gone
or you can smile because she has lived.
You can close your eyes and pray that she'll come back
or you can open your eyes and see all she has left.
Your heart can be empty because you cannot see her
or you can be filled with the love she shared.
You can turn your back on tomorrow and live yesterday
or you can be happy for tomorrow because of yesterday.
You can remember her and only that she is gone
or you can cherish her memory and let it live on.
You can cry and close your mind, be empty and turn your back
or you can do what she would want:
Don't cry, open your eyes, smile, love and go on.*

———————

—Anonymous
Contributed by Hal Stuart
in memory of his mother

3 Dohm, 2000 and Bureau of Labor Statistics.

Chapter 41

THE HARDEST PART OF A 10,000 MILE JOURNEY

THE HARDEST PART OF A 10,000 MILE JOURNEY IS THE LAST MILE

ONE OF MY MOST FAVORITE THINGS TO do in life is to rise up with the chickens and the sun and jog or walk (depending on my energy level) along a spectacular beach located in Negril, Jamaica on the westernmost point of this picturesque Caribbean island. The contrast of the glistening turquoise-blue tranquil water against the powdery white sand just awakens my soul.

When I take my 5-mile jog/walk on this pristine beach, I love to watch as the water gyrates in a rhythmic pattern, playing a game of tag with the sand before it rushes back to the horizon.

There is a point about 2.5 miles into my journey on the beach that inevitably I get a feeling of fatigue. Surprisingly, I know I've reached this certain spot on the beach. I automatically raise my head to break my fixed stare at the white and turquoise colors of the sand and sea and turn it to the left where I behold a little thatched tropical hut. Sure enough the little thatched hut is always right there.

Sometimes upon reaching that spot, I ask myself, "Why did I disturb myself from my great slumber to run and sweat in the Caribbean steaming sunshine?" At that point, my brain reminds me that I'm halfway through the jog. I soon snap into the reality that there are no cars or trucks nearby and realize that the only way I am going to get back to the location from which I started is to finish.

On one hot steaming day, I was truly feeling the heat and the nagging desire to just stop and give up on my run. The beach sand that was usually compact enough to run on had become extra soggy and mushy. My sneakers felt like they had landed in a pile of quick sand. With each step, my feet crunched deeper into a sandy soggy mess. The beach was more moist than normal because a mega-force hurricane—Hurricane Gilbert—had torn through the island and in its wrath ha endowed the seashore with extra water.

It took every ounce of energy in me that day to con centrate on getting through my jog. Bucketloads of swea dripped then clung to every inch of my body. Despair rolled in with a huge sea-blue and white wave that moved to the shore so quickly that my body could not maneuver out of its path in time. Exhausted, discouraged, sneakers drenched with seawater and not knowin how I was going to finish what I had started, I looked uf and saw that all-too-familiar thatched hut. I should have known it would be in my view because of the desperate feelings swirling inside my soul. But this time, I was determined not to cave in to the powers of that thatchec hut spot. In front of me was one of the most beautiful gifts that the sea had ever bestowed upon my eyes.

In the sand, a huge mass of tiny peach and baby pink sea shells glistened like diamonds in the brilliant orange and yellow mass of the Caribbean sun. In an instant, the magnificence of life unfolded before my eyes at the sight of those tiny sea shells. I thought about a quote from the Chinese philosopher Lao-Tse. It reverberated in my mind:

How true, I thought, but the hardest part of a 10,000-mile journey is the last mile, my head echoed.

Think about it: On a 10,000 mile journey, you've taken that first step, often after much consternation. You've gone 9,999 miles and are just *one* mile away from the finish line. Confusion and defeat seep in—why did I think I could tackle something this big? Boy, wasn't I stupid to do this in the first place? Was this really worth all this pain and suffering?

Whatever the 10,000 mile journey is for us—getting a degree, taking on a new job, earning a promotion, starting a business or moving on in a relationship or phase in our lives—invariably life's thatched huts will appear.

During those moments, it is of the utmost importance to take the time to step back for a moment to remember your goal and how close you are to attaining it. We must not lose sight of the peach and pink sea shells of life that glisten like diamonds. They await us at the last step of our 10,000 mile destination.

Adrienne Rumi White of Orlando, Florida, ran her first marathon at age 45. On January 1, 2001, she participated in the Walt Disney World Marathon. She trained with the Pace Training Group for six months. These individuals had vowed to run alongside each other during the race. When Adrienne arrived to run the Marathon, to her horror, she discovered that they were unable to do so because the others had run previous marathons and would be positioned in a place apart from hers. Here is her riveting story about that powerful 10,000 mile-like experience.

Memories of a First

By Adrienne Rumi White

I venture out into the cold, dark morning
bursting with determination and excitement;
hoping for victory,
praying for completion with dignity.
I struggle to fight back the tears as I learn the shocking news…
one red, the rest blue.
What will I do without these souls,
these few whom I have come to trust, depend upon, admire?
Can I make it on my own?
Another group opens their arms to take me in,
and temporary relief washes over me.
I turn to glance back at my group—
"Run well, stay strong," I whisper wistfully.
Then we begin the journey towards the red start.
Many thoughts, questions, fears fill my mind.
"What will I do at the finish line? Will I even see the finish line?
Will my family see me? Can I do it?"
"Don't let it beat you."

Suddenly, we are there.
Mickey Mouse rises from the dark sky,
as my heart races with exhilarating adrenaline.
The fireworks signal it's time…
and we're off!
Dodging, weaving, side-stepping, over, around, between
discarded clothing, dishonest race walkers,
groups running in tight packs,
slower-than-me (or smarter-than-me) runners,
people of all shapes, sizes, colors, ages, mindsets.
Mile after mile of spectators, cheers, entertainment, music, laughter, sighs, grunts and groans, Gatorade, power gels, pit-stops in the bushes, side stitches, riddles, conversation, marathon war stories, periodic disrobing, sun rising higher and higher, getting hotter and hotter, jokes, more jokes, no jokes, long stretches of silent endless highway, cramping legs,

nagging blisters, swelling ankles, group members slipping behind, group members disappearing, sweat, growing aches and pain, agony etched in the faces of those ahead and behind…
"Don't let it beat you."

At mile 21, I break out on my own.
"I can go the distance…" I hear the song down the road,
and I pick up the pace.
Michael, Mary Lou and me.
What a winning team!
I feel good, strong, about to run the farthest distance of my life.
Then, I hit it…
At mile 23, I meet "The Wall."
It looms before me, impenetrable, determined to stop me.
I can't go…my legs won't move…my quads are boulders…
Walk break…long walk break…thoughts of quitting fly in and out.
I want to quit. I need to quit. I am going to quit.
But wait…now I am hallucinating…
That looks like Jeff Galloway…
I struggle to catch up, unsure why, or what I will say.
"What an honor to run alongside you!" I manage to eek out.
He gives me the traditional thumbs up, smiles, and takes off.
I can do this now.
"Don't let it beat you."

Mile 24—I want to drop on the ground right now…what will Jeff think?
There he is, up ahead.
I press on.
Mile 25—no Jeff, no group members, no lime green shirts,
no memory of why I wanted to do this.
Runners massaging side stitches and cramped legs along the roadside.
Runners quitting. Runners giving up.
No glory in this road kill.
No glory at all.
Mile 26. Mile 26. Mile 26.

Suddenly, I hear a voice.
It's my Dad's voice.
"Don't let it beat you."

I feel myself stumble,
I hear myself mumble,
"Daddy, you left and I didn't get to say goodbye."
The tears stream down now,
faster and faster they come…joining the rivers of sweat.
I try hard not to remember his unexpected death, just over one year ago;
but my mind is flooded with memories
of his smile, his laughter, his oversized belly,
his large and callused but oh, so tender hands.
"You're all grown up now, dear daughter.
You're strong, smart, capable and beautiful.
I'm here. I will always be here.
Don't let life beat you, Chicken Little."

25.2—almost there.
"Daddy, this last mile's for you."
I reach down deeper, deeper, deeper,
to the bottom of my very soul,
and pull out just enough to round the bend.
I see the curly jet black hair of my 6 year old son,
propped on the shoulders of my husband;
I catch a glimpse of my football-basketball-track trophy-winning teenager
as he hangs from a tree, camera in hand.
They are searching the crowd for me.
How long they have waited in the cold!
I must finish, and finish with dignity.
I see those six letters just up ahead-
F-I-N-I-S-H.
The line draws closer and closer,
and finally,
I'm home.
I raise my hands up over my head.
I hear my own voice murmur:
"Thank you, Lord.
I love and miss you, Dad.
I did it. I did it. Yes, I did it.
No more, never again…
It didn't beat me!"

And while I lay in the medical tent,
eyes closed in a dehydrated stupor,
an IV pumping much needed fluids into my abused,
damaged frame,
a core body temp of 93.6 and a racing pulse of 88,
legs cramped beyond belief,
yet, even as I lay there,
I am dreaming…
there's Mij with his bell and little red car,
Ruth with her water coolers, cups in tow.
I am back on the road,
running with my partners…
Bob, Ron, Natalie, Jorge, Dino, Jim, Beth.
Into the dark morning on the cobblestone streets of
Winter Park,
we are flying, floating, sailing, laughing…
strong, vibrant, alive.
We are preparing for the race—
this race,
the one that I have now finished.
I keep dreaming, until my rejuvenated body allows
me to awake.
In my hand, I clutch the golden Mickey Mouse.
And I know I will dream of these moments for
many days to come.

…it was all started by a mouse.

—*Walt Disney*

As we finish this marathon book, I'd like to leave you with some final thoughts.

CONCLUSION

WHEN YOUR TIME COMES, HOW DO you want to leave this world? I think a lot about the answer to this question. I hope it is short, sweet and to the point when my day of departure to the afterlife occurs. I also hope I will be missed but not mourned. I want people to remember the happiness and joy of my life—not the sadness of my death.

The story of a man—an alcoholic—comes to mind when I think about the way I desire *not* to die. This man was in his mid-40s when he died in his Cambridge, Massachusetts home about a mile away from Harvard Square. He died alone in a house where the furnace had somehow shut off in the dead of winter. No one knew he had expired for at least a week when they found him stiff and literally frozen to death. I thought that was one of the saddest ways to leave this earth. Imagine you had done so little to make an impact on anyone's life while you were living that no one, not absolutely one person, would miss your existence for a whole week. You were M.I.A.—missing in action—and your absence wasn't felt by a single soul.

REACHING A MILESTONE AGE

For many people, when they reach a milestone age—that special year when Hallmark cards and others have even designed a special card to commemorate the occasion: 13, 16, 21, 25, 30, 40, 50, 60, 65, 75, 85, 100—quite often, something internally starts to happen with our life and career choices. At these milestone moments, some of us seem to magically reflect on what those things have, will, and do mean for us. We feel an urgency to connect the past with the present and future. Often that leads to an internal dialogue that at least for me has gone something like this: "Martha, you've reached 40. You're not a kid anymore, and you may have more years behind you than in front of you. You've got to be serious now and decide what you are going to accomplish with your life. You've got to straighten out some things and tackle some demons in your life right *now* so you're headed down the right road to fulfill your dreams and reach your future destination."

Wise Words

Jessie Shea—Executive Assistant, Fields Associates, Inc.

Work

Never stop dreaming and don't sell yourself short. Within all of us lies a desire to do or become something better than we already are. That's how we progress and grow, striving for the next *best thing* in our lives. And money is not a universal measure of success. Of course, it doesn't hurt to improve yourself financially—but *NEVER* do so at the expense of your emotional and spiritual self. What's better for one person is totally different for someone else.

Follow your heart (and sometimes your gut), and live your life with passion. There always exists an opportunity if you truly want to discover it. Allow yourself to find your purpose within and run with it. If you fail, you'll never regret you tried. But if you never try, you'll always regret it and wonder what could have been. This is your life and your time to live…what are you going to do with it?

Life

Yes, we all have done things in the past that we regret—even hate—about ourselves. However, the key to move forward is leaving those times in the past. You will never forget your past because it has formed who you are today (and made you that much stronger for having gone through it all), but you have the choice whether or not to dwell on it. Use your past to grow and determine how you do and don't want to live in the future. Time goes by fast enough…why waste it pouting? Be happy and help those around you to be happy too. It's so easy to appreciate the little things (like when my parents and I laugh so hard we cry), and it's the little things that often make the biggest difference in trying to LwL². Infect the world with your smile!

Part of traveling down life's path is to understand how to use technology to help you LwL².

Profile of Success

Kevin M. O'Keefe—Owner/Technology Specialist
Beacon Network Technologies

I feel that one of the most important things leading to loving your work and, in turn, your life is to be in control of your destiny. You don't have to own a company to do so. Managers should focus on mentoring their employees and giving them the freedom to "run with the ball," when they demonstrate the ability that they won't "fumble." One of these skills in a client-based business is to be positive, and have a positive outlook on everything that comes your way. This includes being positive in negative situations, as well as with individuals who might not share the same belief, but rather the "glass is half empty" attitude/approach on life. Being negative, or thinking negatively, gets you absolutely nowhere, and never assists in resolving anything, but only brings along doubt in oneself, which leads you down the road to unhappiness in work and life.

As a network consultant, many times I am contacted in "emergency" situations. When these situations occur, I address the large fire, and then put out the small ones strategically. Often, putting out the large fire begins by dealing with the people affected, and letting them know that a solution is close at hand, and that you are there to implement the fix. A positive, confident demeanor is extremely important in these situations…almost as important as the skill required to resolve the problems.

My type of client-based business also revolves around helping people to understand how technology "works," and how it can "work" for them. Technology can be so confusing, especially when companies market their technologies, as "out-of-the-box" solutions. Implementing technology, from antivirus software to wireless access points (hardware) successfully is never that simple. With the aforementioned examples, here are the underlying problems. Antivirus software is not useful without updating the virus definitions. It's comparable to having the ingredients, but not the recipe. Unfortunately, most people realize this only after damage has already been done (by the virus). The other example deals with wireless access points. You can make the necessary connections, and turn these devices on, but the "defaults" need to be modified in order to "secure" the device. This can be compared to the introduction of the electric garage door opener. When they were first installed into homes, people would drive down the street and click the magic button to find other garage doors opening in their neighborhood…opening because they were all programmed from the factory with identical settings. Of course this has all been changed with electric garage door openers, but not so with the wireless access points.

As for the future in my line of business, the buzz word is integration. Everything in our world is about trying to integrate technology into our everyday lives. I can now be on my back porch and send email at high speeds wirelessly vs. in the past, I had to do the same (at analog speeds…slow) with a long telephone cord extending to the nearest phone jack. I can even remember when people laughed at the futuristic gadgets they saw in shows such as *Star Trek.* Now, some of the things we use every day are based on the vision of what we saw in some of those futuristic episodes, such as the similarity between the "communicator" and a flip top cell phone. The speed of technology is rapidly increasing. What people saw as futuristic, and took decades to come to fruition, now only takes months.

In conclusion, I try to take the frustration that comes along with the advancement of technology, away from clients. The main reason behind the name of my company "Beacon Network Technologies" comes from the similarity of a lighthouse leading mariners through difficult waters, while I try and lead people through the complicated waves of technology. I love what the advancements in technology have to offer, and enjoy helping people have a better attitude toward technology. This will hopefully lead to a more enjoyable life…or so I can only hope.

Wise Words

One of my learning experiences from life is any given job is not necessarily the perfect one but each job teaches you what your perfect career path can be.

—*Dima Berdiev, Cambridge Trust Credit Analyst*

Wise Words

"When the student is ready, the teacher will appear."…"Catch people doing something right, then you'll find the magnificence in people."

—Ken Blanchard

"We don't break habits; we replace one behavior with another."

—Dr. Phil

"In the end, things will work out, we just don't know how."

—Martha R. A. Fields

In reference to his illustrious career as a successful musician, Carlos Santana said, "This is what I do, but it is not who I am."

—Carlos Santana, CNN Presents

"Nothing endures but change."

—Heraclitus, ancient philosopher

On October 10, 2003, I had surgery to remove a bunion from my left foot. On Friday, December 12, I was due to see my surgeon who would be giving me clearance to wear regular shoes, exercise and return to the walking world again.

On Sunday, December 7, just days before my life would revert to its regular state; I stepped onto my back porch. I wanted to see what snow needed to be shoveled after two days of one of the worst December blizzards in 112 years. After surveying the winter wonderland, I turned to go inside and BAM! My legs buckled under me and I heard two loud CRACKS as my legs met the snow covered porch. The return to the walking world was not in the cards for me. I had broken my ankle in two places on the same left foot of the bunion surgery. After a scary ride by ambulance to the hospital, I not only faced the release of this book in weeks but months where crutches, wheelchairs, and casts would become my good friends.

A few days after the accident, on Tuesday evening, December 9th, I received a phone call from the principal of my daughter's new school, The Concord Middle School. Why would he be calling me? Upon hearing his warm greeting, I wondered if my daughter had done something very wrong?

Mr. Arthur Unobsky quickly calmed my fears. "I hear you had a bad accident," he said. "I know your family is new to the school and I didn't think you knew about the special program we offer when a member of one of our kid's families is going through a crisis?" He went on to tell me about this special program where a group of parents from the school prepare meals for the entire family during a period of crisis. They get delivered every school day as a way of helping the family in need. Mr. Unobsky went on to say that he would like to extend this offer to me and my family and that a parent representative would call and give me the details. I was touched by his gesture and replied, "What a nice and wonderful thing to do, but you don't have to do that for me." Mr. Unobsky replied, "we want to do that for you. We are just that kind of school and community."

I came to understand the true spirit of a community whose forefathers included the likes of Emerson and Thoreau. Within a short time of saying yes to his proposition, I received a call from parent representative, Janet Lipkin. She reviewed the program details. Then added, "We know you will be unable to get around for a long time and want to make sure you have food every school night from now until Christmas." The date was December 9th and I thought what a commitment to provide food every school night until December 25th! "You real-ly don't have to do this for that long!" I replied. "We want to do it for you, that's the kind of school and community we are!" Janet replied.

I was so touched by this gesture of the Concord Middle School. What a message of caring it sends when the principal (the corporate equivalent is a CEO) takes his personal time to help a student's family during a crisis. What a large statement it makes about the parents who are busy trying to LwL^2 but take time to help others in need.

The meals we received obviously took a long time to prepare. They were not TV dinners. Every school night we received a dinner for the entire family that was elegant, yummy, and often included everything from a salad, entree, and dessert!

This experience with the Concord Middle School not only provided me with an example of a best, interesting, and radical practice for this book, it also made my heart smile. I realized that the true meaning of the Christmas and the holiday season—the spirit of giving back and providing peace on earth to others—is alive and well at the Concord Middle School. One added benefit is that this experience of re-injuring my foot has reaffirmed my LwL^2 secret—you learn as much, if not more, from the downs as the ups.

Recommended Reading

Thomas, Carole Copeland. *Personal Empowerment: How to Turbo Charge your Life Both On and Off the Job.* Woburn, MA: Milormic Press, 2003.

Wise Words

If you had to write a biography of your life, do you believe that anyone would read it? Would you be proud of what it said?

—*Justin Lynch-Colameta*

In this book, we have explored Seven Secrets to LwL². I'm sure that after reading this book, not all of you will get an A in terms of implementing all of them—I won't. But I hope that you will make at least an E for effort. My wish is that you will think about the concepts and apply them to your work and life. In this process, there will be downs, and times when you must remind yourself that the hardest part of a 10,000 mile journey is the last mile.

To LwL², spend some time to shape your personal LwL² work/life plan. Once it is finished, begin to put it into action and realize your career dreams and life's work. Remember, "if you fail to plan, you plan to fail." The most successful people who LwL² have passion around their work and life and take risks and make decisions. I can always count on Oprah Winfrey and Dr. Phil to express wise words that motivate and propel people to success. Heed their words around passion and making decisions.

Wise Words

Sometimes you make the right decision and sometimes you make the decision right!

—*Dr. Phil, Dr. Phil Show, 10/30/03*
www.drphil.com

Any time you hear someone say it's their passion, you can bet they're being successful at it.

—*Oprah, The Oprah Winfrey Show, 10/30/03*
www.oprah.com

Wise Words

Be well within yourself.

—*Larry King, Larry King Live, 10/3/03*
www.cnn.com/cnn/programs/larry.king.live

It's the being well with me.

—*Annie Lennox on Charlie Rose, 6/25/03*

Are you treating your diamond like a glass? Are you a diamond, but being treated like a glass?...Often we need to stop beating ourselves up about what we haven't done and focus on what we've accomplished! Sometimes when you try your hardest not to get there, that's where you end up.

—*Betty Graves*

If everyone lit just one candle, what a bright world this would be.

—*1950s Sunday A.M. TV show*

...ask yourself, is it going to bring me peace?

—*Wayne Dyer on Peace*

Wise Words

God grant me the serenity to accept the things I cannot change,
The courage to change the things I can, and the wisdom to know the difference.
Amen.

Review your progress on completing your plan at least twice a year, preferably at the same two times each year (e.g., January and June, March and August, etc.). This will help you to adjust things so you can remain a continuous learning sponge, mutate regularly and just like the man in the spinning plates act on *The Ed Sullivan Show,* help your work/life spinning plates move smoothly.

In her powerful book, *Personal Empowerment: How to Turbo Charge your Life Both On and Off the Job,* author Carole Copeland Thomas discusses the power of reading and states, "There is no greater resource known to mankind than the power of reading. Through reading you can transform your own ignorance on a subject into an ocean of newfound knowledge. Reading can take you places in the world you never thought existed. Reading can turn your sadness into joy when you select the right book, magazine, newspaper or journal. A ten- to fifteen-minute reading session each day will do wonders for expanding your mind."

It is my fervent wish that your horizons will be expanded by reading this book. I also hope that if you were one of the 98% of people who don't LwL[2], that you've connected with something in this book to change your status.

We've Only Just Begun

We've only just begun to live.
White lace and promises,
A kiss for luck and we're on our way.
And yes, we've just begun.

Before the rising sun we fly…
So many roads to choose.
We start out walking and learn to run,
And yes, we've just begun.

Sharing horizons that are new to us.
Watching the signs along the way.
Talking it over just the two of us.
Working together day to day.

Together. Together.

And when the evening comes, we smile.
So much of life ahead
We'll find a place where there's room to grow.
And yes, we've just begun.

—Words & Music by Paul Williams
& Roger Nichols; Recorded
by The Carpenters, 1970

I'd like to close by leaving you with a passage that I got on a business trip to Princeton, New Jersey. I had a few hours to kill with a wonderful client, Mary Aceto of Boston Coach. We stepped into a quaint shop and I had to purchase a magnet that contained some beautiful words that made my heart smile. I have this magnet positioned on my refrigerator, and it chills my soul every time I see it. I wish you the best of luck Loving your work by Loving your Life. To modify a phrase made popular by the movie *Star Wars*, may a good life and the workforce be with you!

dance
as though no one is watching you;

love
as though you have never been hurt before;

sing
as though no one can hear you;

live
as though heaven is on earth.

—Souza

❧ THE END (01/07/04; 10:10 A.M.) ❧

BIBLIOGRAPHY

Adams, John T. III. "But What About Gen Xers Who Manage Boomers?" *HR Magazine,* December 1999, Vol. 44, Issue 13.

Andre, Rae, Ph.D. and Ward Peter D., J.D. *The 59-Second Employee: How to Stay One Second Ahead of our One-Minute Manager.* Boston: Houghton Mifflin Company, 1984.

Armas, Genaro. "U.S. Survey Shows Rise in Foreign-Born." *Boston Globe,* 3 January, 2001.

Arriens, Angeles, Ph.D. *The Four-Fold Way: Walking the Paths of the Warrior, Teacher, Healer and Visionary.* San Francisco, Harper, a Division of HarperCollinsPublishers, 1993.

Ban Breathnach, Sarah. *Simple Abundance: A Daybook of Comfort and Joy.* New York, Warner Books, Inc. A Time Warner Company, 1995.

Bateson, Mary Catherine. Composing a Life. See www.amazon.com.

Blanchard, Ken and Johnson, Spencer. *The One Minute Manager.* New York: William Morrow, 1982.

Bolles, Richard Nelson. *What Color is your Parachute 2004: A Practical Manual for Job-Hunters and Career.* Berkley, Toronto: Ten Speed Press, 2004.

BrassRing. *TRM: Competing Through Talent. An Anthology for The Talent-Focused Enterprise.* Waltham, MA: BrassRing, LLC, 2002.

Brown, Tracy. *Breaking the Barriers of Bias.* January 1999. See www.amazon.com

Brown, Tracy. Diversity Trends, LLC. Motiversity ™, Motivating while Valuing Diversity. Audio cassette, July 1998. See www.amazon.com

Burns, Kephra and Taylor, Susan. *Confirmation: The Spiritual Wisdom That Has Shaped our Lives.* January 1999. See www.amazon.com

Canfield, Jack, Hansen, Mark Victor and Hansen, Patty. *Condensed Chicken Soup for the Soul.* Deerfield Beach, Florida: Health Communications, Inc. 1996.

Chideya, Farai. *The Color of Our Future.* NY, NY: William and Morrow Company, Inc., 1999.

Cobbs, Price, Turnock, Judith and Reinemund, Steve. *Cracking the Corporate Code: The Revealing Success Stories of 32 African-American Executives.* New York: AMACOM, 2003.

Collins, Jim. *Good to Great: Why Some Companies Make the Leap... and Others Don't.* New York: HarperBusiness, 2001.

Collins, Jim. *Built to Last: Successful Habits of Visionary Companies.* New York: HarperBusiness, 1994.

Covey, Stephen R. *The 7 Habits of Highly Effective People.* New York, New York: Simon & Shuster, 1989

Digh, Patricia. "The Next Challenge: Holding People Accountable." *HR Magazine,* October 1998, Vol. 43, Issue 11.

Digh, Patricia. "Race Matters." *Mosaics,* September/October 1998 (SHRM Diversity Program).

Diversity: Business Rational and Strategies Report No.1083; 1994.

"The Diversity Myth: True Multiethnic Countries are Concentrated in Just a Few Areas." *American Demographics Magazine,* June 1998.

Dohm, Arlene. "Guaging the Labor Force Effects of Retiring Baby Boomers," Monthly Labor Review: July 2000, 17-25. www.bls.gov/opub/mlr/2000/07/contents.htm.

Dyer, Wayne Dr. *10 Secrets for Success and Inner Peace.* Carlsbad, CA: Hay House, 2001.

Dyer, Wayne Dr. *Wisdom of the Ages: 60 Days to Enlightenment.* New York, NY: HarperCollins Publisher, Inc., 1998.

Employee Benefits Research Institute, 2002 Retirement Confidence Survey. http://www.ebri.organization/rcs/2002.

Evans, Gail. *Play Like A Man, Win Like A Woman.* New York, NY. Broadway Books, a division of Random House, 2000.

Evers-Williams, Myrlie with Melinda Blau. *Watch Me Fly.* Boston, MA: Little, Brown and Company, 1999.

Fields Associates, Inc. *The XYZs of How to Become More Diverse: Making Diversity an Organizational and Personal Priority.* (Video) Cambridge, MA: 1998.

Gardenswartz, Lee and Rowe, Anita. *Beyond Sanity and Survival, a Stress Management Workbook.*

Gardenswartz, Lee; Rowe, Anita; Digh, Patricia and Bennett, Martin. *The Global Diversity Desk Reference: Managing an International Workforce.* Pfeiffer, June 2003.

Gardenswartz, Lee and Rowe, Anita. *Managing Diversity: A Complete Desk Reference and Planning Guide.* New York: McGraw-Hill, 1998.

Gill, Lucy. *How To Work with Just About Anyone: A 3-step Solution for Getting Difficult People to Change.* New York, NY: A Fireside Book: Simon & Schuster, Inc., 1999.

Golden, Arthur. *Memoirs of a Geisha.* New York, NY: Vintage Books, a Division of Random House, Inc., 1999.

Graham, Lawrence Otis. *The Best Companies for Minorities. Employers Across America Who Recruit, Train, and Promote Minorities.* New York: A Plume Book by Penguin Group, 1993.

Griggs, Lewis Brown. Griggs Productions. Video Series:

- Valuing Diversity® New Tools for a New Reality. Griggs and Louw, McGraw-Hill, 1995.
- Valuing Relationship®
- No Potential Lost® (Interactive Multimedia Series)
- Humor Energy at Work®, 1995-96
- The Potential is Yours – Internet/Interact Program
- Going International – video series, 1983.
- Global Contrasts, 1996.

Graham, Stedman. *Build Your Own Life Brand! : A Powerful Strategy to Maximize Your Potential and Enhance Your Value for Ultimate Achievement.* New York: Simon & Shuster, January 2001.

Graham, Stedman and Covey, Stephen R. *You Can Make It Happen: A Nine Step Plan for Success.* New York: Simon & Schuster, 2003.

Graham, Stedman. *Teens Can Make It Happen: Nine Steps for Success.* New York: Simon & Shuster, September 2000.

Greene, Robert. *48 Laws of Power.* September 2000.

Hinds, Karen S. *Get Along , Get Ahead: 101 Courtesies for the New Workplace.* Boston, MA: New Books Publishing, 2000.

Hinojosa, Maria. *Raising Raul. An Adventure Raising Myself and My Son.* New York, NY: Penguin Books, 2000.

Hinojosa, Maria. *Crews-Gangs Members Talk with Maria Hinojosa.* See www.amazon.com.

Hubbard, Edward E., Dr. *How to Calculate Diversity Return-on-Investment.* Global Insights Publisher, September 1999.

Hubbard, Edward E., Dr. and Supinsky, Katie (editor). *Measuring Diversity Results.* Global Insights Publisher, April 1997.

Johnson, Spencer, M.D. *Who Moved My Cheese?: An A-Mazing Way to Deal with Change in Your Work and in Your Life.* New York: G.P. Putnam Sons, 1998.

Judy, Richard W. and D'Amico, Carol. *Workforce 2020: Work and Workers in the 21st Century.* Indianapolis, IN: Hudson Institute, 1997.

Katz, Judith. H. *White Awareness: Handbook for Antiracism Training.* University of Oklahoma Press, 2nd edition, September 2003.

Kaye, Beverly and Sharon Jordan Evans. *Love'em or Lose'em-Getting Good People to Stay.* San Francisco: Berrett-Koehler Publishers, Inc., 1999.

Kennedy, Marilyn Moats. "Managing the Deliberately Mute." *Physician Executive,* Jan/Feb 2000, Vol. 26, Issue 1.

Kersey, Cynthia. *Unstoppable: 45 Powerful Stories of Perseverance and Triumph from People Just Like You.* Naperville, IL: Sourcebooks. Inc., 1998.

King, Bernice. *Hard Questions, Heart Answers.* Audio cassette. Bantam Doubleday Dell, 1996.

Kiyosaki, Robert T. with Sharon L. Lechter, CPA. *Rich Dad, Poor Dad. What the Rich Teach Their Kids about Money That the Poor and Middle Class Do Not!* New York: Warner Books, A Time Warner Company, 1998.

Koch, Richard. *The 80/20 Principle. The Secrets to Success by Achieving More with Less.* New York: A Currency Book, Doubleday, 1998.

Lawrence, Paul R. and Nohria, Nitin. *Driven: How Human Nature Shapes Our Choices.* San Francisco, CA: Jossey-Bass, A Wiley Company, 2002.

Masciarelli, James P. *Powerskills: Building Top-Level Relationships for Bottom-Line Results.* Gloucester, MA: Nimbus Press, 2000.

MacDonald, Michael Patrick. *All Souls: A Family Story from Southie.* Boston, MA: Beacon Press, 1999.

Marosky, Myrna. *The Art of Diversity Training.* ProGroup, Inc. May 1998.

McCarthy, Kevin M. *The On-Purpose Person: Making Your Life Make Sense: A Modern Parable,* July 2001.

McCarthy Kevin W. *The On-Purpose Business: Doing More of What You Do Best More Profitably.* April 2002.

McGraw, Phillip C., Ph.D. *The Ultimate Weight Solution: The 7 Keys to Weight Loss Freedom.* Free Press, 2003.

McGraw, Phillip C., Ph.D. *Self Matters : Creating Your Life from the Inside Out.* Simon& Schuster 2001. Hyperion Press, 2001.

Miller, Frederick and Katz, Judith. *The Inclusion Breakthrough: Unleashing the Real Power of Diversity.* Berrett-Koehler Publisher. 1st edition, 2002.

Moen, Phyllis; Erickson, William; Agarwal, Madhurima; Fields, Vivien; and Todd, Laurie. The Cornell Retirement Well-Being Study Final Report 2000. http://www.blcc.cornell.edu/archives/misc/retirement_study.pdf

Moss Kanter, Rosabeth. *Men and Women of the Corporation.* New York, NY: BasicBooks: A Division of HarperCollinsPublishers, 1977.

Muchnick, Marc, Ph.D. *Naked Management: Bare Essentials for Motivating the X-Generation at Work.* 1999.

Newstrom, John and Scannell, Edward. *The Big Book of Team Building Games. Trust Building Activities, Team Spirit Exercises, and Other Fun Things to Do.* New York: McGraw Hill, 1998.

Piven, Joshua and Borgenicht, David. *The Worst-Case Scenario Survival Handbook.* San Francisco, CA: Chronicle Books LLC, 1999.

Poitier, Sidney. *The Measure of a Man. A Spiritual Autobiography.* San Francisco, CA: HarperCollins, 2000.

Rodriguez, Cindy. "Sun Belt Gains Seen in 2000 Census Data." *Boston Globe,* 28 December, 2000.

Robbins, Anthony. *Awaken the Giant Within: How to Take Immediate Control of Your Mental, Emotional, Physical and Financial Destiny.* Free Press, 1992.

Robbins, Anthony. *Unlimited Power: The New Science of Personal Achievement.* Audio cassette. Free Press. February 2000.

Robbins, Steve Long-Nguyen. *Do Diversity Right!* Newsletter. Grand Rapids, MI. http://www.woodrickinstitute.org/doright.shtml

Rosen, Robert; Digh, Patricia; Singer, Marshall and Phillips, Carl. *Global Literacies: Lessons on Business Leadership and National Cultures.* New York: Simon & Schuster, September 1999.

Ruiz, Miguel Don. *The Four Agreements: A Practical Guide to Personal Freedom.* November, 1997.

Scovel Shinn, Florence. *The Game of Life and How To Play It.* Marina del Rey, CA: DeVorss & Company, 1925.

Senge, Peter M. *The Fifth Discipline: The Art and Practice of the Learning Organization.* Audio. September 1994.

Seuss, Dr. *Oh, the Places You'll Go.* New York: Random House, 1990.

Simmons, Terry. CEO Simmons Associates, P. C. Vectors ™, Diversity 360 ™. See www.linkageinc.com.

Smith, Dave (Compiled by). *The Quotable Walt Disney.* New York: Disney Editions, 2001.

Smith, J. Walker & Clurman, Ann. *Rocking the Ages: The Yankelovich Report on Generational Marketing.* HarperBusiness, 1997.

Smith, Lee. "The Diversity Factor." *FORTUNE,* October 13, 2003, pages S1-S12.

Taylor, Mildred D. *Roll of Thunder, Hear My Cry.* New York: Puffin Books, 1991.

Taylor, Susan. *In the Spirit: the Aspirational Writings of Susan L. Taylor.* Perennial. November 1994.

Taylor, Susan. *Lessons in Living.* New York: Anchor Books, a division of Random House. February 1998.

Thomas, Carole Copeland. *Personal Empowerment: How to Turbo Charge your Life Both On and Off the Job.* Woburn, MA: Milormic Press, 2003.

Thomas, David, A. and Gabbaro, John and Thomas, David. *Breaking Through: The Making of Minority Executives in Corporate America.* June 1999. See www.amazon.com

Thomas, Roosevelt with Woodruff, Majorie I. *Building a House for Diversity: A Fable About a Giraffe and Elephant Offers New Strategies for Today's Workforce.* See www.amazon.com.

Thomas, Roosevelt, R. Jr. *Beyond Race and Gender. Unleashing the Power of your Total Workforce by Managing Diversity.* New York, AMACOM, 1992.

Tulgan, Bruce. *Winning the Talent Wars.* Harvard University Press, 2001.

Tulgan, Bruce. *Managing Generation X.* Merritt Company, 1997.

United States General Accounting Office (GAO), Older Workers: Demographics Trends Pose Challenges for Employers and Workers, November 2001. http://www.gao.gov/new.items/d0285.pdf

University of Michigan, Health and Retirement Study, 1998. http://www.umich.edu/~hrswww/docs/hrarr.html

Waterman, Jr. Robert H., Waterman, Judith A., and Collard, Betsy A. "Toward a Resilent Work Force." *Harvard Business Review* July/August 1994.

Weiss, Alan, Ph.D. *Million Dollar Consulting: The Professional's Guide to Growing A Practice.* McGraw-Hill: 2002.

Welch, Jack with Byrne, *John A. Jack: Straight from the Gut.* New York: Warner Books, an AOL Time Warner Company, 2001.

Winfrey, Oprah and Adler, Bill. *The Uncommon Wisdom of Oprah Winfrey: A Portrait in Her Own Words.* January 1997.

Winters, Mary-Frances, Dr. *Inclusion Starts with I.* Chantilly, VA: Renaissance Publishers, Inc. 2003.

Winters, Mary-Frances, Dr. *Only Wet Babies Like Change: Workforce Wisdom for Baby Boomers.* Renaissance Books, June 2002.

Wilder, Hannah S. *The Awakening Executive: A Brief Guide To High Awareness Leadership for Global Business.* Sante Fe, NM; Global Executive Publishing. 2002.

Wilkinson, Dr. Bruce H. with David Kopp. *The Prayer of Jabez. Breaking Through to the Blessed Life.* Sisters, Oregon: Multnomah Publishers, Inc., 2000.

William M. Mercer Company, Capitalizing on an Aging Workforce, 2001. http://wmmercer.com.

Woodward, Nancy Hatch. "The Coming of the X Managers." *HR Magazine,* March 1999, Vol. 44, Issue 3.

Young, Mary B., D.B.A. The Center for Organizational Research, Linkage Learning Network. "Holding On: How the Mass Exodus of Retired Baby Boomers Could Deplete the Workforce. How Employers Can Stem the Tide." White Paper, March 2002. www.cfor.org

LOVE YOUR WORK BY LOVING YOUR LIFE

(LwL²)

Martha R. A. Fields is available to speak at:

- ◆ Conferences
- ◆ Conventions
- ◆ Corporate functions
- ◆ Employee events
- ◆ Executive briefings
- ◆ Non-profit and government events
- ◆ Professional and Trade Association meetings
- ◆ Retreats
- ◆ Workshops

www.MarthaRAFields.com

Martha R. A. Fields

President & CEO Fields Associates, Inc.
Author, Motivational Speaker, Consultant, Entrepreneur and
Expert on the Workforce, Diversity and Globalization

Other books by Martha R. A. Fields:
Indispensable Employees: How to Hire Them. How to Keep Them.
The Career Press, Inc., Franklin Lakes, NJ • ISBN 1-56414-516-6 • ©2001

For more information visit us at *www.MarthaRAFields.com*

About the Author

Martha R.A. Fields

Author, Motivational Speaker, Management Consultant, Entrepreneur and Expert on the Workforce, Diversity and Globalization

Martha is President, CEO and founder of Fields Associates, Inc., which is located in Harvard Square in Cambridge, Massachusetts.

Fields Associates' mission is "to connect Human Resources with business strategies to make a memorable positive difference within people, organizations and the world." Their impressive, international cross-industry client list includes

*The American Red Cross
*Blue Cross Blue Shield of Massachusetts
*Corning, Inc.
*Evergreen Investments
*Fidelity Investments
*The Gillette Company
*Harley-Davidson, Inc.
*Harvard University
*The Massachusetts Bar Association

*National Aeronautics & Space Administration (NASA)
*New England Journal of Medicine
*Partners Healthcare
*Sepracor, Inc.
*Shell Oil Company
*Texas Instruments
A variety of for-profit and nonprofit organizations

Martha has close to 25 years of experience in management and is an internationally recognized expert and leader in the field of Human Resources.

Before starting her firm, she served as a Vice President at a Harvard Medical School affiliated teaching hospital, the Massachusetts Eye and Ear Infirmary. She was also the Director of Human Resources at the Harvard Community Health Plan, and manager of Employee Relations and Training and Development at Boston's Children's Hospital.

An experienced lecturer and writer, Ms. Fields has been quoted in such publications as *FORTUNE*, *The New York Times*, *Kiplinger*, and *The Boston Globe*. The *Boston Herald* called her "a consultant, a coach for change."

As a much-sought-after motivational speaker at corporate functions and member of the National Speakers Association, she has taught college courses and is a frequent keynote speaker at professional association meetings. Martha has addressed audiences as diverse as the Harvard Business School, Chambers of Commerce, The Society for Human Resource Management, United Way, American Red Cross, NICSA – The National Investment Company Service Association, The National Black MBA Association and managers at Harley-Davidson.

Martha prides herself as a "corporate cupid," mentor and strong supporter of social responsibility. Fields Associates partnered with Harvard University to produce a Diversity Recruitment Resource Guide. This guide contains 400 resources and the president of Harvard University wrote its introduction. She has held many board positions including Bentley College's Human Resources Management Program Advisory Board, Harvard Medical Schools' Biomedical Science Career Project, National Human Resources Association and Dimock Community Health Center's Board of Visitors.

She is the former president of the Boston Human Resources Association and is the 2001 recipient of the John D. Erdlen Five Star Award, the most distinguished award given by the NorthEast Human Resources Association/Society for Human Resource Management in recognition of outstanding accomplishments of an individual or organization in the human resources profession. American Airlines included Fields Associates in its 2002 tribute to six of Boston's top companies.

A self-described "citizen of the world," she has traveled widely to such locations as the Amazon Jungle, Jamaica and the Andes Mountains and lived in several parts of the world, including Okinawa. Martha has a degree from Boston University in Sociology and Hispanic studies and undertook doctoral studies there. She draws upon her training, worldwide experiences and skills as a mother of a teenage daughter to assist organizations with strategic and project planning, management development, human resources and diversity and globalization issues.

Martha is the author of the popular book *Indispensable Employees: How to Hire Them. How to Keep Them* and a yet to be released novel, *Dancing with the Sun*. Her latest book is *Love your work by Loving your Life (LwL²)*.

Hiring and Keeping Your Best Employees is Harder and More Important than Ever Before.
***Indispensable Employees* Shows You the Way.**

The book offers best, interesting and radical practices with direct quotes from some of the nation's top companies such as

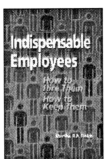

- ◆ Cisco Systems, Inc.
- ◆ Fidelity Investment
- ◆ The Four Seasons Hotel
- ◆ Harvard University
- ◆ Partners Healthcare
- ◆ Texas Instruments
- ◆ Timberland
- ◆ U.S. Army

Indispensable Employees: How to Hire Them. How to Keep Them., shows organizations how to

- ◆ Maximize their recruitment and retention dollars and includes worksheets and action plans to help them figure this out.
- ◆ Decrease costly turnover.
- ◆ Turn employees and managers into goodwill ambassadors and headhunters.
- ◆ Utilize multicultural and segment marketing approaches to recruit and retain a diverse workforce.
- ◆ Prevent competitors from luring key talent away.

"An exceptional handbook with clarifying insight into the complexities of today's competitive labor market."

– Marilyn Fuller, Texas Instruments

"…practical and insightful guidance into what it takes to retain talent…a definitive source on how to make your workplace irresistible."

– Alesia Wilson, Fidelity Investments

To order *Indispensable Employees: How to Hire Them. How to Keep Them.*

Go online or order directly from major bookstores such as AMAZON.Com, Barnes & Noble, Borders Books, etc. or call Career Press at 1-800-227-3371

ISBN 1-56414-516-6 • $14.99 US

Order Form

Love your work by Loving your Life (LWL2)

Share this book with others.

Marmerv Press
Harvard Square

Name_____
      (Please Print)

Company/Organization _____

Title _____

Shipping Address _____

City _____ State_____ Zip Code_____

Email _____

Day Time Telephone (_____)_____-_____   Home Phone (_____)_____-_____

❏ Yes, I want to purchase _____ copy(ies) (Please insert number) at a cost of $29.99 USA/$39.40 (CAN) each plus shipping and handling and applicable sales tax (5% sales tax MA residents only).

$_____ Total Cost

$_____ Plus shipping and handling—$4.00 for the first book and $2.00 for each additional book.

$_____ Plus 5% Sales Tax (MA residents only)

$_____ Total Payment Enclosed

Means of payment enclosed: ❏ Money Order ❏ Check made payable to Fields Associates, Inc.
                           (Note: There is a $25 fee for returned checks.)

Bill my credit card: ❏ American Express   ❏ Visa   ❏ Mastercard

_____   _____
        Credit Card Number   Expiration Date

_____   _____
    Cardholder Name (Please Print)   Signature

❏ Please put me on your mailing list and database to receive future information from Martha R. A. Fields.

❏ Yes, I am interested in seminar/speaking engagement information on Love your work by Loving your Life and other topics. Please contact me.

*   Contact us for special quantity discounts for bulk purchases for educational use, sales promotions, premiums, or fundraisings.

Please mail to: Marmerv Press
                124 Mt. Auburn Street, Suite 200 North, University Place
                Harvard Square, Cambridge, Massachusetts 02138-5900

                or email your order information to: www.MarthaRAFields.com *or* call: (617)576-5733

                Also available wherever books are sold and at Amazon.com and Barnes&Noble.com.

Printed in the United States
49727LVS00003B/2

9 780974 680200